Liberalism and Republicanism in the Historical Imagination

Liberalism *and* Republicanism *in the* Historical Imagination

JOYCE APPLEBY

HARVARD UNIVERSITY PRESS
Cambridge, Massachusetts
London, England
1992

This book is printed on acid-free paper, and its binding materials
have been chosen for strength and durability.

Library of Congress Cataloging-in-Publication Data

Appleby, Joyce Oldham.
Liberalism and republicanism in the historical imagination / Joyce Appleby.
p. cm.
Includes bibliographical references and index.
ISBN 0–674–53012–8 (cloth : acid-free paper). — ISBN
0–674–53013–6 (pbk. : acid-free paper)
1. United States—Intellectual life—18th century.   2. Liberalism—
United States—History—18th century.   3. Republicanism—United
States—History—18th century.   4. United States—History—
Revolution, 1775–1783—Influence.   I. Title.
E163.A67   1992
320.5′1′0973—dc20
91–30897
CIP

For Martha

*In love and gratitude to my sister
who was also my first teacher*

Acknowledgments

IT WAS WITH great delight that I realized that the publication of these essays in book form would give me the chance to thank publicly those cherished friends who have also been thoughtful critics. Academic life is a curious blend of intense isolation and engaged colleagiality. The first is lonely, but necessary to the cultivation of an independent perspective; the latter repairs the loneliness as it broadens and challenges one's singular position.

Although my academic life—and much else—began at Stanford, in a Western Civ class where I met Andrew Appleby, my intellectual debts go back much further, to the time when my sister undertook to tame the savagery of childhood with instruction in literature, French, and the piano. I have dedicated this collection of essays to her because of her enduring interest in what I have thought and how I have expressed it.

Two very fine scholars at Claremont Graduate School, Douglass Adair and Sidney Mead, opened up the eighteenth century to me. If, as Herbert Butterfield said, the historian's chief aim is to elucidate the unlikeness between the past and the present, they are the ones who awakened me to this imaginative possibility. In my first and longest teaching assignment, at San Diego State University, I was extremely fortunate to make friends who not only loved to talk about American history but also acted on their civic values outside the classroom. Dick and Elaine Steele, Dave DuFault, Frank Stites,

Carl Smith, Stan and Giselle Pincetl, Dave Weber, and Bill and Aimee Lee Cheek enriched my life immeasurably.

At UCLA, Scott Waugh, Gary Nash, Norton Wise, Dan Howe, Eric Monkkonen, Ron and Anne Mellor, Philip Huang, Peter Reill, Albion Urdank, Mary Yeager, Ruth Bloch, Debby Silverman, and David Sabean helped me build a new academic home. To Karen Orren, I owe very special thanks. And of course there have been those students whose sympathetic response to ideas has laid the basis for friendships: Cynthia Shelton, Joan Waugh, Susan Neal, Mark Kleinman, Rick Vernier, Hans Eicholz, Tom Thompson, Mary Corey, Robin Lappen, Anne Ustach, Paula Scott, John Majewski, Rob Michaelson, and Roz Remer.

One of the most satisfying aspects of building a life's work around a body of knowledge is the magnetic attraction that body exerts across time and space. For me the magnet of history has drawn in Peg Jacob, Jon Dewald, David Hall, Dagmar and Jeffrey Barnouw, Lynn Hunt, Paul Clemens, Jack Greene, Gordon Wood, John Pocock, Linda Kerber, Michael Kammen, Eric Foner, Tom Hines, James Henretta, Roger Schofield, Tom Haskell, John Higham, David Johnson, Steven Innes, Jack Garraty, Roy and Louise Ritchie, Mike McGiffert, Richard Ashcraft, Pat Bonomi, David Thelen, Mark Kaplanoff, John and Dorothy Thompson, Rick Beeman, John Murrin, Perry Anderson, Sharon Salinger, John Ashworth, Carolyn Dewald, Robert Brenner, Ludi Jordanova, Karl Figlio, and Jack Pole. Ann and David Gordon, Pat and Charles Richards, Jo and Wiley Caldwell, and Phyllis and Bob Green shared much with me along the way.

I would like to thank the fellows of Queen's College, Oxford, who provided the ideal setting for bringing these essays together. My thanks also to Aida Donald for suggesting that they appear as a book.

Dewey Harnish, Frank Appleby, Ann and Jim Caylor; Mark, Heidi, Hannah, and Flora Lansburgh; Martha Avery, Bill Oldham, Carlton and Eileen Appleby, and Harriette Wrye have supported and complicated that most insistent of all historical tasks: understanding one's own family. I am indebted to them all.

J.A.

Contents

Liberalism and Republicanism in the Historical Imagination

Liberalism and Republicanism
in the Historical Imagination

LIBERALISM entered the history of America as a set of powerful ideas; it remained to dominate as a loose association of unexamined assumptions. What in Europe formed the program for a political party became in the United States a description of reality. Core liberal affirmations were expressed explicitly for the first time in the quarter of a century between Independence and the election of Thomas Jefferson. They can be stated simply: Human nature manifests itself universally in the quest for freedom. Political self-government emanates from individual self-control. Nature has endowed human beings with the capacity to think for themselves and act in their own behalf. This rational self-interest can be depended upon as a principle of action. Free choice in matters of religion, marriage, intellectual pursuits, and electoral politics is the right of every individual. Free inquiry discloses the nature of reality, whose laws are accessible to reason. True religion teaches the sanctity of each person and the need to glorify God through the cultivation of one's gifts and talents. The rule of law is binding on all citizens as long as its positive statutes conform to the natural law protection of life, liberty, and property. Vicious tyrannies over the body and mind, established in the infancy of human history, have blocked the spread of knowledge and its liberating potential. And, finally, the human personality presumed in these propositions is male.

Like most American children, I accepted this liberal worldview as a description of reality. The affirmations listed above were part of the given of that world. I could learn to behave as a member of my liberal society, but it was more difficult to accept unthinkingly its factual propositions. Because its norms were explicitly male-modeled, there was a conceptual incongruity between its givens and my self-understanding. With the active social roles reserved for men, I was pushed to the margins where opportunities for observation greatly surpassed those for participation. From this angle, the distortions in the liberal description of human nature were hard to ignore. Its claims to describe how the world actually was could only create in a woman what the psychologists call cognitive dissonance. But what produced confusion in an adolescent became in time a fruitful vantage point for a professional historian.

The specific research that prompted my work on liberalism was prompted by my first teaching assignment at San Diego State University. All first-year students there learned American history from a collection of primary documents. The book we used, *The People Shall Judge,* presented a canon of liberal texts, and from that canon came my question: How had Adam Smith been able to take for granted a description of human nature that would have been utterly unthinkable a century and a half earlier? Neither Puritan or Anglican congregations nor Elizabethan theatergoers were regaled with statements about the steady, reasonable, wholly natural self-interested behavior of all men. Yet such a description of human nature clearly had become a part of Smith's world. Where had it come from? Searching for the elaboration of this concept led me to a new body of seventeenth-century literature: the largely ephemeral writings on commerce. Looking back after a quarter-century, I can see that that question was my Ariadne's thread through the labyrinth of liberal assumptions that had molded my thinking. I began with a straightforward inquiry about the origins of the conception of human nature underlying liberal social theory, and I ended up with an appreciation of the ways in which that theory had decisively shaped Americans' historical consciousness while it insinuated itself into every public discourse. Now both the theory and the history have lost their coherence, forcing us to question how mutually dependent they are.

For a long time American historical writing simply explained how the United States became the territorial embodiment of liberal truths. Instead of narratives describing men and women responding discretely to life's contingencies, historians depicted them as the carriers of ideas that unfolded over time. In political history the story was the extension of the suffrage, the perfection of representation, the creation of the two-party system, and the enunciation of a constitutional jurisprudence. Economic history was devoted to working out complex systems of production and marketing, themselves the result of a natural mechanism that promoted successful applications of human ingenuity. Historians of science featured the solitary discoverer whose bold experiments revealed the unfolding power of the human mind. Intellectual historians produced a great chain of liberating thought. A canon of liberal documents beginning with the seventeenth-century English philosophical tradition of Bacon, Locke, and Newton was assembled to illustrate core ideas and to show as well how the baton of liberalism had passed to the United States at the time of the Revolution. Thus, the authors of the *Federalist Papers* became the true heirs of Locke, and America's democratic statesmen the practical interpreters of Adam Smith.

As social discourse liberalism achieved its fullest explanatory power in the early nineteenth century, when people began to use the rapidly maturing natural sciences as both model and proof of the validity of new theories about the universality of market economics and democratic politics. The emerging synthesis reflected sympathetic affinities more than a coherent philosophy, but it served as the basis for a forward-looking and optimistic modern stance. The quickened expectation of general social improvement brightened the future as it dulled the past, separating the enthusiasts of the new learning from those who saw its destructive implications. Once politicized, scientific inquiries acquired an explosive potential, nicely captured by one of Jefferson's ardent critics, Clement Clarke Moore, who commented that whenever "modern philosophers talk about mountains, something impious is likely to be at hand."[1] But modern philosophers continued to talk about mountains, and with greater certainty. Scientists, as they began to be called, exuded a

1. As cited in Linda Kerber, *Federalists in Dissent: Imagery and Ideology in Jeffersonian America* (Ithaca, 1970), 91. See also Robert Kelley, *The Cultural Pattern in American Politics: The First Century* (New York, 1979), 122–123.

spirit of mastery that redounded to the benefit of the popularizers of science and the social values they endorsed.

Despite Adam Smith's place in the liberal canon, his writings were not influential in the United States until formal economics entered the college curriculum in the early nineteenth century. Rather it was the capacity of the economy to act as a natural moral arbiter that excited attention. The stunningly swift transformation of America's physical environment wrought by private initiatives in the thirty years after 1789 validated the claim that free enterprise built character—habits of planning, work, and thrift—as it built the farms, cities, post roads, and bridges of the expanding nation. Materialism and morality fused as easily as scientific inquiry and political freedom merged to form that web of associated notions which has become known as American liberalism. Jeremy Bentham's utilitarian philosophy, which might seem well attuned to American sensibilities, in fact found little resonance in the United States. The well-being of the individual rather than the mass of the people was being promoted, and that individual was seen as the material embodiment of moral virtue. During these same years evangelical Protestants successfully propagated an individualized Christian message that challenged much of Calvinist orthodoxy.[2] They compared liberation from sin to liberation from tyranny as a kind of individual empowerment, thus providing a Christian foundation for the civil religion forming around natural rights.

For several generations the history of the United States was told as the history of the *progress* of the nation, its people, and its institutions. Individuals personified the developments that marked progress: George Washington, Thomas Jefferson, James Madison, John Marshall, H. D. Thoreau, Ralph Waldo Emerson, Carl Schurz, Abraham Lincoln. Very much like an oral tradition that winnows out discordant story lines through repeated retelling, American history shed illiberal elements. Gone was the proud intolerance of the orthodox Puritans who founded New England, the genteel self-fashioning of parvenu planters in Virginia, and the coercive conformity of one-church communities sprinkled throughout the colonies.

2. Nathan O. Hatch, *The Democratization of American Christianity* (New Haven, 1989), 213–222.

Loyalists were consigned to neglect. Immigrants who had sought nothing more than fertile ground in which to transplant their cherished ways of life were turned into intrepid pioneers voting with their feet on the traditionalism of Europe. Aristocratic ideals of excellence, honor, martial splendor, prescribed deference, and leisured living, so long cherished as the marks of civilization, simply baffled those who encountered their vestigial traces in the colonial past. No explanation of why men endorsed liberal ideas was required. Truth in this historiography was irresistible. Conflict arose when defenders of old ways stood in the way of progress. The obvious clarity of the motives of liberal heroes answered the question of historical causation.

One can hear this seductive reasoning in Jefferson's account of his presidential election. He hailed it as the revolution of 1800, "as real a revolution in the principles of our government as that of 1776 was in its form," and went on to interpret his victory through the striking dichotomies of a new liberal idiom.[3] His opponents looked backward, not forward for improvement, he said. They feared the ignorance of the people, as his party did the selfishness of rulers unchecked by the people. Jeffersonians advocated the reform of institutions in step with the progress of science, maintaining that "no definite limits could be assigned that progress"; "the enemies of reform, on the other hand, denied improvement and advocated steady adherence to the principles, practices and institutions of our fathers which they represented as the akmé of excellence, beyond which the human mind could never advance."[4] With apocalyptic fervor, Jefferson exulted, "We can no longer say there is nothing new under the sun, for this whole chapter in the history of man is new."[5]

Leaving slavery in a conceptual limbo, Jefferson claimed that America stood for free men, free land, free institutions, and free choice—a direction it had been moving toward ever since the May-

3. Jefferson to Spencer Roane, Sept. 6, 1819, in *The Writings of Thomas Jefferson*, ed. Paul L. Ford (New York, 1892–1899), X, 140.

4. Jefferson to Abigail Adams, Sept. 11, 1804, in *Adams-Jefferson Letters*, ed. Lester J. Cappon (Chapel Hill, 1959), I, 278–280; Jefferson to John Adams, June 15, 1813, ibid., II, 332.

5. Jefferson to Joseph Priestley, Mar. 21, 1801, in *Writings*, ed. Ford, XVIII, 54–56.

flower Compact. The Revolution was being fulfilled in the nineteenth century through democratic politics, continental expansion, and material abundance. God had sent choice grain into the wilderness and now there were fruited plains from sea to shining sea. The intentionality of the Almighty merged with the intentionality of all men, when left free to choose. Venerable distinctions between the learned and the vulgar, the virtuous and the ignoble, the authorized and the unauthorized, were dissolving before the imperative to liberate the human potential for self-activation.

Such an interpretation of American history thrust an insignificant country of several million people, three thousand miles from any major civilization, into the foreground of human destiny. Citizens of a provincial outpost, nineteenth-century Americans could transcend their isolation by universalizing and exalting what was peculiar to them: their success in establishing free institutions; their efforts to build communities in the wilderness; their liberation of the ordinary ambitions of ordinary men. What might be construed by Europeans as uninterestingly plebian was elevated by the liberal imagination to a new epoch for mankind.

Told in this way, the settlement of America has all the simple rhythms and repeated choruses of a popular ballad. We can easily see in our mind's eye the undaunted colonists landing in the proverbial wilderness and immediately setting to work to convert natural abundance into marketable commodities, knowing all the while that they were laboring to bring forth a nation that would be the liberal refuge for the world. The story begins with English Pilgrims fleeing persecution and ends with Lincoln's fervid hope that "government of the people, by the people and for the people shall not perish from the earth." It is this version of our national history that prompted Richard Hofstadter to comment that America was the only country which started with perfection and aspired to progress.

We may smile at the naïveté of this first national history, but we would be foolish to underrate its effect. More than a literary production, it created social values and distributed political power. It provided the rationale for displacing the Indians whose ancestral lands lay astride the American march to the West. Its compelling picture of industrious individuals seeking fresh starts in a new land blotted out the memory of those uprooted Africans and cast-off Europeans who had also become Americans. Like liberalism itself, this history contained an attack upon dependency and difference. Disciplined white families made homes for themselves as they moved across the continent, but the solidarity of groups bound by a common religion or birthplace, loyal, even submissive, to the whole, evoked suspicion. Here we see the tensions generated by a history which glorified freedom and taught that the only thing people were free to do was pursue individual ambitions. The universality of this relentless self-improvement was essential if the United States was to serve as a model for the human race.

These assertions which look so dubious in a retrospective view were the weapons with which rebellious intellectuals in the late eighteenth century fought the hierarchical structures, communitarian customs, and aristocratic ideals of their day. Their opponents, defenders of the status quo, could draw upon history, experience, and common sense to explain the permanence of what had always been. It took no effort to accept the givenness of the world and a great exercise of imagination to overcome it. Liberal reformers had to explain away reality if they were to infuse the world with hope. It was not enough to expose the insufficiency and stupidity of the actual in their vendetta against the ancien régime; they had to produce attractive alternatives. Rejecting the tactile and the palpable, they used theories about natural simplicity to promote dissatisfaction with the ornate and byzantine arrangements of traditional society.[6] They dwelt upon abstractions like the social contract, free trade, future progress, and autonomous man, which, following Newtonian cosmology, pointed to a reality hidden by appearances. Their use of analytical reasoning helped them supplant traditional wisdom, but this insistence on universal norms and reliance upon abstract models remained to shape the mature liberal theory.

Conservatives argued for caution, but their pessimism was turned against them. Their negative evaluation of human nature, their persistent belief in the classical cycles of change, their willing sacrifice of individual independence to social stability—all were castigated

6. Jefferson to William Johnson, June 12, 1823, ibid., X, 226n–227n. Still reflecting on the divisions of 1800, he spoke of the other party as believing that experience was a safer guide than "mere theory."

as weapons of oppression rather than the neutral judgments they purported to be. In several critical exchanges—Thomas Paine and Edmund Burke on the significance of the French Revolution, James Madison and the Antifederalists on Montesquieu's small-republic theory, Jefferson and the Federalists on popular sovereignty—the liberals sharpened the contrast between them and their adversaries. These disputes pitted their rational, universalizing, optimistic, progressive, innovative, and analytic approach against an amorphous body of conservative thought characterized as didactic, authoritarian, pessimistic, obfuscating, parochial, and defensive.

Understanding these developments historically has not been easy. More than any other ideology, liberalism has denied its own roots and substituted a genealogy of key ideas. Embedded in the central propositions of liberalism was the history of its own triumph, but it was a peculiarly ahistorical one, which leeched from the record any curiosity about those men and women who could not be given parts in the drama of improvement and discovery. The idea of progress, when it gained currency in the late eighteenth century, had an exhilarating effect upon those who yearned for change. With it the tables could be turned on conservatives who used history to demonstrate mankind's depravity. Their dreary litany of tyrannies, invasions, and revolts could serve as evidence of the depths from which humanity was ascending. People who grasped the idea of progress were easily persuaded that those who had lived before them had also believed in it; hence they eagerly embraced innovations heralding a new day. A new conceptual divide between past and present led to a dramatic reordering of their relation. Shining through the darkness that was the past were liberal triumphs to be recorded, examined, and celebrated. The rest of known history was useless to an enlightened present, its existence a reproach to the human spirit so long enshrouded in ignorance.

These themes, incessantly reworked, made the carriers of liberal ideas appear isolated from their own times, rightfully indifferent to the darkness around them, reaching forward to an imagined future of fulfillment. With this reversal in the emotional investment in the future and past, liberal historians sought out those who could be characterized as pathfinders, inventors, forerunners, dissenters, trailblazers—the lonely outsider or the victim of conventional authority—thus giving liberal history its distinctive proleptic feature. The eagerness to locate anticipators promoted the rhetorical invention of the "precursor"—that idea, event, or person which prepared a way for future developments. The past as a subject worthy of knowing remained undiscovered.

Because of the central role given to reason as the liberating force in human history, liberal scholars presented seminal thinkers as the producers of consistent bodies of thought. The man (and they were exclusively men) and his work became almost indistinguishable. The man existed to think and the thought existed to find human expression. The goal of consistency led historians to reconcile discordant texts, making it necessary sometimes to hive off nonconforming parts of an author's work, such as Adam Smith's science of the legislator or Isaac Newton's interest in alchemy. Individuals were in charge of the contents of their minds; ideas were clear, knowledge unproblematic. Because society now had an agenda, it also acquired "problems" which, like the sciences from which liberal thought so liberally extrapolated, had solutions.

Since the historically significant relationship now was between pioneering figures and future developments, their decontextualization was almost inevitable. It was the future not the past which shed light on personal achievement. The historical construction of Alexander Hamilton as the prescient anticipator of American industrial capitalism reflects this tendency. Founders, fathers—Founding Fathers—forward-looking men leading ordinary men and women out of the maze of wrongheaded thinking of the past were the proper subjects of history. Thus sanitized from contact with their illiberal world, a line of distinguished thinkers—Galileo, Luther, Bacon, Locke, Newton, and Smith—could be wrenched from the "dark and slavish times" in which they lived to be celebrated for their inspiration to all who benefited from progress. Like stones skipping across water, the preserved record touched the surface of the past according to the predictable regularities of the liberal imagination.[7]

Because liberal thinkers constructed their systems around the autonomous individual, their concern with order diverged from

7. See Donald Winch, "Economic Liberalism as Ideology: The Appleby Version," *Economic History Review*, 38 (1985), 287–297, for a discussion of my own liberal tendencies. The quotation is from Thomas Paine, *Common Sense*, ed. Isaac Kramnick (New York, 1982), 68.

traditional schemes. In the social contract treatises of Hobbes and Locke, the free and equal men who founded civil society were given an identity of interests. In his radical naturalizing of society Jefferson found order in the design of nature. "So invariably do the laws of nature create our duties and interests," he told the French economist J. B. Say, "that when they seem to be at variance we might suspect some fallacy in our reasoning." [8] Reluctant to see the release of man's essential freedom as concurrent with an increase in appetitive and aggressive behavior, liberals used the language of progress to define what was undesirable as a lag or remnant. Meanwhile romantic abstractions about the American people popularized in the nineteenth century provided additional secular substitutes for the vital sense of Christian unity which once had provided cohesion. As American Protestantism lost contact with the specificity of Christian doctrine, it was possible for the civil religion of the United States to merge the highly secular strains of liberalism with the evangelical message of personal salvation. At the same time nineteenth-century evolutionary theories placing Anglo-Saxon culture in the forefront of evolving civilizations fused easily with the Hegelian idea of the nation as highest expression of civilization, both helping to explain how America's institutions could be unique as well as exemplary.

The accelerated pace of economic development allowed liberal theory the momentum to outdistance any competing accounts of change in the nineteenth and early twentieth centuries. Its overly determined rendering of events sealed the imagination against alternative explanations of the transformation of the modern world. The search for liberal antecedents dominated the history of the United States, which became the flagship of modernity. Once coalesced into a mutually supporting set of concepts and fantasies, it was easy for liberalism to avoid scrutiny. Unlike Europe, in the United States the word *liberalism* was rarely used. While European liberalism represented a set of national policies, in the United States it became a part of the nation's self-understanding. Its tenets were embraced by the great mass of people who had frequently been deracinated by geographic mobility. Liberalism had the power to evoke the

8. February 1, 1804, in *Writings of Thomas Jefferson,* ed. Andrew A. Lipscomb and Albert Ellery Bergh (Washington, D.C., 1903–1905), XI, 2–3.

behavior it prescribed. National norms acted like a sieve to strain from the fellowship of the liberal-minded those immigrants and native-born Americans who failed to exhibit the energetic qualities of the free and independent man. Having supplied the givens for a worldview, liberalism disappeared into the underground foundations of American thinking.

By the middle of the twentieth century the highly selective memories that formed Americans' historical understanding stood in the way of further understanding. The masculine personality that was highlighted left no room for women's experience, while the emphasis upon independence devalued the cohesion of ethnicity, class, and commitment. Not only did liberal theory contain a reductionist concept of the human personality, it also mandated the exclusion of much of the colonial record. Where historical events unassimilable to the liberal story were originally ignored, with the passing of the revolutionary generation they were forgotten altogether. The impoverished reality of liberal theory frustrated efforts to comprehend contemporary society. Thus cut off from the exercise of critical intelligence, the liberal tradition in America finally became what Louis Hartz poignantly described in 1955 as an illiberal and conformist cast of mind.[9]

HISTORICAL scholarship resembles nothing so much as the layering of cities on an ancient site. Like the river confluences and defensible escarpments that have drawn successive waves of city-builders to the same location, ideologically potent issues attract cohorts of historians to the same topics. Historiography, in this view, is a form of archaeology. Understanding the history of the history of an event involves digging through the remains of previous historical accounts. With that effort comes an increasing awareness of the way in which the original foundations have shaped the constructions of latter-day builders. No scholar—at least no scholar working today at the end of three centuries of intense historical consciousness—begins his or her work fresh. Prior interpretations structure curiosity, point out sources, and define what makes a

9. Louis Hartz, *The Liberal Tradition in America* (New York, 1955).

plausible explanation. In the case of national history, more than a debt is involved; there is a collective responsibility to make history illuminate the character of the people. For almost two centuries in the United States this character was assumed to be liberal; yet since the 1960s historians, influenced by the crosscurrents of contemporary thought, have sought a disengagement with liberalism.

America's first major historian, George Bancroft, devoted ten volumes to explaining how the United States—undistinguished by its art, literature, military exploits, or contributions to science— was, nonetheless, God's chosen nation. Both the individual and humanity were ennobled by the American liberation from the shackles of poverty, superstition, and tyranny. Bancroft's foil was Europe, whose towering cathedrals and ancient cities proclaimed an impressive past, but a spirit that was debilitated. Feudalism may have lingered long in Europe, but it lingered even longer in American political discourse where it became the code word for everything that differentiated Old World atavism from New World innovation. Well after the last of the feudal remnants had disappeared, they were evoked in American writings to create the fixed darkness upon which to project the bright prospects of the United States. Europe's past defined its future; America's past was prologue.

Bancroft merged the discrete revolutionary participants into a collective noun—the American people—and described how they mounted a heroic protest against wicked and tyrannical British ministers. Tracing the origins of the freedom-loving passions of his American people took him and other nineteenth-century historians back to the elections of kings by migratory Germanic tribes, the juridical practices of medieval English hundreds, and the town-meeting culture of colonial New England.[10] The thread of democratic self-governing stitched revolution, Constitution, and Jeffersonian party politics into a seamless fabric. The disembodied idea and the fully bodied champions of progress supplied the *dramatis personnae* of history.

Confronted with the self-congratulatory opaqueness of patriotic

10. A fascinating account of how late-nineteenth-century historians resisted methodological advances when writing about the American Revolution is contained in Sydney G. Fisher, "The Legendary and Myth-Making Process in Histories of the American Revolution," *American Philosophical Society Proceedings,* 51 (1912), 53–75.

histories, Progressive historians in the early part of the twentieth century decided to build in a different part of the city. The American Revolution, they insisted, could not be described as the patriotic response of an undifferentiated people, because the colonists had been differentiated by class and region. Nor could their motives be taken at face value. "Man as a political animal acting upon political as distinguished from more vital and powerful motives is the most insubstantial of all abstractions," Charles Beard announced.[11] Making interest-group conflicts the pistons in the engine of change, the Progressives described the Revolution as the culmination of a two-stage conflict: first between the capitalist ruling classes in Great Britain and the colonies, and subsequently between the merchant princes and landed magnates of the colonial elite and the disenfranchised masses. The American Revolution was, in Carl Becker's clever phrase, about "home rule and who shall rule at home." Nor could the Constitution be interpreted as the fulfillment of the Revolution, as Bancroft had done. Rather it was the product of a rivalry between proto-capitalists and plain farmers, a conflict Progressives believed animated politics throughout the nineteenth century. Disaggregating Bancroft's "whole people," Progressives reassembled historical figures into occupational and income groups. They did not, however, abandon the liberal fixation with progress. Instead they substituted lower-class democratic aspirations for the patriots' drive for self-government as the forward-looking force that manifested itself in the Revolutionary era. Not unlike their predecessors, they universalized American experience, although now the nation exemplified the scientific laws of evolution, working through conflict, to carry mankind to new levels of rationality and productivity.

Historians encamped in the Progressives' part of the city found ample room for expansion. Their tools permitted them to unearth new records. The earlier city of Bancroft and his peers was deemed old-fashioned, devoid of the modern inventions of utility and short-range gain, burdened with outdated philosophical doctrines and ornate political oratory. No one built in the old part of the city any more; historians spread to new fields of inquiry where one could

11. As quoted in Max Lerner, "The Constitution and Court as Symbols," *Yale Law Journal*, 46 (1937), 32.

support a sophisticated appetite for economic motives. Soon new structures, bulging with vital class interests and clashing legislative contests, overshadowed the old historical constructions about evolving political forms and constitutional principles, now crumbling from neglect.

Archaeologists often puzzle over why one group of people quits living in a site or why, years later, another contingent of builders brings human habitation back to an old location. Not being so ancient an undertaking, the writing of American history reveals the reasons for its moves more readily. The Progressives' utilitarian reconstruction of the past proved too cramped to contain the variety of experiences and aspirations present in revolutionary America. Doing research in areas neglected by their Whig predecessors, the Progressives added enormously to our knowledge of the constituent parts of colonial society, but they also uncovered artifacts which jarred with the clean lines of their economic determinism. Buildings erected to house debtors and creditors turned out to be occupied by New and Old Lights; corridors designed to link economic interests and political choices were unexpectedly blocked by atavistic sensibilities and attitudes.

The exploited lower classes, center of gravity for Progressive historiography, began to appear more facade than solid foundation. Robert Brown discovered that the preponderance of white male colonists, thought to be disenfranchised, actually could vote. [12] Worse yet, revolutionary participants did not seem to be firmly connected to the profit motive. Without the disenfranchised masses, the edifice of class conflict in the American revolution began to crumble. In its place a jerry-built structure of consensual middle-class democracy was erected, but its fragility quickly became apparent. The fact that ordinary white men voted for their social superiors raised doubts about the democratic character of colonial politics. To explain this seemingly undemocratic practice Jack Pole introduced the concept of deference and opened up a new way to think about thinking and about how it enters into the historical process. [13] The nineteenth-

12. Robert E. Brown, *Middle Class Democracy and the Revolution in Massachusetts* (Ithaca, 1955).

13. J. R. Pole, "Historians and the Problem of Early American Democracy," *American Historical Review*, 67 (1961).

century attention lavished upon political thought began to appear less old-fashioned. Careful readings of the pamphlets of the American Revolution only multiplied the questions. Why, for instance, did the political rhetoric from supposedly liberal pathbreakers contain so many perplexing references to ancient prudence and civic virtue?

Out of this confusion emerged a wide-ranging curiosity about colonial society. Freed from the teleology of progress, a liberation which owed more to intellectual currents of the mid-twentieth century than to any feature of historical scholarship, historians could begin to entertain the idea that America had not been born free, rich, and modern. Further, liberalism itself might have been a construct of the early-nineteenth-century imagination deployed backward to the colonial era in an effort to find antecedents worthy of an enlightened, progressive age. Without the urgency to find trailblazers or unmask interest-group conflicts, a new generation of scholars began to reconstruct colonial society as a subject worthy of study for itself. From this perspective the yearning of America's original settlers to recreate the traditions of their European homes became increasingly apparent.

Directing their attention to the private lives of ordinary colonial men and women, social historians discovered the power of community in the charter settlements through their land usage, farming practices, family patterns, and ways of worship. In many instances the humble and poor were far more likely to cleave to beloved customs than were their social superiors, destroying the old conceit that the elite imposed venerable institutions upon the people who were actually ready to get on with the business of being free and independent Americans. Instead of traveling light to the New World, the original settlers brought a full complement of cultural baggage with them and succeeded against great odds in clinging to the familiar ways of their homeland. Indeed the contrast between Europe moving at glacial speed away from old customs, while the America avalanche encompassed every passing innovation has very nearly been reversed. American patriarchs ruled over their wives and adult children longer than in Europe, if only because of their extended life span. It took population pressure to force young men and women away from birth communities, and the recurrent religious revivals of Protestant America always summoned people to return to the faith of their fathers.

Among the colonial elite there was a conspicuous influence exercised by what Jack Greene has called "the mimetic impulse," that imitative imperative felt by a provincial gentry toward the beau ideals and stylized behavior of metropolitan leaders.[14] A wonderful collection of folkways and gentry imitation had been successfully transplanted from the Old World to the New, so successfully that preserving them had been a prime goal for many Americans right through the Revolutionary era. Well might the Baptist John Clarke exclaim, "while Old England is becoming New, New England is become Old."[15] Clarke's contemporary remark seemed true of the entire colonial experience as it was being reconstructed in the 1970s. The reversal of fortunes of progress and continuity in American historiography produced the disturbing conclusion that the most radical invention of New World colonization might have been the institution of slavery.

Once departure from the conventional liberal perspective seemed both possible and necessary, it was easier to see how invisible liberal foundations had structured the historical stories raised upon them. The historians' use of deference is an example of the way in which an analytical construct—in this case a borrowing from English history—could expand beyond its intended purpose. Used to explain why ordinary colonial voters perpetuated a system of elite rule, the concept of deference pointed to a link between internalized norms and external responses. The assumption that rational self-interest could serve as a universal explanation for behavior was suddenly exposed. If a study of eighteenth-century political language revealed that certain convictions held by common colonial voters about who should hold office eliminated themselves from consideration, what was the relation between these personal convictions and the free play of rationality? If historically specific beliefs determined behavior, what role did self-interest play? If it were constrained by cultural norms, what did the historian need to know about those norms in order to explain events? The old intellectual history offered little

14. "Political Mimesis: A Consideration of the Historical and Cultural Roots of Legislative Behavior in the British Colonies in the Eighteenth Century," *American Historical Review,* 75 (1969).

15. As quoted in Sidney Mead, *The Lively Experiment: The Shaping of Christianity in America* (New York, 1963), 25–26.

help in answering these questions. Within that scholarly tradition historians had assessed formal thought in terms of coherency and connectedness to a larger body of literature; the mundane cerebrations of ordinary life were left to be comprehended under the motivation of self-interest. Now the thought of major thinkers and ordinary sentient beings alike seemed to be mediated by a complex of ideas which could be ascribed to something called culture.

CONFRONTED with speculations like these, a new cohort of historians in the 1960s sought theoretical insights from the sociology of knowledge, cultural anthropology, and structural functionalism.[16] The liberal interpretation of the relation between the individual and society had become problematic for these disciplines. As social scientists, they were preoccupied with social change, particularly the momentous one that turned simple, small, poor, face-to-face, undifferentiated communities into parts of large, complex, wealthy, class-structured, literate nations. Without the guidance of the liberal idea of progress, these scholars assumed that individuals began life as members of a particular society and that each society left its indelible impress upon their personalities. Just how the acculturation process was activated in social life had been the focus of the great sociological works of Karl Marx, Emile Durkheim, and Max Weber. Their seminal writings became the basis for a variety of reworkings after the Second World War, when Western intellectuals became more and more engaged in explaining the varieties of social experience.

For American intellectual historians two social scientific presuppositions were particularly uncongenial to the liberal assumptions written into American historiography: that reality was socially constructed, and that it took ideas to inform people wherein their

---

16. These postwar developments can be followed in *History and Theory* and the *Journal of Interdisciplinary History*. See also Robert Berkhofer, Jr., "Clio and the Culture Concept: Some Impressions of a Changing Relationship in American Historiography," in *The Idea of Culture in the Social Sciences*, ed. Louis Schneider and Charles M. Bonjean (Cambridge, 1975); H. Stuart Hughes, "The Historian and the Social Scientist," in *Generalizations in Historical Writing*, ed. Alexander V. Riasanovsky and Barnes Riznik (Philadelphia, 1963); and Quentin Skinner, "Meaning and Understanding in the History of Ideas," *History and Theory*, 8 (1969).

interests lay. Both pointed to individuals' dependence upon society, now conceived as a creative force. A new kind of sophisticated relativism entered historical writing. If the goal of history was to account for change over time, and if what people thought determined what they did, then the truth and falseness of a given proposition was not nearly so important as the consequence of people's having believed it. The possibility was now open of exploring the nature of consciousness without the strictures of liberal assumptions about the free and independent man in control of his mind and bent on extending his interests and the ambit of freedom for acting upon them.

Ideology emerged as an appealing concept to clarify these perplexities. It also offered some conceptual tools for probing the elusive character of the invisible world of values and convictions, styles and sensibilities, embedded within each member of society. Its provenance was Marxist, derived from the proposition that systems of production determined the relations of classes and that those relations determined consciousness. According to Marx, the dominant class maintained its sway in part by fashioning an elaborated set of beliefs, or ideology, which justified the existing distribution of wealth and power. The false consciousness of the proletariat which accepted the ideology of the ruling class was proof of the malleability of human nature and the bad faith between social classes. Although important work was done within this Marxist framework, particularly after Antonio Gramsci's elaboration of the idea of hegemony, most new scholarship was inspired by an anthropological notion of ideology.

Max Weber had originally challenged the mechanistic aspect of Marx's thought because, he argued, it left unexplained how a dominant class could create an effective nexus of beliefs and institutions and why, once created, other classes would passively accept it.[17] Rather than assume the plasticity of believing, Weber insisted that all individuals possess an inner need to comprehend the world as a meaningful cosmos and to know what attitude to take toward it. This need provides the stimulus for human culture, which draws

17. Norman Birnbaum, "Conflicting Interpretations of the Rise of Capitalism: Marx and Weber," *British Journal of Sociology*, 4 (1953); "The Sociological Study of Ideology (1940–1960)," *Current Sociology*, 9 (1960).

upon the values people attach to their activities. Weber's man, the anthropologist Clifford Geertz commented, "is an animal suspended in webs of significance he himself has spun." [18] Culture ministers to what sociologists Peter Berger and Thomas Luckmann have called the "craving for meaning" because it permits understanding of the human enterprise through religious doctrines, philosophical princi- ples, and social theories. Functionally powerful, culture provides the repertoire of norms and forms that make coherent social action possible.

At the level of personal psychology, culture is seen as mobilizing the raw material of emotions into enthusiasms, commitments, and prejudices. It embodies the enduring manifestation of an ever- present demand for understanding. In these theoretical explorations culture lost any reference to visible artifacts; increasingly it came to denote the transmitter of systems of meaning through symbols, signs, codes, narratives, iconography, and public theater. A sponsor of Weberian studies in post–World War Two America, the soci- ologist Talcott Parsons, reworked Weber's ideas into a concept of ideology that shed the Marxist association with class interest for a stronger connection with social solidarity. In this view the identity of membership in society as a whole took precedence over class- consciousness. All societies have a particular way of organizing real- ity, and being a social creature is to participate in that particular- ity. [19] Some may benefit more than others, but for all, ideology is a passport to social membership.

Tied to literacy and commerce, the handmaidens of modernity, ideology is seen as supplying an invisible coherence to a vast and disparate body of social information about laws, roles, responsi- bilities, and the workings of that system of systems which is society. Ideological history differs from intellectual history in its concern with that structuring of consciousness which shapes identity and channels emotions. As Geertz has explained, "ideology is ornate, vivid, deliberately suggestive: by objectifying moral sentiment through the same devices that science shuns, it seeks to motivate action." [20] Reason, which the Enlightenment celebrated as the means

18. "Thick Description," in Geertz, *Interpretations of Culture* (London, 1973), 9.
19. I have discussed some of the implications of this use of ideology in Chapters 4 and 11.
20. "Ideology as a Cultural System," in Geertz, *Interpretations of Culture,* 219.

of liberation, was folded back into sentiment and opinion. Now it was seen as operating within a given construction of reality instead of presiding as a critical presence outside the socially given.

This concept undermined the proud structure of Enlightenment thought. The propositions of liberalism—the independent faculty of reason, the free and independent man, the unfolding idea of liberty, the relentless march of progress—could no longer support a new and more compelling view of human experience. The recovery of earlier systems of thought conducted under the aegis of ideology encouraged the abandonment of liberalism's conceptually lean, rational, autonomous, self-improving individual in favor of a social creature given to passion, responsive to symbols, animated by moral imperatives, and bonded to others by shared worldviews. After the single melody of liberal progress, the rich symphony of ideology, orchestrated by human needs and harmonized by social institutions, was music to the ears of a generation which had discovered culture.

Although he employed neither the concept of ideology or of culture, Perry Miller earlier had transformed the study of seventeenth-century Puritans by suspending disbelief in their spiritual longings and intellectual hubris. Rejecting the liberal perspective of his predecessors, he debunked the champions of religious freedom and precursors of democracy that had long peopled American colonial history. Accepting that the Puritans lived in a different conceptual universe, he explored that universe for the secret springs of their actions. Reconstructing with rare sensitivity their preoccupation with covenant theology and free grace, he put the God-intoxicated, Calvinist-inspired founders of New England back into American history—if not exactly on their terms, then certainly on terms totally unassimilable to the liberal tradition. This was as apparent in the substance of the Puritan ideas he detailed as in the range of emotions—jealousy, hope, malice, rapture, rage—that he evoked to explain the elaboration of Puritan intentions over time. By employing a rhetoric that highlighted the passions Miller recovered the sense of sin that had so thoroughly permeated the consciousness of the Puritans. His masterpieces pointed a way for later revisions of the liberal tradition in American history.

Neither mindless traditionalists nor progressive entrepreneurs, Miller's Elect of the Massachusetts Bible Commonwealth were hybrids who bore no relation to modern personality types. They had to be approached as strangers, something American historians had been loath to do with their ancestors. These strangers on an "errand into the wilderness" betrayed a profound distrust of nature, self-interest, and other liberal enthusiasms. Their exalted ambition to found a Bible Commonwealth made them peculiarly vulnerable to failure, which Miller explored under the rubric of declension. Miller's concept of declension suggested that before the idea of progress came to prevail in America, there were men and women who were more familiar with noble defeats.

It was against the background of new social scientific explorations of ideology and the towering achievement of Perry Miller's scholarship on the Puritans that Bernard Bailyn and Gordon Wood undertook a major reinterpretation of America's nation-building acts of revolution and constitution-writing. Jettisoning the search for liberal roots, they began to examine what eighteenth-century Americans seemed to be saying in their writings. The rhetoric and references led them to a conceptual universe which structured political discourse around the models of the ancient world. As explicated most fully by J. G. A. Pocock, classical republicanism made civic virtue—the capacity to place the good of the commonwealth above one's own—the lynchpin of constitutional stability and liberty-preserving order. In the life of the polis men realized their full humanity. The rest of humankind—the young, the female, the economically dependent—had to rely upon the civic humanism of an elite to protect them from the terrors of history: plagues, famines, usurpations, tyrannies, and conquests.

Educated Englishmen had turned to the interpreters of classical politics—Aristotle, Polybius, Machiavelli, and Harrington—after burning their bridges to their own political traditions with the execution of Charles I in 1649. Critical to their new situation was the realization that their nation was in history and hence subject to the vicissitudes and decaying processes of time. This "Machiavellian moment," as Pocock has called it, created a new historical consciousness that produced a heightened sense of the dangers of corruption. Civil society was treated like a fragile vase, an artifact of high civilization that required the most exquisite care. Particularly threatening to England's constitutional government was the new class of moneyed men who had sprung up through the expansion of public credit in the 1690s. Their machinations enhanced the power and glory admired by the court, while in the country an opposition party read their abandonment of public virtue as a sign that England too would be pushed into the Polybian cycles of degeneration.[21]

During the eighteenth century, when remarkable innovations in economic and social life were occurring, England's Country party, guided as its members were by a Renaissance ideology hostile to change, experienced these novelties as an alien intrusion. Commentaries about luxury, degeneration, loss of virtue, decaying standards, and fear of enslavement can be understood as part of this classical discourse, but they also invite exploration as reactions to the economic developments which were rendering the models of antiquity totally irrelevant to modern Europe.

In America the republican polarities of virtue and corruption, disinterest and interestedness, public spirit and private ambition, participation and passivity, structured the world of politics, as one by one the colonies extended their range of competence at the expense of imperial authority. Far more than a set of moral precepts for an opposition party, this colonial strain of republicanism provided a language for discussing all actions in the public realm. Where English republicans were engaged in a quarrel with history, Americans were seeking to define the parameters of their polity in the uncertain dependent status of the present.

True to the theoretical underpinnings of the concept of ideology, scholars who have written about classical republicanism during the past twenty years have presented eighteenth-century Anglo-Americans not as possessing ideas so much as being possessed by them. Their historical figures have not been in command of the contents of their minds as liberal heroes had been. In their reinterpretation of the history of the American Revolution, the level-headed, lawyerlike Revolutionary leaders of a previous historiography have been replaced by anxious and frenzied patriots obsessed by the fear of British corruption.[22] Mindful that liberal and Marxist historians

21. *The Machiavellian Moment: Florentine Political Thought and the Atlantic Republican Tradition* (Princeton, 1975), viii.

22. Republicanism is featured prominently in Chapters 4, 11, 12, and 13.

depended upon champions of progress to carry forward the history of modern society, the republican revisers adroitly removed from eighteenth-century ideology a favorable disposition to change. Like Miller's Puritans, Bailyn's patriots and Wood's Founding Fathers were nostalgic about the past, devising ways to save what was best from a social transformation beyond their control and beneath their civilized standards.

Classical republicanism offers late-twentieth-century men and women an attractive alternative to liberalism and socialism. Both substantively, in the recovery of a Renaissance discourse of politics, and theoretically, in the reliance on an anthropological understanding of how societies structure consciousness, the republican revision has inspired a whole generation of scholars in history, political science, literature, and law.[23] Because it demonstrates colonial support for a political order that emphasizes virtue, participation, and deliberation, the revision has changed our perceptions about what was possible in the eighteenth century and, by inference, what might be possible today. Standing outside the liberal field of imagination, it has become a vantage point for assessing that field. Like a magnet, republicanism has drawn to it the filings of contemporary discontents with American politics and culture. Unlike Marxism, it has done this by establishing its origins before Independence and hence establishing authentic American roots.

THERE IS YET one more facet of the story of liberalism to be looked at: capitalism. The radical force which provoked the quarrel with history and made the ahistorical liberal paradigm possible in the Anglo-American world of the eighteenth century was economic development. Spectacular changes in the material world marked the beginning of the modern era. From the seventeenth century on men and women began to express wonder at the volume and variety of goods that graced their lives. Cheap books, maps, and pictures rolled off an ever-increasing number of printing presses. Colorful calicoes embellished the appearance of people and their homes. New

23. My own response to this body of scholarship informs a number of the essays in this collection. See particularly Chapters 5, 6, 10, 11, 12, and 13.

foods, new eating utensils, new tools, and new fads provoked the curiosity and excited the imagination of contemporaries. It also triggered a negative discourse on luxury.[24]

Population grew, as it had many times before in human history. Now, however, instead of the accordianlike pattern typical for four millennia, new levels of population were sustained after the mid-eighteenth century. A vital revolution, that continues to this day, had begun. Even more remarkable, the output of goods in Great Britain surpassed population growth. People crowded into cities; cultivation of the countryside became more intense. Familiar tasks were reorganized for greater efficiency. New networks were elaborated to distribute products and consummate bargains. By the end of the eighteenth century British use of pumps, engines, and mechanical devices for milling and weaving began to revolutionize production as they simultaneously increased the volume and variety of commodities circulating through the market. Theirs, like ours, was a constantly changing world.

The major task of modern history has been to make sense of these changes. The profound rupture in venerable institutions which the material changes entailed gave birth to the social sciences. They flowered first in Scotland, then in France, Great Britain, Germany, and the United States. By following a single story line, like that of American liberalism, we can see a fascinating counterpoint between history and social science, as first one, then the other, plays theme to accompaniment in the accounts of the modern transformation of the Western world. But neither could escape the influence of its own genesis.

R. H. Tawney shrewdly pointed out that the modernization of English society took place over so long a period of time that the categories of thought associated with the new forms of life appeared as timeless forms imprinted on the very stuff of the human brain.[25] The market, which had existed for centuries within the interstices of traditional society, had established itself in England and America as a near autonomous social system so slowly that Adam Smith's

24. John Sekora, *Luxury: The Concept in Western Thought, Eden to Smollet* (Baltimore, 1977).

25. "Essays in Bibliography and Criticism: XIII. A History of Capitalism," *Economic History Review*, 2 (1950), 307.

observation of the "natural propensity to truck and barter" seemed a truism about human nature. When the idea of progress became paramount near the beginning of the nineteenth century, earlier worldviews embedded in Calvinist tracts, Elizabethan drama, and republican notions of civic humanism either had been forgotten or had been filed away as evidence of a preenlightened era.

Tawney's implicit contrast was with Europe. While two centuries of agricultural and commercial development preceded British industrialization, the Germans, French, and Italians saw their economies wrenched from an age-old structure within a single generation. This dimension of time affected the perception of change powerfully. For those on the continent, industrialization was a radical transformation that required new explanations; for the British the final stages of advanced economic development seemed the end of a natural progression. The English could comprehend relations in this modern economy through the laws of nature, applicable to all societies and discoverable through empirical investigation. On the continent modernization appeared as a historical event rather than a natural process; in the European sociological tradition the shaping fingers of society replaced the invisible hand of the market. This European theory did not intrude upon American consciousness until the end of the nineteenth century. At that time capitalism, as distinct from economic development or modern progress or material prosperity, entered historical writing as part of a polemic whose traces can be found in all subsequent efforts to tell the story of economic change in the early modern era.

For Karl Marx capitalism represented the mode of production which determined the character of nineteenth-century bourgeois society. Its principal features were the private ownership of capital in a capital-intensive system and the dependence of the propertyless upon a ruling class of capitalists animated by the drive to maximize profits. Upon this fundamental social relationship rested the ideology, legal institutions, and political order of European nation-states. Marx turned capitalism into an entelechy, an organic system with its own inexorable laws and hierarchy of functions. With this potent concept he challenged liberalism's dependence on the inevitability of progress.

The overpowering effect of both Marxist and liberal theories has been to treat changes in ways of work and the deployment of social resources as parts of an unfolding historical process. With a fully mature industrial economy depicted as the end point, the past could be ordered into preparatory stages. Because material advance is cumulative and interactive—abundant harvests do sustain a larger population, lower food prices do impinge on decisions about investing—it has been particularly difficult to break the mental habit of treating economic development in mechanistic terms. Once the market ceased to be a palpable affair of visible products and noisy bargainers and became instead an abstraction about human responses and the establishment of prices, it was possible to cover up the tremendous variation in exchanges from moment to moment and place to place. The rich record of men and women resistant to standardization was ignored in favor of an analytical mode which diverted attention from people to numbers.[26] At the same time a shift in economic analysis away from definable groups such as manufacturers, laborers, and landlords toward the abstract individual of marginal-utility theory lent the field a specious certitude comparable to that of the physical sciences.[27] Lost in all this was the actual indeterminacy of human affairs and the acute sense that people, in making economic decisions as in other matters, move into an unknown future.

Although Marx shared in the liberal assumption that improvements in productivity promoted by the market were part of an inevitable historical development, his economic determinism was charged with moral outrage at the degradation of the human spirit which had accompanied Europe's vastly increased wealth-creating capacity. This powerfully negative appraisal of industrialization has darkened the treatment of the entire modern period. Marx attributed the material advance of the Western world to the rise of a new class of men hostile to the ascriptive excellence of an aristocratic society and indifferent to the just aspirations of the working class. The

26. For brilliant critiques of this tendency in historical writing, see William Reddy, *The Rise of Market Culture: The Textile Trade and French Society, 1750–1900* (Cambridge, 1984), and Robert Brenner, "The Origins of Capitalist Development: A Critique of Neo-Smithian Marxism," *New Left Review,* 104 (1977).

27. On this point see Ronald Meek, *Economics and Ideology* (London, 1967); Nicholas Xenos, *Out of Paradise: Scarcity and Modernity* (New York, 1990).

moral stigma he placed on commercial development has dichoto-
mized the way scholars have presented economic choices.

The history of capitalism has been written in the shadow of
industrialization, with its "dark, satanic mills," degraded proletariat, and ruthless destruction of the familiar round of rural routines
which replaced humans and animals with machines. Because earlier
agricultural and commercial transformations have been linked
to industrialization, the motivations underlying them have been
homogenized, as though the seventeenth-century men who decided
to grow more grain for the market knew they were putting their
feet upon a conveyer belt that would lead their descendants to the
factory door. Assuming the naturalness of industrialization, liberal
and Marxist historians have treated the timing, form, and occasion
for economic change in particular communities as examples of a
process rather than a genuine historical situation. The final transformation has been attributed either to the intensification of market
relations by proto-capitalists with a market mentality or to the
release of a pent-up market id within all men and women once
institutional, physical, or technological barriers had been overcome.

In his *Protestant Ethic and the Spirit of Capitalism* Weber opened
up a way for breaking out of these interpretative schemes by assessing the choices people made, acting without the knowledge of
future developments.[28] Weber's decision to study the economic
behavior of a highly differentiated religious group, the Calvinists,
reflected his conviction that human beings approach all phenomena
within a dominant framework of meaning. In the early modern
period this framework was almost always religious. Weber did not
believe in the uniform motives of economic man; he considered the
compulsion to make money irrational because there was no end to
it, in both senses of the word. The rationale for capitalist behavior
had to come from some other source. Weber located his "spirit of
capitalism" in a range of characteristics associated with Calvinism:
the desire to glorify God in a calling; the commitment to a strenuous
life; the psychological isolation of the religious rebel; the desacraliz-
ing of the world; and the attendant insistence upon rationalizing

28. Daniel Vickers in "Competency and Competition: Economic Culture in Early
America," *William and Mary Quarterly*, 47 (1990), demonstrates the possibility of recovering
the meaning of economic choice in eighteenth-century America.

all human activities. In this stunning reorientation of premodern values Weber felt he had found an essential accompaniment to the material changes necessary for modern economic development: a capacity to infuse morality into the previously denigrated qualities of hard work, pleasure-denying frugality, wise investment, and steady accumulation of wealth.

What made Weber's study enduringly influential was the renewal of curiosity about how the free market could have flowered in a social environment so inhospitable to its norms and imperatives. As long as capitalism was viewed as a natural process, it was hard to rouse interest in the choices and reactions of early modern men and women. Take away the innate desire for progress, and scholars had to examine economic changes as they took place in a social order that was God-centered, hierarchical, and deeply attached to the folk wisdom of an earlier era.

The social effects of economic opportunities can be read in the laments of critics. Planning for profitable exchanges, even if it was just adding to one's livestock, engaged people's attention. Here were "the unweaned affections" Puritan divines bewailed. As an imaginative area where plans were devised, the market created new interests and spread the consciousness of change. As the distributor of goods, unmediated by authority, the market promoted individuality as well; paradoxically, it was an individuality that removed distinctions.[29] In the long run the marks of superiority upon which authority in a hierarchical society rested began to seem less important than the shared propensities of all men. Patriarchy began to yield to the freemasonry of independent men. Because power relations were affected by these shifts, the novelties that began in the marketplace intruded upon politics just as the need to understand the constantly altering conditions of life called forth new social theories.

THE HISTORICAL consciousness that prompted early modern Anglo-Americans to preserve civic order out of fear of the terrors of

29. For an extended treatment of the psychological effect of the market, see Colin Campbell, *The Romantic Ethic and the Spirit of Modern Consumerism* (Oxford, 1987).

history was overlaid a century later by a liberal doctrine that removed the terror from history by teaching that all change is development. It is hard for us to appreciate the brilliance of this accomplishment, because the very triumph of liberalism spelled oblivion for the intellectual traditions which had preceded it. The deep historical consciousness of the earlier age was expunged from the record. Yet in the bosoms of America's Revolutionary leaders there dwelt lively fears about the dangers of priestcraft and aristocrats, of seventeenth-century enthusiasm and Laudian oppression, of Roman tyrants and Athenian mobs. From our perspective this long eighteenth-century "memory" of inappropriate historical precedents seems puzzling unless we can think our way back to a world that took its soundings about what could happen from what had already done so.

Liberal reformers argued that their propositions were simple dictates of nature; our retrospective view suggests that they were creative responses to the urgent need to bring a constructive theory of change to a changing world. Paradoxically, the republican revision which revealed the indebtedness of America's revolutionary elite to a classical view of politics has made it possible to see liberalism as the compelling intellectual artifact that it was. It is now possible to conjecture that, whereas the adoption of a classical political idiom reflected a resistance to commerce and its social entailments, the acceptance of liberalism announced an attitudinal shift with its cultivation of expectations of sustained improvement. Modern categories of thought had been worked out for those confronted by the incessant transformations of modern times.

Obviously the liberal hero was male. Less obviously liberalism relied on gender differences to preserve the purity of its ideal type. Dependency, lack of ambition, attachment to place and person— these qualities were stripped from the masculine carrier of inalienable rights and conferred upon women. In this ideological division of labor women became the exemplifiers of the personal and intimate, maintainers of family cohesion, and repositories of romantic fantasies about the past. This allowed the unsentimental, self-improving, restlessly ambitious, free, and independent man to hold sway as a universal hero. Without women to accept what was denied in men, the assertion of a uniform human nature could not have been maintained. Nor could society have been analyzed in the social scientific mode without scattering to the periphery the poetic, the sensuous, the indeterminant—in short, the experiential burden carried by women.

As in the return of the repressed, the scholarly imagination has flooded back to the parched lands of a preliberal sensibility. Historians of our generation have reconstructed the diversity of past American lives, exposing the many divergences from liberal stereotypes. They have also produced an embarrassment of riches for those seeking a unified national history. There are so many recorded meanings to the American experience that earlier efforts to confine the record to torchbearing individuals seem more and more dubious, morally and intellectually.

Outside historical scholarship, but impinging upon it, have been new theoretical assertions that language does not just structure our thinking, but actually constitutes our world. As the reigning ideology in the United States, liberalism has been subjected to the most penetrating analysis of rhetoric and conceptualization. In exploring the way discourses confine or enlarge the ambit of our imagination, the deconstructionists have revealed a new domain of discursive power. However, having undermined faith in the stability of language and the constitution of knowledge, they have left us somewhat powerless to use our new analytical tools to break up the linguistic structures that hold us in thrall. Thus the critics of liberalism have been working at cross-purposes. Social histories have opened up new fields of knowledge which have forced a broadening of categories, but they have not created a historical synthesis to illuminate the meaning of the American experience. Those who have examined liberalism as a historical discourse have undermined confidence in more than liberalism, for their deconstructive weapons have been trained upon the whole conception of bodies of knowledge.

This encounter between scholarly research and philosophical skepticism in the writing of American history is but our national version of a crisis in Western thought. Having completed its historic mission of preparing people to live with profound, cumulative processes of development, liberalism seems expendable. Its preoccupation with progress and individualism appears an impoverished reality. Its middle-class and northern European bias has been thoroughly exposed, although it would be a mistake to minimize the capacity of liberalism to cross racial and ethnic boundaries to win adherents to its personal characteristics. Liberalism's dependence on an epistemology of objectivity reveals the awkward connection between assertions of fact and value.

Richard Rorty has posed the insistent question that springs from this crisis: Can democratic societies prevail without the philosophical foundation upon which they have rested for two hundred years?[30] The answer is that we do not know until we have moved onto this new terrain, but we are forced into the experiment through a lack of attractive alternatives. This brings us to the irony that the perdurability of liberalism and its supportive systems of capitalism and democracy have been demonstrated for much of the world at the very time that in its homelands doubt about the virtues of liberalism are widespread.

National histories rest on a volatile mixture of the moral and the instrumental. Because they aim to establish order through shared sentiments, they seek consensus, but because they partake in scholarly traditions inimicable to propaganda, they encourage critical reasoning. National histories are also weathervanes of the climate of opinion. Where they point, the larger public will look. It is not just that historians necessarily participate in the intellectual trends of their age, but rather that engaging with the meaning of experience occupies the center of a nation's intellectual life. Speaking in the deflating voice of the social scientist, Mary Douglas has commented that any "institution that is going to keep its shape needs to control the memory of its members."[31] But that control, as the scholarly trends in American history demonstrates, cannot be maintained in a democratic society except through the conspiracy of successive generations bound to certain silences by the moral imperatives of their times.

Born liberal as a nation, the United States did not appreciate the pain of that birth until the republican revision made us aware of the vitality of a classical political tradition within the colonial societies that sought Independence. That revision—and its enthusiastic reception—indicates a readiness of Americans to detach them-

---

30. *Objectivity, Relativism and Truth* (Cambridge, 1991), 175ff.
31. *How Institutions Think* (Syracuse, 1982), 112.

selves from the liberal perception of reality. Critics of liberalism have pointed to its grandiosity in claiming to represent universal norms and its indifference to human experience outside the great drama of progress. Perhaps it is time to return to the eighteenth-century inspiration, before liberalism was made to do the work of a national ideology.

The original passion of liberal reformers was outrage: outrage at institutions that interfered with free inquiry; outrage about the tyranny that groups exercised over individuals; outrage with the human debasement in the aristocratic assumption of innate superiority. Between its animating spirit and its deliquescent complacency, liberalism held the ground for a powerful, if contradictory, commitment to equality and freedom. Historically associated with the free-market economy and participatory politics, liberalism helped produce the West's mixed legacy of wealth-making and empowerment, exploitation and manipulation. As its cognates suggest, liberalism also had affinities with both liberation and liberality, qualities that resonate with meaning in our world. It offered an openness to change to a society that was changing without a supportive ideology. It applied the principle of hope to a world afflicted with that pessimism which comes from too great an awareness of the past.

To return to my archaeological metaphor, historians go back to certain sites because it is there that a beginning can be found. To locate a national beginning is to give the nation an identity enveloped in a history. For six generations the envelope of American identity was liberalism, with its proud assertion that the enlightened eighteenth century marked a break with the Old World and the old regime. Not since Noah's ark, according to Thomas Paine, had humanity such an opportunity for a fresh start. Historical writing on republicanism not only demolished the idea that American values had always been modern; it also endowed America's revolutionary leaders with intentions incompatible with the nation's myth of creation.

In every truth there is liberation. Freed from the burden of explaining American origins, the values of liberalism have much to commend them. But can they be retained without the certainties of Western metaphysics and scientific positivism? And when American nationalism and liberalism have gone their separate ways, will the nation flounder without its heroic birth in enlightenment freedom? Do the robustly male virtues of liberalism depend on a belief in their universality in order to continue as the promoters of constructive change? Can a hatred of injustice, once premised on the concept of inalienable natural rights, coexist with an understanding of cultural differences? These questions pull us back to the foundational sites of our history, where memory and imagination play a part in the closing and opening of the American mind. But in returning to our historic roots we should not forget that the spirit invoked at Independence was that of experimentation and hope, tolerance and outrage, common sense and uncommon expectations.

1

Political and Economic Liberalism in Seventeenth-Century England

DURING THE last two decades of the seventeenth century—ninety years before the *Wealth of Nations* appeared—a number of British writers challenged the central premises of the balance-of-trade theory for economic growth. The currency crisis and the craze over Indian cottons had sharpened a sense of conflicting interests among Englishmen, and these divisive issues called forth a body of writing which attacked the principles underlying the mercantile system. Examining in a new way the operation of the market, Dudley North, Nicholas Barbon, Dalby Thomas, Henry Martyn, Francis Gardner, James Hodges, Henry Layton, John Houghton, and several anonymous pamphleteers produced explanations of economic relations which were far more sophisticated than the prevailing theories, anticipating at many points the premises of Adam Smith's monumental synthesis.

Yet despite this new plateau in economic reasoning, the conceptually flawed balance-of-trade theory, with its built-in corollary that economic regulation was essential to national security, became even more firmly fixed in the public mind in the eighteenth century. The ideological implications of the rejection of these writings have not been explored. Scholars have assumed the science of economics had to wait for the path-breaking geniuses[1] or that the balance-of-

1. Eli Heckscher, *Mercantilism* (London, 1935), I, 104ff; Jacob Viner, *Studies in the Theory of International Trade* (New York, 1937), 90, 117–118. This interpretation is implicit in Bruno Suviranta, *The Theory of the Balance of Trade in England* (Helsingfors, 1932).

trade critics were too exceptional to treat as a significant group.[2] Charles Wilson has described Dudley North as a swallow who did not produce a summer.[3] The analogy is worth pursuing. Taking a closer look at the birds in hand, it is possible to conclude that it was not the lack of swallows that counted, but the distaste for summers, that, in fact, economic thought ran ahead of social developments, and the analytical insights of the balance-of-trade critics were dismissed because they threatened the fragile social order in England during the country's critical passage into a fully capitalistic society.

The balance-of-trade explanation of how nations grow wealthy had focused attention upon production in such a way as to obscure the dynamics of consumption. Inside England the most noticeable consumers were the very rich and the very poor, and there was little in their patterns of spending to encourage a reevaluation of consumption. As landowners, the rich could tap agricultural revenues first. Their rent rolls were the principal source of capital, but they spent rather than invested their income.[4] The very poor were a conspicuous drain upon the economy because there were so many of them, and their subsistence needs were paid for through taxes.[5] Gregory King's estimate that half the families in England could not pay for their living indicates the dimension of the problem of underemploy-

---

See also Alexander Gershenkron, "History of Economic Doctrines and Economic History," *American Economic Review,* 59 (1969), 2; William Letwin, *The Origins of Scientific Economics* (London, 1963), 144–148.

2. J. D. Gould, *Economic Growth in History* (London, 1972), 220–222; Charles Wilson, *England's Apprenticeship, 1603–1763* (New York, 1965), 184.

3. Ibid., 266.

4. Sir William Petty referred to transferring wealth through taxation "from the Landed and Lazy, to the Crafty and Industrious," *A Treatise of Taxes and Contributions* (London, 1661), 19. A similar sentiment was expressed by Sir Dalby Thomas in *An Historical Account of the Rise and Growth of the West-India Colonies* (London, 1690), in *The Harleian Miscellany* (London, 1809), II, 359. He explained that when it is said "people are the wealth of a nation, it is only meant, laborious and industrious people; and not such as are wholly unemployed, as gentry, clergy, lawyers, serving men, and beggers, etc." See also Sir Francis Brewster, *Essays on Trade and Navigation* (London, 1965), 52.

5. For contemporary estimates of the Poor Law burden, see [William Carter], *England's Interest Asserted, in the Improvement of its Native Commodities* (London, 1669), 10; [Sir Humphrey Mackworth], *England's Glory* (London, 1694), 24. For a modern estimate, see Wilson, *England's Apprenticeship,* 235.

ment.[6] These realities made plausible the argument that since domestic consumption took from the store of English capital through luxury buying and the maintenance of the poor, markets for English goods should be sought outside the country. In other words, let the social overhead and upper-class vanity of other nations return a profit to England. Such a prescription fit well with the endemic political rivalries of seventeenth-century European states. Blocked from appreciating the role of domestic consumption, economic thinkers slipped easily into the assumption that consumption was a necessary evil, growing—if at all—in response to population growth.

Thomas Mun, Gerald de Malynes, and Edward Misselden had analyzed the influence of demand upon prices in their famous debates over the foreign exchange in the 1620s. In *England's Treasure by Forraign Trade,* Mun also drew attention to the way elasticity of demand influenced foreign consumption, as did Mun's contemporary, Rice Vaughan. But none of these writers of the early seventeenth century or their immediate successors dealt comprehensively with the relation of supply and demand.[7] As long as domestic trade was considered analogous to taking in each other's washing, there was no way to consider increased spending as beneficial.[8] Instead total demand appeared inelastic. The rich were expected to buy their luxuries, the poor to have enough to subsist. The possibility that at all levels of society consumers might acquire new wants and find new means to enhance their purchasing power which could generate new spending and produce habits capable of destroying all tradi-

6. King's figures are reproduced and analyzed in Peter Laslett, *The World We Have Lost* (New York, 1973), 36–40.

7. Thomas Mun, *England's Treasure by Forraign Trade* (London, 1664), 84–86; Rice Vaughan, *A Discourse of Coin and Coinage* (London, 1675), in *A Select Collection of Scarce and Valuable Tracts on Money,* ed. John R. McCulloch (London, 1856), 82.

8. For contemporary assertions that selling to one another is "mere consumption" without enrichment, see Sir Thomas Culpeper, *A Discourse, Shewing the Many Advantages Which Will Accrue to This Kingdom by the Abatement of Usury* (London, 1668), 2–3; Sir William Petty, *Political Arithmetick* (London, 1690), 82ff; John Cary, *An Essay on the State of England* (Bristol, 1695), preface; [John Pollexfen], *England and East India Inconsistent in their Manufactures* (London, 1697), 20; *The Profit and Loss of the East-India Trade* (London, [1699]), 8–9; *Certain Considerations Relating to the Royal African Company of England* ([London], 1680), 1; Brewster, *Essays,* 50–52. In the 1690s the word "consumption" loses its pejorative connotation.

tional limits to the wealth of nations was unthought of, if not unthinkable.

During these same years that the balance-of-trade theory served as the principal explanation of economic growth, important social sentiments had become embedded in the prevailing ideas of how nations grew wealthy and powerful. Behind the balance-of-trade theory, there lay a model of the national economy which supplied the principal moral support for mercantilistic regulation. Since national wealth was believed to accrue only from the annual net gain from foreign trade, the whole economy could be conceived of as a kind of national joint-stock trading company. In this view, members of society did not interact with each other, but rather participated, one with another, in England's collective enterprise of selling surplus goods abroad. As in a company, the administration was formal. There was little of Adam Smith's awareness of individuals with personal motives working purposively on their own. Rather economic writers approached the problem of promoting national growth much as a factory foreman might view meeting a production quota. Reading through dozens of proposals for promoting English production one is forcibly struck by the absence of concern for the problem of marketing the projected increase in goods. Emphasis fell exclusively upon mobilizing labor and exploiting new resources: lowering interest rates would stimulate land improvements; attracting foreign craftsmen would introduce technical skills; agricultural diversification would relieve dependence upon outside suppliers.[9] With such a model at the back of their heads, these writers repeatedly elaborated schemes for putting people to work. Houses for the "orderly management of the poor" was a favorite theme. Even more indicative of the national management attitude were the frequent suggestions for a national fishery. Not only would it absorb the labor of weavers' apprentices in off-season, but one writer even suggested that the footmen of the gentry could rise early and employ

9. For example, see Culpeper, *A Discourse*, 5; Samuel Fortrey, *England's Interest and Improvement* (London, 1673), in *A Select Collection of Early English Tracts on Commerce*, ed. John R. McCulloch (London, 1856), 234–236; *Britannia Languens* (London, 1680), in ibid., 298ff; *Angliae Tutamen* (London, 1695), 29. Suviranta, *Theory of the Balance of Trade*, 153–154, errs, I think, in saying that prior to Jacob Vanderlint little attention was paid to the economic value of land.

their idle hours making nets, as could "disbanded soldiers, poor prisoners, widows and orphans, all poor tradesmen, artificers, and labourers, their wives, children, and servants." [10]

This joint-stock enterprise was a powerful image, for it provided symbolic cohesion to a society being atomized by the market. Merchants and industrialists were able to establish their place in the social order in reference to this model, and the laboring poor could find in their disciplined effort an avenue of grace. Effortlessly entwining religion with the social benefits of productivity, Slingsby Bethel railed at popular feastings because they provoked the wrath of God, wasted time, dulled wits, and made men "unfit for action and business, which is [the] chief advancer of any Government." [11] Where religion failed to secure the necessary habits, laws were expected to supply the deficiency. William Sheppard urged double indemnity for those who bought wares knowing that they could not pay for them. Those who lived high, he said, should be taxed as long as they continued their excesses. [12] In a similar vein John Scarlett proposed discriminating among defaulters on the basis of the use made of the dissipated funds, those running into debt for riotous living being subject to the "utmost extremity" of the law. [13] The morality of the market was quietly fused with the morality of the marketman's God.

The balance-of-trade theory explained how increasing exports alone could increase England's wealth and at the same time provided a rationale for organizing labor and legislating market patterns. Associated with it were appeals to patriotism and a justification of existing economic roles. Where the theory failed was in its ability to explain English economic growth. In the closing decades of the seventeenth century, real income, domestic spending, and foreign exports rose together. From John Graunt in 1662 to William Petty in 1682 to Charles Davenant in the next decade the wealth of

10. James Puckle, *England's Path to Wealth and Honor* (London, 1700), in *A Collection of Scarce and Valuable Tracts,* ed. Walter Scott (London, 1814), II, 380. See also Roger Coke, *A Detection of the Court and State of England* (London, 1694), II, 494–495; *Reasons for a Limited Exportation of Wooll* (n.p., 1677), 18–20; Richard Haines, *England's Weal and Prosperity Proposed* (London, 1681), 6–7.

11. [Slingsby Bethel], *The Present Interest of England Stated* (London, 1671), 12–13.

12. William Sheppard, *Englands Balme* (London, 1657), 147, 148.

13. John Scarlett, *The Stile of Exchanges* (London, 1682), 321.

England drew comment.[14] Every index of economic growth showed an advance—agricultural output, capital investment, imports from the Indies and the New World, and the range and quantity of home manufacturing.[15] Most striking was the abounding evidence of a rise in domestic consumption. What had happened to the store of wealth consumed by the London fire? Contemporaries saw it splendidly replaced before their very eyes. And the rebuilding of London was but the most spectacular testimony to the fact that Englishmen were generally enjoying a higher standard of living. This growth posed questions beyond the explanatory power of mercantilist theory.

In the 1670s some writers, responding to the obvious, if uneven, economic growth, began to speculate upon the dynamic effect of increasing demand. The word "markets" in their pamphlets subtly changed from a reference to the point of sales to the more elusive concept of expandable spending. In the next decade a controversy over East Indian imports grew into a raging debate on domestic consumption. According to traditional writers, the villain of the piece was the East India Company. Not only did the company enjoy a monopoly of the trade to India, but the nature of its trade—exporting bullion in return for imports competitive with English goods—ran athwart the most cherished principles of the balance-of-trade concept. From the point of view of those in the English woolen and silk industries the company's greatest crime was introducing the English public to the light, colorful, cheap fabrics of India. By 1690, the taste for chintz, calico, and muslin had reached epidemic proportions. What had begun as an inconspicuous use of cotton for suit lining had given way to a gaudy display of printed draperies, bedspreads, tapestries, shirts, and dresses.[16] With marketing exper-

14. K. G. Davies, "Joint-Stock Investment in the Later Seventeenth Century," *Economic History Review*, 4 (1952), 284–285; for contemporary comment, see Petty, *Political Arithmetick*, 96–99; [Charles Davenant], *An Essay on the East-India-Trade* (London, 1696), 8–10; [William Carter], *The Great Loss and Damage to England by the Transportation of Wooll to Forreign Parts* (n.p., 1677), 12.

15. Wilson, *England's Apprenticeship*, 185; R. M. Hartwell, "Economic Growth in England Before the Industrial Revolution," *Journal of Economic History*, 29 (1969), 25; Gould, *Economic Growth*, 156–157.

16. P. J. Thomas, *Mercantilism and the East India Trade* (London, 1963), 30, 51; Suviranta, *Theory of the Balance of Trade*, 7. Both Thomas and Suviranta pointed out the stimulus of the East India trade to economic reasoning in the seventeenth century.

tise equal to Macy's, in the twentieth century, the managers of the East India Company had sent English fabric designers to India to direct the Indian craftsmen in reproducing patterns especially admired at home. The impact upon employment in England was strong. The popularity and competitive advantages of imported cottons led to a glut in the home market for woolens and silks. Contemporaries complained that thousands of workers in the two domestic industries were thrown onto the parish for support. The affected producers wanted a flat prohibition on domestic imports of Indian cottons. Their advice to the East India Company was to sell their calicoes abroad where cheap textiles would undermine the native industries of Great Britain's trade rivals.[17]

Although it is difficult to learn from contemporary pamphlets whether the poor were important for working up manufactures or manufacturing important for employing the poor, increasingly after 1660 the emphasis fell upon the importance of expanding opportunities for work. Bans on the export of English raw materials and proposals for replacing foreign imports with domestic substitutes were advanced on the ground that they would increase employment. From this point of view, items requiring more labor were socially more useful than those requiring less. Even labor-saving devices were suspect. The woolen and silk manufacturers drew upon this rationale in fighting the East India Company. They stressed the unfairness of searching out places which could undersell English commodities and questioned why manufacturing ought not be promoted "in England [rather] than in India."[18] Charles Davenant was obviously thinking within the traditional theoretical framework when he asserted that cheap imported textiles "freed" more English woolens for foreign export, but other writers recognized that the clothiers could only be convincingly answered by moving outside the balance-of-trade logic altogether.[19]

In *Considerations on the East-India Trade,* Henry Martyn made a full

17. *The Great Necessity and Advantage of Preserving our Own Manufacturies* (London, 1697), 6–10; [Thomas Smith], *England's Danger by Indian Manufactures* (n.p., [1698]), 2–7; [Pollexfen], *England and East India,* 18–20; *Reasons Humbly Offered for the Passing of a Bill* (London, 1697), 7–23; *An Answer to the Most Material Objections* (n.p., [1699]), 1.

18. Ibid., 2.

19. Thomas, *Mercantilism and the East India Trade,* 81.

frontal attack on the theory of the social utility of high labor costs by examining the differentials in domestic consumption. Conceding that Indian imports "abate the price of English Manufactures," he maintained that this abatement stimulated other segments of the economy. Laborers who bought Indian cottons would have more money available from their wages to spend on those items produced more efficiently by the English. Even if English laborers were thrown out of work, the greater competition for jobs would lower wages and push down the cost of other English products. Driving home his cost-advantage theory, Martyn stressed that any law which forced the English to consume only English goods forced them to pay more for their needs than was necessary. He likened this to denying the benefits of new inventions or the obvious savings from the division of labor or rejecting wheat sent as a gift from God.[20] Martyn explored the relation between earning and purchasing power with unprecedented analytical skill. Many of his observations had been anticipated by earlier commentators. For example, Dalby Thomas had extolled the labor-saving ingenuity which the desire to acquire called forth, and John Houghton had disputed Samuel Fortrey's strictures against French imports by pointing out that even foreign luxury items satisfied genuine consumer demands and made people work harder.[21] These writers legitimized domestic competition because they perceived that England was not a giant workhouse but a giant market whose individual members had differing needs.

In focusing attention on these new market relationships, the pamphlets on Indian imports revealed those areas of conflict between manufacturers and merchants which the predominating concern with foreign trade had so long obscured. Driven no doubt by self-interest, the defenders of the East India Company put forth a justification for "a good buy" which amounted to a defense of domestic consumption. Here the issue became critical to the whole structure of ideas associated with the balance-of-trade theory, because the idea of the English economy as a collective undertaking was being challenged. This line of attack cut deeper than the superficial clash of

20. [Henry Martyn], *Considerations on the East-India Trade* (London, 1701), in *Early English Tracts on Commerce*, ed. McCulloch, 606, 578–586.

21. [Thomas], *An Historical Account*, 361–362; *England's Great Happiness* (London, 1677), 18–20.

interests. The actual social atomization which came with the seventeenth-century transition to a market economy had been ameliorated by an imaginative model of economic unity organized around national production and fortified by religion and patriotism. Psychological atomization could be forestalled as long as this image retained its credibility. When individuals began to think of their separate needs and demands as acceptable social considerations, the coherence of the earlier model would disappear. The benefits of the English consumers' having access to cheap East Indian imports depended upon the rejection of the view that society was an interlocking set of producers and distributors and the acceptance of the alternative view that the economy was an aggregation of self-interested individual producer-consumers. The boldest proponents of Indian imports perceived this difference and advanced a theory of economic growth based upon this perception.

When the maverick spirit of fashion revealed itself in the craze over painted calicoes the potential market power of previously unfelt wants came clearly into view. Here was a revolutionary force. Under the sway of new consuming tastes, people had spent more, and in spending more the elasticity of demand had become apparent. In this elasticity, the defenders of domestic spending discovered the propulsive power of envy, emulation, love of luxury, vanity, and vaulting ambition. On the other hand, as long as demand was viewed as more inelastic than elastic, the static conception of wealth held good. England then could only grow richer by selling a larger share of her surplus abroad, that is, by controlling a larger share of the international market. Once consumption was construed as a constructive activity, the connection could be made between progressive levels of spending or effective demand and a self-sustained momentum for economic growth. Writing in 1690, Nicholas Barbon bubbled over with the new possibilities: "The Wants of the Mind are infinite, Man naturally Aspires, and as his Mind is elevated, his Senses grow more refined, and more capable of Delight; his Desires are inlarged, and his Wants increase with his Wishes, which is for every thing that is rare, can gratifie his Senses, adorn his Body, and promote the Ease, Pleasure, and Pomp of Life."[22]

22. [Nicholas Barbon], *A Discourse of Trade* (London, 1690), 15.

From Dudley North came a similar expression: "The main spur to Trade, or rather to Industry and Ingenuity, is the exorbitant Appetites of Men, which they will take pains to gratifie, and so be disposed to work, when nothing else will incline them to it; for did Men content themselves with bare Necessaries, we should have a poor World."[23]

Less euphorically, Francis Gardner explained that while frugality was no doubt a commendable thing, "where People grow Rich, they will spend more largely, and it is better they should do so than to slacken their Industry and Diligence in Trade."[24] These sentiments even crept into the writings of conventional balance-of-trade writers such as John Cary, who affirmed that the growth of pride and luxury was the principal quickener of trade and extended his analysis down to "our poor in England" who can spend more on clothes and furnishings when they are paid more and hence increase the consumption of the very goods they manufacture.[25] An early convert to the power of consumption, John Houghton asserted that "Our High-Living is so far from Prejudicing the Nation that it enriches it." Describing the deadly sins as economic virtues, Houghton cited pride, finery, vanity, shows, play, luxury, eating, and drinking high as causing "more Wealth to the Kingdom, than loss to private estates."[26] "Desire and want increase with riches," Barbon observed, "a Poor Man wants a Pound; a Rich Man an Hundred."[27]

Not content merely to catalogue the psychological stimulants to demand, these writers drew attention to the specific economic function of each emotion. Foreign imports were justifiable because they dazzled people with their novelty and promoted industry by way of

---

23. [Sir Dudley North], *Discourses upon Trade* (London, 1691), 14.

24. [Francis Gardner], *Some Reflections on a Pamphlet* (London, 1696 [1697]), 24, as cited in Richard C. Wiles, "The Theory of Wages in Later English Mercantilism," *Economic History Review,* 21 (1968), 119. Usually identified simply as "Gardner," the author was probably Alderman Francis Gardner of Norwich, who was consulted by the Privy Council on the question of recoinage, according to J. Keith Horsefield, *British Monetary Experiments, 1650–1710* (Cambridge, Mass., 1960), 52, and appears among those voting against the recoinage measure in [Thomas Wagstaffe], *An Account of the Proceedings in the House of Commons* (London, 1696), 13.

25. Cary, *An Essay,* 143ff.

26. Houghton, *A Collection of Letters* (London, 1681), 60.

27. Nicholas Barbon, *A Discourse Concerning Coining the New Money Lighter* (London, 1696), 3.

the acquisitive instinct. Analyzing the rationale for banning foreign imports, Barbon explained that it was based on the fallacious idea that if Englishmen could not buy foreign luxuries they would consume domestic goods. This was not true, he said, because it "is not Necessity that causeth the Consumption, Nature may be Satisfied with little; but it is the wants of the Mind, Fashion, and desire of Novelties, and Things scarce, that causeth Trade."[28]

Dalby Thomas made the same point when he objected to those who wanted England to live on its own without imported luxuries. They were not the source of sin, he said, but "true spurs to virtue, valour, and the elevation of the mind, as well as the just rewards of industry."[29] Competition prompted men to invent things to reduce labor costs, Martyn asserted. "If my Neighbour by doing much with little labour, can sell cheap, I must contrive to sell as cheap as he."[30] North described envy as a goad to industry and ingenuity even among the lowest order. When the "meaner sort" see people who have become rich, they "are spurr'd up to imitate their Industry." Even the man who goes bankrupt emulating his neighbor is a national benefactor, for the public gains from "the extraordinary Application he made, to support his Vanity." Fashion, Barbon said, promotes trade because it "occasions the Expence of Cloaths, before the Old ones are worn out." Rejecting sumptuary laws, North commended consumption for its stimulus to trade. Nations never thrive more than when "Riches are tost from hand to hand."[31]

Behind these endorsements of early obsolescence and conspicuous consumption lay a new confidence in society's productive powers. Where Adam Smith would use the self-sustaining power of consumption without extolling it, these writers of the 1690s actually praised prodigality. A "Conspiracy of the Rich Men to be Covetous, and not spend, would be as dangerous to a Trading State, as a Forreign War," Barbon proclaimed.[32] When John Pollexfen, an

28. Barbon, *A Discourse of Trade,* 72–73.
29. [Thomas], *An Historical Account,* 362.
30. [Martyn], *Considerations on the East-India Trade,* 590.
31. [North], *Discourses upon Trade,* 15; [Barbon], *A Discourse of Trade,* 65; [North], *Discourses upon Trade,* 15. See also Fortrey, *Englands Interest* (London, 1682), 6.
32. [Barbon], *A Discourse of Trade,* 63.

unreconstructed balance-of-trade thinker on the Board of Trade, used the old moralistic arguments against luxury consumption, Gardner replied that there was "no other use of Riches, but to purchase" what served "our Necessity and Delight."[33] The dour disapproval of self-indulgence was countered with the happy intimation of a new society of consumer-producers. "The more the merrier," Humphrey Mackworth proclaimed, "like Bees in a Hive, and better Cheer, too."[34] Moreover, the writers who promoted domestic consumption stressed the essential reciprocity of international trade. Rather precipitately labeling balance-of-trade notions as dead, the author of the Preface to North's *Discourses upon Trade* announced that the whole world of trade was but as one nation, concluding from this that "the loss of a Trade with one Nation, is not that only, separately considered, but so much of the Trade of the World rescinded and lost, for all is combined together."[35] After asserting that either foreign or domestic consumption was good for the nation, Houghton explained in his *Letters* that import consumption enabled foreign countries to buy of England.[36] Henry Martyn's cost-advantage defense of the East India Company also emphasized the mutuality of international commerce.

Accompanying the pamphlet war over Indian imports was a debate over money which pointed up the inadequacy of the mercantilist definition of wealth. According to the balance-of-trade theory, gold and silver alone were wealth, and countries without mines could become wealthy only by a carefully managed foreign trade which brought in more specie than went out. This explanation of wealth undergirt the notion of the sterility of domestic trade and led to an evaluation of all economic activities in terms of their contribution to a net balance of payments. As early as 1650, William Potter had emphasized the commodity exchange that lay at the base of commercial transactions,[37] but the writers of the 1690s

33. [Gardner], *Some Reflections on a Pamphlet*, 7.

34. [Mackworth], *England's Glory*, 20–23.

35. [North], *Discourses upon Trade*, viii. William Letwin, "The Authorship of Sir Dudley North's 'Discourses upon Trade,'" *Economica*, 18 (1951), 35–45, suggests that Roger North wrote the preface to his brother's essay.

36. John Houghton, *A Collection of Letters for the Improvement of Husbandry and Trade* (London, 1681), 52–53.

37. William Potter, *The Key of Wealth* (London, 1650), 2.

stressed the utility of money as a means to the goods men desired. Roger Coke put it succinctly: "The wealth of every Nation consists in Goods more than Money, so much therefore as any Nation abounds more in Goods than another, so much richer is that Nation than the other, for Money is of no other use, than as imployed in Trade, and the defence of the Nation."[38] "To distinguish rightly in these points," Dalby Thomas explained, "we must consider money, as the least part of the wealth of any nation, and think of it only as a scale to weigh one thing against another."[39] Carrying the analysis further, Francis Gardner maintained that "some Goods are more acceptable in some Countries, at sometimes, than Money."[40]

The repeated assertions that money was only a means for satisfying one's desire for goods was but a step away from the position that consumption was the logical end of production. As Henry Martyn put it: "The true and principal Riches, whether of private Persons, or of whole Nations, are Meat, and Bread, and Cloaths, and Houses, the Conveniences as well as Necessaries of Life . . . These for their own sakes, Money, because 'twill purchase these, are to be esteemed Riches; so that Bullion is only secondary and dependent, Cloaths and Manufactures are real and principal Riches.[41]

Speaking directly to the balance-of-trade maxim that commerce was only beneficial when more goods were exported than imported, Thomas Papillon maintained that this would only be true if gold and silver were the sole stock and riches of the kingdom: "Whereas in truth the Stock and Riches of the Kingdom, cannot properly be confined to Money, nor ought Gold and Silver to be excluded from being Merchandise, to be Traded with, as well as any other sort of Goods."[42] John Houghton asserted that money in coin was "good for nothing, but potentially is good for everything."[43]

During the debates which preceded the 1696 recoinage of Eng-

38. Coke, *A Deduction*, II, 522.

39. [Thomas], *An Historical Account*, 359.

40. [Gardner], *Some Reflections on a Pamphlet*, 7.

41. [Martyn], *Considerations on the East-India Trade*, 558.

42. Thomas Papillon, *The East-India-Trade a Most Profitable Trade to the Kingdom* (London, 1696), 4 (published anonymously in 1677).

43. Following this logic, Houghton, *A Collection of Letters*, 24–25, recommended bringing in goods rather than money to balance accounts, since money is unable to satisfy any real human needs.

land's clipped silver, attention passed to the question of whether gold and silver possessed an intrinsic and unique value which made bullion synonymous with wealth, or whether the use of money for exchange purposes made the extrinsic value derived from official minting the more important. In this clash of opinions John Locke found himself ranged against North, Barbon, James Hodges, Henry Layton, Sir Richard Temple, and William Lowndes. Because Locke's recommendation for recoinage was based in part on the metalist view of wealth, his opponents dug away at this point. Money, Layton said, was as much a measure between items to be bartered and a commodity itself as the "natural, unalterable measure of Commodities," which Locke had made it.[44] Hodges said Locke's system of coin was built on the common error of considering the estimate of worth to be its intrinsic value rather than its usefulness.[45] Attacking Locke's belief that trade was valuable only as a means of attracting bullion, Barbon called the notion "altogether a mistake." Gold and silver were "but Commodities; and one sort of Commodity is as good as another, so it be of the same value."[46]

By depriving gold and silver of their unique qualities, the balance-of-trade critics opened the way for appreciating the contribution of domestic trade to economic prosperity. Daniel Defoe developed this position most thoroughly in *Taxes No Charge*. Setting forth an elaborate plan for pumping money into the economy by taxing misers and pleasure spenders, Defoe argued that if the benefit of foreign trade is to bring in commodity for commodity then that can be done at home without exposing people to the hazards of the sea.[47] Lowndes, Layton, and an A. Vickaris similarly drew attention to the fact that money is only uniquely prized as a means of foreign exchange, and that within the internal market the intrinsic value of gold and silver is immaterial.[48] Carrying the argument still further, Dudley North said that it was absurd for people to say that

44. [Henry Layton], *Observations Concerning Money and Coin* (London, 1697), 12.

45. [James Hodges], *The Present State of England as to Coin and Publick Charges* (London, 1697), 135.

46. Barbon, *A Discourse Concerning Coining*, 40.

47. [Daniel Defoe], *Taxes No Charge* (London, 1690), 17.

48. [William Lowndes], *A Report Containing an Essay for the Amendment of the Silver Coins* (London, 1695), 81–82; *Observations*, 12–14; [A. Vickaris], *An Essay for Regulation of the Coyn* (London, 1696), 22–23.

money was short. If there were a demand for it, it would be man-ufactured like anything else, since there was free coinage and plenty of gold and silver around in plate.[49] With increasing sophistication, these writers assessed the economic role of money. In shifting atten-tion away from money as a store of wealth, they moved closer to recognizing the dynamic elements in the economy. The debate over money—often with the same debaters—thus reenforced the theoret-ical advances made in the India imports controversy. What was needed next was to examine how the latent consuming capacity of the public at large might become an engine for sustained growth.

The idea of man as a consuming animal with boundless appetites, capable of driving the economy to new levels of prosperity, arrived with the economic literature of the 1690s. By going behind the new tastes to explore the human motives regulating personal spend-ing, some writers discovered both a human dynamic and a market mechanism which undermined the static, specie-oriented mercan-tilist view. Unlike the number of working days in a person's life, energy and ingenuity organized under the stimulus of desire appeared almost limitless. Since man could satisfy his new wants only by increasing his purchasing power, what desire ultimately produced was an incentive to be more competitive in the market. From such a spring economic activity could function without outside direction. Where earlier writers had recognized the impact of taste and delight upon the market price of items, they never saw the effect of these influences upon total demand. Nor did they move to an appreciation of the role played by domestic consumption in stimulating production and total national growth.[50] This required a new definition of wealth and a new model of economics as a self-sustaining complex of internal relationships in which foreign trade represented accessibility to desired goods rather than the only source of riches.

The material for building a new economic theory was presented in the 1690s, but these ideas were not worked out in the succeeding

---

49. [North], *Discourses upon Trade,* postscript. See also [Mackworth], *England's Glory,* 5–6; Sir Richard Temple, *Some Short Remarks upon Mr. Locke's Book* (London, 1696), 4–10; John Cary, *An Essay on the Coyn and Credit of England* (Bristol, 1696), 5–12.

50. See Marian Bowley, "Some Seventeenth Century Contributions to the Theory of Value," *Economica,* 30 (1963), 122–139.

decades. Instead the old formulas of the balance-of-trade theory survived with undiminished strength well into the eighteenth century. Fragments from the controversies over Indian imports can be found in the polemics over the French treaty of 1713, in the voluminous economic writings of Daniel Defoe, and in a different vein in Bernard Mandeville's *Fable of the Bees.* Clearly, to conceive of economic growth in terms of goods and services annually produced, purchased, and consumed was difficult for Englishmen long accustomed to the pot-of-gold image of wealth. Even after these ideas had been published, there still remained obstacles—circumstantial as well as ideological—to the idea that society was an aggregation of self-interested individuals tied to one another by the tenuous bonds of envy, exploitation, and competition.

It lies in the nature of historical investigation that developments which could be expected to take place, but do not, are rarely given the same attention as actual events. Yet a break in a development offers important clues to the nature of social change. The lacuna which needs to be explained here is the failure of writers to build upon the insights and arguments of the seventeenth-century critics of the balance-of-trade theory. Between the 1620s, when Mun, Malynes, and Misselden probed the mechanism of the exchange, and the 1690s, when the popularity of Indian cottons and the recoinage became issues, a host of journalists, reformers, merchants, bank promoters, royal officials, London developers, members of Parliament, mathematicians, improving landlords, clothiers, and lawyers published a steady stream of tracts and treatises. Their writings paralleled revolutionary changes in the English economy: the extension of the internal market, the development of the colonial trade, the spectacular growth of London, the striking increase in agricultural productivity, the founding of the Bank of England, and the redistribution of people and production centers. As could be expected from such a motley assortment of would-be experts, the quality of the description and analysis is uneven. There is, nonetheless, an increasing sophistication in the conceptualization of wealth, commerce, and money which challenged the central premises of the mercantilist theory. The failure of others to take up this fruitful line of reasoning is the historical fact which remains unexplored.

The usual treatment of this puzzle is to appeal to the slow spread of new ideas, to minimize the amount and thoroughness of the criticism, or to refer to residual Puritan scruples against spending. Of course new ideas often spread slowly, but the rate and unevenness in intellectual currents is what we would like to understand better. The same is true of the enduring strength of old ideas such as the Puritan legacy in Restoration England. There were many beliefs and values in the complex of Puritan thought. Why did some survive into the Restoration and others not? The waning and waxing of Puritan ideals require investigation. As for the more common scholarly tendency to see the mercantilist critics of the late seventeenth century as brilliant exceptions, the range and number of their publications belie this.

The answer, I believe, is that the values embedded in the alternate theories of economic growth were incompatible with the ideological imperatives of English society. Ideology, I define as a shared and coherent view of the world which provides solidarity by assigning and rationalizing the various roles people fill in society. The moral cohesion provided by common beliefs cannot be dispensed with, particularly in a society where custom has been largely replaced by conscious decisions. In a time of profound social change, such as England was experiencing, the shared explanations which an ideology offers become all the more important because they prepare people to assume new functions. They also facilitate the integration of new ideas with old ones. The volitional nature of belief means, however, that new explanations must satisfy a range of needs before they will be willingly accepted. The uprooting of much of the English peasantry and the geographic redistribution of workers made social control a critical issue. Ideas which explained and justified that control to both the controllers and the controlled were essential if order was to be maintained through a time of change. The new economic ideas undermined the rationale for lower-class discipline and upper-class direction. The divisiveness of competition among groups within the economy threatened a political structure already strained by clashes with the crown. Mercantilism, unlike the more intellectually impressive ideas of its critics, created morally satisfying roles in the new market society. It prescribed a path of economic development more compatible with social stability. It also deflected awareness of the tensions between economic groups within England.

From this perspective, the balance-of-trade theory became economic orthodoxy in the first half of the eighteenth century not because it explained the market to contemporaries—it had ceased to do this by 1680—nor for want of better explanations, but because it offered a rationale for coercing the poor, controlling the direction of growth, and subordinating the competition among groups to the goals of economic nationalism.

Capitalism in the first part of the seventeenth century had proved compatible with traditional social stratification. The lower order became the laboring poor, while merchants, clothiers, bankers, shippers, and processors acquired the gentility formerly reserved for the landed class.[51] Subtle shifts in values had occurred, but the two-tiered world of the propertied and the propertyless had not been undermined. A consumption-oriented model of economic growth, on the other hand, threatened major interests of the ruling class that had coalesced in Restoration England. Dangerous leveling tendencies lurked behind the idea of personal improvement through imitative buying. The notion that the wealth of nations began with stimulating wants rather than organizing production robbed intrusive social legislation of a supporting rationale. Once it was suggested that spending in the home market was more beneficial to the economy than domestic parsimony the social benefits of statutory wage levels could be questioned. If English consumers had a right to a good buy in Indian cottons, as Martyn suggested, why could they not demand commercial policies which would protect them?

It is no accident that the men who advanced these novel opinions about domestic consumption were merchants—either outspoken defenders of the East India Company or, like Dudley North, an experienced Turkey merchant, associated with foreign trades which grew with the spread of new tastes. They were not involved, as were manufacturers, in the mobilization of labor. The important variables of their commercial world were markets, prices, shipping costs, and interest rates. The manufacturers whose numbers grew with the increase in industrial processing shared the clothiers' concern with

---

51. Lawrence Stone, "Social Mobility in England, 1500–1700," *Past and Present*, 33 (1966), 52–55.

employment problems. The lower class loomed larger to them as potential workers than as likely customers. In this regard the industrial capitalists shared the interest of farmers and landed gentry, who relied upon the availability of day laborers at critical seasons of the year. Unlike the foreign merchants, these members of the ruling class had powerful reasons to maintain the credibility of the balance-of-trade explanation of national wealth. Before patriotism was the last refuge of the scoundrel, it was the valued ally of English manufacturers and landlords, creating a free labor force from the copyholders, tenants, mechanics, and craftsmen of an old order. Moreover, conventional mercantilist formulas supplied a rationale firmly based on national security for the protectionist legislation which came into full force after 1713.[52] To entertain the idea that "the whole World as to Trade, is but as one Nation or People" was to bring into question not only the entire Navigation System but also the wisdom of England's calculatedly aggressive national posture.

This new challenge to mercantilist thought also bore upon the more subtle problem of social control in a liberal society. Through the course of the seventeenth century, upper-class Englishmen had disentangled themselves from the constraining ties of a corporate society and embraced instead the ethos of liberalism. Slowly the individual's right to be free of inherited social obligations had gained precedence over the older notion of society's primary claim upon its members. While liberal ethics freed property and property owners from traditional social restraints, it also undermined the justification for some people's being invested with permanent authority over others. Instead, all in the society were conceived to be free and individually responsible. In arguing for this personal liberty, however, upper-class liberals had delivered most of the propertyless into the hands of a new master—the market through which they sold their labor and bought their bread. At the same time that the spirit of "possessive individualism"—to use C. B. Macpherson's insightful phrase—shattered institutional responsibility for social survival, developments in the economy separated most workers from their

52. For an interesting discussion of the repatterning of English trade under the protectionist impulse, see Ralph Davis, "English Foreign Trade, 1700–1774," *Economic History Review,* 15 (1962), 294–295.

tools or their access to land. Without these, they were forced to sell their labor. Since only through these transactions could people feed themselves, the unseen market replaced the visible and personal authority of the previous era.

Contemporaries recognized this coercive power of the market. In 1641, Henry Robinson had defended higher food prices because the "Husbandman would hereby be brought to a frugall dyet or stirrd up to become more industrious." Likewise, farmers could "discharge a rackrent by multiplying the fruits thereof through industry."[53] Evaluating the effects of a poll tax, Petty adduced an added benefit from the fact that it encouraged men with many children to set them "to some profitable employment upon their very first capacity, out of the proceed whereof, to pay each childe his own Poll-money."[54] Francis Gardner put the low wage argument in a nutshell: "The Poor, if Two Dayes work will maintain them, will not work three: and our Manufactures are never so well wrought as, in a time of dull Trade, when we pay less for Workmanship, and yet the Poor live as well then as in time of greatest Plenty, if they have but a full stroke of Work."[55]

The efficacy of the market as an implement of control in a technically free economy depended, however, upon whether it was a buyer's or a seller's market. As John Locke commented, mechanics and apprentices lived such a "hand-to-mouth" existence that they were forced to accept food for wages rather than starve.[56] Another writer feared their excessive freedom and described the poor within a fifty-mile radius of London as idle and surly and willing to work only "if two days pay will keep them a week." Others suggested an excise tax on food and drink to make the poor work a full week.[57] Against this background the danger of a consumption formula for

53. Henry Robinson, *Englands Safety, in Trades Increase* (London, 1641), 7–8.

54. [Petty], *A Treatise of Taxes,* 3. See also Thomas Manley, *Usury at Six Per Cent. Examined, and Found Unjustly Charged* (London, 1669), 24–25.

55. [Gardner], *Some Reflections on a Pamphlet,* 16.

56. [John Locke], *Some Considerations of the Consequences of the Lowering of Interest* (London, 1692), 34.

57. *The Trade of England Revived; and the Abuses Thereof Rectified* (n.p., 1681), 8. See also E. P. Thompson, "Time, Work-Discipline, and Industrial Capitalism," *Past and Present,* 38 (1967), 56–97; Keith Thomas, "Work and Leisure in Pre-Industrial Society," ibid., 24 (1964), 61–62.

economic growth can be assessed better: it threatened the most effective form of class discipline in a liberal society. The capitalistic organization of the economy could force men and women onto the labor market since that was the only place where they could earn the means of subsistence, but the amount of labor they were forced to sell depended upon the wage rate.

The employers' need to control the labor force reveals the incompatibilities between liberalism and capitalism. Liberalism asserted the right of each person to the enjoyment of himself and the fruits of his labor. It did not matter whether laborers were predisposed toward leisure or consuming. But the economic growth which the capitalistic system promoted required a disciplined and expandable work force. Leisure preferences could be as inhibiting to growth as archaic Poor Laws. Employers did not seek conditions of political and moral freedom for the working class. In fact, as they well perceived, transporting workers to centers of employment was much more efficient than relying upon necessitous, but free, workers to go where the jobs were.[58] While much has been made of the congruence between freedom and capitalism, it was the freedom of property owners from social obligations which was critical to capitalistic growth in the seventeenth century. Ideas which promoted free choice among the poor were inherently dangerous to the entrepreneurs. The writers who extolled the advantages of domestic spending in the fight over Indian imports implied that human behavior could be shaped by the impulse to consume, but such optimistic reliance upon envy and emulation must have appeared inadequate to the task of controlling laborers described as idle and surly and willing to work only if two days' pay would keep them a week. Since the old social justification for ordering all economic relations had been destroyed in the fight to make property private and property-owners free, economic theory had to supply the reasons for statutory regulations.[59] This

58. Sir Josiah Child, *A New Discourse of Trade* (London, 1693), 67; [Petty], *A Treatise of Taxes*, 48–49; Robinson, *Englands Safety*, 44–45.

59. For Edward Coke's role in endowing economic freedom with a constitutional sanction, see David Little, *Religion, Order, and Law* (New York, 1969), 203–217, 243–246; Barbara Malament, "The 'Economic Liberalism' of Sir Edward Coke," *Yale Law Journal*, 76 (1967), 1321–1358; Donald O. Wagner, "Coke and the Rise of Economic Liberalism," *Economic History Review*, 6 (1935), 30–44.

was the role which the balance-of-trade dogmas played in the eighteenth century.

The critical difference between Adam Smith's theory of economic growth, which was anticipated in the closing years of the seventeenth century, and that of the mercantilists was the constructive value given to consumption. This constructive value in turn rested upon the assumption that all men wished to maximize their market power because that and that alone offered an avenue of self-improvement. Although Smith's sympathies lay strongly with the savers and investors, the propensity to consume provides the linchpin for his whole system.[60] Externally, it creates the effective demand which calls forth production systems large enough for specialization and division of labor. Internally, the drive to truck and barter—to buy and sell—directs individual energies toward the market and away from other human satisfactions. So axiomatic is it to Smith that self-improvement will be fulfilled through economic activity that he does not even entertain ideas about alternate means to improve oneself, much less alternate goals. One improves through market power, but market power rests upon producing power. The more one produces, the more one can satisfy wants. Since self-improvement, as Smith defined it, has no natural limit, there is no limit to man's endeavors. In Smith's model, people as producers and people as consumers act like an alternating electrical current, throwing a steady flow of impulses into the economy. The flow can be taken for granted because it came from human qualities assumed to be universal.

The acceptance of the idea of universal economic rationality was the key step in the triumph of modern liberalism, because the natural economic laws depended upon natural modes of behavior. Before the laws could be accepted, the description of human nature supporting them had to be credible. Historically, however, before economic rationality became a learned pattern of response, explicit

---

60. "Consumption is the sole end and purpose of all production; and the interest of the producer ought to be attended to, only so far as it may be necessary for promoting that of the consumer. The maxim is so perfectly self-evident, that it would be absurd to attempt to prove it." Adam Smith, *An Inquiry into the Nature and Causes of the Wealth of Nations* (New York, 1937; originally published in 1776), 625. For Smith's ambivalence on the subject of consumption, compare this quotation with those in ibid., 321–325.

control was necessary to secure working-class discipline. The laboring poor had to be managed. The spendthrift with a feast or famine mentality had to be transformed into the shrewd saver, and the saver had to become an orderly, but compulsive, investor and consumer. Market thinking could be relied upon only after the variety of forces influencing personal preferences in the use of time and wealth had been ruthlessly narrowed to one—the likelihood of gain. This radical reductionism was the essence of Smith's economic rationality. The economically rational person was the one who subverted all other drives to the economic one of gaining more power in the market.

During the first part of the seventeenth century, when invested capital moved England toward a market economy, only the vanguard of entrepreneurs operated as economic rationalists. To them, the rest of the society represented a problem demanding external control and direction. To meet this challenge, moreover, they relied upon a model of economic growth which obscured the possibility that the extension of economic rationalism to the working class was either desirable or possible. Rather the economic irrationality of the poor was assumed; the solution was to train them up to habits of work. When the writers in the closing decades of the seventeenth century proposed unleashing the acquisitive instincts of all classes, they were proposing a route to economic growth fraught with perils. The idea of self-improvement through spending implied genuine social mobility. The assertion that "the meaner sort" could and should emulate their betters suggested that class distinctions were based on little more than purchasing power. The moral implications of growth through popular spending were even more suspect. Unlike the work ethic which called upon powerful longings for self-discipline and purposeful activity, the ethic of consumption rested upon a moral base so shallow as to threaten the whole complex of conventional religious precepts. Calvinism had joined an ancient Christian ascetic impulse to a modern reorganization of work; the psychology of consumption offered nothing more than a calculating hedonism.

The moral anemia of appeals to consume was inextricably tied up with questions of control. Liberalism had posited man's freedom and responsibility. Capitalism required unrelenting personal effort in the marketplace. The two could meet only if the poor, like the rich, were converted to possessive individualism and economic rationality. Until this transition had been made, class discipline needed the support of economic theories bolstered by religion and patriotism. When capitalism and free choice were joined by Adam Smith, they were compatible because Smith could theorize from a human model in which the drive for economic self-improvement predominated. This conception of man was the antithesis of freedom, for it presumed a compulsive market response. In recommending the democratization of consumption in the 1690s, the proponents of a spending model of economic growth were revealing for the first time the tensions that lay beneath the values and sensibilities associated with the producing and consuming sides of capitalism. Only when economic rationalism had become internalized by the working, as well as the investing, class could liberal economics support the onus of its amorality. The ideology of mercantilism in the meantime blunted the force of new ideas.

2

Locke, Liberalism, and the
Natural Law of Money

IN THE nineteenth century the idea that natural laws determined social relations informed all thinking on politics and economics. Central to this theory was the belief in inexorable regularities that derived their power from human propensities beyond the reach of thought or will. The iron law of rent, the law of supply and demand, Malthus' laws of population, the law of diminishing returns, the invisible hand of the market, and the irresistible human urge to truck and barter are all concepts which assume that natural forces overrule positive law, moral injunctions, and personal choice. As Karl Polanyi described it, "human society had become an accessory of the economic system" and "the laws of commerce were the laws of nature and consequently the laws of God."[1] The old idea of civilization as created artifact or of human existence as a dramatic struggle between moral and natural man collapsed before the intellectual appeal of a mechanistic social order.

From our vantage point this nineteenth-century faith that universal laws governed society requires explanation. Through what process did the Western philosophical tradition once suffused with rationalism and didacticism give way to a belief in the unseen, uncontrollable, mindless power of nature? What undermined the

---

1. Karl Polanyi, *The Great Transformation: The Political and Economic Origins of Our Time* (Boston, 1944), 75, 117.

age-old wisdom that social living involves conscious human planning and explicit direction? Since belief that natural social laws are capable of integrating the discrete activities of egocentric individuals is simply a belief and in no way demonstrable, the adoption of it must be seen as a selective act on the part of individuals, groups, and finally a whole society. The time and setting for the change is not in doubt. In England it began in the late seventeenth century and culminated with the publication of *The Wealth of Nations* and the elaboration of Adam Smith's ideas by Malthus, Bentham, Ricardo, and Townsend. The process itself is more obscure. In this chapter I will explore one of the turning points: the polemical battle over the recoinage in 1696 of England's clipped silver money and the subsequent triumph of John Locke's theory of the natural value of money. On the surface this dispute concerned the choice between recoining the battered silver shillings at the old denomination and reducing the silver content of the coins to reflect the actual amount in the clipped coins in circulation. Beneath the surface was an intellectual and ideological conflict about the nature of money and the regulatory power of the government.

My point of departure for arguing that an extraordinarily tedious debate over mint ratios and money values represents a major milestone on the road to nineteenth-century liberalism is the belief that the steady expansion of the market in seventeenth century England presented contemporaries with a serious intellectual challenge. The market itself was a dislocating force not unlike an invading army. People were torn from customary homes and ways of working. Alien values intruded upon well-established mores. Theoretical explanations of behavior, human purpose, and social organization were challenged. The ambitious attached themselves to the new power, threatening normal social arrangements. The market, indifferent to persons but responsive to appropriate personal behavior, upset the prescriptive system of rewards. Traditional bonds of social responsibility between king and people, master and worker, father and children, were broken. Since the social dislocation caused by the expanding market economy preceded an understanding of its operation, constructing a theory of the new economy was inevitably implicated in the problems and opportunities accompanying its spread. One solution was to let the market solve the problems it had created by giving free reign to economic forces. This meant treating men and land as commodities to be utilized according to the logic of the market, yet there was little in the Western philosophical tradition to lend support to the adoption of a market ethic which would dethrone authority and unravel the fabric of social responsibilities. As formal propositions the imperatives of the market could not be legislated, for they flew in the face of established norms. However, as facts about nature, they could be discovered. It is here that the idea of natural law came into play. In the Western concept of nature and the nature of God's created universe lay a potential rationale for supplanting the laws of man by the laws of impersonal economic forces. If it could be demonstrated that the new market system represented an economic order rooted in the nature of man and capable, like other natural systems, of achieving its own equilibrium, then efforts to control it could be viewed as both futile and arrogant.

It is within this context that I intend to examine the debate of 1696 over recoinage. The argument over reminting shillings contains a key part of the theory of natural social laws which transformed English thought. The transformation itself involved a rejection of human purposefulness and an acceptance of natural forces as the arbiters of social decisions. The full articulation of such a system required repeated discoveries of the natural mechanisms which obviated individual choice and social authority. The polemics over recoinage produced just such a discovery. In the face of an impressive amount of evidence to the contrary, John Locke successfully asserted that the denominational value of English shillings could not be changed because the value of money was rooted in nature. The dispute is significant not only because of what it reveals about the creation of economic liberalism but also because it illuminates how deeply theoretical choices were embedded in the social situation. Despite the superior reasoning of Locke's opponents, Parliament, as we shall see, followed Locke and spurned his critics. A fruitful line of inquiry was subsequently stifled, and the independent natural value of money took its place in the elaboration of the theory of a self-regulating market.

*   *   *

THE DRAMA OF the silver shilling began in a tangled skein of commercial troubles encumbering English trade at the end of the seventeenth century. Gold and silver coin were in short supply relative to England's needs for currency. The outbreak of war with France in 1689 aggravated the shortage of coin because the English government sent regular shipments of money to the continent to pay soldiers' wages and to supply England's allies in Flanders, the Piedmont, and on the Rhine. The causes of the long-term shortage of coin were more complex. Contemporaries blamed the adverse balance of trade with France, but as the gravity of the shortage became more severe, attention focused upon the money mechanism itself. To understand how official policy encouraged the outward flow of silver requires some background information and a lot of patience on the part of the reader. Although England's money of account was silver, the mint had been issuing gold guineas since 1663. Unlike silver coins, guineas were allowed to find their own level, that is, people could exchange them for shillings at the going market rate. Since gold and silver were used for a variety of things besides minting coin, bullion prices fluctuated like those of any other commodity traded on the market. In England the mint ratio—that is, the face value or denomination put on a certain quantity of silver— was too low and that put on gold too high. Silver was undervalued and gold was overvalued. This created an incentive to melt down English silver coin and export it as bullion to Europe where it received a higher price. Foreigners or those who had accounts to settle outside England could do this as part of their business; or one could simply trade in money, shipping silver bullion out of England, exchanging it abroad for gold, which imported into England could be used to buy up cheap silver coin.[2] Exporting English coin was illegal, but it was widely recognized as a common, if felonious, practice which "anyone's conscience permits" when profits are so great.[3]

2. *Select Tracts and Documents Illustrative of English Monetary History, 1626–1730,* ed. William A. Shaw (London, 1896), v–vi. Shaw says that merchants could buy up good money with bad and in a "retail way sell piece by piece the coin of one country to another country." For a contemporary account, see Anon., *A Letter from an English Merchant at Amsterdam to His Friend at London* (London, 1695).

3. A. V[ickaris], *An Essay for Regulating of the Coyn* (London, 1696), 3; William Hodges, *The Groans of the Poor* (London, 1696), 15; [Henry Layton], *Observations Concerning Money and Coin* (London, 1697), 10.

The coin shortage and the enhanced value of silver abroad promoted a further fraud. Enterprising Englishmen discovered that they could clip off the edges of their hammered silver shillings and half-crowns, saving or melting down the clippings for profitable export. This private whittling was age-old, but the 1690s saw more of it and the accompanying inflation brought the crisis to a head.[4] Although contemporaries generally acknowledged that the clipped coins passed freely[5]—no doubt because of the acute shortage of coin—the increasing lightness of silver coins enhanced the value of unclipped gold guineas. These guineas, which had been exchanged for twenty years at 21*s.* 6*d.*, rose to 30*s.* in 1695. One more factor complicated the English monetary system. In 1663 the mint began milling coins instead of hammering them into shape. The milling process was a technological advance which among other things produced coins with milled edges which could not be clipped. In practical terms this meant that the new milled coins, chiefly half-crowns, had a nominal value exactly the same as hammered coins, but a silver content as much as twice that of the battered and clipped hammered ones. Unclipped milled silver coins in relation to clipped hammered coins were like hard money to soft. The clipped coins drove the milled coins out of circulation. However, they were not hoarded as Gresham's Law would have it, but rather, because of the higher price for silver on the continent, the newly minted coins were melted down and exported as bullion to be sold at a higher price abroad. Thus every market factor served to promote a drain of English silver coin.[6]

In 1695, when the king's ministers addressed themselves to the

4. For a scholarly discussion of the inflation, see C. R. Fay, "Locke versus Lowndes," *Cambridge Historical Journal,* 4 (1933), 149–155; J. Keith Horsefield, *British Monetary Experiments, 1650–1710* (Cambridge, Mass., 1960), 47–60; Sir Albert Feavearyear, *The Pound Sterling* (Oxford, 1963), 119–122; William Letwin, *The Origins of Scientific Economics* (London, 1963), 69–74.

5. Neither Fay, "Locke versus Lowndes," 145, nor Feavearyear, *The Pound Sterling,* 121, agrees with Letwin, *The Origins of Scientific Economics,* 69–74, in saying that the coins were rejected. Contemporary evidence is overwhelming that they passed freely: Hodges, *The Groans of the Poor,* 14; [William Patterson], *A Review of the Universal Remedy* (London, 1696), 24; Anon., *A Letter from an English Merchant,* 8; and Anon., *The Bank of England, and Their Present Method of Paying Defended from the Aspersions cast on them in a Late Book Entitled a Review of the Universal Remedy* (London, 1697), 9.

6. Shaw, *Select Tracts,* viii–x.

twin problems of the shortage of coin and the battered condition of the remaining silver money, the situation was acute. Thomas Wagstaffe, a Member of Parliament, put the case succinctly: there was not enough money both to drive trade at home and to ship coin abroad. "If the King wants it Abroad, and the Necessities of the People cannot spare it from Home, 'tis plaine, one of them must be great sufferers."[7] Rising prices for guineas and continued clipping of silver shillings aggravated the problem. Fears of recoinage upon terms as yet undefined added an unwelcome element of panic.[8] In the summer of 1695 the Privy Council sought the advice of William Lowndes, who had been secretary of the Treasury for sixteen years. Lowndes responded with a report which was a model of monetary analysis. He first traced the history of English money, noting the ups and downs in the amounts of silver officially designated or denominated for each coin. After detailing why the divergence of the prices of bullion and coin promoted the melting down of silver coins, Lowndes concluded with a recommendation that the clipped coin be called in and reminted with a devaluation of 25 percent, that is with 25 percent less silver denominated for each coin. As long as bullion is worth more by weight than coin, Lowndes explained, silver in bulk will never be brought to the mint for coining, which was what England needed to increase the circulating medium. Rather the opposite would take place: coin, already in short supply, would be melted down and shipped out as bullion, illegalities notwithstanding.

Lowndes's point was simple, but is hard to grasp in an age accustomed to paper money. Several facts must be sorted out. First, the name shilling is an arbitrary designation given to a certain weight of silver. The designation is made in the form of an order to the officials of the mint to accept silver bullion and coin it at a particular standard of purity and weight. In the 1690s officers of the mint coined five shillings from an ounce of silver. Contemporaries believed that people exchanged goods for a particular sum of silver, but the behavior of Englishmen during the last part of the

7. [Thomas Wagstaffe], *A Letter to a Gentleman Elected a Knight of the Shire* (London, 1694), 9.

8. [Thomas Wagstaffe], *An Account of the Proceedings in the House of Commons, in relation to the Recoining the clipp'd money* (London, 1696), 7ff.

seventeenth century had pushed to the fore two new economic facts: the exchange value of money does not depend upon its silver content, and the exchange value of silver differs according to its form, that is, whether it is minted into coin or sold as bullion. These relationships were perplexing to men and women used to thinking of wealth in static, metallist terms, so Lowndes's *Report* excited comment as much for bringing to the surface these apparent paradoxes as for his suggested remedy of removing the incentive for the export of English silver by reminting with less silver in each coin.[9]

The court party led by Lord Keeper John Somers was not altogether happy with Lowndes's *Report* and sought advice elsewhere. Among the new advisers was John Locke, who vigorously opposed Lowndes's recommendations.[10] Lowndes's *Report* and Locke's *Further Considerations Concerning Raising the Value of Money* were published, and issue was joined. The writings on the coin crisis which followed in short order—four hundred separate titles in all—form an impressive collection of late-seventeenth-century expertise.[11] Isaac Newton, Dudley North, Nicholas Barbon, James Hodges, Richard Temple, John Cary, A. Vickaris, Francis Gardner, Henry Layton, Charles Davenant, John Briscoe, and Roger Coke all entered the fray. Sharply divided on whether or not the clipped coins should be reminted at the old standard or raised to a higher denomination to match the

9. [William Lowndes], *A Report containing an Essay for the Amendment of the Silver Coins* (London, 1695), repr. in *A Select Collection of Scarce and Valuable Tracts on Money,* ed. John R. McCulloch (London, 1856), 206–214. The actual continental price of silver was equal to 6*s.*, 5*d.*, but Lowndes reasoned that the two-pence difference was negligible and could be ignored. Although Lowndes is usually said to have been called upon in the summer of 1695, he in fact became involved in the question in January, when the Privy Council referred to him "A Project for Reforming our Coin," in which the author, Lewise Gervaize, had proposed a recoinage at the old standard with a two-year transition period at an enhanced face value: Brit. Lib., Add. MS. 18759, "Papers Relating to the British Coinage and the Mint, 1652–1769," fo. 108r–v. Cf. Lewis Gervaize, *A Proposal for amending the Silver Coins of England* (London, 1696).

10. Peter Laslett, "John Locke, the Great Recoinage, and the Origins of the Board of Trade: 1695–1698," *William and Mary Quarterly,* 14 (1957), 378–385; Feavearyear, *The Pound Sterling,* 136–149. For a critical, contemporary account written by a Member of Parliament and accompanied by a listing of the division see [Wagstaffe], *An Account of the Proceedings.*

11. [John Locke], *Further Considerations concerning Raising the Value of Money* (London, 1695). For subsequent writings, see the extensive bibliography in Horsefield, *British Monetary Experiments,* and *Kress Library of Business and Economics Catalogue* (Boston, 1940).

devaluation by chisel, the antagonists carried the conceptualization of the past fifty years to a new level of sophistication.

Locke's refutation of Lowndes followed the argument of his earlier treatise against statutory limits on usury: legislation is unavailing because men will seek their own gain, which in both loan rates and money exchanges is set in the market. Both interest and specie, Locke said, had a natural value which legislators and kings were unable to change.[12] The difference in his reasoning about these two natural price mechanisms, however, was that in the case of interest rates Locke had included all the forces affecting the supply and demand of lendable money, whereas in the case of money he defined coin in such a way as to exclude key factors in the determination of its market value. Mankind, Locke explained in a crucial assertion, had consented to put an imaginary value upon gold and silver. This unique and imaginary value had created the possibility of money exchanges. The intrinsic, unique value of specie had created the utility of money because it made possible a standard for all other commodities. Because men held gold and silver in unique esteem, they were willing to trade useful goods for them. Market values were thus set in relation to the quantity of gold and silver for which goods were exchanged: by "the quantity of silver, Men measure the value of all other things."[13] There was only one source of value in coin, Locke was saying, and that was its silver content. Thus any change of denomination would be fruitless, and its perpetration by government a fraud. For Locke, shillings were silver in another guise and that guise was totally irrelevant to the value of the coin. This being the case, there was logically no possible way to affect the behavior of people in relation to silver coin by altering the mint ratio as Lowndes had suggested. Silver coins, Locke went so far as to say, represented a fixed value which was the share of the wealth in silver in the world at large![14]

The basic assumption Locke built into his case was faulty: that people exchanged goods for quantities of silver. Rather people exchanged goods for quantities of coin. The quality of being legal

12. [John Locke], *Some Considerations of the Consequences of the Lowering of Interest and Raising the Value of Money* (London, 1691), 32.

13. [Locke], *Further Considerations*, 3.

14. Ibid., 22.

tender added value to the silver content or the clipped coins would not have been accepted at face value for more than three decades. Coin, being separable from silver, had a different market value. If the quantity of silver alone measured the exchange of goods, there would have been no reluctance to use milled coins in daily trade, no melting down of coin, no export of bullion, no variety in the silver content of the variously clipped coin passing at face value, no fluctuating relation between gold and silver coin. Locke's position involved the rejection of three discrete facts of English commerce in the 1690s: the passing of clipped coins at face value; the different price per pound of silver in English coin and silver in bullion; and the movement of gold or silver bullion in response to its own international market. Just as rigidly as he insisted upon a single intrinsic value of money, Locke maintained that money came into England only in response to the balancing of trade accounts.[15] Given his assumptions, the illicit trade in coin and bullion was a conundrum, for how could silver be traded if it had one universal standard of value?

Locke's errors were obvious to the dozen or more writers who rushed into print to challenge the great philosopher. For the most part merchants and entrepreneurs, Locke's opponents were willing to start with the evidence that coin had a source of value in addition to its silver or gold content. In the debating terms of the day, this extrinsic value caused the divergence between prices of coin and bullion. Breaking free from Locke's dogmatic association of money and silver, they were prepared to accept the definition of money as a medium of circulation, separable from precious metals. In their rebuttals of Locke they made explicit ideas which had been hovering at the edges of economic writings throughout the century. Specifically, the pamphlet dispute over recoinage brought into full view both the extrinsic and commodity value of money. Locke's principal opponents reversed his cause-and-effect explanation of the use of money. Where Locke had said that mankind's esteem for gold and silver had created the value of money, they said that the utility of having a medium of exchange had prompted the use and hence the value of gold and silver. Their refutations of Locke emphasized the

15. Ibid., 63.

role that silver and gold played as money rather than as commodities. After a half-century of fixation upon foreign trade, the devaluationists recognized that money was not always the passive follower of foreign-trade balances. They also distinguished between factors affecting money within the national economy and money in international exchanges, a distinction categorically rejected by Locke. More important, they responded to the evidence of daily commercial life which indicated that governmental policies could influence the value of money. In 1696 these men were not ready to take the modern leap of faith with Locke and assert the existence of natural social laws which operated automatically and independently of man-made institutions.

"The mony of every Country, and not the Ounce of Silver, or the intrinsick value, is the Instrument and Measure of Commerce there," Sir Richard Temple wrote. In one of the pithiest responses to Locke, Temple noted that time, place, and circumstance, as well as minting costs, the price of bullion, and the demand for a particular national currency will raise or lower what Locke called the intrinsic value of money. Indeed, Temple said that the proposition that an ounce of silver will buy an ounce of silver is an absurd proposition since there would be no occasion for such an exchange. It is the transformation of silver into coin which gives rise to the exchange of an ounce of silver for an ounce of coin, and the relative value of the two will depend upon the need for a particular form of silver which in the case of coin is its extrinsic value as legal currency.[16] Locke's system of coin, according to James Hodges, was built upon the "common error" of considering the estimate of worth to be equal to intrinsic value. Hodges reduced Locke's argument to a meaningless syllogism: silver is the measure of commerce by its quantity; the quantity is the measure of its intrinsic value; therefore the same quantity of silver must always be equal in value to the same quantity of silver. Asserting to the contrary, that extrinsic value arose from a coin's capacity to circulate as a legal medium of exchange, Hodges went all the way and declared that "Silver, considered as Money, hath, speaking properly, no real intrinsick value at all," for "the

16. Sir Richard Temple, *Some Short Remarks upon Mr. Lock's Book in Answer to Mr. Lounds* (London, 1696), 4.

whole value that is put upon Money by Mankind, speaking generally, is extrinsick to the Money" and derives from the good it is capable of because of what it can buy.[17] John Cary, a model of conventional thinking, pursued a similar point. Money, he said, was sought as a standard of trade, "the Excellency whereof was not to arise so much from an intrinsick value in its self, as from the usefulness of it to answer that end."[18] Nicholas Barbon covered the same ground with impressive thoroughness. Beginning with a précis of Locke's argument, Barbon charged him with failing to see the difference between silver defined as a commodity without "any fixt or certain Estimate that common consent hath placed on it," rising and falling in value "as other commodities" on the one hand, and money which is "the Instrument and Measure of Commerce," deriving its authority from the government and valued by men for its stamp and currency rather than the quantity of fine silver in each piece.[19] By insisting that the value of money arose from an imaginary value placed upon silver and was thus determined by the quantity of silver in each coin, Locke was ignoring the fluctuations in the value of particular currencies and the impact of the demand for goods upon the value of money. Money, Barbon maintained, was a commodity like anything else and its value arose from its use. Plenty or scarcity in respect to their occasion or use determined prices, Barbon said, and the plenty or scarcity of one commodity will not alter the price of another if they do not serve the same uses.[20] James Hodges also attacked Locke's insistence that prices were determined by the quantity of silver. Silver, Hodges explained in contradistinction to Locke, receives its value in relation to what it buys. It does not have the same value if wheat is scarce even if the quantity of silver remains the same.[21] John Cary indicated that the true value of silver cannot be said to rise or fall or be worth more in one place or another for it always responds in relation to another

17. [James Hodges], *The Present State of England as to Coin and Publick Charges* (London, 1697), 135–147.

18. John Cary, *An Essay, on the Coin and Credit of England* (Bristol, 1696), 5.

19. Nicholas Barbon, *A Discourse Concerning Coining the New Money Lighter* (London, 1696), "The Contents."

20. Ibid., 7.

21. [Hodges], *The Present State of England*, 142.

commodity "because the Buyer must pay for the Commodities he wants, suitable to his Necessity, and their Scarcity."[22] Although in his "Memorial Concerning the Coin of England," Charles Davenant agreed with Locke in denying the extrinsic value of coin, he too emphasized the passivity of money: "the worth of money will always Take its Rule from the Necessity Men have of other Commodities."[23]

Two crucial theories were entwined in the discussion of the value of money: one concerned the source of the value of money and the other the connection between money and wealth. Although separable concepts, there were logically paired affinities. The first position had been that the accumulation of treasure in specie was the aim of economic life; people produced and exchanged in order to acquire money. Such a view naturally predisposed its holder to assume that coin was valued for its specie content. The second view focused upon the exchange value of money—its command over goods. The best thinkers joined this emphasis upon what money could buy with a conception of wealth in terms of capital investments: "Land at Farm, Money at Interest, or Goods in Trade," as Dudley North put it.[24] Locke's view, that is that a man's wealth represented his proportion of the world's gold and silver, was already old-fashioned when he advanced it. Long before the coin crisis of the 1690s most English writers on economics had maintained that things useful to people's needs or delight were the real objects of economic activity.[25] Money had been recast as a convenience in the process of exchanging what was not wanted for what was wanted. Money was defined by 1653 as a medium of commerce between those who have no reciprocal wants.[26] Thomas Papillon was even more exact in calling money a

22. Cary, *An Essay*, 11–12.

23. *Two Manuscripts by Charles Davenant*, ed. Abbott Payson Usher (Baltimore, 1942), 20.

24. [Dudley North], *Discourses upon Trade* (London, 1691), 24.

25. The persistence of the notion that writers on economics in the late seventeenth century conceived of the accumulation of gold and silver as the appropriate goal of economic life is puzzling. Locke's position is the exception, not the rule. Writing on this same point of confusion, Bruno Suviranta, *The Theory of the Balance of Trade in England: A Study in Mercantilism* (Helsingfors, 1923), 118–119, noted that McCulloch criticized the mercantilists for their slavish adoration of gold and silver in almost the same words as one of the accused mercantilists used to lampoon the same idea! *A Select Collection of Early English Tracts on Commerce*, ed. John R. McCulloch, (London, 1856), vii.

26. Anon. [Cressy Dymock?], *An Essay upon Master W. Potters Designe* (London, 1653), 27.

measure of the value of commodities. "The Stock and Riches of the Kingdom," he wrote in 1677, "cannot properly be confined to Money, nor ought Gold and Silver to be excluded from being Merchandise, to be Traded with; as well as any other sort of Goods." While it is true that riches are accounted for in money terms, this, Papillon explains, is rather in imagination than reality: "A Man is said to be worth Ten Thousand Pounds" in money, but in fact the figure represents other real possessions of the man.[27] Edward Leigh, writing in 1671, gave another pithy description of money. It "answereth for all" things, yet, according to Leigh, the Indians indicated by trying to eat money and spitting it out that "they would not part with their Commodities for money unless they had such other Commodities as would serve their use."[28] "Money is of no other use, than as imployed in Trade, and the defence of the Nation; and therefor wherever the Market is Money will follow," Roger Coke maintained, adding that money "is that by which all Commodities are valued; and is of no other use: if therefore a man should give me £100 never to make use of it, I should scarce thank him for it."[29] "To distinguish rightly in these points," Dalby Thomas wrote, "we must consider money as the least part of the wealth of any nation, and think of it only as a scale to weigh one thing against another."[30] An anonymous writer, probably the same Alderman Gardner of Norwich who was among those consulted by the Privy Council, wrote that the treasure of the nation consists not just in money, "but in Money's Worth. Silver and Gold serve as the measure of other Commodities, and is valuable only in proportion to them."[31] When John Houghton claimed that money is anything "the Government of each Dominion set a mark and value

27. [Thomas Papillon], *A Treatise Concerning the East-India Trade* (London, 1677), 4.

28. Edward Leigh, *Three Diatribes or Discourses* (London, 1671), 36.

29. Roger Coke, *England's Improvements* (London, 1675), 58.

30. [Dalby Thomas], *An Historical Account of the Rise and Growth of the West-India Collonies* (London, 1690), in *The Harleian Miscellany,* ed. W. Oldys and T. Park, 10 vols. (London, 1808–1813), II, 359.

31. *Some Reflections on a Pamphlet, Intitled, England and East-India Inconsistent in their Manufactures* (London, 1696), 6. Gardner favored devaluation and left his ideas in a manuscript (no. 536 in Horsefield's bibliography). [Wagstaffe], *An Account,* 13 (actually 21), in his publication of the division in the Commons on reminting at the old standard, lists a "Fran. Gardiner" from Norfolk among those voting in opposition.

on," and that coin "is good for nothing, but potentially is good for everything," he was expressing a common view on the subject which made entirely reasonable his recommendation that goods rather than money be imported to balance accounts since money is unable to satisfy any real human need.[32] Barbon also attacked Locke's twin points that trade was valuable as a means of attracting bullion and that only a favorable balance of trade could correct the coin shortage. "That the Overplus is paid in Bullion, and the Nation grows so much the richer, because the Balance is made up in Bullion," he said, "is altogether a mistake: for Gold and Silver are but Commodities; and one sort of Commodity is as good as another, so it be of the same value."[33]

Presumably, in Locke's logic, trade never would have developed beyond commodity-bartering had gold and silver not inspired a unique and universal admiration among mankind. Locke's opponents who were attempting to account for the monetary fluctuations of the past decade came to an opposite conclusion: money was valued because it was useful. To go one step further, its usefulness could be traced to its specific property of being the legal tender in the trade of a particular country, an extrinsic value added by sovereign authority. The free coinage Act of 1663, which permitted anyone to bring bullion to the mint to be converted into coin without charge, had greatly facilitated the conversion of bullion into coin. The profit to be made by feloniously melting down undervalued English silver coin into bullion for export had promoted the reverse conversion of coin into bullion. This experience had driven a conceptual wedge between the intrinsic and extrinsic value of coin.

The clipped silver coins passing at face value had further suggested the possibilities of money-substitutes. "Money is but a medium of Commerce, a Security which we part with, to enjoy the like in Value," an anonymous bank-promoter announced. "And such is a Bank-Bill, it will obtain what we want; and satisfie where we are indebted, and may be turned into Money again when the Possessor pleaseth, and will be the Standard of Trade at last."[34]

32. John Houghton, *A Collection of Letters for the Improvement of Husbandry and Trade* (London, 1681), 24–27.

33. Barbon, *A Discourse Concerning Coining*, 40.

34. *England's Glory* (London, 1694), 5. This pamphlet was probably written by Humphrey Mackworth.

James Hodges could write of money "or its equivalent"; and William Hodges, lamenting the retirement of the old money in *The Groans of the Poor,* concluded that "though the old money was exceeding bad yet it served to Trade with, and go to Market: And as many use to say, if it was Leather, if it would pass, it would serve."[35] In daily commercial transactions people had demonstrated that "that which would pass, would serve." Not the intrinsic, but the extrinsic value predominated. The value-conferring role of the sovereign, banished by Edward Misselden and Thomas Mun during the famous debate on the Royal Exchange in the 1620s, had reappeared in the 1690s.[36] James Hodges could ask ingeniously why people should object to the sovereign changing the value of money when the loss of specie upon the sinking of an East India merchantman or a dearth similarly influenced the value of their money, but John Locke, the political philosopher, could not so easily accept this power over property.[37]

Locke had attempted to dissociate the value of money—gold and silver—from the value of other commodities. Goods were sought for their usefulness; gold and silver were given an imaginary and unique value by mankind, but because this value was universal, he reasoned, specie could serve as a pledge in the exchange of goods. Locke's opponents rejected this view. Barbon called it a "popular" but false notion, Hodges "a Fundamental mistake in the Notion of Money," Henry Layton a simple "mistake."[38] Having participated in a sustained effort to master the relationships of a market economy, they had come to accept the fact that all value lay in the imagination. "Things have no Value in themselves," Nicholas Barbon said, "it is opinion and fashion brings them into use, and gives them a value."[39] "There is no other use of Riches but to purchase what serves our Necessity and Delight . . . and some goods are more acceptable in

35. [James Hodges], *A Supplement to the Present State of England* (London, 1697), 9; Hodges, *The Groans of the Poor,* 14.

36. For a discussion of this earlier pamphlet debate, see Barry Supple, "Currency and Commerce in the Early Seventeenth Century," *Economic History Review,* 10 (1957–1958), 239–255.

37. [Hodges], *Present State of England,* 177.

38. Barbon, *A Discourse Concerning Coining,* 36; [Hodges], *A Supplement,* 10–11; Temple, *Some Short Remarks,* 10; [Layton], *Observations Concerning Money and Coin,* 12.

39. Barbon, *A Discourse Concerning Coining,* 43.

some Countries, at sometimes, than Money," as another writer put it.[40] Locke's theory of the value of money was central to his conception of wealth and, as we shall see, his larger theory of natural law. Money, which he defined strictly as gold and silver, had a unique, universal, and imaginary value. All three qualities were important in his overall scheme. If the value of money was imaginary, it could not arise from utility. If it was unique, it could not be replaced. If it was universal, it could not be influenced by the extrinsic trappings of particular minting processes. Due to these three qualities, all men were willing to accept gold and silver as a pledge "to receive equally valuable things to those they parted with."[41] Uniquely desired, their accumulation could be the unquestioned aim of commerce, and only through trade could this accumulation be achieved: "In a Country not furnished with Mines there are but two ways of growing Rich, Either Conquest, or Commerce . . . Commerce therefore is the only way left to us, either for Riches or Subsistence . . . Trade then is necessary to the producing of Riches, and Money necessary to the carrying on of Trade."[42]

The argument was circular and outdated. Locke's view prevailed, not because it explained the economic phenomena of his day, but rather because of the compelling association he drew between economic and political freedom, an association predicated upon the dogma of natural, universal, inexorable laws working outside the purview and power of human legislators. His triumph at the practical level lay in the harmony between his ideas and the vested interests of the parliamentary magnates who decided that the clipped silver coin would be called in and reminted at the old standard.

IN THE 1620s the growing awareness of the importance of foreign trade to the English economy had called attention to the power of

40. *Some Reflections on a Pamphlet,* 7.

41. [Locke], *Some Considerations,* 31. Wrestling with the "imaginary" quality in the value of money, Locke, ibid., 23, added jewels to gold and silver as truly treasure, but said they were inappropriate as money because their value was not measured by their quantity.

42. [Locke], *Some Considerations,* 16–17. Further on (32) Locke specifically excluded bills of exchange as money "Because a Law cannot give to Bills that intrinsick Value, which the universal Consent of Mankind has annexed to Silver and Gold."

specie to transcend national boundaries and impose its value upon the international market. The sovereign right to mint coin shrank before the sovereign passage of gold and silver from country to country in response to trade. It was this passive response of money which had prompted Thomas Mun in *England's Treasure by Forraign Trade* to assert that coin would only come and "abide" in a country when it was sent there to settle accounts.[43] By the 1690s, however, it had become apparent that if gold and silver fetched a higher price in another country, they would be sent there as would any other commodity. As Locke's critics correctly pointed out, coin had two sources of value: its silver content and its status as legal tender in a particular country. Neither, they insisted in contradiction to Locke, was unique; both sources of value were similar to that of other commodities which serve "our Necessity and Delights." As commodities, both precious metals and coin responded to their own markets. Because this was so, the balancing of trade could in no way solve the problem of the coin-drain. This fact had been realized in the 1620s: "when your Money is richer in substance and lower in price than the silver in the Low Countries," Rice Vaughan had written, "how can you expect that the Merchant, who only seeketh his profit, will ever bring hither any Silver." Lowndes, Barbon, Hodges, Temple, Vickaris, and Layton elaborated the point with more sophistication. As long as there was a profitable trade in exporting undervalued English silver, the settling of other accounts would never solve the problem. Correctly predicting the immediate melting down that would follow a recoinage at the old standard, Henry Layton wrote that "nothing that England can do is able to alter the price of Silver in other places of Europe, from whence we must acquire and obtain it."[44]

This dispute over the nature of money impinged upon the theory of economic growth which has been associated with the name of mercantilism. The essential point of the theory is that only a favorable balance of foreign trade can attract gold and silver to a country without mines. As the analogy to a mechanical balance suggested, the balance of trade worked through automatic and autonomous

43. Thomas Mun, *England's Treasure by Forraign Trade* (London, 1664), 54–55.

44. Rice Vaughan, *A Discourse of Coin and Coinage* (London, 1675; originally written in the 1620s), 76; [Layton], *Observations Concerning Money and Coin,* 39.

adjustments. Monarchs and parliaments could not alter this economic order, although they could adopt policies to enhance its workings.[45] A more subtle implication of this balance-of-trade analogy was that all men benefited or suffered equally from its operation. To curse the need to maintain a favorable balance of trade was to curse the rain. Locke set his theory of money within this representational model of the market, but at the end of the century in which he wrote many no longer believed that attracting gold and silver was the goal of commerce. More significantly, some writers had come to recognize that the nation encompassed different economic groups whose interests were not always compatible.

Throughout the seventeenth century Englishmen had felt the full force of the economic variables in a market society. Imports of silver from the New World and increased demand for corn had played havoc with prices; employment had followed trade cycles; gluts had produced depressions; clipped coins had passed at face value; inflation had eroded returns from rents and loans. The close observation of these new phenomena had sharpened the perception of economic interests. Despite the mercantilists' rhetorical claim that a favorable balance of trade brought uniform prosperity, astute commentators had discerned and advertised the differing effects of trade flows, money exchanges, and policies affecting agriculture, manufacturing, and commerce. When the wild fluctuations in prices of 1695 prompted Parliament at last to act on the problem of coin-clipping, many responded by asking not how the nation would correct the situation, but rather who in the nation would benefit from the remedy. Reminding his "superiors" that the price-inflation due to West Indian silver had redounded to the benefit of merchant shopkeepers and tradesmen rather than to the crown, church, nobility, and landed gentry, an anonymous pamphleteer urged the rejection of Lowndes's recommended devaluation.[46] While those who were in favor of reminting at the old denomination tried to rest their case on Locke's argument that devaluation would be ineffective, they inconsistently argued that deflation would help landlords and creditors

45. See Letwin, *Origins*, 178ff, for an incisive discussion of the difference between a belief in a natural economic order and the inference of a laissez-faire policy.
46. Anon., *The Proposal for the Raising of the Silver Coin of England from 60 Pence in the Ounce to 75 Pence* (London, 1696), 11.

who otherwise would be defrauded of their due if the currency were inflated.[47]

Lowndes had argued that changing the mint ratio would be the least disruptive policy, since the denomination he suggested reflected the average silver content of the coins passing at face value at the time. Landlords and creditors would receive less value, but no less than in the present currency.[48] In a similar vein, Vickaris carefully weighed the different effects of raising a tax to make good the loss in clippings or raising the denomination as Lowndes had suggested and concluded that the latter was preferable. He explained away the loss to landlords and creditors by saying that the tax would have been a loss to them as well.[49] The author of *A Proposal for Amending the Silver Coins of England,* more concerned about the landed and the lending, advised devaluation but proposed that the old denomination be restored after two years.[50] Drawing more polemical conclusions, Layton charged that Locke "extends his Care to Creditors and Landlords, not regarding the Cases of Tenants or Debtors; Men for this four or five years last past, have borrow'd many Thousand Pounds in Clipt Money, but he notes no unreasonableness or injustice in compelling them to pay such Debts again in heavy Money, perhaps of twice the weight."[51] Much of this awareness of the discriminatory effect of inflation had been advertised by a cluster of popular writers who had been advocating inflation for inflation's sake for over two decades. These writers, although having little impact upon the debates over recoinage, did draw attention to the critical difference between money circulating in an internal market and money used to settle international accounts.

Unlike Lowndes and the other devaluationists who were responding to an actual devaluation brought about by clipping, many earlier writers had urged changes in the mint ratio artificially to stimulate the economy. Touting a land bank scheme, William Potter extolled

47. Anon., *Decus & Tutamen* (London, 1696), 27; Anon., *Some Considerations about the Raising of Coin* (London, 1696), 20.

48. [Lowndes], *Report,* 206ff.

49. [Vickaris], *Essay for Regulating of the Coyn,* 26.

50. Gervaize, *A Proposal.* Other pamphlets supporting Lowndes were [Samuel Prat], *The Regulating Silver Coin Made Practicable and Easie* (London, 1696); Anon., *Select Observations of the Incomparable Sir Walter Raleigh, Relating to Trade, Commerce and Coin* (London, 1696).

51. [Layton], *Observations Concerning Money and Coin,* 13.

its capacity to increase stock, lower interest rates, and set more people to work, "for quick returns makes a small stock equivalent to a great with slow returns."[52] Another bank promoter, Humphrey Mackworth, asserted that "there is no doubt, that the Consumption of the People is not so much as the Product of their Labours, which is the real Riches and Strength of the Nation, and the more the merrier, like Bees in a Hive."[53] Richard Haines wrote repeatedly about the economic stimulus to be had from inflating and thereby increasing the currency.[54] In *Taxes No Charge,* Daniel Defoe, an ardent pump primer, recommended tax policies designed to pluck idle money from hoarders and pleasure-seekers. Declaring that even the meanest sort of person who paid taxes would be rewarded by the increase of trade occasioned by well-spent tax money, he underscored his point by claiming that there was far more treasure at home than the potential in trade abroad.[55] While these writers did not contribute to the debates over recoinage, they did emphasize two relevant and important points: the differing impact of devaluation in domestic and foreign trade and the growing importance of the internal market to English prosperity. As Richard Haines pointed out, "money is principally intended for the Conveniency of Traffique between persons of the same Nation onely, and to them it is all one, since the same is made Currant by Authority."[56] Lowndes had made explicit this fact when he explained that the common propensity to speak of money in terms of foreign exchange ignores its more common use in domestic trade.[57] The anonymous authors of *Decus & Tutamen* and *Letter from an English Merchant at Amsterdam* recognized the differences, but did not draw connections between this difference and the effect upon various segments of the

52. This comment is made in a tract edited by Samuel Hartlib: *Samuel Hartlib his Legacie of Husbandry,* 3d ed. (London, 1655), 294.

53. *England's Glory,* 20–21.

54. [Richard Haines], *The Prevention of Poverty* (London, 1674); [Haines], *The Uses and Abuses of Money* (London, 1671).

55. [Daniel Defoe], *Taxes No Charge* (London, 1690), 18.

56. [Haines], *Prevention of Poverty,* 19.

57. [Lowndes], *Report,* 81–82. Nor did Lowndes make the mistake that T. B. Macaulay attributed to him of not recognizing that foreign balances were settled by weight, rather than by denomination: T. B. Macaulay, *History of England,* ed. C. H. Firth, 6 vols. (London, 1913–1915), V, 2752.

economy.[58] Vickaris, on the other hand, said that inflating the currency officially would have no impact upon the domestic economy except to discourage foreign imports, while Layton associated specific resistance to inflation with the fact that certain merchants would have to spend more coins of lighter silver to pay for foreign goods.[59] The conflicts of interests cloaked by the balance of trade theory stood forth briefly during the debate over recoinage just as the different behavior of money in the domestic and international markets was momentarily disclosed and examined.

PARLIAMENT finally acted in January 1696. It determined that after May, later extended to June, clipped coins would not be accepted as legal tender. Before that date, clipped coins would be accepted at face value in payment of taxes and loans to the king. The clipped coins brought in during this period would be reminted at the old standard. Thus English silver currency, with an estimated face value of £4.7 million, was reduced in 1696 to £2½ million reminted at the old full weight.[60] The folly and disaster predicted by Locke's critics was realized in full. Much of the newly minted silver was melted down as soon as it was coined and sent abroad to realize a profit as bullion. The actual minting could not keep pace with the demand for a medium of circulation, and wage-earners and shopkeepers found themselves desperate for some kind of money. The halving of the face value of silver coin caused a drastic deflation. Prices fell, and landlords and creditors reaped the benefits that had been expected. Others, the bulk of the population, could only exchange their clipped coins at face value during the five-month period of grace by selling them to the privileged taxpayers. Those who had no opportunity to unload or who had to hold on to some ready cash suffered the loss when the deadline came. The shortage of money pressed particularly hard on the poor. Rioting broke out in Kendal and Halifax and among Derbyshire miners. The government had difficulty paying its soldiers. Trade contracted in the cold

58. *Decus & Tutamen*, vii; *Letter from an English Merchant at Amsterdam*, 8.

59. [Vickaris], *Essay for Regulating of the Coyn*, 24; [Layton], *Observations Concerning Money and Coin*, 11.

60. Feavearyear, *Pound Sterling*, 136–149; [Wagstaffe], *An Account*, 8–10.

winds of deflation and money shortage. Debtors and tenants saw their obligation increase overnight while money profiteers turned again to melting down English coin.[61]

The recoinage could be seen as an ingenious tax upon the property-less. The inflation of 1695—estimated at 25 percent—had badly hurt landowners and creditors, the men who were shouldering the burden of financing William's war. If, as is generally conceded today, the inflation was caused by the dramatic increase in credit accompanying the first year of successful operation of the Bank of England, then the cost of putting royal finances on a sound basis was also borne by the same men. Transforming a rapid inflationary movement in prices to an equally rapid deflationary one reversed the fortunes of the moneyed men who paid the bulk of the taxes and supplied the loans to the king. These men, moreover, did not just profit from deflation; they enjoyed a net transfer of income from the recoinage. During the five-month period when silver coin was accepted at face value, the Exchequer paid out £2,200,000 to the taxpayers and subscribers to royal loans who brought in their clipped coin for new, full-weight milled coins. Eventually this cost was made up by a window tax.[62] This subsequent development may have been fortuitous. It is certain that no intended goal of recoinage was achieved except for Locke's abstract and novel one of turning a mint standard into an immutable fact of nature. Considering the venerability of the gold standard in the next two centuries it was an ironic triumph of mind over matter by one of the major architects of

61. Feavearyear, *Pound Sterling,* 140–147; *Seventeenth-Century Economic Documents,* ed. Joan Thirsk and J. P. Cooper (Oxford, 1972), 707–708. Writing in 1694, Thomas Wagstaffe had complained that even with bad money there was not enough coin to drive trade. *A Letter to a Gentleman Elected Knight of the Shire,* 9.

62. For a discussion of recent literature on the subject, see Mark Blaug, "Economic Theory and Economic History in Great Britain, 1650–1776," *Past and Present,* 28 (1964), 111–116. While D. Vickers, *Studies in the Theory of Money, 1690–1776* (Philadelphia, 1959), Feavearyear, *Pound Sterling,* Horsefield, *British Monetary Experiments,* and Letwin, *Origins of Scientific Economics,* touch upon the dislocations following Parliament's deflationary recoinage and call attention to the fallacies in Locke's reasoning, they do not analyze the decision itself. Horsefield (*British Monetary Experiments,* 68) acknowledges that the followers of Locke never go beyond his theoretical dogmatism, but concludes without evidence that neither "the dogmatic subtleties of Locke [n]or the pragmatic justifications of Lowndes" were influential. "In the end it was the fear of change, the instinct of conservatism, which won the day for Restoration."

empiricism. The reminted silver did not provide England with a good currency; silver left the country, and the overvalued gold and vastly increased use of banknotes supplied the deficiency. Trade was not eased nor war-finance made more convenient. Nor did the burden fall like the gentle rain on rich and poor alike. Yet historians, writing under the spell of Whig political theory and nineteenth-century classical economics, have been loath to explore the extent of the disaster. Rather than look at the recoinage in terms of the event itself, they have fixed upon one totally unintended conse-quence: the driving out of silver currency and subsequent depen-dence upon gold. To quote Peter Laslett, "it is surely time we recognized that explanations in terms of unconscious anticipations are not explanations at all." [63] What needs to be examined critically are Locke's reason for recoining at the old standard and the lingering predisposition of historians to view the process of modernization as inevitable. If Locke's conception prevailed because of his brilliant integration of monetary theory and the philosophy of natural rights, then this is a fact of great importance in understanding the triumph of liberalism. If ideology rather than ideas shaped the development of English economic theory in the eighteenth century, that too is worth investigating.

To DISCUSS the recoinage of 1696 as an ideological issue requires some clarification. More is intended than a mere reference to the fact that the recoinage had a different effect upon different interest groups within English society of the time. Rather I would like to explore the argument between Locke and his opponents in terms of the value-judgments that lay embedded in the apparently value-free assertions they made about the behavior of silver coin in a commer-cial economy. Norman Birnbaum has defined ideology as a set of statements about society which contain, usually by implication, evaluations of the distribution of power in that society. [64] Ideology, in this view, is the articulation of propositions which subtly veil

63. Laslett, "John Locke, the Great Recoinage and the Origins of the Board of Trade," 397, n.8.

64. Norman Birnbaum, "The Sociological Study of Ideology," *Current Sociology*, 9 (1960), 91.

particular policies or selective interpretations of nature and society. Locke's convictions about money were not simply parts of a scientific analysis of economics; they contained important ideological assertions about power, property, and political norms.

Locke's position on money was foreshadowed in his famous *Second Treatise of Government*. There Locke confronted a fundamental problem: how to disprove the traditional notion, exemplified in Robert Filmer's *Patriarcha*, that monarchy had a biblical warrant because of Adam's God-given dominion over the world. After refuting Filmer's biblical reasoning in the *First Treatise*, Locke, in the *Second Treatise*, had to resolve the difficulties implicit in his own claim that God had not given the world to Adam, but rather to mankind in general as a common resource for sustenance.[65] How, as John Yolton has expressed Locke's dilemma, is it possible to get from what is common that which is private and particular.[66] Locke's ingenious answer was that each of us has a property in ourselves. Our property in ourselves is not shared in common, and through our own exertions—our labor—we make from common property private property. Furthermore, this particularizing of the public through private labor is fully in concert with God's aims since it is only through labor that the earth's resources are transformed into life-giving sustenance. "And will any one say he had no right to those acorns or apples he thus appropriated," Locke asked of his hypothetical man in the state of nature. "Was it a robbery thus to assume to himself what belonged to all in common? If such a consent as that was necessary, man had starved, notwithstanding the plenty God had given him."[67] Man thus serves God's purposes as he serves himself, making private that of the commons which he needs. However, since man's sustenance is the reason for the gift of the earth, all private appropriation is limited to what man can use.[68] Waste is an evil. How then were some men able to expand their private property beyond their daily use? Because there developed an

65. As Peter Laslett has demonstrated in his Introduction to *Two Treatises of Government* (Cambridge, 1960), Locke wrote his *Two Treatises* before 1683 and not long after the posthumous publication of Robert Filmer's *Patriarcha* (London, 1680).

66. John Yolton, *Locke and the Compass of Human Understanding* (Cambridge, 1970), 195.

67. Locke, "Second Treatise," sect. 28.

68. Ibid., sect. 31.

attraction to gold and silver which "by mutual consent, men would take in exchange for the truly useful but perishable supports of life."[69] Thanks to this peculiar affection, Locke was able to legitimate individual concentrations of wealth through man's common consent to value gold and silver, while at the same time he drew upon God's gift of the earth to mankind in general to substantiate the existence of natural rights independent of any sovereign power.

Thus the universal human agreement to value gold and silver formed a key step in Locke's explanation of how property rights preceded and transcended civil authority. Mankind voluntarily consented to the unequal sharing of what God originally gave as a gift in common. Every time a poor man traded his labor for a silver sixpence, he was consenting to the esteem in which gold and silver were held and thus indirectly—or tacitly, as Locke put it—supporting the accumulation of riches beyond the needs of consumption. Locke's almost solitary rejection of the extrinsic value of money in the recoinage debates, seen from the perspective of his major political treatise, was not an offhand contribution to an ephemeral issue; it was integral to his whole philosophy. His contemporaries— men not undertaking a sweeping reconstruction of reality—might keep their feet on the ground and their eyes on the daily market fluctuations of bullion prices. For Locke this was not possible, perhaps literally unthinkable. The debate over extrinsic value was quite simply about the nature and extent of sovereign authority, not, however, couched in terms of what this power should be, but rather what this power in fact was. For Locke's opponents money had both intrinsic and extrinsic value; the former coming from the silver content and influenced by movements of trade in bullion; the latter from its minting as legal tender and conditioned by political decisions. They had no difficulty accepting what to Locke was repugnant: the power of the sovereign to influence the creation of property.

Barbon traced the value of money to the utility it acquired from being named money by public authority. Noting that anything which is convenient and can be preserved from counterfeiting could be made into money, he said, "tis the Publik Authority upon the Metal that makes it money; and without such Authority, Silver

---

69. Ibid., sects. 46–47.

would not more pass for money than gold."[70] Lowndes equally conceded the establishment of mint value to the king, "to whose regality the Power of Coining Money, and Determining The Weight, Fineness, Denomination and Extrinsick Value there of doth Solely and Inherently Appertain."[71] Touching on the role of demand in affecting value, James Hodges wondered that anyone should doubt that the king could alter the value of money for his reasons just as individuals alter it in their market transactions.[72] Replying directly to Locke's question about the difference between paying in clipped money or in authorized light money, Layton replied that "one is a Payment in lawful and good Money, and the other is the contrary; and therefore one sort will be accepted and the other rejected, not only or principally for their difference of weight, but for that the Publick Authority allow the one, and condemns the other." Recognizing Locke's effort to make the value of silver coin fixed in nature, Layton scorned him for pretending "that the Government had no more power in Politicks than they have in Naturals."[73] This, of course, went right to the heart of the matter: Locke was denying that money was a creature of politics.

Money occupied a crucial place in Locke's political philosophy. Its definition impinged upon his conceptions of the natural order and the essence of civil society. Locke could not be indifferent to the ideological implications of assigning to money an extrinsic value manipulatable by the sovereign. The distinguishing character of man, for Locke, was his capacity for reasoning, and the full development of human rational capacity demanded independence from the will of others. This independence rested upon property, and, as we have seen, it was money which enabled men to accumulate property—indeed to free themselves from that hand-to-mouth existence which characterized society without gold and silver to store wealth. For Locke, the freely acting, fully rational man created property. Private property had a moral base in the labor of its acquisition, but equally important, the possession of property enabled men to be independent of the will of others. Property was the reward for

70. Barbon, *Discourse Concerning Coining*, 25.
71. [Lowndes], *Report*, 175.
72. [Hodges], *Present State*, 149.
73. [Layton], *Observations*, 13, 15.

man's initiative and effort, and the reward itself permitted men freely to exercise their God-given powers. The need to have an access to the means of creating property in order to be fully human, and of protecting property once acquired also created the need for government in Locke's scheme. This need, as Geraint Parry has forcefully argued, creates the central problem of politics for Locke, for the efficacy of government rests upon its coercive power, creating a situation where government threatens to invade "the condition it is intended to preserve."[74] To secure property and the independence which makes true civil society possible, men enter a contract to create government, but in so doing they create a power capable of restraining their liberty. Locke resolved this problem at the theoretical level by assigning all that is important to the development of human nature to the realm of nature and confiding to government only those powers which God's natural order requires for its preservation. In detailing how private property arose from God's original gift of the world, Locke revealed for his contemporaries how fidelity to God's creation required a political order run for and by men who would be equally free, independent, rational, and propertied.

Historically, Locke confronted a situation in which government was already in possession of powers that impinged upon Englishmen's control of their property. The determination of the weight, fineness, denomination, and extrinsic value of coin which Lowndes had ascribed to the king's regality was just such a sovereign right. A supporter of devaluation, John Briscoe, exposed the ideological nerve of the problem. When the sovereign manipulates the coin, he wrote, the subject "lives merely at the Mercy of the Prince, is Rich or Poor, has a Competency, or is a Beggar, is a Free-man, or in Fetters at his Pleasure."[75] Locke could have maintained that sovereigns ought not to tamper with the coinage, as Briscoe did, but his system was only truly coherent if the natural value of money prevailed whatever the government did. His political philosophy required of him precisely that with which Layton charged him: pretending that kings had "no more power in Politicks than they had in Naturals." As with the rate of interest, Locke labored to create a value for money which arose in the state of nature in accord

74. Geraint Parry, "Individuality, Politics and the Critique of Paternalism in John Locke," *Political Studies,* 12 (1964), 169.

75. [John Briscoe], *A Discourse of Money* (London, 1696), 18.

with the order of things. He was not condemning extrinsic value; he was denying it. In *The Origins of Scientific Economics,* William Letwin identifies the turning point in economic thought as that moment when certain thinkers, notably Locke, "forcefully suspended all judgments of theology, morality and justice" and were "willing to consider the economy as nothing more than an intricate mechanism, refraining for the while from asking whether the mechanism worked for good or evil." [76] This scientific detachment, however, is rooted in an ideological stance. Locke's willingness "to consider the economy as nothing more than an intricate mechanism" was inseparable from his effort to create a new social reality in which property rights stood outside the control of sovereign authority. His ideas on interest, money, and the balance of trade formed the economic side of his political liberalism. What Locke denied was central to his philosophy: that money had an extrinsic value coming from public authority, that men could trade in money independently of goods, that conscious decisions relating to larger social purposes could affect the free workings of the market. As Sir Albert Feavearyear has astutely pointed out, what Locke created was not a scientific foundation but a new mode of reverence: "This sanctity which Locke attached to the Mint weights was something new. Before his time few people regarded the weights of the coins as in any way immutable. The king had made them; he had altered them many times; and doubtless if it suited him he would alter them again . . . Largely as a result of Locke's influence, £3. 17s. 10½d. an ounce came to be regarded as a magic price for gold from which we ought never to stray and to which, if we did, we must always return." [77]

In the Dedication to his *Further Considerations Concerning Raising the Value of Money,* Locke appealed to the unbiased justice of Lord Keeper Somers to reject a measure which would "deprive great Numbers of blameless Men of a Fifth Part of their Estates, beyond the Relief of Chancery." Locke of course refused to acknowledge what Layton called the case of tenants and debtors compelled to pay debts contracted in clipped money "in heavy Money, perhaps of twice the weight." It was central to Locke's argument to deny that clipped coin ever passed at face value, and considering the cacophony

76. Letwin, *Origins,* 147–148, 170ff.
77. Feavearyear, *Pound Sterling,* 148–149.

of experts trying to explain the causes of the inflation Locke's insistence that it was due totally to clipped coin was not devoid of plausibility. Moreover, in arguing for government policies so trustworthy that men of wealth would not hesitate to venture their money in royal loans, Locke was sounding a note that anyone reasonably knowledgeable about fiscal matters could appreciate. Why then did Locke's opponents—men no less susceptible to ideological persuasion than he—disavow his natural law of money? Why did Nicholas Barbon, Dudley North, Henry Layton, A. Vickaris, Francis Gardner, John Briscoe, James Hodges, and Richard Temple reject out of hand the idea that gold and silver enjoyed a unique and imaginary value which alone could store the wealth created by labor? The fact that many of Locke's opponents were London merchants and financiers does not really explain their loyalties in this battle because the king's creditors did as well as landowners in exchanging clipped coin for new milled pieces. The fact that deflation restricted the volume of retail sales probably fell harder on merchants than landlords, but no one could have predicted that the recoinage itself would get bogged down in two years of bureaucratic muddling. The explanation for their resistance to Locke's logic lies in part with the fact that merchants involved in daily commercial transactions through the 1690s had more difficulty denying the reality of clipped coins passing at face value. More important, Locke held hostage for his economic theory a new conception of wealth which had gained ground in the preceding decade.

By insisting that gold and silver alone were money, Locke not only dismissed the power of civil authority to create value, he also avoided consideration of that value which came from utility and which fluctuated with demand. His contemporaries perceived that because money facilitated the exchange of what people wanted and what they did not want, anything would serve for money that would pass at face value; but Locke was insisting that bills of exchange could not serve for money "because a Law cannot give to Bills that intrinsick Value, which the universal Consent of Mankind has annexed to Silver and Gold." [78] Moreover, Locke's theory of money

78. [Locke], *Some Considerations,* 32. According to Michel Foucault in *Les mots et les choses* (Paris, 1966), translated as *The Order of Things* (New York, 1973), 174–189, 208–211, money had a representational character for the mercantilists, yet the substance of money as

did not stand alone; it was entangled in the balance-of-trade conception of wealth. Some Englishmen, particularly in the earlier part of the century, had advocated national policies which directed the kingdom's economic energies toward the production of goods designed for sale in foreign markets. The restriction of imports, the organizing of labor resources, and the strict watch on wage rates all flowed from the same goal of growing wealthy by maintaining a favorable overall balance of trade. Implicit in this view was the sterility of domestic trade, the inelasticity of demand, and the beggar-thy-neighbor approach to international commerce. As Locke's recoinage opponents demonstrated, this static, substantialist view of wealth was no longer widely shared by the end of the century. Instead writers spoke of wealth in terms of productive capacities and the enjoyment of things which satisfy human wants. Moreover, during the 1670s and 1680s Englishmen had witnessed a slowly rising standard of living, the amazing rebuilding of London after the fire, and such consumer crazes as the fashion for East Indian calicoes. The importance of the domestic market as a source of commercial profit made itself felt. In the desire to consume, writers like North and Barbon, Dalby Thomas, John Houghton, and Henry Martyn detected a new dynamic to economic growth and development. Ingenuity, inventiveness, and industry appeared as promoters of new productive powers. As their writings on recoinage suggest, utility, desire, and imagined wants offered a truer picture of economic forces to these men than the old image of stored wealth bought with unremitting effort and parsimony. As I have argued elsewhere, the merchants and speculators responded to the new theories of wealth, while manufacturers and landlords, beset with the problems posed by a laboring force more inclined to buy leisure than acquire the tastes of their betters for consumption, found in the balance-of-trade theory political support for protective tariffs and statutory limitations on wages.[79]

If Locke wrote about money with one eye on the political implications of his definition, his readers read him with their minds on

---

a real segment of the world's wealth was a notion of critical importance to Locke's theory of natural economic relations.

79. I have discussed these writings in detail in Chapter 1.

banking schemes and the profits to be made in the East India trade. The debates over recoinage had concentrated economic discourse around a fundamental issue—the definition of money. Ambitions, conflicting interests, and indeed the direction of national economic policies were concerned not with how to recoin the currency but with how to justify and explain what was to be done. Had Locke based his recommendation upon preferred action rather than assertions of fact, the dispute would have been less portentous. Locke's view prevailed for good practical reasons, but the facts he chose implicated other facts and rested upon a model of economic relations which threatened a particularly fruitful line of economic development: the cultivation of a rising class of consumers and the expansion of purchasing power through currency-inflation. The rigidity of Locke's position as well as the modernity of his opponents provides an unexpected twist to the origins of liberalism. Locke, the empiricist, stands forth as the creator of a system whose moral basis was more important than the observable phenomena it attempted to explain. If you want to understand any forceful thinker, J. M. Clark said, you must discover what it is that he is reacting against.[80] For Locke the answer seems simple—arbitrary, unlimited power. And his reaction was impressive. In the face of pervasive evidence of formal, unlimited, sovereign authority, he asserted the reality of natural inalienable rights. Against the power of the modern state he pitted the moral claims of the free individual and extracted from these claims a rationale for limited government. To do battle against the powers that were, Locke chose science—the disciplined, rational inquiry into the nature of things. In the natural order Locke found equal rights to the fruits of the earth, private property, money—all existing prior to the formation of civil government and operating independently of its authority. In this context Locke's reluctance to recognize the extrinsic value of money is less puzzling.

In defending the autonomous value of money, however, Locke slipped an expandable wedge between natural property rights and the rational social purposes used to explain their genesis. In his original formulation, private property was connected with a moral

80. J. M. Clark, "Adam Smith and the Current of History," in *Adam Smith 1776–1926* (Chicago, 1928), 57, as cited in G. S. L. Tucker, *Progress and Profits in British Economic Thought 1650–1850* (Cambridge, 1960), 5.

end: God's desire to provide sustenance for man. The labor which made the common gift into private property executed God's design. The picked apple facilitated nourishment at the same time that it became private. The introduction of money, however, destroyed the moral purpose associated with God's gift of the earth, for it removed the check on accumulation. Nor did the creation of money rest on any formal or rational purpose—it was merely the result of a natural human attitude. In a finite world the removal of a check on the accumulation of property actually worked against God's purposes. The conceptual weaponry Locke used to trim sovereign power worked equally to repel any social scrutiny of private property. In turning the recoinage battle to good account for political liberalism, Locke launched a theory of money which went a long way toward freeing basic economic relationships from social control.

Money, above all, was power, and the extent of its power grew during the seventeenth century as the market intruded into areas of life previously the domain of the family, custom, and central authority. The autonomy of men in their market relations meant that aggregates of people in pursuit of private goals determined public policy. In the *Second Treatise* Locke did away with the formal, rational, unlimited power of Filmer's *Patriarcha* to make room for the impersonal and invisible tyranny of the market. In the recoinage debate he forged the link between political and economic liberalism by removing money from the realm of politics and making it a creature of nature. The fact that Locke's contentions were incompatible with observable phenomena and that his errors were widely publicized points to the role of choice in the gestation of liberalism. Men believed in natural economic laws not because the facts led them to that conclusion but because of the social, political, and intellectual implications of their possible existence. An ironic corollary to Locke's successful assertion about the natural value of money is that its triumph breathed new life into the moribund theory of the balance of trade. It took a further eighty years and the genius of Adam Smith to develop an ideological preference for natural laws into an empirically satisfying model of their operation. In the meantime economic reasoning came to a halt at the halfway house that Locke had built.

3

Modernization Theory and Anglo-American Social Theories

"MODERNIZATION THEORY," Alexander Gerschenkron once remarked, "obstructs rather than promotes the understanding of processes of economic change." [1] Far from being a startling judgment, Gerschenkron's comment only signals that another distinguished scholar has joined the theory's detractors. The marked failure of modernization theory to predict how less developed countries would react to incentives for material advance explains the growing chorus of criticism. This indeterminate response from third-world peoples has quite properly raised doubts about how well we understand what is involved in the reorientation of a society's habitual practices. The blight of disconfirming evidence, according to E. I. Eisenstadt, has now led to the abandonment of hope that breakdowns in modernization would be followed by resurgences toward modernity. [2] The rapid fading of a flowering intellectual persuasion reflects the early obsolescence of most things in postindustrial society. One might be tempted to say "let it pass," were it not for the fact that the theory represents the culmination of a century of sociological inquiry into the systematic nature of social change.

At the heart of modernization theory are two contrasting models

1. Alexander Gerschenkron, "Europecentrism and Other Horrors: A Review Article," *Comparative Studies in Society and History*, 19 (1977), 111.
2. E. I. Eisenstadt, "Studies of Modernization and Sociological Theory," *History and Theory*, 13 (1974), 235–241.

of society, the traditional and the modern. In the early decades of the twentieth century, sociologists used these types as means for comprehending the full range of dislocations brought on by European industrialization. Assuming that all societies possess networks of interlocking systems from the various routines of human interaction, these scholars sought the ordering principle working within traditional and modern societies. Through this effort emerged the familiar paired differences of community and association, ascriptive status and achieved status, adherence to custom and rational calculation, varied self-sufficient work and economic specialization. Each form of society was apprehended as a coherent unit, and basic to the integration of the parts was a reigning consensus on goals and values. The critical shift in this structural-functional approach came after the Second World War, when the models of traditional and modern societies were turned into real stages in an evolutionary course.[3] Then the ideal types became steps in a common social process by which small, simple communities moved through successive phases of differentiation, disruption, and reintegration to become large, complex nation-states. Invoking what one critic has called the teleology of adaptation, modernization theorists held that societies will adopt more complex forms of social interaction to meet new situations, and then sustained pressure toward more efficient social mechanisms can be expected to lead eventually to a modern social organization.[4] Thus survival demands a new form, and the form produces the sequential events we study as history.

The strength of modernization theory lies in the underlying commitment to account for the totality of changes involved in the creation of a modern nation. Where liberal social theory and classical economics encouraged scholars to analyze change from the perspective of the isolated individual—his wants, his nature, his means— the pioneers of sociology began with society and recognized in the

3. Anthony D. Smith, *The Concept of Social Change: A Critique of the Functionalist Theory of Social Change* (London, 1973), 14–15, 68–77; Dean C. Tipps, "Modernization Theory and the Comparative Study of Societies: A Critical Perspective," *Comparative Studies in Society and History*, 15 (1973), 202–204.

4. Smith, *Concept of Social Change*, 66. See also Robert A. Nisbet, *Social Change and History: Aspects of the Western Theory of Development* (New York, 1969), 240ff; Jonathan M. Wiener, "Modernization Theory and History: Achievement and Limitations," paper delivered at the Social Science History Association Meeting, Madison, Wisc., April 23, 1976.

patterned behavior of men and women the presence of structures which, though intangible, were nonetheless objects to be studied scientifically.[5] Building on this view, modernization theorists have been able to draw attention to the way that progressive economic developments necessarily impinge on family loyalties, personal behavior, the distribution of power, and the assignment of prestige. Once the impressive morphology of their social types has been studied, no simple narrative of political decisions or technological triumphs will satisfy as an explanation for the emergence of modern societies. So valuable has been the corrective offered by modernization theory that today some scholars—particularly historians—are reluctant to let go of the theory's basic contention that progressive increases in per-capita productivity set in motion political, familial, and personality changes whose similarities are great enough to merit consideration as a common modernizing process. Moving to the high ground of successful modernizations in the West, these scholars have suggested retaining the theory for its usefulness in the restricted sphere of European and American history.[6]

Before this retreat from sociological to historical generalizations is made, however, it would be important to consider a striking weakness in modernization theory: its neglect of the intellectual response to modernizing forces. Like its ideological opposite, Marxism, the theory assumes that changes in the organization of work will call forth corresponding changes in attitudes and perceptions. Left implicit is the plasticity of the human intellect ready to register in new thoughts the impressions left from new social experiences. It is true that the striking contrast between the mentalities of men and women in traditional and modern societies has confirmed the acuity of Marx's observation that it is not the consciousness of men which shapes existence but the existence of men which shapes their consciousness. Yet neither the presence of contrasting mentalities nor their congruence with other social realities explains how, or if,

5. Emile Durkheim, *The Rules of Sociological Method,* ed. George E. G. Catlin (New York, 1964), 1–13. See also Anthony Giddens, "Classical Social Theory and the Origins of Modern Sociology," *American Journal of Sociology,* 81 (1976), 703–721.

6. Richard D. Brown, "Modernization and the Modern Personality in Early America, 1600–1865: A Sketch of a Synthesis," *Journal of Interdisciplinary History,* 2 (1972), 201–202; Harry S. Stout, "Culture, Structure, and the 'New' History: A Critique and an Agenda," *Computers and the Humanities,* 9 (1975), 213–230.

they come into being. Central to the functional-structuralist core of modernization theory is the importance placed on values as the integrators of coherent social action. Shared values can do this only because they convey shared intelligibility or meaningfulness.[7] Yet there is no place in the theory for analyzing how meaningfulness is created and, once created, is adapted to changing circumstances. The expectation that modernization will promote rationality as a mode of thought is more tautological than descriptive: where rationality appears, modernization takes place; where it does not, modernization has not taken place. Moreover, rationality is not all of one piece. The particular conceptual bridges men and women build to carry them into the unfamiliar territory of a radically altered future must be examined as discrete developments because there is nothing in modernization theory to account for them as parts of a process.

To give empirical substance to this line of criticism, I wish to compare the ideological responses of England and America in the pivotal eighteenth century. Both countries embraced the ideal of economic advance, but different ways to interpret this revolutionary prospectus were chosen. Hence the form of their modernity was shaped in part by what was said about it. New circumstances made possible new thoughts. In the expression of these thoughts possibilities were explored, consequences clarified, and conflicts sharpened. As Clifford Geertz has reminded us, it is just when societies leave the governance of tradition that ideologies emerge and take hold.[8] But which ideologies emerge and, more important, which take hold? It is just because the creation of a modernizing ideology is so problematic that the investigation of the English and American experiences has something to reveal about the larger process. Because in the realm of the imagination, new approaches may be suggested in anticipation of structural rearrangements, we may also get a look at the beginnings of those shifts of consciousness which in full course appear as inexorable reactions.

Ideology has become a kind of code word for ideas converted into social forces, but the precise causal relation remains unclear.[9] Pre-

7. Talcott Parsons, *The Structure of Social Action* (New York, 1937), 768.

8. Clifford Geertz, "Ideology as a Cultural System," in *Ideology and Discontent,* ed. David E. Apter (Glencoe, Ill., 1964), 64.

9. Ibid.; George Lichtheim, "The Concept of Ideology," *History and Theory,* 4 (1964), 164–195.

vailing usage indicates that ideology refers to the system of ideas which serves as the conduit for a given society's wisdom on the questions of authority, behavior, and social purpose. Marx's idea of false consciousness is not entirely gone, for the unequal distribution of power in a society is most often justified covertly through mediating values.[10] In both the consensual and conflict models, however, ideology implies functioning ideas: ideas which serve discernible public and private needs. This emphasis upon the function of an ideology leads to another distinction. An ideology can only serve as a cohering force when it has preempted other interpretations of reality. Truths must be shared to create the solidarity that undergird cooperative action. As Bernard Bailyn has written, political values do not influence behavior unless they are in the form of ideology, that is, unless they are capable of organizing the consciousness of the individual by fusing interests with beliefs and ideals.[11] This transformation of a value into a social influence involves the coercive, I must; the intellectual, I understand; and the spiritual, I believe.

Viewed broadly, the commercialization of the European economy created two political and hence two ideological problems. First, it greatly enhanced the possibility of political centralization by providing a network of communication through which goods and payments moved. New wealth-producing activities also could be most easily tapped by the ruler and manipulated by him or her to strengthen monarchical authority. The sovereign could buy new weaponry, employ a bureaucracy for more efficient control, and implement fiscal and commercial policies. Thus the range and intensity of political power grew, and the problem of tyranny was raised in a new form by economic developments which proved more favorable to kings and queens than to their traditional rivals, the nobility.

At the same time the expansion of trade brought new power to the plain members of society because of their private dealings in the market. As Harrington wrote of Henry VIII's England, "the yeomanry or middle people . . . were much unlinked from depen-

10. Norman Birnbaum, "The Sociological Study of Ideology," *Current Sociology,* 9 (1960), 91.

11. Bernard Bailyn, "The Central Themes of the American Revolution: An Interpretation," in *Essays on the American Revolution,* ed. Stephen G. Kurtz and James H. Hutson (Chapel Hill, 1973), 11.

dence upon their lords" whose estates became "so vast a prey into the industry of the people" as to upset the balance of kings, lords, and people.[12] As Harrington also perceived, trade intruded upon the monarch's imperium as well. Where formerly the sovereign had been the final arbiter of rewards, now the market competed as a distributor of wealth. Changes in marketing, in the terms of tenantry, and in the employment of labor narrowed the sovereign's control of economic rewards, while evasions of regulatory statutes were so flagrant for so long that offenders, according to a seventeenth-century writer, "are ready to prescribe use and custome" in justification of their acts.[13] Commerce increased the total wealth of the society and distributed it without reference to sovereign authority.

Despite the unchallenged assumption that the English government had the right and the responsibility to regulate economic activities in the interest of the common good, the ambit of private initiative widened considerably during the seventeenth century. Circumstances—usually in the form of a political crisis—permitted men to pursue their private profit with little official interference. The only enduring policy decision in the economic domain came early in the century when, as Barry Supple has detailed, "as far as official doctrine was concerned, all thoughts of unduly restraining the processes of industrialization had disappeared."[14] Once diversification and the exploitation of new markets were seen as preferable to the protection of a stable agrarian order, opportunities for enterprise grew at a much more rapid rate than the capacity of government to oversee them. Enclosures continued to provoke protests just as depressions prompted government inquiries, but relief from distress usually came from the economy itself. Proposals to reform the Poor Laws expired with the Rump Parliament, and thenceforth the relief of the poor was sought in an increase in employment rather than in curtailing grain sales. Industrial legislation, too, lagged

12. *The Commonwealth of Oceana*, in *The Political Works of James Harrington*, ed. J. G. A. Pocock (Cambridge, 1977), 197–198. For a fine exploration of this development, see Elizabeth Fox-Genovese, "Psychohistory versus Psychodeterminism: The Case of Rogin's Jackson," *Reviews in American History*, 3 (1975), 407–418.

13. [Robert Powell], *Depopulation arraigned* (London, 1636), 111.

14. Barry Supple, *Commercial Crisis and Change in England, 1600–1642* (Cambridge, 1959), 235.

behind innovations.[15] Retrospectively the second half of the century appears as a period of circumstantial laissez-faire.

In the absence of political direction, the informal incentives of gain guided men toward new avenues of investment and new ways of mobilizing resources. In commerce whole new trades grew up outside the monopoly restrictions of the great companies.[16] Englishmen enjoyed a free hand with their money as well after the free coinage Act of 1666. A largely unintended consequence of the English Civil War was the neglect of laws prescribing industrial, agricultural, and labor practices. The ordinance which lifted the burden of feudal dues from the country's principal landlords strengthened the attitude that property was a private rather than a social resource, but the lapses in economic regulation must be ascribed simply to the weakness of successive governments. These same political conditions made possible a free discussion of public issues. Throughout the century an increasingly sophisticated commentary accompanied changes in the economy, for the vigorous press which served religious and political debates lay ready at hand for the publication of tracts on trade. Thus the interpenetration of political, economic, and intellectual developments associated with modernization is nowhere better documented than in seventeenth-century England.

The steady integration of England's many local economies into a single great market furnished the most palpable evidence of change to observers. By the end of the seventeenth century shopkeepers everywhere were stocking the textiles, foodstuffs, metals, and building materials that announced England's participation in a worldwide trade. Behind these expanded inventories lay a human network of buyers and sellers who had become attuned to serving each other's needs as they served their own. Without official mandate, or even public encouragement, more and more people had become involved in exchanging goods over longer distances, more regularly through the course of the year. Common men and women who had been reared to follow orders and assume their subordinate station in a very

15. J. P. Cooper, "Social and Economic Policies under the Commonwealth," in *The Interregnum*, ed. G. E. Aylmer (London, 1972), 121–142.

16. Robert Brenner, "The Social Basis of English Commercial Expansion, 1550–1650," *Journal of Economic History*, 32 (1972), 361–384.

local setting had somehow seen a chance to act on their own and had done so long enough to bring into being new patterns of exchange. The aggregation of private initiative had led over time to new concentrations of purchasing power along with the cost advantages of specialization and the redistribution of capital to effective competitors.[17] A complicated social organization had taken form, uncoerced, but patterned; untraditional, but not disordered; unrestrained, but not without its own regulation.

Critical to new ways of thinking about the economy were the food surpluses of Restoration England. A half-century of agricultural improvement had led to a total increase in productivity which found England in most years a net exporter of grain.[18] Depressed prices for food and fibers kept farm incomes down, but others—rural and urban wage earners—had more money to spend. More important, the successive years of abundance broke the conceptual link between agriculture and social survival. It still existed, of course, but being able to take food supplies for granted liberated the imagination and challenged the rationale for control. Tudor economic legislation rested on the fundamental proposition that the social importance of food production required that an authoritarian watch be kept on all economic activity. The vitality of the government's concern about dearth and the reliance of the poor upon the magistracy reinforced traditional attitudes, but when scarcities disappeared so too did the urgency of official action. As the fear of famine receded, food lost its special character and became a commodity like all others.[19]

The enhancement of agricultural productivity in England also involved a consolidation of landholdings and a decline in the number of laborers needed in agriculture.[20] The success of England's agricul-

---

17. On these developments, see E. A. Wrigley, "A Simple Model of London's Importance in Changing English Society and Economy, 1650–1750," *Past and Present*, 37 (1967), 44–70, and my *Economic Thought in Seventeenth-Century England* (Princeton, 1978), 158–198.

18. W. G. Hoskins, "Harvest Fluctuations and English Economic History, 1620–1759," *Agricultural History Review*, 16 (1968), 15–31, esp. 21.

19. John Walter and Keith Wrightson, "Dearth and the Social Order in Early Modern England," *Past and Present*, 71 (1975), 22–42.

20. F. M. L. Thompson, "Landownership and Economic Growth in England in the Eighteenth Century," in *Agrarian Change and Economic Development*, ed. E. L. Jones and S. J. Woolf (London, 1969); Eric Kerridge, *Agrarian Problems in the Sixteenth Century and After* (London, 1969), 124–125.

tural revolution had shaken the redundant sons and daughters of peasants from their traditional social niches, but the rate of growth in commerce and industry was not fast enough to absorb them all in new occupations. Squatting in forest villages and filling the London slums, they constituted an enduring problem.[21] By the 1660s many began to realize that these displaced men and women would never return to the rural England of their parents and grandparents. The wandering, masterless men of Elizabethan times had acquired a new visibility as the unemployed poor. In fact, the propertyless in seventeenth-century England were divided between those who were finding a place in the infrastructure of the new commercial economy and those poised in a kind of limbo outside both the old and the new economic orders. From the margins of rural tenantry came a steady stream of persons to swell the numbers of the unemployed, but as the progressive commercialization of agriculture filled this pool, so opportunities in trade and industry drew away some of these men and women into an embryonic industrial work force.

The undeniable evidence that productivity had become a major social goal in Restoration England led many men to probe for its causes. In this imaginative work they had to impose an order on the phenomena they wished to explain, which means that they had to convert the activities under their observation into meaningful generalizations. While their writings reflect no intention of revamping conventional wisdom on social relations, they nonetheless put into circulation new thoughts about human behavior as a by-product of their effort to lay bare the workings of a commercial economy. The word "market" acquired a new meaning in their publications. The image of village stalls and peasant hawkers gave way to that of a huge conveyor belt continuously moving goods and payments through an unceasing flow that girdled the globe and crisscrossed the English countryside. This market was treated as an abstraction which represented the aggregation of all market bargains condensed from time to time into a price which went back along the lines of communication to influence people's decisions about what to plant,

21. Alan Everitt, "Farm Labourers," in *The Agrarian History of England and Wales 1550–1640,* ed. Joan Thirsk (Cambridge, 1967).

where to sell, and from whence to order goods. "Let me sell as the market goes" was the husbandman's philosophy, according to John Cook.[22] Dudley North noted that men would "not endure to be under a force to Sell at lower . . . than the Free Market of things will produce."[23] Nicholas Barbon told his readers that "the market is the Best Judge of Value."[24] In these references the market appears as an independent, often an inexorable, force. Thomas Mun gave classic expression to this idea earlier when he insisted that tampering with the royal exchange would not influence trade. "Let the meer Exchanger do his worst; Let Princes oppress, Lawyers extort, usurers bite, prodigals wast . . . so much treasure only will be brought in . . . as the Forraign Trade doth over or under balance," he wrote, concluding with an assertion of great significance for the reconceptualization of economic life: "and this must come to pass by a Necessity beyond all resistance."[25]

Only natural forces could be construed as impervious to human intentions, and this is exactly the identification which economic writers made. As one man said of imitating the Dutch, "we must not think to do that by compulsion . . . which with them is done by nature."[26] Roger Coke proclaimed that he never would believe that "any man or Nation ever will attain their ends by forceable means, against the Nature and Order of Things."[27] Charles Davenant invoked nature to explain why statutes cannot set prices. If person B did not pay a price, he said, C or D would and concluded by way of emphasis, "Nor can any law hinder B. C. & D. from supplying their Wants [for in the] Naturall Course of Trade, Each Commodity will find its Price," to which he added, "The supream power can do many things, but it cannot alter the Laws of Nature, of which the most originall is, That every man should preserve himself."[28]

To reduce the multifarious details of economic life to a set of gen-

---

22. John Cook, *Unum necessarium* (London, 1648), 7.

23. [Sir Dudley North], *Discourses upon Trade* (London, 1691), viii.

24. [Nicholas Barbon], *An apology for the builder* (London, 1685), 32–33.

25. Thomas Mun, *England's Treasure by Forraign Trade* (London, 1664), 218–219.

26. *Interest of money mistaken* (London, 1668), 21–23.

27. Roger Coke, *England's improvements* (London, 1675), 57.

28. Charles Davenant, "A Memorial Concerning the Coyn of England" [1695], in *Two Manuscripts by Charles Davenant*, ed. Abbott Payson Usher (Baltimore, 1942), 20–21.

eral laws represented an imaginative leap of great consequence. A mastery was achieved when the evanescent acts of buying and selling were construed as parts of a real, if invisible, process. More important, treating economic activities as parts of a natural order led analyzers to search for the source of regularity which they found in a predictable human response—self-interest. The consistency of the profit motive undergird all of the generalizations about investment returns, market prices, and interest rates. Because of the presumed dependability of human beings to seek their own gain, economics acquired that coherence which, as William Petty put it, made the subject worthwhile for a man "to imploy his thoughts about it."[29]

What made the pursuit of profit so salient in the seventeenth century was obviously the number of occasions for acting upon it. By 1692 John Locke could present it as an undeniable proposition that it "will be impossible by any Contrivance of Law, to hinder Men from purchasing Money at what Rate their Occasions shall make it necessary for them to have it."[30] Moralists fumed at this rationalization of self-willed behavior. They pointed out the confusion between an unopposed tendency and an unopposable force,[31] but economic writers went beyond mere acceptance of self-interest; they refashioned it into a constructive mediator of human will. John Houghton explained the widening of the market through the operation of self-interest. Our ambition, he said, "puts us all upon an industry, makes everyone strive to excell his fellow, and by their ignorance of one anothers quantities, make more than our markets will presently take off which put them to a new industry to find a foreign Vent, and then they must make more for that market; but still having some overplus they stretch their wits farther."[32] Defending a mid-century enclosure, Joseph Lee claimed that if left on their own men would automatically supply the needs of the market, for "it's an undeniable maxime, That everyone by the light of nature

29. Sir William Petty, *A treatise of taxes* (London, 1662), 33.

30. [John Locke], *Some considerations of the consequences of the lowering of interest* (London, 1692), 1–2.

31. *Sir Thomas Colepepers Tracts concerning Usury Reprinted . . . with some animadversions on the writings of Dr. Lock* (London [1709]).

32. [John Houghton], *A collection of letters for the improvement of husbandry and trade* (London, 1681–1683), 60.

and reason will do that which makes for his greatest advantage."[33]
If there are unprofitable trades, "private individuals will stop it,"
Dudley North said, from which he concluded that "wherever the
Traders thrive, the Public, of which they are a part thrives also."[34]
John Briscoe said that people have a quick sense of "the Profit of
their Labour, and will bestow their Cost and Pains in Proportion
to the Worth of the Subject Matter and the Benefit they gather for
their industry."[35] Even men with no propriety in the soil were said
to have "a distinct and peculiar interest in the General wealth of
the nation" because of the benefits that came to them from manufacturing and trade. "Every Man's own experience is the best director
for such purposes," this writer went on to say, "and every Man's
private Interest is the strongest persuasive to the promotion of his
own Concerns."[36]

Competition also appeared in a constructive light. Nicholas
Barbon said that butchers, brewers, drapers, mercers, bricklayers,
and carpenters could do better than provide a livelihood; they could
grow rich because "there ariseth an emulation among them to out-
live and out-vye one another in arts . . . [which] forceth them to
be industrious and by industry they grow rich."[37] "If my Neighbour
by doing much with little labor, can sell cheap," Henry Martyn
wrote, "I must contrive to sell as cheap as he."[38] Along with this
favorable reevaluation of self-interest and competition came an
equally enthusiastic endorsement of the expansive human appetites.
North said that the main spur to industry and ingenuity were "the
exorbitant appetites of men which they will take pains to gratifie
and so be disposed to work when nothing else will incline them to
it."[39] Dalby Thomas claimed that love of luxury was the true spur
"to Virtuc, Valour and the Elevation of the Mind, as well as the
just rewards of Industry."[40]

33. Joseph Lee, *A vindication of a regulated enclosure* (London, 1656), 9.

34. [North], *Discourses upon Trade,* viii.

35. [John Briscoe], *A discourse of money* (London, 1696), 22.

36. *Discourse of the nature, use and advantages of trade* (London, 1693), 8–12.

37. [Barbon], *An apology for the builder,* 32–33.

38. [Henry Martyn], *Considerations upon the East-India trade* (London, 1701), 67.

39. [North], *Discourses upon Trade,* 14.

40. [Sir Dalby Thomas], *An historical account of the West-India Collonies* (London, 1690), 6.

These writers were articulating a new social reality in which human beings possessed an internal regulator more effective than master or magistrate. Wishing to explain the evident enhancement of English productivity, they pointed to self-interest redefined as a universal goad to effort, a discipliner of the will, a promoter of business acumen, and a force giving consistency to market relations. They rarely addressed political questions, but they nonetheless created a new rationale for freedom. The importance ascribed to the pursuit of profit, like Mun's earlier assertion about autonomous trade flows, redirected attention away from political authority and its comprehensive purposes to the market behavior of individuals seeking private satisfactions. Without challenging reigning truths, these economic writers created a striking picture of the liberty of the market economy where individuals used their own powers, moved freely toward desired objects, planned for change, and set in motion a series of activities with the simple aim of private gain. No threat of chaos lurked behind this depiction of human freedom, for the strivings of men and women in the market were orderly because the market itself channeled energies towards work, rewarding efficiency and the intellectual mastery of economic relations.

Despite the obvious gradations of wealth and status and the deep divisions of class and rank in England, many economic pamphleteers blithely imputed a market morality to all. "Every man in society, even from the King to the peasant, is a merchant," one writer declared, which, according to him, put each under a necessity of taking care of his "Reputation."[41] Another asserted that differences of birth, age, and sex were irrelevant to trade because "all Persons are under a possibility of improving their Fortunes, in proportion to their Parts and Industry."[42] In a similar vein many linked the prosperity of the nation to the spread of a utilitarian mode of thinking. These same pamphleteers argued forcefully that rises in the standard of living in response to ambition were potentially more stimulating to economic growth than policies designed to protect English industry and restrain the price of wages. Extending this logic, Dudley North said "that the loss of Trade with one Nation,

---

41. [Thomas Sheridan], *A discourse of the rise and power of Parliaments* ([London] 1677), 225.

42. *A discourse of the nature, use and advantages of trade*, 15.

is not that only, but so much of the Trade of the World rescinded and lost, for all is combined together."[43] Where earlier writers had defined wealth as the store of gold and silver and assumed that acquiring specie was the motive behind economic acts, prosperity in the second half of the century revealed a different picture. It became evident that people went through coin to goods. Money appeared more and more to be a medium of trade; wealth the capacity to produce marketable goods.

The depiction of the natural, self-generating buoyance of commerce came most typically from the pens of merchants, bank promoters, and real-estate developers, men happily placed to benefit from the Restoration prosperity and the likely prospect of expansion. For the clothiers who represented England's largest industrial interest, the situation was less rosy. The 1660s and 1670s brought increased competition in European markets from continental woolen manufacturers, while at home the free importation of printed Indian fabrics cut into domestic sales.[44] Spokesmen for the clothiers used Mun's idea that wealth followed the settling of international trade accounts to make a case for the protection of English industry. If it was the favorable balance which increased the national store of treasure, they argued, then decreasing foreign imports and making good the loss through domestic manufacturing would produce the same effect. Figures purporting to represent England's annual trade deficit with France were published.[45] Despite this gesture to the new interest in statistics, most of the clothiers' arguments were practical: cottager families were without work; manufacturing could create jobs for the unemployed men, women, and children who would otherwise become a public burden; the state should act positively in the interests of the whole nation to exclude luxuries and those foreign imports which could be produced at home.[46] Responding to a short-run dislocation in their trade, the clothiers rejected the

43. [North], *Discourses upon Trade*, viii.

44. P. J. Thomas, *Mercantilism and the East India Trade* (London, 1963), 30, 51.

45. *A scheme of trade as it is at present carried on between England and France* [London, 1674]. On this, see Margaret Priestley, "Anglo-French Trade and the 'Unfavorable Balance' Controversy, 1660–1685," *Economic History Review*, 4 (1951–1952).

46. *The great necessity and advantage of preserving our own manufacturies* (London, 1697); *The great loss and damage to England by the transportation of wooll to forreign parts* (n.p., 1677); *Reasons humbly offered for the passing of a bill* (London, 1697).

merchants' contention that economic freedom would cause prosperity because ordinary people would work harder and with more ingenuity in order to satisfy their new consuming tastes. Rejected too was the possibility of harmony from undirected effort. A staple assertion of clothier tracts was that men frequently grew rich while the nation went bankrupt. Here in economic terms was the old religious fear of self-willed behavior.

The clothiers' laments about economic freedom in Restoration England did not lead to any significant change in legislation or enforcement, but events in the critical quarter-century after 1689 brought about a dramatic reorientation of economic life—and thinking about it—in eighteenth-century England.[47] First war, then a new political arrangement, and finally a national economic policy raised ideological barriers to further speculations on the benefits of economic freedom. The balance-of-trade theory, which had long ago ceased to reflect the realities of international commerce,[48] became what it had never been before: the orthodox explanation of how nations grow wealthy. William III's accession to the throne not only plunged England into a general European war, it also signaled the beginning of a century of Anglo-French confrontations around the world. The free-ranging published discussions on market relations were among the casualties of this sustained hostility. The immediate impact of the war was devastating. French privateers wreaked havoc on English shipping. Much of the capital created during the prosperous 1670s and 1680s was wiped out. Many merchants withdrew their money from trade rather than risk running the gauntlet of enemy ships in the Channel.[49] Financing the war created major problems as well. The expectation of a short war had encouraged the ministry to pay high interest rates for short-term loans, an

---

47. On these shifts of economic orientation, see G. N. Clark, *Guide to English Commercial Statistics* (London, 1938), xiii–xiv; Ralph Davis, "England's Foreign Trade, 1700–1774," *Economic History Review*, 15 (1962), 295–303; Thomas, *Mercantilism and the East India Trade*, 172–173.

48. Jacob Price, "Multilateralism and/or Bilateralism: The Settlement of British Trade Balances with the North, c. 1700," *Economic History Review*, 14 (1961), 254–274; J. Sperling, "The International Payments Mechanism in the Seventeenth and Eighteenth Centuries," ibid., 446–468.

49. D. W. Jones, "London Merchants and the Crisis of the 1690s," in *Crisis and Order in English Towns 1500–1600*, ed. Peter Clark and Paul Slack (London, 1971), 333–338.

expediency that brought on a fiscal crisis. At the same time, the press for funds had prompted the government to raise the traditionally low custom duties to unprecedented, high levels.[50]

Under these multiple pressures several programs were worked out which were to have long-range implications for economic development and theories about it. In quick succession Parliament created the Bank of England, undertook a general recoinage, overhauled the enforcing mechanisms for the navigation laws, and created a royal Board of Trade.[51] With these measures the king and his ministers gained effective control of the monetary and commercial systems of the nation. In succeeding years the attractiveness of public securities lured investors away from company shares.[52] The wartime custom rates, which were a departure from England's traditional policy of low levies, were systematically reworked to provide protection for English industry.[53] Tariff barriers went up throughout Europe, and the principal trading nations began to look to their colonies and the far-flung markets of Asia and Africa for customers and suppliers. These new policies were put to the test at the end of the War of the Spanish Succession when Queen Anne's Tory ministers negotiated a commercial treaty with France. Those who benefited from tariff protection added their weight to the already strong opposition to closer relations with France, and implementation of the treaty was blocked in the Commons.[54] In the next decade the level of tariff protection was extended, as were the provisions of the navigation system. At the beginning of the eighteenth century the government became the principal influence upon the direction of economic development in Great Britain.

50. P. G. M. Dickson, *The Financial Revolution in England* (New York, 1967), 6–17; Ralph Davis, "The Rise of Protection in England, 1689–1786," *Economic History Review*, 19 (1966), 306–317.

51. Dickson, *Financial Revolution*, 8–22; Peter Laslett, "John Locke, the Great Recoinage, and the Origins of the Board of Trade," *William and Mary Quarterly*, 14 (1957), 370–402.

52. Jones, "London Merchants and the Crisis of the 1690s," 338–343; Dickson, *Financial Revolution*, 257–259.

53. Davis, "Rise of Protection," 313–317.

54. D. C. Coleman, "Politics and Economics in the Age of Anne: The Case of the Anglo-French Trade Treaty of 1713," in *Trade, Government and Economy in Preindustrial England: Essays Presented to F. J. Fisher*, ed. D. C. Coleman and A. H. John (London, 1976).

During these same years the great Whig magnates were able to consolidate their power and check the more open, participatory politics of the previous half-century. Through a series of legislative and political maneuvers they reduced the size of the electorate and the frequency of elections, thus laying the foundation for a self-perpetuating oligarchy.[55] When the Tories were discredited as Jacobites in 1715, the Whig oligarchy was finally in a position to exploit to the fullest the political advantages of the wartime economic policies. The founding of the Bank of England, the expert management of the national debt, and the revaluation of the currency gave the Whigs the monetary tools with which to forge a vital link between the government and City wealth. At the same time the growth of bureaucracy greatly facilitated oligarchic rule.[56] The administration of the navigation system and the national treasury increased the number of places at the disposal of the ministers, who could then substitute corruption for cooperation in the management of Parliament. The economic and political initiatives of the Whig rulers were complementary. They used the power of the purse to secure political power and political power to enlarge the purse by aggressively pursuing British economic development at home and abroad.

If, as Michael Walzer has said, "politics is an art of unification," then Britannia, that symbol of waxing commercial prowess, was the Whig unifier. Here was the representation of a modern, national goal summoning all classes and regions to the mundane tasks of increasing the productivity of Great Britain and her empire. Theoretical justification for these new economic policies lay at hand in the balance-of-trade idea that specie alone constituted wealth and that a country without mines could only add to its stock of gold and silver through a favorable trade balance. John Locke lent the considerable prestige of his name to this idea when he defended parliamentary recoinage in 1696.[57] In subsequent years it became a fixed feature of official pronouncements about protective tariffs and

55. J. H. Plumb, "The Growth of the Electorate in England from 1600 to 1712," *Past and Present*, 45 (1969), 90–116.

56. J. R. Western, *Monarchy and Revolution: The English State in the 1680s* (London, 1972), 3.

57. [Locke], *Some considerations*, 16–17.

navigation laws. Little then was heard of the liberals' model of a natural economic order with its own inner propulsion toward growth and development. The positive evaluation of economic self-interest faded, while the ideal of enhancing national profit and power was evoked to commend the deployment of force against economic rivals around the world.

The rejection in the early eighteenth century of the English liberals' conception of market relations offers a rare glimpse of the intersection of culture and society. Through an elusive process of screening facts, the interests of the powerful, the sensibilities of a larger, but dominant group, and the needs of ordinary men and women are accommodated in a single formulation of reality. In this case an intellectual advance—for there is no doubt that the liberal model more adequately accounted for the role of money, of multilateral trade balances, and of market behavior—was repelled in deference to an explanation that met a broader range of ideological demands. The liberals had entwined their analysis with a radical social vision. Their facts implicated values and their optimism rested on the acceptance of economic virtues as measures of social worth. The means used to stop further speculations along liberal lines are obscure. Contemporaries suggested that ambitious men echewed free-trade views after the seventeenth century because of official endorsement of mercantilistic policies.[58] The financial revolution which saw public securities preempt private company shares as preferred investments undoubtedly influenced the merchants and bank promoters who had earlier promoted an expansion of trade. The fact that the licensing act controlling publications was allowed to lapse indicates that persuasion was enough to discourage unwanted economic discourse. There were, moreover, aspects of the social vision of the liberals which invited opposition on practical grounds.

The belief that economic development could best be promoted through individuals seeking their own interests in constructive activity rested upon the assumption that, if given the opportunity, human beings would discipline themselves in order to profit thereby. In this view, there is a natural, and hence dependable,

---

58. On this, see William James Ashley, "The Tory Origin of Free Trade Policy," in *Surveys, Historic and Economic* (London, 1900), 295–299.

striving for self-improvement planted in every human breast. The operation of the market, as it were, could call forth a second nature whose tendencies were so compatible with the economic goals of the nation that the institutional apparatus for coercion could be abandoned. The pamphleteers who had suggested that society could be naturally free, orderly, and prosperous had projected upon the entire human race the economic rationalism they saw around them. What began as an analysis of the most modern aspects of the English economy had ended as a theory of human behavior with profound social implications. The difficulty with the liberal vision of economic freedom, as it was expressed at the end of the seventeenth century in England, was that the capacity of the market to act as a voluntary integrator of social tasks depended upon the number of jobs it offered. The idea of a society of avid consumers and eager workers was hypothetical at best. Self-discipline and private economic planning were latent human qualities requiring careful nurture in youth. As with any socialization process, the results were problematic, particularly when the economy could not be relied upon for the reinforcement of gainful employment. In the short run, the lure of personal ambition was a less certain discipliner and a more subversive incentive than the rod of the magistrate. To liberalize the economy was to rely upon a common psychological orientation toward self-improvement. Thus the liberal alternative to more conventional methods of controlling the lower class had the effect of advertising the implicit egoism of the market society. It is not difficult to see why a propertied class could generate its own antipathy to such a program independent of the government.

The insufficiencies of the balance-of-trade explanation of market relations, on the other hand, should not be allowed to obscure its very real ideological merits. By defining wealth as specie—a fixed sum in the world—the theory endowed the endemic international rivalries with a rationale, while providing a theoretical justification for subordinating private interests to national goals. Following the ineluctable logic of their propositions about economic development, liberal writers had anticipated the irenic sentiments of the nineteenth century. John Houghton, for instance, had stressed that it was better "for England to have Ireland Rich and Populous, than Poor and sparce," while he and others had given a constructive role to the trade in French luxuries.[59] When liberals suggested that prosperity might best be promoted through a Donnybrook of self-interested competitors, they came dangerously close to challenging the hereditary, hierarchical order of the kingdom. Mercantilism, on the other hand, with its emphasis upon tangible wealth was congruent with political and social distinctions based upon property. There was also in its focus upon corporate economic goals the presumption of an identity of interests which helped screen the competitive aspects of the market economy. Within the balance of trade logic, moreover, the mobilization of labor for private industry took on the appearance of a national program. Mercantilism also retained the negative evaluation of self-interest embedded in Christian morality. It is worth noting in this regard that the spirit of the manufacturer differed markedly from that of the merchant. From the merchants had come the paeans to free trade, increased consumption, and personal competition. Manufacturers and landlords were more concerned about the work habits of the poor and the cost of wages. Thus the adoption of legislation to protect English industry joined public policy to the interest of employers, that is, the managers of others' labor. Lower-class men and women henceforth attracted more attention as workers in need of discipline than as consumers in an upwardly mobile society. The balance of trade theory offered a justification for this concern couched in the modern terms of profit and power rather than traditional ideas of an unchanging order.

The price to be paid for the adoption of the balance-of-trade theory was the substitution of sentiment for science and the consequent loss of the means for acquiring a more adequate description of economic phenomena. In this suspension of critical analysis there is a parallel in eighteenth-century political thought. As Quentin Skinner has so adroitly shown, Whig assertions about the history of the English constitution were totally at variance with historical evidence.[60] Paradoxically because a particular interpretation of the past was so important to the Whigs, they could not afford to pursue open-ended historical investigation. Similar too was the contradiction between constitutional theory and political practice. While the

59. Houghton, *A collection of letters,* 43–49.

60. Quentin Skinner, "History and Ideology in the English Revolution," *Historical Journal,* 8 (1965), 151–178.

Whigs celebrated government by consent, they narrowed the popular political base, replaced argumentation with manipulation in parliamentary decisionmaking and fused executive and legislative powers. While the cosmetic of ideology hid the true face of English politics, it would be wrong to conclude that the myths of mercantilism and Whig history were adopted for their beauty. Rather it seems more likely that the implicit understanding of the English political nation undergirded the exercise of authority. The collective memory of the instability and divisive controversies of the previous century acted as the hidden persuader for patently distorted presentations of reality. At home, awareness of the disjuncture between actualities and affirmations could be deflected by a common appreciation of civil peace, but the economic policies defended by balance-of-trade considerations could no more stand up under rigorous examination than constitutional arrangements justified by a unique historical inheritance. It was, in fact, an ideological package too fragile to travel, as the British were to discover in the last quarter of the century.

To return to the original proposition that it is through ideas that men and women grasped the meaning of modernization, we have found by canvassing the intellectual response to the commercialization of the English economy evidence of the way a social accommodation was reached. Those able to influence public discourse rejected the naturalistic depiction of the new economic order. In its place they put the balance-of-trade theory, using its fixed-pie, specie-centered propositions to enlist patriotism and conventional morality for the cause of organizing the nation's productive resources. What is remarkable about the modern restructuring of British society is not the establishment of political stability through oligarchic rule, but rather the successful blend of progressive economic policies and traditional notions about place. Without undermining upper-class rule at the local level, the Whig magnates pushed the independent country gentlemen to the backwater of national life. The electorate was narrowed and participatory politics checked, but the "productorate" was enlarged and in the market economy grew unabated.

English entrepreneurs continued to enjoy a wide ambit of freedom in their dealings, but as public policy cut off many profitable exchanges in Europe, investments poured into the channels of trade cut by the navigation system. Markets for English exports were aggressively cultivated in Africa, Latin America, the East Indies, and the colonies.[61] The elaboration of an Atlantic communications and transportation network created an imperial market to complement the market at home. By at last providing effective means for protecting the monopoly of colonial commerce in 1696, Parliament paved the way for British wealth to prime the economic pumps of the New World. With the redirection of future expansion toward the Atlantic, British officials, British credit, British land speculators, and British merchants began to exercise a powerful influence upon American economic development.

Rapid colonial growth was first felt in the plantation economies of the South and the West Indies. The Caribbean sugar plantations offered an excellent model for the kind of intensive agriculture most responsive to market incentives. An increased demand for sugar in Europe led to a doubling of the sugar islands' slave force early in the century.[62] With Britain firmly in control of the African slave trade Chesapeake planters moved quickly to replace a white-servant work force with slaves. When after 1713 the French demand for Virginia and Maryland tobacco was added to the British, production in the Chesapeake trebled and quadrupled.[63] In South Carolina a commercial boom followed close on the heels of successful rice and indigo cultivation. These "factories in the fields" of the Antilles, Carolinas, and Chesapeake in turn promoted the commercialization of agriculture in the northern colonies. The more specialized the staple colonies became, the more they depended upon the market to supply their needs for food, lumber products, and horses, the natural surpluses of Pennsylvania, New York, and New England. The dynamic which John Houghton described for Restoration England was repeated: men not knowing the quantity a market would bear overproduced and consequently sought out new markets for their goods. By the second quarter of the century, American-built ships laden with American cargoes called regularly in the ports of the extended Atlantic trade world that linked the littorals of four continents.

61. Davis, "England's Foreign Trade, 1700–1774."

62. Philip Curtin, *The Atlantic Slave Trade* (Madison, 1969), 140, 216.

63. Jacob Price, "The Economic Growth of the Chesapeake and the European Market, 1695–1775," *Journal of Economic History*, 24 (1964), 496–516.

By the third decade of the eighteenth century the growth of population in Europe had created that demand for food which was to underwrite the territorial expansion of America for the next century.[64] First in the West Indies, then in southern Europe, and by the 1750s in the British Isles, food shortages repatterned trade connections. As demand at home increased, the British curtailed their grain exports and American farmers from South Carolina to Rhode Island moved to supply the markets once served by English ports. From the middle colonies came wheat, flour, biscuits; from New England salted fish and meat. Throughout the South lands of marginal efficiency for tobacco production were planted in wheat and corn. Whole new urban networks took form in response to the demand for New World foodstuffs. The backcountry of the Carolinas and the interior valleys of Pennsylvania, Maryland, and Virginia were drawn into the Atlantic trade world almost as quickly as the colonists pushed westward. The trade in grains was particularly promising, for only rice came under navigation act restrictions. Nor were colonial food growers pushed by foreign competition like the British West Indian sugar growers. Indeed, as European population began its steady climb, North American farmers stood to become the principal beneficiaries of the vital revolution. Well might Thomas Paine exult in 1776 that America would always have a commerce to enrich herself "while eating is the custom of Europe."[65]

The colonists, for their part, responded to the considerable scope for economic initiative opened up in the eighteenth century and throve. Marc Egnal has analyzed available data on the American economy and discerned two long swing periods of growth and development.[66] The first period, from 1720 to 1745, was characterized, he reports, by the expansion of the total output; the second twenty-five-year period by a rise in the standard of living. Per capita income grew during the same period that population doubled, going

---

64. Carville Earle and Ronald Hoffman, "Staple Crops and Urban Development in the Eighteenth-century South," *Perspectives in American History*, 10 (1976), 34.

65. Thomas Paine, *Common Sense, The Works of Thomas Paine* (London, 1796), 12.

66. Marc Egnal, "The Economic Development of the Thirteen Continental Colonies, 1720 to 1775," *William and Mary Quarterly*, 32 (1975), 191–222. See also John J. McCusker, "Sources of Investment Capital in the Colonial Philadelphia Shipping Industry," *Journal of Economic History*, 32 (1972), 146–157.

from one million to two million. In the latter period there was also a significant increase in the amount of credit extended to the colonies, and the flow of English investments spilled over its regular channels, reaching new commercial debtors among small farmers and tradesmen. The great Atlantic trade world underwrote continuous exploitation of the natural resources of North America. Developments in Great Britain's economy were also propitious for a broadly based colonial prosperity. Long-term credit and cheaper manufactured goods brought both enterprise and new consuming tastes within the reach of the great body of middling colonists. Eighteenth-century economic development in the colonies thus involved an extension and an intensification of the commercial influence. Ready access to markets in the Atlantic provided strong inducements to those individuals willing to cultivate the opportunities available to them. The profit motives of English merchants brought enterprising possibilities to an ever-increasing number of colonists whose ambitions created strong personal ties to economic growth.

As in England, the quickening pace of commercial growth disrupted old social patterns, provoked extended commentary, and put pressure on the existing distribution of power. Unlike England, the men and women most affected by economic change were not the displaced persons of a waning agrarian order, but the migrants and immigrants who pushed onto the uncultivated lands in successive waves. People in the colonies were not displaced; they moved. Everywhere in the eighteenth century there is evidence of movement. Over a hundred towns were newly platted in the middle decades in Massachusetts.[67] Through the port of Philadelphia alone some 7,000 immigrants passed annually between 1730 and 1750.[68] Thousands of westward-moving families poured into the interior valleys of Pennsylvania, Maryland, and Virginia. Dotted through the back country of the middle and southern colonies were communities called into being by the requirements of marketing foodstuffs, hides, and timber—the first fruits of frontier settle-

67. P. M. G. Harris, "The Social Origins of American Leaders: The Demographic Foundations," *Perspectives in American History*, 3 (1969), 234–236.

68. Gary B. Nash, "Slaves and Slaveowners in Colonial Philadelphia," *William and Mary Quarterly*, 30 (1973), 227–228.

ments.[69] Despite the rise in tenantry, farm ownership grew through-out the century.[70] Land held out hope of personal independence; it conveyed political rights; its widespread ownership democratized a social order based on property. The wholesale experience with founding new towns, moreover, had educational value: it demon-strated the ease with which societies of working men and women could be formed.

Without a ruling group powerful enough to impose its program for growth, political decisions in the colonies were frequently deter-mined by elections. The 40-shilling freehold qualification which acted as a limitation on the electorate in England conferred the vote upon half of the adult white males in the colonies. The divisive conflicts peculiar to an entrepreneurial economy turned this exten-sive electorate into an active one. Questions of land, banks, and money embroiled communities and whole colonies in factional poli-tics. The increase in commercial transactions made specie short and created a demand for government to issue paper money.[71] Eager for a more rapid growth, many colonists endorsed various banking schemes to convert immovable wealth into movable funds for invest-ment. Through their market transactions ordinary colonists acquired an awareness of how political decisions affected them. Land com-panies, licensing acts, the incorporation of towns, access to freeman-ship, warehousing and inspection laws, regulation of auctions, tax proposals, debt collection—all were economic issues capable of mobilizing men into political action. No body of leaders in the colonies possessed the authority of the Whig magnates to reduce the size of the body politic and restrict the number of elections. Instead contending groups of colonial leaders frequently enhanced the political power of their constituents by enlisting their help to oppose rivals or British officials. As Gary Nash has shown, urban politics were transformed in the middle decades of the century

69. Earle and Hoffman, "Staple Crops and Urban Development," 56; Robert D. Mitch-ell, "The Shenandoah Valley Frontier," *Annals of the Association of American Geographers,* 62 (1972).

70. David Allen Williams, "The Small Farmer in Eighteenth-century Virginia Politics," *Agricultural History,* 43 (1969), 93; James Lemon, *The Best Poor Man's Country: A Geographical Study of Early Southeastern Pennsylvania* (Baltimore, 1972), 94.

71. Richard A. Lester, "Currency Issues to Overcome Depressions in Pennsylvania, 1723 and 1729," *Journal of Political Economy,* 45 (1938), 324–375.

because office-holders began to woo votes and unwittingly turned the deferential, politically passive common man of Whig theory into a ticket-managing, slogan-spreading, ballot-stuffing, caucusing political animal.[72] The solidarity of a closed ruling group was repeatedly shattered when gentlemen, eager to carry an issue, turned out-of-doors for political allies.

Although Americans showed little interest in theoretical questions, the economic arguments they used in political disputes give some hint of how the market influenced their thinking. The colonial experience with money was unique. Chronically short of specie and pressed for a circulating medium, almost every colony turned at one time or another to paper money issues. Far from accepting it as an expediency, many colonists adopted an instrumental definition of money and in words echoing the English liberals praised inflation for its capacity to invigorate trade and spread economic opportunity.[73] The idea of engineering prosperity drew support from tangible and repeated evidence that new trades promoted population growth and that population growth raised land values. Like the English economic liberals, many colonists reevaluated the role of self-interest, ascribing to it both the power of an irradicable natural force and an engine behind individual productivity.[74] Neither economic opportunities nor political power was evenly distributed in colonial America, but their accessibility to plain, white members of society was pervasive. When that accessibility was blocked, as in Georgia under the Trustees, men were prepared to argue that they had a right to an unrestrained participation in the market.[75] In these instances colonial responses to economic developments sound like

72. Gary B. Nash, "The Transformation of Urban Politics, 1700–1765," *Journal of American History,* 60 (1973), 605–632.

73. [John Wise], "A Word of Comfort to a Melancholy Country," and [Benjamin Franklin], "A Modest Enquiry into the Nature and Necessity of a Paper Currency," in *Colonial Currency Reprints, 1682–1751,* ed. A. M. Davis (Boston, 1911), II, 186.

74. Edward M. Cook, Jr., "Social Behavior and Changing Values in Dedham, Massachusetts, 1700 to 1775," *William and Mary Quarterly,* 27 (1970), 578; Richard Bushman, *From Puritan to Yankee: Character and the Social Order in Connecticut, 1690–1765* (Cambridge, Mass., 1967), 276–280; Beverly McAnear, "Mr. Robert R. Livingston's Reasons Against a Land Tax," *Journal of Political Economy,* 48 (1940), 73.

75. [Thomas Stevens], "A Brief Account of the Causes that Have Retarded the Progress of the Colony of Georgia in America," in *Collections of the Georgia Historical Society,* 2 (1892).

echoes from the liberal writings of the seventeenth century, but champions of economic individualism did not have the field to themselves. There were still strong centers of community life held together by a presiding local gentry or a shared submission to the discipline of the church. Up until the 1740s, religious uniformity was the rule within villages and parishes; even in newly formed towns the congregation often exercised a powerful moral authority over the individual. Defenders of a traditional social order were blind to the virtues of self-assertion so necessary in the market economy. Nor was it easy to reconcile the Calvinist concept of a calling with the unweaned worldly affections of free enterprise. The consuming tastes that enhanced trade could also be construed as vanities, and the competition that increased production was often seen as socially disruptive. Laments over economic growth produced their own peculiar genre. In the most thorough study of this body of writing, J. E. Crowley has traced the conflict between two views of work: work as a moral force binding the members of society, and work as a means to personal profit.[76] The yearning for cohesion and for a reaffirmation of human purpose beyond mere self-improvement died hard, Crowley found. Late in the colonial period people still clung to the hope that commerce could cement rather than divide their communities. Unlike the English economic writers, American writers did not construct a model of economic relations. Their predominating concern with the moral implications of market behavior took them to the heart of the ideological problem of liberalism: how to maintain a unifying social purpose under the atomizing pressures of a capitalistic economy. Success in the market required the capacity to organize resources on one's own behalf, yet the assertiveness involved was frequently discordant with reigning ideas about religious and political authority. This meant that an increasing number of colonists experienced a disjuncture between their everyday lives and the ideals that acted as ethical reference points.

Each of the thirteen colonies had a distinctive past. Totally separated political connections with Great Britain enhanced this historical distinction. Different and often inimicable religious loyalties

76. J. E. Crowley, *This Sheba, Self: The Conceptualization of Economic Life in Eighteenth-Century America* (Baltimore, 1974), 76–127.

divided the colonies still further. The conversion to slave labor introduced into the southern population a racial component of profound significance. Some colonies grew through natural increase; others by a heterogeneous influx of immigrants. Topography, size, and climate further differentiated them, but commercial expansion in the middle decades of the eighteenth century had a homogenizing influence upon this cluster of markedly dissimilar societies. Everywhere the rapid growth, the trade cycles, uncertainties about price, the variable worth of land and the shift to new crops created a common awareness of changing times. The uncertainty attendant on commercial enterprise also undermined the solidity of status. While commercial developments led to greater spreads between the rich and the poor, it did not strengthen class divisions. As G. B. Warden has found in Boston, the ups and downs of business meant that investments were not well secured nor poverty an inescapable fate.[77] Widespread too was the colonists' experience with the alternating waves of credit and consumption, depression and debt. In the North and South a code of thrift and moderation was extolled, but new borrowing took place just as fast as old accounts could be settled.[78] The peculiar form of instability generated by a buoyant market economy produced a common set of private anxieties and material aspirations. Varied as their backgrounds were, the colonists were confronting very similar problems and possibilities.

By 1763, the economies of Great Britain and her American colonies were well tuned to the commercial rhythms of the great Atlantic trade world, but their differing ways for accommodating indigenous economic development had put them on a collision course. In England, as we saw, after a half-century of commercial ebullience, a segment of the propertied class acquired the power necessary to steer the nation's development into those areas where growth was compatible with upper-class privilege and lower-class discipline. Through the control of finance and commerce, the government had been able to check the centrifugal tendencies of an unregulated,

77. G. B. Warden, "The Distribution of Property in Boston, 1692–1772," *Perspectives in American History,* 10 (1976), 111.

78. Ibid., 97. See also Edmund Morgan, "The Puritan Ethic and the American Revolution," *William and Mary Quarterly,* 24 (1967), 3–43; C. Vann Woodward, "The Southern Ethic in a Puritan World," ibid., 25 (1968), 343–370.

preindustrial market economy. The ideology of mercantilism, embalmed in the preambles of successive commercial statutes supplied the theory for subordinating private interests to the corporate goal of state-building. Prosperity, patriotism, and pride in English victories over rival nations kept critics at bay. From the British perspective the Sugar, Stamp, and Townshend acts were elaborations of established policies, designed at most to make the imperial tax base more equitable and enforcement of the navigation system more effective.[79] To the colonists they appeared successively as unwarranted intrusions, violations of charter rights, and finally extraconstitutional usurpations of power by Parliament. Pressed to justify these laws, English leaders did not demonstrate the coherence between their economic policies and their political traditions. They relied instead upon the reiteration of an imperative: submit to the indivisibility of Parliamentary sovereignty. The theories which came to dominate English thinking in the early eighteenth century could not survive the Atlantic crossing, for their persuasiveness lay less in what they said than in what they prevented being said. Subordination to Parliament was not an isolated ideal. It was inextricably tied up with the balance-of-trade definition of national wealth and the Whig interpretation of English history. Critical examination of these ideas was to be averted, even at the cost of an empire.

Edmund Burke observed that it is a sign of an ill-governed state when people begin to examine their rights. It is also a sign of a very faulty theory of rights—in retrospect—that after a decade of questioning the colonists were so ill-satisfied by the answers they had received.[80] Defenders of Parliamentary sovereignty made the colonists aware of how positivist theories of law endangered their own peculiarly free and undirected path toward modern development, but they were unable to make accessible to them the logic of the British Empire. The assertions of British authority only revealed to Americans the tenuousness of their own political privi-

79. Robert J. Chaffin, "The Townshend Act of 1767," ibid., 27 (1970), 90–121; and on this point, see Jack N. Rakove, "The Decision for American Independence: A Reconstruction," *Perspectives in American History,* 10 (1976), 217–275, esp. 274–275.

80. On this point , see L. F. S. Upton, "The Dilemma of the Loyalists' Pamphleteers," *Studies in Burke and His Time,* 18 (1977); H. T. Dickinson, "The Eighteenth-Century Debate on the Sovereignty of Parliament," *Royal Historical Society Transactions,* 26 (1976).

leges. The long decade of colonial agitation has been characterized as the defense of a principle, but it would be more accurate to describe it as the search for a set of principles which could explain and rationalize lives which had been repatterned by economic change. The shortened tether of imperial control introduced an urgency to the more fundamental need the colonists had to articulate their own theory of social order.

It is fruitful to distinguish three concurrent responses to the 1764–76 crisis: resistance, independence, and revolution. Almost every colonial leader from Patrick Henry to Thomas Hutchinson disapproved of the new British measures and recommended some action to express that disapproval. Repeatedly, colonial writers relied upon venerable ideas about the English constitution and the rights of Englishmen to justify resistance. Through the work of Bernard Bailyn, the peculiar idiom of colonial protesters has been recovered and connected to the conceptual world of the English Opposition.[81] The vocabulary of degeneration, corruption, power lusts, usurpations, and enslavement which pamphleteers employed was encoded in a Renaissance scheme of thinking in which a balanced rule of kings, lords, and commoners alone could produce stability. Future loyalists as well as future patriots subscribed to this view of the English constitutional virtues, and the pervasiveness of Opposition sentiment helps explain the unanimity behind resistance to the Stamp Act. However, the logic of the Opposition position also set the parameters of protest. As long as the colonists continued to assert their loyalty to the English constitution, grievances growing out of an alleged subversion of that constitution could act as a rallying force. Concerns for prescriptive rights and constitutional purity could fuel a resistance movement; they could only brake a drive for separation.

Independence as a response to the imperial crisis divided the colonial gentry, requiring a complete change of government in Pennsylvania and Maryland and calling forth a Loyalist group in all the colonies. For some of the new band of American patriots, independence was an act of separation with minimal ideological impli-

81. For a summary of his position, see Bailyn, "Central Themes of the American Revolution." Pertinent here is Pauline Maier, "Why Revolution? Why Democracy?," *Journal of Interdisciplinary History*, 6 (1976), 715.

cations. These men continued to espouse the theory of balanced government with its institutional recognition of the division between the few and the many. In their view the maintenance of order required active intervention from government. Given the enduringly problematic nature of human beings, they chose to rely upon the guidance of strong institutions and the discipline of social superiors to achieve moral goals. This restricted intellectual response to the imperial rupture persisted well into the life of the new nation, surfacing most prominently in the 1790s, when the French Revolution raised in a new and insistent form questions about the meaning of American independence.

The revolutionary response to the Anglo-American conflicts of the 1760s appeared early and grew unsteadily until events after 1774 favored those least attached to the monarchial tradition. Then more colonists were willing to use the imperial dispute as the occasion for airing new ideas about human rights. Locke's rationalistic explanation for the origins of civil society acquired new friends and new enemies.[82] In the decisive early months of 1776 Americans officially broke with the conceptual order of English Whiggery. By jettisoning the notion of historic rights the American legislative bodies put liberty into a very different philosophical context—one from which American individualism acquired a moral force. The Levellers in the seventeenth century had failed to shift the ground for rights from history to reason, but American radicals had what they lacked: a social reality which reflected the rationalist argument from equality, uniformity, and utility. The need for a consensus and the credibility of natural rights brought the is and the ought together. The thirteen resistance movements became one revolution with the adoption of the Declaration of Independence, for here was a rationale for rebellion which contained a new vision of political obligation.

Two abstractions—nature and freedom—formed the basis of the Americans' conception of government, and both of them owed their eighteenth-century reworking to social changes wrought by the

---

82. Edward Countryman, "Out of the Bounds of the Law: Northern Land Rioters in the Eighteenth Century," in *The American Revolution: Explorations in the History of American Radicalism,* ed. Alfred Young (De Kalb, Ill., 1976), 48; Jonathan Boucher, *A View of the Causes and Consequences of the American Revolution* (1779).

market. One of the distinguishing features of a market economy is that its coercion is veiled. The apparently voluntary nature of commercial transactions creates the illusion that participants are free to choose. The fact that people must earn before they can eat is a commonly recognized link between need and work, but it appears to be a natural link embedded in the necessity of eating rather than issuing from a particular social arrangement for distributing food through a system of private bargains. Despite the fact that men and women must buy and sell to live, the voluntary aspects of the market remain more salient. It is the individual who makes choices, takes risks, and suffers or enjoys the consequences of these decisions. Commercial expansion increased the number of private transactions, and the market reached through groups to the single members of society, turning them into individuals who had rights to life, liberty, and the pursuit of happiness.

The market also supplied the solution to the political problem of order. Its capacity to engage men and women in productive activities offered an attractive alternative to overt social control. In the presumed naturalness of market behavior lay the key to converting self-interest from a moral defect to an organizing principle of nature. An English pamphleteer in the seventeenth century nicely explained the utility of self-interest when he claimed that giving surety for good behavior created a stronger bond than conscience, religion, or honor. "In these," he wrote, "we are sure there may be Hypocrisie, but in Interest we know there is none." [83] Americans were prepared to go much further. As Bernard Friedman has shown for New York, lower-class resisters emphatically rejected gentry notions about human irrationality and redefined reason as a normal competence to look after oneself. Where gentlemen declaimed against the power of self-interest, their inferiors hailed it as a "universal law." [84] The possibility of infusing self-interest with a moral value lay in just this quality of universality which could be equated with the uniform operation of natural laws. The term, human nature, came into wide use at the end of the century to convey this discovery of basic human tendencies. For many, the natural man of

83. [Briscoe], *A discourse of money*, 136.
84. Bernard Friedman, "The Shaping of Radical Consciousness in Provincial New York," *Journal of American History*, 56 (1970), 789, 792.

Christian drama was replaced by the natural man of an orderly universe. And individual freedom, so long hedged in by political and ecclesiastical authority, became the secret spring of the liberal system. When the rights of Englishmen were abandoned for the rights of man, colonial revolutionaries detached "the universal principle of self-interest" from its debasing association with sin and placed it in the center of a new social theory.

The most remarkable expression of this new vision was Thomas Paine's *Common Sense*. Here in lucid prose Paine set forth the political implications of economic liberalism: government should be a simple thing because society is natural, produced by our wants and sustained by the peaceful interaction of independent, autonomous individuals. Feet firmly planted in the future, Paine described how commerce could replace war in international relations. He combined, as J. R. Pole noted, the radical's hatred of inherited rank with the liberal's enthusiasm for economic development.[85] The blend was not idiosyncratic; it came from the first enthusiastic appraisal of the social relations produced by the market. The expansion of freedom, like the expansion of commerce, rested upon the capacity of the free market to integrate the essential social tasks which formerly had been secured through the exercise of authority, but the perception and propagation of that possibility required ideas and the occasion to turn them into an ideology.

To return to a consideration of modernization theory, in both England and the American colonies conspicuous economic growth produced changes which led to public discussions of their significance. Novelties were examined in the light of established truths; they were also pondered as elements in a new social reality. But the social leverage of the market did not raise a uniform intellectual response. The elaboration of distinctive theories of modernization in England and America does not reveal a social form calling forth a single explanation. Rather the working out of a shared understanding of how to accommodate modern pressures involved the selective acceptance and suppression of competing views. Not only did the content of their theories differ; so too did the source of legitimacy,

---

85. J. R. Pole, "Review of Merrill Jensen, *The American Revolution Within America*," *William and Mary Quarterly*, 33 (1976), 157. See also Eric Foner, "Tom Paine's Republic: Radical Ideology and Social Change," in *American Revolution*, ed. Young, 200ff.

and the differences mattered. In the discrete events in which England and America acquired modernizing ideologies we are in the presence of indeterminate historical processes where chosens are as important as givens. The resistance movement in America acted as a catalyst in the formation of a social theory capable of dissolving the contradictions between behavior and belief. The British theories that facilitated modernization at home provoked the colonists to turn freedom and autonomy into natural rights and to identify their desired social arrangements with nature itself. The similarities in the English and American experiences are also worth noting, for in both countries men produced new social theories, and with these conceptual representations of social patterns they achieved a measure of mastery over them. This intellectual response may in fact be the critical factor in the reorientation of a society's values. With the capacity to objectify human relations, to demythologize and turn them into natural phenomena, men in Western societies could manipulate their social and material environment. This means, then, that modernization theory in twentieth-century scholarship is more a sign of modernization than a theory about it.

4

Ideology and the History
of Political Thought

MORE THAN TWO decades ago, J. G. A. Pocock described a
radical transformation going on in the study of political thought.
Although he made passing reference to many historians and
philosophers, this particular transformation can in fact be traced to
a handful of men, each in some way connected with Cambridge
University. In addition to Pocock, the group included Peter Laslett,
John Dunn, and Quentin Skinner. What gave collaborative cohesion
to their scholarship, besides the consanguinity of Cambridge ties,
was their shared élan at undermining the received wisdom of the
day. In particular they attacked the conventional depiction of
Thomas Hobbes as the brilliant but ignored iconoclast and John
Locke as the runaway winner in the seventeenth-century debate on
government. The result of these challenges has been a new appreciation of the complexity of the intellectual matrix in England's century of revolution which has unavoidably raised questions about the
origins of liberalism. Pocock and Skinner have also written exten-
sively on the need for an analytical framework that would embrace
political thought and political action.[1] Eschewing the Lovejoyian
textual and the Marxist contextual approaches, they have urged
instead the adoption of a methodology springing from social linguis-

---

1. J. G. A. Pocock, *Politics, Language, and Time* (New York, 1971); Quentin Skinner,
"Meaning and Understanding in the History of Ideas," *History and Theory*, 8 (1969); "History
and Ideology in the English Revolution," *The Historical Journal*, 9 (1965); "The Ideological
Context of Hobbes's Political Thought," ibid.

tics. Under their collective prompting both intellectual history and the history of ideas have given place to the study of ideology conceived of as a structure of meaning expressed through a historically specific system of communication.

Substantively, the revisionist effort that began with Laslett's redating of the composition of Locke's *Second Treatise of Government* has culminated in what might be called a rout of the Whig tale once wound around it. Working with the famous Lovelace collection of Locke papers, Laslett initiated a reassessment of the Exclusion Crisis and went on to argue that Locke's real target was Robert Filmer's *Patriarcha,* not Hobbes's *Leviathan.*[2] Congruent with Laslett's emphasis upon the vitality of Filmer's theory during the Restoration was John Dunn's further muting of the radical sound of Locke through his showing that Locke's intended audience, the faint-hearted gentlemen of England's landed class, would never have drawn the revolutionary conclusion later read into the *Second Treatise.*[3] At the same time Pocock's *Ancient Constitution* brought to light intellectual preoccupations difficult to comprehend in the old scenario of liberty-loving Whigs doing battle against the Tory defenders of the king's prerogative.[4] Far from being swept away by contract theories, Pocock found the preponderance of reading Englishmen still thinking about politics in historical terms, a finding which moved Locke from the center to the eccentric. While the famous philosopher's seventeenth-century intentions were being reinterpreted, his eighteenth-century influence was remeasured. Indeed, Louis Hartz had hardly settled the American consensus on the firm foundation of Lockean liberalism before Dunn gave the base a nasty shock with his contention that the fame of the *Second Treatise* hardly survived its illustrious author's death. Simultaneously with this pruning of the vinelike sprawl of Locke's reputation, Skinner discovered a group of proto-Hobbists whose success in popularizing the conquest theory of political obligation made Hobbes appear more a power than a pariah to his contemporaries.[5] With all this, the celebrated story of liberty became less clear and the triumph of the social contract more problematic. But room had been made

2. *Two Treatises of Government by John Locke,* ed. Peter Laslett (Cambridge, 1960).
3. John Dunn, *The Political Thought of John Locke* (Cambridge, 1969), 47.
4. Pocock, *The Ancient Constitution and the Feudal Law* (Cambridge, 1957).
5. Skinner, "Ideological Context of Hobbes's Political Thought."

for the study of previously neglected groups: Skinner's de facto theorists, Laslett's patriarchalists, and, above all, Pocock's civic humanists. With Locke's political rationalism in eclipse, Anglo-American political thought could be reclaimed for the Renaissance, leaving liberalism bereft of roots.

Along with the flow of articles and books setting the record straight came a stream of prescriptive pieces arguing the case for ideology as the proper organizing principle for students of political writing. In the structure of men's thought, these scholars insisted, we could learn not only what they wanted to do but, even more ambitiously, what they could conceive of doing. Pointing to the new fluidity of the subject, Pocock wrote that the object of attention should be "the changing function, context and application of conceptual languages . . . found in particular societies at particular times." The study of political expression should become the study of symbolic action and the sociology of knowledge the sociology of meaning, for, as Clifford Geertz said, what is socially determined is not the nature of the conception but the vehicle of the conception.[6] Clearly history's pursuit of the particular was more relevant here than the philosopher's love of logical connections or the sociologist's search for the distribution of power and status. As one would expect from these new emphases, language began to take on the characteristics of the chameleon, its accessibility constantly being threatened by the human tendency to turn all general vocabularies into local codes. Its study, nonetheless, promised an aperçu into the fusions of reason and rhetoric, belief and behavior, experience and its interpretation. The exemplification of the ideological approach was awaited in Pocock's *Machiavellian Moment*[7] and Skinner's *Foundations of Modern Political Thought*[8] whose publication prompted Lawrence Stone to conclude that "the history of the political thought in the west is now being rewritten, primarily by J. G. A. Pocock, Quentin Skinner, and Bernard Bailyn."[9]

6. Geertz, "Ideology as a Cultural System," in *Interpretations of Culture* (London, 1973), 219.

7. Pocock, *Machiavellian Moment* (Princeton, 1975).

8. Skinner, *Foundations of Modern Political Thought,* 2 vols. (Cambridge, 1978).

9. Stone, "The Revival of Narrative: Reflections on a New Old History," *Past and Present,* 85 (1979), 14.

With the appearance of the *summa ideologica,* it is perhaps appropriate to take stock of what has been transformed and rewritten. Relevant too is the degree to which method and material have been joined in these two crowning works. In both his earlier *Ancient Constitution* and the *Machiavellian Moment,* Pocock has treated ideas as intellectual strategies. He has argued that an indigenous English political philosophy arose from the acute need to justify opposition to the king. Much like Geertz's claim that ideologies tend to emerge and take hold when societies free themselves from the governance of tradition, Pocock's research has focused upon the intellectual and moral exigencies posed by the shift from men's being subjects to their becoming citizens. This felt need to rationalize their new behavior made Englishmen peculiarly receptive to the civic humanism revived in quattrocento Italy. From Florentine writers Englishmen were also introduced to a historical consciousness. This heightened awareness of the profound changes wrought by the passage of time carried with it a recognition of the inherent instability of all institutional arrangements. As in Florence, so in England, a search for a secular political theory swiftly followed the collapse of the chiliastic politics of Savonarola and Cromwell. Approaching social theories as the means men use for resolving the tensions between moral imperatives and practical necessities, Pocock implies that once an ideological problem has been solved, the resolution is capable of inhibiting the acceptance of nonconforming propositions. For instance, when *homo rhetor,* the ideal political figure of ancient Greece, replaced *homo credens* as the Englishman's model, it was difficult to make room for other conceptions of public life. Republicanism arrives, Pocock has written, "when a political society envisages itself as a community of active beings and is led to create its own morality." [10] Both the historical consciousness stimulated by Renaissance studies and the English preoccupation with an ancient constitution made Harrington's writings, not those of Locke, the source of an enduring ideology. Thus Pocock has taken the Whig story of England's constitutional monarchy and placed it in a Renaissance context laden with emotive force. Egregiously indifferent to both the antiquity of the common law and the historical roots of

10. Pocock, *Machiavellian Moment,* viii.

government, Locke failed to achieve paradigmatic influence because he failed to capture the imagination of those Englishmen imbued with classical republican values.

What is important to Pocock's larger design is that the "Machiavellian moment" lasted over a century in England. The political solutions propounded by Harrington, Harringtonians, and neo-Harringtonians riveted the attention of three successive generations to the civic humanist drama of public virtue imperiled by what Pocock has called "the zone of secular irrationality"—that territory where men sought wealth, power, pleasure, and novelty. While the expanding role of commerce transformed the material world around them, a significant number of Englishmen became captives of an ancient concept of politics which prejudiced them against disruptive change. When the worldly—and presumably unideological—Whig oligarchs embraced the modern goals of power and wealth through trade, those outside the charmed circle at court mounted a vigorous counteroffensive in the name of civic virtue. Pocock acknowledges that innovations in trade and manufacturing could be accommodated to country views, but he fails to show how the consequent economic developments affected country thinking about society. Only political ideas seem to have traveled. In Pocock's scheme the English country-minded alerted their colonial brethren to the dangers emanating from the court and gave them grounds for opposing imperial policy.

Although similar in approach to Pocock, Skinner has laid greater stress upon recreating the intentions of the writers themselves. Every statement, he has said, is "the embodiment of a particular intention, on a particular occasion, addressed to the solution of a particular problem and thus specific to its situation." Understanding political thought, it follows, involves not only a knowledge of the contemporaneous events but also a familiarity with the means of expression—the literary conventions, popular idioms, unexamined assumptions, and eternal verities shared by author and audience. So historically nuanced is language in Skinner's view that it is not possible to study disembodied political writings, for their meaning is accessible only through the particular intellectual code of their author's milieu. It is from this perspective that Skinner has derided studies which treat the history of political thought as the supra-terrestrial movement of great ideas through the ages. Less critical of the contextualist approach, he has insisted nonetheless that knowledge of the relevant social structure cannot unlock what is actually being expressed in political writings. Having developed these insights in two brilliant articles, it comes as something of a shock to discover that his much-heralded *Foundations of Modern Political Thought* contains little of the intellectual detective work his prescriptions call for.

The foundations Skinner finds for modern thought are deep and narrow; they extend back to the eleventh century and rest principally on the footings set out by northern Italians. Recapitulating his thesis in a brief conclusion, Skinner names the principal result of these writings as the emergence of the state as the supreme object of analysis for political writers. Preconditions for this development were envisioning politics as a distinct branch of moral philosophy and recognizing each particular ruler as an autonomous lawgiver. The first precondition, he suggests, required the recovery of Aristotelian thought and the second the elimination of the competing claims of secular authority made by feudal lords, the Holy Roman Emperor, and the Church. These are judicious conclusions arrived at after a careful examination of the voluminous writings of successive groups of humanists, scholastics, reformation leaders, historians, and jurists. One searches in vain, however, for the exploration of the authors' intentions, their language games, or conceptual codes about which he has written so persuasively elsewhere. When motive is discussed at all, it usually appears as a straightforwardly instrumental reason for doing something unconnected with any particular perception of reality. The power of precedents is repeatedly pointed out, and one comes away believing memory to be a greater intellectual force than imagination. Thus we are told that the early advice books set the pattern for mirror-for-prince literature; the humanists crystallized their identity through hostility to the scholastics; French jurists drew their inspiration from Florentine legal writings; and Huguenot revolutionaries turned to scholastic and Roman law traditions for their radical constitutionalism. The influences described as playing upon the authors seem bland, almost trite: love of liberty, admiration for virtue, dislike of luxurious habits, literary confidence, study of the law, civic pride, and patriotism. Skinner's reticence amounts to evasion, for antecedents are not causes, nor does the existence of an earlier expression of an idea explain the decision that led to its subsequent expression. Considering that some ideologies involved the explicit rejection of tradition, the constant reversion to inherited beliefs that Skinner finds requires its own explication. "Nothing can be taken for granted" should be the motto of ideological studies, if, as Skinner and Pocock have argued, meaning is elusive and modes of thinking evanescent.

Skinner has produced a first-rate account of how two evolving bodies of writing inspired by Renaissance humanism and Reformation politics converged on the state as the embodiment of men's social aspirations. True to his announced purposes he has examined the texts of hundreds of writers rather than those of a handful of great philosophers, and he has provided a running evaluation of recent scholarship on the subject. While he uses the word "ideological" frequently, it appears in contexts where intellectual would be more exact. The most widely accepted distinction between ideological and intellectual turns on ideas being used to rationalize and explain experience and ideas as parts of a system of thought. In the former the emphasis is upon function; in the latter upon elucidation. Some examples may clarify the difference. The reader learns that fifteenth-century humanists addressed all of their fellow citizens and that subsequently Florentine writers extolled the virtues of equality and popular political participation. Yet there is no discussion of the actual or perceived social structure, no indication of the ideal or real parameters of citizenship, no hint of political alignments affected by these democratic impulses. Similarly language as an object of analysis is virtually ignored although opportunities abound. For instance, we are told that after the ideal of Providence as the ruling force in human affairs has been rejected, Fortuna returns to fill the void. Machiavelli dilated upon Fortuna in highly sexual terms: because Fortuna is a woman she favors ardent, less circumspect men; because Fortuna is a woman the aim of the man of virtue must be to best and coerce her. Surely a scholarly approach that delights in the exploration of normative vocabularies should expatiate on this stunning shift of imagery from *deus absconditus* to accessible female. What is puzzling is that, covering much the same body of literature with the same agenda, Pocock ferreted out paradigmatic imperatives and conceptual contingencies where Skinner found straightforward assertions and compelling precedents.

These diverging practices from a shared prospectus invite a closer look at the organizing theme of ideology. Pocock, drawing upon Thomas Kuhn's *Structure of Scientific Revolutions,* has called ideologies political paradigms which operate as systems of communication and authority. For example, the Aristotelian and humanist values omnipresent in early modern England had the power, according to him, to hamper the development of the role of citizen for the capitalist. Skinner has also emphasized the confining power of existing worldviews. Men and women, he says, not only tailor their normative language to fit their projects, they also tailor their projects to fit the available normative language. Bailyn, the third scholar in Stone's list of pathbreakers, also has stressed the psychological over the intellectual. Formal discourse, he has written, becomes politically powerful "when it becomes ideology . . . when it crystallizes otherwise inchoate social and political discontent and thereby shapes what is otherwise instinctive . . . when it clarifies, symbolizes and elevates to structured consciousness the mingled urges that stir within us." [11]

More evocative of what ideology does than is, these descriptions hold little hint of what general social and human tendencies call forth ideologies. The obvious source for a theory of ideology of course is Marx. His famous statement that it is not the consciousness of men that determines their being, but on the contrary their social being that determines their consciousness, is certainly compatible with the emphasis that Pocock, Skinner, and Bailyn have placed upon the socially determined character of human thought and expression. What has been less assimilable has been Marx's corollary that socially constructed realities are the work of ruling classes seeking to legitimate their power. In the Marxist perspective ideologies involve a division of intellectual labor. The dominant elite produces beliefs and the exploited multitude consume them as false consciousness. As Norman Birnbaum has written, ideologies appear "wherever systematic factual assertions about society contain

11. "The Central Themes of the American Revolution," in *Essays on the American Revolution,* ed. Stephen G. Kurtz and James H. Hutson (Chapel Hill, 1973), 11.

(usually by implication) evaluations of the distribution of power." [12] Statements about the moral uplift of farming, the frailty of women, or the ineffectiveness of economic regulations are thus ideological because general assent to them promotes acceptance of specific social arrangements. This definition makes salient the relation of ideology to authority, and it provides a way of distinguishing ideological statements from random observations. Marxists make this connection even stronger because of their a priori assumption that ruling classes propagate beliefs in order to justify their rule. For Skinner this drastic reductionism is made possible by the faulty logic of believing that to know the motive behind a statement elucidates the meaning that is being communicated. In swimming against this Marxist tide, however, the new historians of ideology have run the risk of creating a mirror reductionism in the implication that understanding the meaning of a statement is tantamount to understanding its social purpose and effect.

Quite apart from these theoretical questions, the radical transformation of the study of political thought which Pocock saluted has resulted in a conservative reinterpretation of the early modern period. In the most literal sense the revisions have been conservative because of the potency ascribed to inherited intellectual traditions and reigning political paradigms. In a rare speculative mood, for instance, Skinner asks why Luther's message proved so widely attractive and answers that for the historian of political ideas the most important consideration is the fact that Luther's doctrines were based upon a number of deeply rooted traditions in medieval thought. For Pocock the force of an existing worldview is epistemological: "Men cannot do what they have no means of saying they have done; and what they do must in part be what they can say and conceive that it is." [13] These methodological premises have tended to strengthen the case which has been made for the historical-mindedness of seventeenth-century Englishmen. This interpretation in turn has placed the giants of the century—the rationalists, Hobbes and Locke—in something of a conceptual limbo. Locke has

12. "The Sociological Study of Ideology (1940–1960): A Trend Report and Bibliography," *Current Sociology*, 9 (1960), 91.

13. "Virtue and Commerce in the Eighteenth Century," *Journal of Interdisciplinary History*, 3 (1972), 118.

been given paradigmatic stature only when he could be assimilated within "the solid continuous historical order of the English polity."[14] One sometimes gets the impression that Pocock entered the world of civic humanism as a scholar and remained to become a partisan. Locke must be banished because he is offensive to the sensibilities cultivated by classical republicanism.

Strengthening the conservative tenor of the new revision has been the application of a very conventional definition of what constitutes political thought. In their prescriptive pieces Skinner and Pocock have been far more adventuresome. "A complex plural society will speak a complex plural language," Pocock has written, "each carrying its own biases as to the definition and distribution of authority." One of the strands in the "complex plural language" in seventeenth-century England came from writings about the nature of the market. While not strictly speaking political, the frequently made assertions that trade possessed its own natural laws and hence was not susceptible to regulation carried profound implications about government's authority. Indeed, one might say that if, as Pocock has insisted, the supremacy of civic humanist values forestalled the appearance of a bourgeois ideology with the entrepreneur as citizen, so the study of economics disclosed a way for making that paragon of civic humanism—the disinterested citizen—an irrelevant figure. In literature as well as economic writings ideologically potent languages appeared. Ian Watt, in *The Rise of the Novel* has found signs of a new individualism in the fictional handling of ordinary men and women in the early eighteenth century. These examples suggest that new inquiries and new genres may have acted as the avenue of novelty, a matter of some importance given the weight placed upon inherited patterns of thought by Skinner and Pocock.

Minimizing the importance of Hobbes and Locke has had the effect of nearly eliminating what was distinctively English about early modern political thought and, in this form, represents the ultimate rejection of Whig historiography. As Skinner's deflating remarks about the "exegetes" of classical texts indicate, he has been unhappy all along with the notion of venerable ideals like justice or liberty transcending the limits of time and place. What is histori-

14. Dunn, *The Political Thought of John Locke,* 47.

cally relevant from the ideological perspective is not the enduringly instructive but the immediately influential. The sophisticated antidote to Whiggism is making human beings the agents of culture. Their preference for freedom, if it exists at all, then becomes attributable to their society's values. The same structures that have reduced the importance of Locke have also made the Glorious Revolution appear less a historical turning point. Even Skinner's conclusion that the concept of the state is the seminal foundation of modern political thought runs athwart the old liberal story of the individualistic origins of political society. So too England's balanced government—that triumph of civility in the age of absolutism—has become less a unique national achievement than the culmination of venerable intellectual traditions revived in the Italian Renaissance. One would not know from this version of the history of political thought that England produced the first capitalist economy, the first constitutional monarchy, the first modern society. And the disturbing implication here is that these momentous developments are seen as impinging so lightly on the thinking of the time.

The organizing principle that has wrought this revision is not Marx's definition of ideology but rather the one used by linguists, philosophers, anthropologists, and students of religion. This provenance has much to say about the loose connection between social and intellectual context, for these disciplines explain the existence of structured consciousness as part of the general human "craving for meaning." Thus universalized, consciousness has lost the Marxist qualifier of false. The articulate elite may benefit from the political paradigm it creates, but everyone enjoys the order supplied by a shared worldview. Anthropologists have emphasized ideas functioning for the benefit of the whole society rather than separate groups. Consensus not conflict is the seedbed for triumphant ideologies. What serves society serves its members, and ideologies prevail and endure because they are widely believed, not because they issue from a dominant class. In recent years ethnomethodologists have denied the existence of a single cultural perspective operating in societies, but the indispensability of the concept seems to have overridden doubts about its empirical base. This tendency to view ideologies as single overarching belief systems has been strengthened by the sociologists' preoccupation with societal forms. If societies are most crucially affected by their being traditional or modern, then differences within a given society seem by comparison to be trivial. Ideology as a cultural system has thus offered deliverance from the mechanical association of belief and self-interest without encumbering its users in a contemporary ideological dispute.

Metaphor has now become more important than methodology. Seemingly as ineffable as the spiritual longings to which they minister, ideologies have been compared to cameras, compasses, triggering devices, maps of problematic social reality, computers, and switchboards, while the imagery of deep structures and middle levels of belief has been employed to suggest the human site where ideologies operate. What this evocative language furnishes is not an explicit theory open to empirical testing but a vehicle for smuggling insightful observations about human thinking into scholarly studies. Overshadowed by these subliminal aspects of experience, the reality of power relations has faded away much like the Cheshire cat, leaving nothing behind but the smile of culture.

In their explorations of conceptual orders and normative vocabularies, Skinner and Pocock have laid greater stress on the paradigmatic authority detailed by Thomas Kuhn than the potentiality for discovery and novelty which Noam Chomsky has ascribed to language use. By drawing our attention back to meaning, they have forced us to take seriously the complexity of social communication. The autonomy they have conferred upon worldviews, however, has obscured the struggles for power that go on behind the adoption of those views. Nor have they pursued words serving radical purposes or words giving shape to visions of what might be in order to raise standards for judging what is. As Nancy Streuver has pointed out, the rule-governed creativity of language holds out hope of transcending the dilemma of freedom versus determination in favor of a model of culture that is "rich, dynamic and open ended." [15]

J. G. A. POCOCK responded to these foregoing remarks of mine in a later issue of the *Intellectual History Group Newsletter*. [16] Reading

15. "The Study of Language and the Study of History," *Journal of Interdisciplinary History*, 4 (1974), 415.

16. "An Appeal from the New to the Old Whigs? A Note on Joyce Appleby's 'Ideology and the History of Political Thought,'" *Intellectual History Group Newsletter* (Spring 1981), 47–51, to which I responded in "Response to J. G. A. Pocock," ibid. (Spring 1982), 20–22.

his "Appeal from the New to the Old Whigs," I was reminded of an incident in my near youth, when I had just finished graduate work. Having taken a field in political philosophy, I was both fascinated by the subject and disappointed by most learned treatments of it. Too many books presented the history of political thought as the transfer of great truths from one generation to another. Individual thinkers were depicted as men very much in charge of the content of their minds, freely choosing their views from the world's store of wisdom. There must be a more authentic way to deal with political belief I told myself as I prepared to leave for a year in France. As if in answer to my wishes, the day of my departure the latest issue of the *William and Mary Quarterly* arrived. Happy for a brief respite from the relentless succession of decisions about what to take, what to store, and what to give away, I sat down amid the packing boxes and began to read an essay by a J. G. A. Pocock entitled "Machiavelli, Harrington and English Political Ideologies in the Eighteenth Century." [17] The simple choices about house plants and tennis shoes gave way to a real dilemma, for here was the exemplification of a bold, new way to deal with political thought. I could not possibly take another journal with me, but neither could I wait the months (perhaps years?) before the article became accessible at the Bibliothèque Nationale. Like Buridan's Ass I was poised between two equal pressures; but, unlike Buridan's Ass, I had a plane to catch. I seized the lovely, mint-white *Quarterly* and ripped out the Pocock piece. With such acts (even of destruction) we pay tribute to seminal thinkers.

In his "Appeal" Pocock expressed the conviction, which I certainly share, that our differing interpretations could be brought together and made mutually illuminating. He agreed that I had rightly seen that the effect of his work would be "the dethronement of the paradigm of liberalism, and of the Lockean paradigm associated with it," but he rejected my view that his was necessarily a conservative reinterpretation of the early modern period. Elaborating on this point, he emphasized that he saw a very early perception of capitalism challenging the classical republican paradigm in the

17. Pocock, "Machiavelli, Harrington and English Political Ideologies," *William and Mary Quarterly*, 34 (1965).

period from 1690 to 1720. This perception focused upon the invest-ment of capital in public funds and did not involve John Locke because Locke had not participated in these debates.

In surveying the English economic literature of the seventeenth century I discovered that writers had created an imaginative model of commerce which not only shaped the discussion of trade and finance but also introduced a dramatically different conception of the economy.[18] Embedded in these early tracts was the view that human nature led to uniform behavior in the marketplace and that human beings had the capacity to pursue their self-interest in an orderly, rational way. Through this literature the now familiar, but peculiarly Western, worldview could be examined as a socially con-structed reality. Much to my surprise the fruitful line of analysis that I had traced for a half-century came to a halt in the early eighteenth century. Then the old discredited balance of trade theory reappeared, giving Adam Smith his paper tiger—the mercantile system—to stalk through the pages of *The Wealth of Nations.*

Thus Pocock and I are in agreement that capitalism and the social reflections it provoked did not sail smoothly into English conscious-ness in the modern era. Where we differ is in our accounts of when and how capitalism presented itself. For Pocock its intensely troubling introduction came between 1690 and 1720 and was associated principally with public funds open to political manipula-tion. Because it was tainted by the state-building program of the court Whigs, capitalism provoked an ideological counteroffensive undertaken by a country party employing classical republican ideas. As a consequence, Pocock has said that capitalism plunged the English into a quarrel with history which took the form of a per-ceived dichotomy between commerce and virtue.

By insisting that this is how Englishmen first took cognizance of capitalism, Pocock suggests that they were conceptually boxed in. They did not see in the new wealth-producing system the promise of abundance, for instance, because they were forced to respond to the threat of corruption or the subversion of their much-vaunted constitution. They could not construe the capitalist as a citizen because their classical paradigm carried with it an idealization of

18. See Chapters 1, 2, and 3 for an elaboration of this work.

the public man. As opposed to this picture, I have stressed that Englishmen had been discussing the economy of private enterprise for over sixty years before the financial revolution put funds at the disposal of Whig magnates. As early as the 1620s, members and advisers of Parliament used an analytical model of private market exchanges in their policy disputes. Instead of prompting a quarrel with history, this method of reasoning disturbed settled ways of thinking about status, wealth, and sovereign authority. It also involved a drastic reformulation of the human personality which touched upon questions of autonomy, responsibility, and freedom. Later on this sophisticated way of analyzing economic phenomena, as I have noted, was arrested. I have speculated that it may have been the incongruence between the theoretical proposition that ordinary men and women were naturally endowed with the means of running their own lives and the social attitudes of the English ruling class that accounts for the lacuna in the development of liberal theory.[19]

Pocock and I have dealt with the reception of two different responses to capitalism in early modern England: the state-building balance-of-trade theory of the Whigs, and the early adumbration of classical economic theory. The one does not exclude the other. Their dual presence, however, complicates the picture and makes it less tenable to think that there was a single struggle going on between the court patrons of commerce and the country celebrators of virtue. However much court and country disputants monopolized conventional political discourse, fragments of the liberal paradigm found lodging in other inquiries. The idea of a uniform human nature and the assumption that human beings have a natural tendency to think rationally about their self-interest spread, as did the larger conviction that social relations were susceptible to analysis as systems of behavior. It is of no small importance that John Locke contributed significantly to these developments.[20] The existence of this alternative conceptual mode throws into high relief the question of choice, motive, and interest. For if men could say these things about the market economy, why they do not continue to do so must intrigue us.

19. See Chapter 1.
20. See Chapter 2.

Pocock has built a strong case against the old view of English history as the progressive unfolding of the free political institutions envisioned in the writings of John Locke and Adam Smith. He has astutely argued that Marxists have accepted this version as readily as liberals because it provides a way of ushering in the real conflict between capitalist and worker. Instead of these geniuses and their admirers, he has described an English ruling class in a crisis of self-perception, divided against itself, in its Machiavellian moment of historical consciousness. There is certainly a struggle for power here. But I would insist that there was simultaneously a struggle being waged against this form of historical consciousness by those outside the political nation. Because the originators of liberal ideas began with a critical stance toward government regulation of the economy, they ended up with propositions subversive to traditional authority and those privileged to exercise that authority both at court and in the country. An exploration of eighteenth-century Anglo-American thought limited to the classical paradigm is in danger of missing this other, more radical intellectual response to English capitalism and thereby mistaking its beginning. The rationalistic depiction of economic life regulating itself through the competition of self-interested individuals organizing private resources in the pursuit of profit through market exchanges did in time become the Western explanation of material progress. We no longer believe that it represents fact, and we have been taught that it did not sweep all before it. From the historical perspective, however, the liberal model must be addressed as a brilliant and powerful conception, even if its claim to scientific validity has been undermined. What we in the late twentieth century have lost as nature, we must now recover as art.

5

Liberalism and the
American Revolution

THE SPECIFIC problem confronting historians of the American
Revolution is to explain that event without relying upon the
assumptions embedded in the revolutionary legacy. The heirs of a
revolution are at a disadvantage, for they have received the revolutionary tradition as a set of unexamined assumptions. The fact that
men would resort to the violent overthrow of their government for
personal liberty is such an assumption. The preeminent place which
the Founding Fathers gave to individual freedom has been accepted
as natural, and if the principles set forth in the Declaration of
Independence have not always been taken as self-evident truths,
they have rarely been approached as radical ideas requiring explanation. This does not mean that the historiography of the American
Revolution has remained where George Bancroft left it. For more
than two hundred years of writing on the subject, powerful currents
of European thought interrupted the tendency to examine American
events within a closed cultural context. However, the Progressive
historians' effort to interpret liberal ideology as a mask behind
which diverse economic groups struggled for power foundered on
the rock of specific proof. More enduring as a challenge to the Whig
explanation for the Revolution was the scholarship of the Imperialist
school associated with Charles Andrews. These colonial historians
effectively demonstrated that the tyranny the revolutionary pamphleteers evoked could more accurately be described as a legitimate

endeavor by British policymakers to bring the old colonial system up-to-date. The bewilderment of American Tories over the radical response of their compatriots has supplied contemporary validation to the Imperialists' claim that the British connection was capable of evoking affection and loyalty. Still the Revolution did take place, and the imposing intellectual and moral stature of the men who led it has survived popular and scholarly scrutiny for some two centuries. During the last forty years, a new revisionist group has confronted the problem of reconciling revolutionary rhetoric with the realities of British rule. Accepting man as a culture-creating being, the Neo-Whig historians have looked at the period as a socially constructed reality. Their interpretation, nonetheless, hangs upon liberal assumptions about human nature.

By taking seriously the colonists' expressions of purpose and motive, Edmund Morgan, Bernard Bailyn, Richard Buel, Jack Greene, and Gordon Wood have moved with historical imagination to recapture the way the revolutionaries themselves perceived their situation. In their view, the English Commonwealth literature furnished the colonists with a model of republicanism and a critique of government power.[1] The Neo-Whig interpretation is idealist, emphasizing the role which colonial assumptions and values played in determining behavior. As Wood said of Bailyn, he found that "ideas counted for a great deal, not only being responsible for the Revolution but also for transforming the character of American society."[2] The concept of ideas transforming American society, however, should be examined as a logical proposition. The English Commonwealth tradition has done yeoman service for American historians, but it is after all a passive complex of concepts unable to move men by itself. It cannot be used like some *deus ex machina* to explain the causes for belief. Examining the content of the revolutionary mind does not relieve the historian of the responsibility for explaining what compelled belief, what triggered reac-

---

1. See Jack P. Greene, "The Flight from Determinism: A Review of Recent Literature on the Coming of the American Revolution," *South Atlantic Quarterly*, 61 (1962), and Robert E. Shalhope, "Toward a Republican Synthesis: The Emergence of an Understanding of Republicanism in American Historiography," *William and Mary Quarterly*, 29 (1972).

2. Gordon Wood, "Rhetoric and Reality in the American Revolution," *William and Mary Quarterly*, 23 (1966), 22.

tions, what stirred passions, and what persuaded the colonists of the truth of their interpretation of events. One might accept the Commonwealthmen's description of political reality while refusing to break into a formal legislative session with a seditious speech, join a crowd to coerce the resignation of a crown commission-holder, countenance the destruction of private homes, connive at the burning of one of His Majesty's schooners, organize public meetings to mobilize town sentiments against constituted authorities, or risk the loss of self-governing privileges by thwarting the commands of the British Parliament. These are acts flowing from a revolutionary consciousness, a state of mind which accepts, almost embraces, a suspension of the normal rules of conduct and justifies nonordinary behavior by referring to the extraordinary nature of the times. There is no power in the Commonwealth tradition by itself to produce this response.

We are necessarily thrown back to the social situation which prompted a significant number of colonists to endorse these actions as a legitimate response to justifiable fears. Although the Neo-Whigs began with an explicit rejection of the Progressives' efforts to locate the cause of the Revolution in the American social structure, they nonetheless have related their idealist explanation to an interpretation of colonial society. More by inference than explicit demonstration, they have used the idea of colonial maturity to explain the colonial protest movement. According to their interpretation, colonial society had diverged slowly from British norms through the seventeenth and eighteenth centuries. This imperceptible process of differentiation became clear in the turbulent years after the French and Indian War and explains the aggressive behavior of the colonists when new British policies were laid down. Intellectual developments in the decade before Independence, Bailyn has written, "led to a radical idealization and conceptualization of the previous century and a half of American experience."[3] Such an interpretation necessarily understates the risks, the social tensions, the skewed relations and personal anxieties generated when legitimate authority is challenged. It also leaves unanswered why the

---

3. Bernard Bailyn, *The Ideological Origins of the American Revolution* (Cambridge, Mass., 1967), vi.

particular conception of personal liberty and government legitimacy set forth in the revolutionary literature should have seized the American imagination and carried sober men to violent protest and the resort to arms.

By not answering these questions, the Neo-Whig explanation of the American Revolution is necessarily tied to liberal assumptions. It relies upon the liberal concept of human nature and the proper relationship of the individual to social authority. Yet the personal detachment implied in liberal theory runs athwart what we know about the social nature of men and women: their dependence upon integrating institutions and their need for social cohesion. The only form of social tension which liberalism recognizes is that generated by the explicit and unwarranted intrusion of authority upon individual freedom. If the universality of this tension is assumed, then it is not necessary to seek far for an explanation of the American Revolution. Its causes are contained in the rationale for independence: governments are instituted among men to protect individual liberties and destroyed by those same men when the governments fail to achieve this goal. If, on the other hand, liberalism is a cultural perspective which triumphed through the successful American Revolution and not the expression of a constant and basic relationship between man and society, we are forced to ask what conditions would have prompted the adoption of the liberal vision of the good society. The Neo-Whigs have immeasurably enriched our knowledge of the way colonial patterns of thought mediated between the colonists' anxieties and the resolution of those anxieties in a program of action. We still need to explain the nature and origin of their anxieties and the circumstances which made extralegal violence in the interest of a radical theory of individualism tolerable.

Recent scholarship has begun to coalesce around a new interpretation of prerevolutionary society. Instead of the slowly diverging process of cultural differentiation associated with the colonial maturity view, there is now evidence of a disjuncture in colonial life in the second quarter of the eighteenth century. A social order of due subordination incumbent in varying degrees upon all members of the community gave way in the decades after 1730 to an atomized society. The disruption of the contained, community-oriented societies which had been established in the seventeenth century produced new circumstances of far-reaching importance. For a large number of men coming of age in the 1740s and 1750s the contrasting statuses of free and unfree, dependent and independent, came to represent stark alternatives. To be dependent in a society of interdependence was quite a different thing from being dependent or fearing dependence in a society in which institutions no longer integrated people's lives into a satisfying social order. This new social situation made contemporaries peculiarly sensitive to threats against their personal freedom. Among the many satisfying human goals, liberty came to overshadow all others. This changing balance between the demands of the community and the individual helps explain two puzzling American developments in the revolutionary era: why the colonists reacted with such frenzied apprehensiveness to Parliamentary efforts to enforce imperial controls, and why liberalism with its core affirmation of the individual's claim upon society to protect his natural rights could so easily have displaced the devotion to order which animated colonial life a half-century earlier.

Historical research on the seventeenth century has enabled us to appreciate more fully the efforts colonists made in that century to establish traditionally structured, interdependent communities. Informed by a more sophisticated understanding of social organization, some colonial historians have been able to break from the liberal perspective which promoted a search through colonial records for evidence of individual self-assertion and antiauthoritarian stands. They have demonstrated the importance colonists attached to order and their consequent willingness to give up personal freedom to achieve stability. Evidently social cohesion was a widely shared goal, and the drive for local autonomy in the New World served to build strong communities rather than to liberate individuals. The microscopic studies of towns in Connecticut and Massachusetts have revealed that community authority determined farming practices, religious establishments, land allocations, and social responsibilities.[4] Michael Zuckerman has made a good case for interpreting the apparently democratic suffrage as an operational device for

4. Sumner Chilton Powell, *Puritan Village: The Formation of a New England Town* (Middletown, Conn., 1963); Richard L. Bushman, *From Puritan to Yankee: Character and the Social Order in Connecticut, 1690–1765* (Cambridge, Mass., 1967); John Demos, *A Little*

assuring conformity and social control in communities lacking any other coercive force.[5] As Timothy Smith has pointed out, religious groups doctrinally opposed to civil sanctions in religious matters, turned to political authority to shore up congregational discipline when faced with the "threat of social disorder, of barbarization, which hung over their common enterprise."[6] In Virginia the self-made men of the short-lived tobacco boom did not solidify their power. This was largely because they lacked the capacity to command respect or the ability to create the integrative institutions lacking in the raw frontier of the Chesapeake before 1670.[7] In Maryland the proprietor's authority supplied much of the direction for social organization, whereas in Pennsylvania the most effective social arrangements grew out of the sectarian discipline of the Quakers and Baptists.[8]

If we abandon, or at least suspend, belief in the notion that the American colonists arrived with the conscious desire to break with

Commonwealth (New York, 1970); Kenneth A. Lockridge, *A New England Town: The First Hundred Years* (New York, 1970); Philip J. Greven, Jr., *Four Generations: Population, Land and Family in Colonial Andover, Massachusetts* (Ithaca, 1970). See also T. H. Breen and Stephen Foster, "Moving to the New World: The Character of Early Massachusetts Immigration," *William and Mary Quarterly*, 30 (1973), 217–219, and "The Puritans' Greatest Achievement: A Study of Social Cohesion in Seventeenth-Century Massachusetts," *Journal of American History*, 60 (1973).

5. Michael Zuckerman, "The Social Context of Democracy in Massachusetts," *William and Mary Quarterly*, 25 (1968), 3–30. David Grayson Allen, "The Zuckerman Thesis and the Process of Legal Rationalization in Provincial Massachusetts, with a Rebuttal by Michael Zuckerman," *William and Mary Quarterly*, 29 (1972), 465ff, notes the decline of community cohesion as the eighteenth century progressed.

6. Timothy L. Smith, "Congregation, State, and Denomination: The Forming of the American Religious Structure," *William and Mary Quarterly*, 25 (1968), 164. See also Sidney Mead, "From Coercion to Persuasion: Another Look at the Rise of Religious Liberty and the Emergence of Denominationalism," *Church History*, 25 (1956).

7. Bernard Bailyn, "Politics and Social Structure in Virginia," in *Seventeenth-Century America: Essays in Colonial History*, ed. James M. Smith (Chapel Hill, 1959); Wesley Frank Craven, *The Southern Colonies in the Seventeenth Century* (Baton Rouge, La., 1949), 269–299.

8. Gary Nash, *Quakers and Politics: Pennsylvania, 1681–1726* (Princeton, 1968). See also James T. Lemon, *The Best Poor Man's Country: A Geographical Study of Early Southeastern Pennsylvania* (Baltimore, 1972). Although Lemon's "poor man's country" is characterized throughout as one "free of external restraint" (5, 13), he also suggests repeatedly that the sectarian discipline in Quaker and Mennonite communities accounted for their superior economic growth and social stability (20–21, 71, 224).

European corporate traditions, we must question why the social order established in these discrete colonial communities broke down. Why did the group-centered social organization, the deferential political system, and the orthodox congregational establishments which characterized seventeenth-century colonial society fail to survive intact through the second third of the eighteenth century?[9] A tentative answer is that demographic and economic changes overwhelmed these communities' adaptive capacities. Richard Bushman estimated that Connecticut's population grew by 58 percent between 1670 and 1700 and by 380 percent between 1700 and 1730, and "the increase in town planting placed extraordinary pressures on the colonial government."[10] Examining the demographic history of Andover, Massachusetts, Philip Greven found an explosive population rate in the last decades of the seventeenth century followed by slower, but sustained, population growth in succeeding decades. As long as the land resources of each town were sufficient to distribute to the bumper crop of surviving children, population growth did not present a social problem. According to Greven, "the small rural agricultural towns like Andover probably proved to be excellent places in which to realize the goals of order, hierarchy, and the closely-knit community" until the middle decades of the eighteenth century, when population outran the town's allocation of land and young men "reached maturity sooner, married younger, established their independence more effectively and earlier in life, and departed from the community with even greater frequency than in earlier generations."[11] In Dedham, Massachusetts, a town subjected to a similarly close scrutiny, Kenneth Lockridge found the same pattern.[12] While population growth among the Pennsylvania Quakers did not match the extraordinary fertility of New Englanders, the

9. A critical step in the undermining of deferential politics was the shifting of attention of the colonial leaders from imperial authorities to domestic constituencies. This subtle process is illuminated somewhat by Robert M. Calhoon and Robert M. Weir, "The Scandalous History of Sir Egerton Leigh," *William and Mary Quarterly*, 26 (1969), and David Curtis Skaggs, "Maryland's Impulse Toward Social Revolution: 1750–1776," *Journal of American History*, 54 (1968). See also Bushman, *From Puritan to Yankee*, 122–143; Lockridge, *A New England Town*, 119–138. I am using the term "congregational" here in the generic sense rather than in specific reference to the Puritan churches.

10. Bushman, *From Puritan to Yankee*, 83.

11. Greven, *Four Generations*, 270–272.

12. Lockridge, *A New England Town*, 147ff.

demographic studies of Robert Wells indicate a fertility rate which would have made it difficult for parents to provide for all of their adult children. The conservative transmission of culture from one generation to another was challenged by the unprecedented number of children growing to maturity.[13] Population growth forced a change in rural society. The "outlivers" of Bushman's seventeenth-century Connecticut became the norm as independent farmers, even squatters, moved onto the land outside of town boundaries. The style of town planting changed drastically too. If one compares the founding of Sumner Chilton Powell's Sudbury with that of Charles Grant's Kent, the social consequences of land distribution by town planners in contrast to colony auction becomes apparent.[14] And the qualities of Kent were represented in the dozens of frontier towns that marked the migration of surplus population into northwestern Connecticut, western Massachusetts, New York's Mohawk Valley, and the southern tier of Maine, Vermont, and New Hampshire.[15]

In the middle decades of the eighteenth century the demographic structure of the colonies was changed not only by the spectacular growth of native population in the rural communities of the North but also by the total increase from immigration. Philadelphia, a city of 12,000 in 1730, began receiving immigrants from Germany and Ireland at the rate of 7,000 a year, an average maintained for the next two decades![16] While Philadelphia was the prin-

---

13. Robert Wells, "Family Size and Fertility Control in Eighteenth Century America: A Study of Quaker Families," *Population Studies,* 25 (1971); "Quaker Marriage Patterns in a Colonial Perspective," *William and Mary Quarterly,* 29 (1972). See also John Demos, "Families in Colonial Bristol, Rhode Island: An Exercise in Historical Demography," *William and Mary Quarterly,* 25 (1968); Kenneth A. Lockridge, "The Population of Dedham, Massachusetts, 1636–1736," *Economic History Review,* 19 (1966); Philip J. Greven, Jr., "Family Structure in Seventeenth-Century Andover, Massachusetts," *William and Mary Quarterly,* 23 (1966).

14. Powell, *Puritan Village,* 102–113; *Democracy in the Connecticut Frontier Town of Kent* (New York, 1961), 12–39.

15. Jackson Turner Main, *The Social Structure of Revolutionary America* (Princeton, 1965), 11ff; P. M. G. Harris, "The Social Origins of American Leaders: The Demographic Foundations," *Perspectives in American History,* 3 (1969), 234–236. According to Harris' computation of towns recognized by the Massachusetts Legislature, there were 23 new towns between 1696 and 1722; 40 between 1723 and 1746; and 67 between 1747 and 1770.

16. Gary B. Nash, "Slaves and Slaveowners in Colonial Philadelphia," *William and Mary Quarterly,* 30 (1973), 227–228, n. 11. See also A. E. Smith, *Colonists in Bondage* (Chapel Hill, 1947), 308–337.

cipal port of debarkation for white immigrants in the eighteenth century, New Castle, New York, and Boston also felt the impact of Europe's second great westward migration.[17] Although many of the immigrants, of whom probably half were redemptioners or indentured servants, stayed where they landed, these ports also served as distribution centers. Philadelphia particularly offered access to the inland valleys of the Susquehanna, Shenandoah, and other intermountain valleys of western Maryland, Virginia, and North Carolina. In Charleston the principal immigrant of the 1720s and 1730s was the black slave who of course could more easily be brought under social control. The increase in the slave population after 1710, however, called forth measures to restrict even more than previously the slaves' freedom of action. Colonial legislatures, not individual masters, defined the conditions of black and white servitude. Despite these efforts, South Carolina remained vulnerable to the fear of slave rebellions.[18] Both South Carolina and the Chesapeake experienced a dramatic demographic transformation between 1700 and 1740. Not only was there an absolute increase of 51 percent in the first decade, 30 percent in the second, 37 percent in the 1720s, and 38 percent in the 1730s, but the black population in this forty-year period increased by 500 percent to reach a ratio of one black for every three people in the Chesapeake and two in three in South Carolina.[19] Many of the landless whites and marginal family farmers were pushed out into the areas of Southern subsistence farming described by Jackson Turner Main.[20] Edmund Morgan's contention that the yeoman farmer came into his

17. J. Potter, "The Growth of Population in America," in *Population in History*, ed. D. E. C. Eversley and D. V. Glass (London, 1965), 644–646; Wayland F. Dunaway, "Pennsylvania as an Early Distributing Center of Population," *Pennsylvania Magazine of History and Biography*, 55 (1931); Clifford Shipton, "Immigration to New England, 1680–1740," *Journal of Political Economy*, 44 (1936); Erna Risch, "Joseph Crellius, Immigrant Broker," *New England Quarterly*, 21 (1939).

18. M. Eugene Sirmans, "The Legal Status of the Slave in South Carolina, 1670–1740," *Journal of Southern History*, 28 (1962); Herbert Aptheker, *American Negro Slave Revolts* (New York, 1943), 174–175, 184; *South Carolina: A Documentary Profile of the Palmetto State*, ed. Elmer D. Johnson and Kathleen Lewis Sloan (Columbia, S.C., 1971), 110–111.

19. United States Bureau of the Census, *Historical Statistics of the United States* (Washington, D.C., 1960), 756. For the impact of immigration on Maryland, see Skaggs, "Maryland's Impulse," 771.

20. Main, *Social Structure*, 49ff.

own in Virginia during the eighteenth century is obviously applicable to those who could hold out through the changeover from white to black labor.[21] Nor does it take into account the social dislocations involved in such a wholesale switch of labor and land usage.

Economic forces lay behind many of the demographic changes of the 1720s and 1730s. While the striking decline in the infant mortality rate in the Northern rural communities is partially explained by fortuitous conditions, prosperity also contributed by raising living standards. Economic growth obviously stimulated both white and black immigration. European famines and economic distress created a pool of potential immigrants, but the rapid growth in the Atlantic commerce in foodstuffs and timber promoted the demand for servants, tenants, and land buyers which turned the shipping of passengers into a major business.[22] Economic growth raised incomes, brought all but the most remote frontier outposts into connection with the great Atlantic commerce, rewarded enterprise, and generated impressive local capital accumulation.[23] These same results put severe pressures upon social stability. Rising land values stimulated waves of land speculation from Georgia to New Hampshire which undermined the conservative development of land resources. Possibilities for profit promoted enterprise, but introduced competitive attitudes that destroyed group solidarity. Land

21. Edmund Morgan, "Slavery and Freedom: The American Paradox," *Journal of American History*, 59 (1972), 28.

22. Smith, *Colonists in Bondage*, 44–55, 113ff; D. A. Farnie, "The Commercial Empire of the Atlantic, 1607–1783," *Economic History Review*, 15 (1962); George R. Taylor, "American Economic Growth Before 1840," *Journal of Economic History*, 24 (1964); James G. Lydon, "Philadelphia's Commercial Expansion, 1720–1739," *Pennsylvania Magazine of History and Biography*, 91 (1967); Ralph Davis, "English Foreign Trade, 1700–1774," *Economic History Review*, 15 (1962); Lemon, *Best Poor Man's Country*, 179ff.

23. Aubrey Land, "Economic Base and Social Structure: The Northern Chesapeake in the Eighteenth Century," *Journal of Economic History*, 25 (1965); James Henretta, "Economic Development and Social Structure in Colonial Boston," *William and Mary Quarterly*, 22 (1965); Jacob Price, "The Economic Growth of the Chesapeake and the European Market, 1695–1775," *Journal of Economic History*, 24 (1964); Edward Edelman, "Thomas Hancock, Colonial Merchant," *Journal of Economic and Business History*, 1 (1928); Lemon, *Best Poor Man's Country*, 222ff; Bushman, *From Puritan to Yankee*, 122–133; Main, *Social Structure*, 61, 281ff; Gary Walton, "New Evidence on Colonial Commerce," *Journal of Economic History*, 28 (1968); William S. Sachs, "Interurban Correspondents and the Development of a National Economy before the Revolution: New York as a Case Study," *New York History*, 36 (1955).

values climbed steadily but caused dissension over the distribution and organization of agricultural acreage.[24] Paper money, land banks, and credit extension created opportunities, democratized competition, unleashed the acquisitive instinct, and encouraged personal ambition—all corrosives to a community order which valued continuity, solidarity, and stability. In addition to the demographic and economic changes affecting the colonies, for eighteen of the twenty-four years between 1739 and 1763, England's rivalry with Spain and France erupted into open hostilities. The frontier communities of New York, New England, and Pennsylvania were subject to enemy attacks. Privateering and profiteering skewed normal patterns of trade throughout the colonies. Georgia and South Carolina were not only exposed to military threats but also felt the repercussions of slave unrest stimulated by Spanish invitations to desert.[25]

The characteristic colonial society of 1700 subordinated the individual to the group and regulated his activities in accordance with traditional purposes usually defined by the local church or the ruling class. Prosperity, new economic opportunities, immigration, population growth, and the pressures of war undermined efforts to perpetuate this social pattern. Religious establishments in the South were unequal to the task of providing ministers for the new communities in the hinterland. Immigrants recreated their native religious affiliations with delay and great difficulty.[26] Within the

24. Bushman, *From Puritan to Yankee,* 143; Kenneth A. Lockridge, "Land, Population, and the Evolution of New England Society, 1630–1790," *Past and Present,* 39 (1968); Charles S. Grant, "Land Speculation and the Settlement of Kent, 1738–1760," *New England Quarterly,* 28 (1955); Michael Zuckerman, *Peaceable Kingdoms: New England Towns in the Eighteenth Century* (New York, 1970), 89–91; Lockridge, *A New England Town,* 145–156; Main, *Social Structure,* 16; Lemon, *Best Poor Man's Country,* 86–89.

25. Howard H. Peckham, *The Colonial Wars, 1689–1762* (Chicago, 1984), 81–155; Edelman, "Thomas Hancock"; Sachs, "Interurban Correspondents"; Grant, *Democracy in Kent,* 6–9; Bushman, *From Puritan to Yankee,* 139–140; Aptheker, *American Slave Revolts,* 184; *South Carolina,* ed. Johnson and Sloan, 110–111; Arthur Pierce Middleton, "The Chesapeake Convoy System, 1662–1763," *William and Mary Quarterly,* 3 (1946).

26. *The Carolina Backcountry on the Eve of the Revolution: The Journal and Other Writings of Charles Woodmason,* ed. Richard J. Hooker (Chapel Hill, 1953), 67–81; Smith, "Congregation, State, and Denomination," 171–176; George M. Brydon, *Virginia's Mother Church* (Richmond, 1947), I, 127ff; Wesley M. Gewehr, *The Great Awakening in Virginia, 1740–1790* (Durham, N.C., 1930); Joseph Henry Dubbs, "The Founding of the German Churches of Pennsylvania," *Pennsylvania Magazine of History and Biography,* 17 (1893), 256ff.

established churches the changing nature of colonial life presented itself as a challenge. The one great effort to reassert the religious focus of the community aroused such passions that its effect was more disruptive than ameliorative. The succession of revivals which swept over the colonies between 1728 and 1741 were directed to bringing people back to God-centered lives, but in appealing to individual sensibilities, the Great Awakening boomeranged. The dissension it aroused bred contempt for much of the church hierarchy, and the voluntary nature of the conversion experience undermined authority. The aftermath of the Awakening was an explicit recognition of religious pluralism.[27]

It is difficult to estimate the relative importance of the purposeful and the contingent in the breakdown of the social order of seventeenth-century America. Our liberal historiographical bias has led to an emphasis upon the purposive. Eighteenth-century opportunities no doubt encouraged men and women to free themselves from the restraint of family, church, and town government, but the acceleration of economic and population growth forced freedom upon others. There was no room in the established towns for the surplus population of the third and fourth generations. Immigrants were cultural outsiders. Slaves and Indians were hostile groups by definition. Whether the transformation of colonial society came about principally from conscious effort or necessary adjustments, the historian must weigh the effect upon the perceptions, sensibilities, and expectations of the people who grew up through this period.

The middle decades of the eighteenth century brought challenges to the political authority and the deferential social structure in the colonies, created choices of religious loyalties, including the possibility of not belonging to a church at all, forced young adults from the protective control of their families, and added thousands of

27. Edwin Gaustad, *The Great Awakening in New England* (New York, 1957), 113–135; J. M. Bumsted, "Revivalism and Separatism in New England: The First Society of Norwich, Connecticut, as a Case Study," *William and Mary Quarterly,* 24 (1967), 600ff; "Religion, Finance, and Democracy in Massachusetts: The Town of Norton as a Case Study," *Journal of American History,* 57 (1971), 829–831; Perry Miller, "Jonathan Edwards' Sociology of the Great Awakening," *New England Quarterly,* 21 (1948); Leonard J. Trinterud, *The Forming of an American Tradition: A Reexamination of Colonial Presbyterianism* (Philadelphia, 1949), 71–98; Bushman, *From Puritan to Yankee,* 235ff.

black and white aliens to the native population. These changes, however, did not expand the range of personal opportunities. Neither vertical nor horizontal mobility increased with growth and prosperity during these years. Sketchy as our knowledge is of the exact details of the distribution of wealth, several studies indicate that the trend of the eighteenth century was toward greater economic stratification. As it became more difficult for the colonists to find personal meaning through traditional social institutions, the alternative possibilities for individual fulfillment as independent farmers, artisans, and merchants were decreasing. The size of farms in New England shrank from an average over 100 acres to less than 50.[28] New opportunities for town founding were checked by the hostile activity of the Spanish, French, and their Indian allies in the Northeast and along the southern frontier. As capital accumulated in the hands of the wealthier merchants in the major colonial ports, chances for success for the unsponsored young man diminished. The landless and disenfranchised population in Boston and Philadelphia grew throughout the century.[29] Tenant farming increased in New York, New England, Maryland, and Virginia, as people pushed into the western areas where farsighted investors had patented large tracts of land. The opportunity for indentured servants to acquire land and assume civic responsibilities decreased rather than increased

28. The decline in size of agricultural holdings is confirmed in the studies of Lemon, *Best Poor Man's Country,* 87–94; Lockridge, "Land, Population, and the Evolution of New England Society." Although rising land values could compensate for declining size of holdings, Lockridge argues persuasively that rising land values would have exacerbated the situation by making it more difficult for the landless to acquire land. See Stanley D. Dodge, "The Frontier of New England in the Seventeenth and Eighteenth Centuries and Its Significance in American History," Michigan Academy of Sciences, Arts, and Letters *Papers,* 28 (1942).

29. Main, *Social Structure,* 31–43, 44–46. Although Main argues that opportunities were great in revolutionary America, the morphology of social structure he develops would indicate that economic opportunity decreased with the growth, complexity, and wealth of America, as a result of the concentration of wealth in urban areas, the conversion of some frontier areas to commercial farming, and the movement westward into lands held by speculators or large absentee landlords. These implications are borne out by Henretta, "Economic Development and Social Structure in Colonial Boston"; Land, "Economic Base and Social Structure"; Gary Nash, *Quakers and Politics,* 321ff; Lemon, "Urbanization and Development of Eighteenth-Century Southeastern Pennsylvania and Adjacent Delaware," *William and Mary Quarterly,* 24 (1967); Allan Kulikoff, "The Progress of Inequality in Revolutionary Boston," *William and Mary Quarterly,* 28 (1971), 381ff.

with time.[30] Colonial society was becoming liberalized in the middle decades of the century, but the prospect of becoming a fully free man in that society was conditioned by forces largely outside individual control.[31] In an earlier time some people had had more authority than others, but few were free from the restraints of the community. After 1740 more colonists were free from authoritarian restraints, but they did not necessarily have greater control over the decisive forces in their lives.

Let us analyze the social structure of the American colonies in forms of personal freedom. There was not the tapestry of shaded ranks which European society presented. Nor had colonial America produced the elaborate social usages which enabled an Englishman to exercise a vocabulary of verbal class distinction every time he greeted a fellow countryman. But if the breadth of personal freedom is used as the gauge of social distinctions, America offered a range of statuses unique for its extremes. The continuum would begin at one end with the slave who was formally stripped of all rights and informally dependent upon the will of a master. Next on the continuum was the white servant whose status was defined by contracts binding him or her to personal service up to seven years. Indentured servants had legally enforceable rights relating to work, punishments, living conditions, and freedom dues, but the person who owned a servant's contract could exercise control over a whole range of personal liberties dealing with property, selection of friends, use of free time, and supervision of behavior. A. E. Smith has estimated that between half and two-thirds of the several hundred thousand immigrants of the eighteenth century entered into indentured service either before or after their arrival in the colonies.[32] Next to indentured servants on the continuum of personal freedom were

30. Land, "Economic Base and Social Structure"; Russell R. Menard, "From Servant to Freeholder: Status Mobility and Property Accumulation in Seventeenth-Century Maryland," *William and Mary Quarterly*, 30 (1973); Main, *Social Structure*, 45, 50, 61–65, 278–279; Skaags, "Maryland's Impulse Toward Social Revolution."

31. See Michael G. Kammen, "Essay Review: Intellectuals, Political Leadership, and Revolution," *New England Quarterly*, 41 (1968), 590ff, for an interesting suggestion about unemployed intellectuals in revolutionary situations. At the opposite extreme, for evidence of the increase in "idlers and vagabonds" on the frontier, see *The Carolina Backcountry*, ed. Hooker, 167–168.

32. Smith, *Colonists in Bondage*, 336.

dependent sons, young men who reached maturity but did not possess a craft or a freehold which could make them independent of their fathers' support.

Figures on the number of dependent sons or the number of years of their dependency are difficult to establish. Several factors, however, contributed to the importance of this group. The demographic profile of rural society north of Maryland was marked by longevity and large families.[33] This meant that usually sons in their late twenties had living fathers still in possession of the family farms and that there was competition for land among the potential heirs. Recent scholarship has made it difficult to generalize about dependency trends.[34] Where fathers in one community left evidence of controlling their children through bequests or gifts of land, in other towns the aged parents' fear of neglect suggests that grown sons had great freedom of movement. The undulating cycles of population growth could affect the personal freedom of young people in two contrasting ways. Population growth could stimulate town planting which might give migrating young couples early independence from their parents, or population pressure could create a land scarcity which inhibited young people from leaving the security of a prospective share in the family farm.[35] The fact remains that land resources of eighteenth-century America were controlled by proprietors or corporate bodies, and decisions about opening up land were made by the older generation. Despite the apparent economic opportunity, preindustrial society offered a limited range of self-supporting occupations to men without land, and real property was essential to personal freedom defined both economically and politically. If the average colonist under twenty-seven or twenty-eight was neither slave nor servant, neither was he free.

This calibration of personal dependency might appear as an elaboration of the obvious truth that society involves subordination were

33. See note 13 above.

34. Compare, for instance, Greven with Demos, "Notes on Life in Plymouth Colony," *William and Mary Quarterly*, 22 (1965), and Linda Auwers Bissell, "From One Generation to Another: Mobility in Seventeenth-Century Windsor, Connecticut," *William and Mary Quarterly*, 31 (1974).

35. Contrast Grant, "Land Speculation and the Settlement of Kent," and Bushman, *From Puritan to Yankee*, 83, with Lockridge, "Land, Population, and the Evolution of New England Society."

it not for the fact that at the end of the continuum were thousands of the freest individuals the Western world had ever known. These people were not members of an elite, but average white men whose childhood, youth, and maturity had paralleled the disruption of the previous, conservative social order. Neither family, state, nor church could lay fundamental claims upon them, for the terms of group membership in colonial life had become voluntary, short range, and unintrusive. Already in the 1760s and 1770s there was in adumbrated form the qualities of a liberal society which Tocqueville described so well three-quarters of a century later: "As social conditions become more equal, the number of persons increases who, although they are neither rich nor powerful enough to exercise any great influence over their fellows, have nevertheless acquired or retained sufficient education and fortune to satisfy their own wants. They owe nothing to any man, they expect nothing from any man; they acquire the habit of always considering themselves as standing alone, and they are apt to imagine that their whole destiny is in their own hands." [36]

If we can accept this picture of the qualitative changes in colonial society before the Revolution, and can entertain the idea that the removal of traditional social restraints would make the categories of free and unfree crucial to personal satisfaction, then it is possible to see how British imperial reforms could be viewed as menacing acts demanding immediate and forceful repudiation. The proof of these conjectures lies deep in the consciousness of the revolutionary generation, but the language of their protests offers some clues. Acceptance of Parliamentary authority is repeatedly compared to slavery in the political pamphlets of the 1760s. Servile is the description for accommodation. The imagery of subjugation, submission, and subordination courses through the literature that marked the way to Independence. Stephen Hopkins evoked the prospect of slavery in *The Rights of Colonies Examined:* "Liberty is the greatest blessing that men enjoy, and slavery the heaviest curse that human nature is capable of," explaining later on in his pamphlet that "those who are governed at the will of another, or of others, and whose

36. Alexis de Tocqueville, *Democracy in America,* ed. Richard D. Heffner (New York, 1956), 194 (taken from Part II, Book Two of the original Henry Reeve translation).

property may be taken from them by taxes or otherwise without their own consent and against their wills are in the miserable condition of slaves."[37] His critic, Martin Howard, Jr., answered Hopkins with a statement of the conservative view of society: "every connection in life has its reciprocal duties; we know the relation between a parent and child, husband and wife, master and servant, and from thence are able to deduce their respective obligations."[38] But the idea of slavery stayed firmly fixed in the colonial imagination. "Slavery," "slavish," "enslave," appeared throughout James Otis' *The Rights of the British Colonies Asserted and Proved.* "The people," he asserted, "never entrusted any body of men with a power to surrender [their liberty] in exchange for slavery." Slavery was so vile and miserable an estate of man that Otis found it hard to believe that an Englishman would plead for it.[39]

In his *Summary View of the Rights of British America,* Jefferson claimed that the series of oppressions by Parliament "too plainly prove a deliberate and systematic plan of reducing us to slavery." Were the British Parliament to succeed, he said, Americans would "suddenly be found the slaves, not of one, but of 160,000 tyrants."[40]

Jonathan Mayhew, the liberal Boston minister, wrote *A Discourse Concerning Unlimited Submission and Non-Resistance to the Higher Powers* to refute the orthodox religious argument for obedience to authority. His pamphlet is an exegesis on the meaning of "submission" and "subjection," but he also used the imagery of slavery: "Resistance was absolutely necessary in order to preserve the nation from slavery, misery, and ruin"; "In plain English, there seems to have been an impious bargain struck up betwixt the scepter and the surplice for enslaving both the bodies and souls of men"; not to resist the English king "would be to join with the sovereign in promoting the slavery and misery" of the colonies, passive obedience is a "slavish

37. *Pamphlets of the American Revolution, 1750–1776,* ed. Bernard Bailyn (Cambridge, Mass., 1965), I, 507–508.

38. Martin Howard, Jr., "A Letter from a Gentleman at Halifax," ibid., 534–535.

39. *Pamphlets,* ed. Bailyn, 477, 424, 434–435, 429, 447, 439, 440, 443. Although this pamphlet appeared before Howard's "Letter from a Gentleman at Halifax," Otis did answer Howard with "A Vindication of the British Colonies, against the Aspersions of the Halifax Gentleman," ibid.

40. *Tracts of the American Revolution: 1763–1776,* ed. Merrill Jensen (Indianapolis, 1967), 264–265.

doctrine," and disobeying the civil powers in certain circumstances is "warrantable and glorious" if it involved freeing oneself and "posterity from inglorious servitude and ruin."[41] Writing principally to protest the "servile" judicial tenure of "during pleasure," the anonymous author of *Letter to the People of Pennsylvania* insisted that the colonists should profit from what the histories of Europe had to say about the designs of arbitrary princes for "quelling the spirit of liberty and enslaving their subjects to their will." "If Charles and James dispensed with penal statutes in order to introduce popery," colonial governors, he said, have suspended laws "in order to introduce slavery." Those who cooperated with royal officials were "slaves" preparing a "slavish condition" for Americans who "will become slaves indeed, in no respect different from the sooty Africans, whose persons and properties are subject to the disposal of their tyrannical masters."[42]

Benjamin Church was equally insistent that slavery awaited the colonists. In *Liberty and Property Vindicated,* he claimed that "every action which should tend to promote the freedom of Britons is most notoriously made use of to enslave and plague them." "Britons never must be slaves," he intoned and, warming to his topic, recommended to his readers that if they find a man "in any post that unjustly grinds the face of the poor or that contributes to your slavery, ask him peaceably to resign it, and if he refuses to, use him in such a manner that he will be glad to do anything for a quiet life."[43] Oxenbridge Thacher raised the specter that the colonists had shed their blood in the French and Indian War only "to bind the shackles of slavery on themselves and their children."[44] The author of *The Constitutional Courant* described the Stamp Act as a design to "change our freedom to slavery." "What then is to be done?" he asked rhetorically. "Shall we sit down quietly, while the yoke of slavery is wreathing about our necks? He that is stupid enough to plead for this," he answered, "deserves to be a *slave*." "What is a slave, but one who depends upon the will of another for the enjoyment of his life and property?" The English Parliament that "can lay

41. *Pamphlets,* ed. Bailyn, 241, 245, 232, 222.
42. Ibid., 259, 269, 271, 272.
43. Ibid., 592, 596.
44. Oxenbridge Thacher, "The Sentiments of a British American," in ibid., 490.

burdens upon us," he warned, "can also, if they please, take our whole property from us, and order us to be sold for slaves." The fate of the colonists will be unrelieved. "Let us not flatter ourselves, that we shall be happier, or treated with more lenity than our fellow slaves in Turkey." [45] Far less radical than the author of *The Constitutional Courant,* John Dickinson, nonetheless, devoted the last of his *Letters from a Farmer in Pennsylvania* to a discussion of the slavery that awaited the colonists. [46] Even the young Alexander Hamilton found slavery the most appropriate analogy for the colonial situation. "Were not the disadvantages of slavery too obvious to stand in need of it," he declaimed in his *Full Vindication,* "I might enumerate and describe the tedious train of calamities inseparable from it." Appealing to farmers on the grounds that they would be most oppressed in a country where slavery prevailed, he asked, "Are you willing, then to be slaves without a single struggle?" [47] John Adams as "Novanglus" put the case most succinctly: "There are but two sorts of men in the world, freemen and slaves." "The very definition of a freeman," he went on to explain, "is one who is bound by no law to which he has not consented." [48]

As the inheritors of the point of view expressed in these writings, we often have been uncritical of its genesis. Surely no one today would defend so stark an assertion as that there are only two sorts of men in the world, nor would the colonists' contemporaries in the other New World colonies or in Europe have agreed. By contrasting freedom to slavery the revolutionaries were giving an absolute value to freedom which it had not previously possessed, even in the intellectual tradition from which they drew. Our understanding of the Revolution in part hinges upon our capacity to discover what experiences would have prompted this apocalyptic attitude about freedom. Social upheaval by itself does not produce radical notions about individual rights. One could guess that the social instability occasioned by population pressures, high rates of immigration, the

45. *Tracts,* ed. Jensen, 87, 82, 83, 90, 89.

46. *The Writings of John Dickinson,* ed. Paul Leicester Ford (Philadelphia, 1895), I, 397–406.

47. *The Works of Alexander Hamilton,* ed. Henry Cabot Lodge (New York, 1904), I, 15, 34–35.

48. *Tracts,* ed. Jensen, 315–316.

increased use of slaves, wartime dislocations, and religious revivals would cause a conservative reaction. Perhaps, on the other hand, the individual energy recently freed from familial, congregational, and community restraint supplied the force for liberalization rather than reaction.

Because law enforcement had always been weak in the Anglo-American colonies, community coercion had supplied the social control normally exercised by superior authorities. Local autonomy had served group, not individual, goals, but the effectiveness of such a system of control depended upon the capacity of the larger society to create new locales of community control to keep pace with growth. Rapid and diversified population growth strained the system. The controversies over the Great Awakening undermined the consensual basis for religious discipline. Economic opportunity beckoned to the ambitious. American society was maturing, but its maturation was not that of the acorn, for the oak had not yet been prefigured. Perhaps the prosperity and economic growth of the middle decades provided the possibility of a new order which would minimize social control and maximize the individual ambit of choice and responsibility. In such a context, any threat to the expectations generated by a liberal vision of society could induce panic and encourage violence. Such threats could also be widely accepted as tyrannical, unjust, unnatural, and unacceptable. This at least is what the revolutionary rhetoric suggests was the prevailing response.

Historians of the American Revolution who have devoted themselves to reconstructing the discrete steps that led to "the seizure of power over a governmental apparatus by one group from another" are understandably reluctant to see the careful definitions of the last two decades of scholarship disappear into a quagmire of explanations which rely more upon theories of social psychology than evidence supporting a connection between presumptive cause and discernible effect.[49] Their capacity to disentangle causes from prior events has been demonstrated by Jack Greene. Addressing himself again to the

49. Jack P. Greene, "The Social Origins of the American Revolution: An Evaluation and an Interpretation," *Political Science Quarterly*, 88 (1973), 19. Just how wide the parameters of social explanations for the American Revolution can be is demonstrated in Kenneth A. Lockridge, "Social Change and the Meaning of the American Revolution," *Journal of Social History*, 6 (1973).

implications of Gordon Wood's assertion that the rhetoric of the American Revolution indicated "the most severe sort of social strain," Greene astutely distinguished between the modernization of American society and the American Revolution.[50] Few would contend that this modernization process which produced a sweeping social revolution throughout western Europe would not have taken place in America without a political break from Great Britain, as Greene points out. However, distinguishing these two revolutions for purposes of analysis is not the same as demonstrating that contemporaries experienced them as separate forces. Modernization is inseparable from the demographic and economic changes which sapped the cohesion of the first colonial communities. The transformation of values which accompanied the intrusion of the market into social relations can scarcely be distinguished from the liberal philosophy which found expression in revolutionary rhetoric. One aspect of a change from an ascriptive to an achieving basis of social ranking is the anxiety generated by fears about one's personal access to avenues to achievement. Frenzied concern for individual liberty makes little sense unless the meaning of freedom is related to the specific social context which gives it preeminent importance. Even if it is agreed that the modernization of colonial society would have continued without the American Revolution, can the converse be dismissed? Would the American Revolution have taken place without the tensions generated by social atomization and a spreading commercialism? Can we understand the revolution without exploring how personal ambition was elevated to a fundamental right in Jefferson's tellingly modern phrase "the pursuit of happiness."

50. Ibid., 4–5; see also Greene's "Search for Identity: An Interpretation of the Meaning of Selected Patterns of Social Response in Eighteenth-Century America," *Journal of Social History,* 3 (1970); "Williams Knox's Explanation for the American Revolution," *William and Mary Quarterly,* 30 (1973); "An Uneasy Connection: An Analysis of the Preconditions of the American Revolution," in *Essays on the American Revolution,* ed. Stephen G. Kurtz and James H. Hutson (Chapel Hill, 1973).

6

The Social Origins of American Revolutionary Ideology

THE REIGNING ideas of the American Revolution are now being characterized as premodern. This judgment comes at the end of more than a decade of scholarly probing into the ideological origins of the colonial resistance movement. The origins that Neo-Whig historians Bernard Bailyn, Richard Buel, Jack Greene, and Gordon Wood have discovered are not simple and Lockean, as once believed, but complex and atavistic growing out of the rich English intellectual traditions of the Dissenters, radical Whigs, Classical Republicans, Commonwealthmen, Country party, or more simply, the Opposition.[1] Dramatically reorienting the scholarship on the Revolution, Bailyn has reconstructed the interpretive scheme which dominated the colonists' minds, triggered their emotions, and pushed them into resistance.[2] The revolutionary force of this scheme lay, in Wood's words, with "its obsession with corruption and disorder, its hostile and conspiratorial outlook, and its millennial vision of a regenerated society."[3] These of course are the qualities that have prompted J. G. A. Pocock to question whether the Amer-

1. See Robert E. Shalhope, "Toward a Republican Synthesis: The Emergence of an Understanding of Republicanism in American Historiography," *William and Mary Quarterly*, 29 (1972), 49–80.
2. Bernard Bailyn, *The Ideological Origins of the American Revolution* (Cambridge, 1967).
3. Gordon S. Wood, "Rhetoric and Reality in the American Revolution," *William and Mary Quarterly*, 23 (1966), 26.

ican Revolution ought not to be considered as "the last great act of the Renaissance" rather than "the first political act of revolutionary enlightenment."[4]

Originally undertaken as a corrective to the shallow economic determinism of Progressive historiography, the revisionary work of the Neo-Whigs has ended up sapping the foundation of their alma mater, the Consensus school.[5] Taking ideas seriously and treating them as parts of a socially constructed reality, the Neo-Whigs have challenged the Consensus historians on two grounds: the mode of thinking attributed to Americans, and the alleged content of the American mind. Where Consensus historians Daniel Boorstin and Louis Hartz had emphasized the pragmatic wisdom of Americans along with their intuitive grasp of reality and their dislike of elaborate philosophical constructions, Bailyn and Wood have tracked Revolutionary rhetoric through a labyrinth of classical republican allusions. Far from grasping reality, it seems, educated colonists were in the grasp of a "peculiar inheritance of thought," which forced them to interpret the British measures in the light of "the known tendencies of history." The Parliamentary acts of the 1760s became evidence of evil policies designed as a deliberate assault against liberty through "the destruction of the English constitution, with all the rights and privileges embedded in it."[6] From the English Opposition literature, the colonial gentry had absorbed the classical republican fears about the encroachments of power and were compelled to respond violently to the British tax acts because, in their minds, these acts were portents of tyranny.[7] By going beyond the colonists' words to the complex of assumptions that makes their apprehensions intelligible, the Neo-Whig historians have demonstrated that ideas should be approached as the necessary mediators between experience and action.

4. J. G. A. Pocock, "Virtue and Commerce in the Eighteenth Century," *Journal of Interdisciplinary History*, 3 (1972), 120.

5. Compare Bernard Bailyn's recent work with that in a more consensual mode. See Bernard Bailyn, "Political Experience and Enlightenment Ideas in Eighteenth-Century America," *American Historical Review*, 67 (1962), 339–351.

6. Bailyn, *Ideological Origins of the American Revolution*, 95.

7. J. G. A. Pocock, "Civic Humanism and Its Role in Anglo-American Thought," in J. G. A. Pocock, *Politics, Language and Time* (New York, 1971), 80–103.

The discovery of this ornate intellectual tradition in the "articulate colonial mind" brings into question the Consensus historians' contention that only the simple affirmations of Lockean liberalism ever sank deeply into the collective American consciousness. In the enormously influential *Liberal Tradition in America,* Hartz had maintained that, without natural enemies in America, John Locke's philosophy had grown luxuriantly, leaving no room for competing ideas. In a wry commentary on the completeness of the liberal triumph, Hartz had noted that "the American historian at practically every stage has functioned quite inside the nation . . . an erudite reflection of the limited social perspectives of the average American himself."[8] The Neo-Whigs have succeeded in breaking free of this intellectual vise, but their scholarship poses problems for those working in later periods of American history. For, in truth, they have come up with a colonial past ill-adapted to serve as the story of the beginnings of what was to come.

There is more at stake than historiography in these conflicting interpretations of the ideological origins of the American Revolution. If a classical republicanism imbued with traditional notions of political authority dominated colonial thinking, where are the roots of that liberalism which flowered so quickly after independence?[9] Having eschewed intellectual history for the study of consciousness, the Neo-Whigs have unavoidably provoked curiosity about the relation of ideas to the social context in which they were held. Does a premodern revolutionary ideology argue for a premodern colonial society as well? If the Revolution was fought in a frenzy over corruption, out of fear of tyranny, and with hopes for redemption through civic virtue, where and when are scholars to find the sources for the aggressive individualism, the optimistic materialism, and the pragmatic interest-group politics that became so salient so early in the life of the new nation?

Broadening the search into the ideological origins of the American Revolution may help answer this question. There were com-

8. Louis Hartz, *The Liberal Tradition in America: An Interpretation of American Political Thought since the Revolution* (New York, 1955), 29.

9. These questions have been raised persistently by Jackson Turner Main. See his review of Gordon S. Wood, "The Creation of the American Republic," *William and Mary Quarterly,* 26 (1969), 604–607.

peting ideologies in the Anglo-American world of the eighteenth century. In addition to the classical republican tradition that the Neo-Whigs have explored, there was a body of seventeenth-century English literature on economic topics that nurtured a very different attitude toward human nature and the terms of social stability. To this source scholars should look for the world view characterized as liberal. Like the thinking on republicanism, ideas from these writings crossed the Atlantic and helped shape the consciousness of some colonists. To appreciate fully, however, the extent to which liberal and classical republican thought presented ideological options to the Americans, it is important to examine them as intellectual responses to the modern restructuring of England and her North American colonies.

The eighteenth-century English patrons of classical political theory were using ideas to oppose the immediate threat of Sir Robert Walpole's management of Parliament and the more elusive dangers that a dynamic capitalism posed for England's traditional leaders. The members of the Opposition—radical Whigs, Dissenters, Tories—wrote as reactionaries. Their ideas fueled what Isaac Kramnick has called "the politics of nostalgia."[10] Their targets were the great Whig magnates who were enthusiastically pursuing a new national destiny through commercial expansion. The Renaissance vocabulary of power, corruption, degeneration, virtue, stability, and balance lay ready to advertise the urgency of checking Whig policies. Not always in agreement, Walpole's opponents nonetheless used a common ideological legacy to argue that only strict adherence to England's mixed constitution offered protection against the fatal usurpations of power.[11] According to the theory, which blended notions about England's ancient constitution with the strains of civic humanism from sixteenth-century Florence, the classic forms of government—monarchy, aristocracy, and democracy—were sub-

10. Isaac Kramnick, *Bolingbroke and His Circle: The Politics of Nostalgia in the Age of Walpole* (Cambridge, 1968), 39–83.

11. Pocock, "Civic Humanism"; Bailyn, *Ideological Origins of the American Revolution,* 55–93. Quentin Skinner has built a case for Bolingbroke's patriotic vigilance as representing the only strategy open to an opposition leader in the period. Quentin Skinner, "The Principles and Practice of Opposition: The Case of Bolingbroke versus Walpole," in *Historical Perspectives: Studies in English Thought and Society in Honour of J. H. Plumb,* ed. Neil McKendrick (London, 1974), 94–110.

ject to degeneration into their debased alter egos, tyranny, oligarchy, and anarchy. Hope of breaking with this fated corruption lay with combining the known forms into a constitutional arrangement in which the monarchical, aristocratic, and democratic elements acted as checks upon each other.[12] This checking would take place, however, only if the three elements were independent of one another and if members of the political body possessed the necessary civic virtue to place constitutional duties above private concerns.

Because of the critical importance of virtue, the proponents of the mixed constitution analyzed the ways to enhance men's capacity to place the public weal before their own self-interest.[13] Since the principal means of subverting virtue were bribes and places of profit, it was concluded that virtue could only exist among those who were not dependent upon others for such favors. Opposition writers warned of two kinds of dependency: the one of the servant whom necessity made servile, and the other of the ambitious man whose pursuit of profit extinguished a concern for the common good. Thus the simple propositions of the mixed constitution led to a consideration of the economic organization and social structure that could preserve the constitutional order.[14] In the light of these truths, the virtuous citizen became a kind of mythic finger to plunge into the crumbling dike of the hereditary social order.

The corruption that Walpole's critics described was not the old one arising from human flaws but a new one made possible by the market economy.[15] On a scope unheard of before, private enterprise supported by government policies could create wealth in a variety of ways. And the bogeys of the opposition press were precisely the instruments of the new capitalist economy—the Bank of England, the funded debt, the expanding national bureaucracy, and the

12. J. G. A. Pocock, *The Machiavellian Moment: Florentine Political Thought and the Atlantic Republican Tradition* (Princeton, 1975), 361–400; Quentin Skinner, "History and Ideology in the English Revolution," *Historical Journal*, 8 (1965), 151–178.

13. W. H. Greenleaf, *Order, Empiricism and Politics: Two Traditions of English Political Thought 1500–1700* (Oxford, 1964), 196; Richard Buel, Jr., "Democracy and the American Revolution: A Frame of Reference," *William and Mary Quarterly*, 21 (April 1964), 165–190.

14. Pocock, "Civic Humanism"; J. G. A. Pocock, "Early Modern Capitalism—the Augustan Perception," in *Feudalism, Capitalism and Beyond*, ed. Eugene Kamenka and R. S. Neale (Canberra, 1975), 63–83.

15. Kramnick, *Bolingbroke and His Circle*, 245–247.

plethora of investment opportunities that led to stock-jobbing. From the viewpoint of classical republicanism these were the engines of corruption. They were also elements of a fairly coherent national policy to promote the productive possibilities of Great Britain in an expanding world trade. In fact, nothing could have been more antithetical to the goals of the Opposition than the most progressive developments of the century: the extension of the market, the increase in the division of labor, the enhanced productivity of reorganized labor, the commercialization of agriculture, and the conversion of the English peasantry into a mobile, free labor force. Participation in this growing market required constant attention to one's self-interest. Self-interest, moreover, ran along the tracks of dependence, for it quickly led to an awareness of the importance of government policies in the newly emerging economic structure— policies affecting the money supply, the terms of trade, the protection of markets, the awarding of lucrative contracts. Thus the unmistakable direction of English growth involved modes of behavior and political stances diametrically opposed to the constitutional ideal of the disinterested citizen living on his own, cultivating the public weal, and committing his virtue to the maintenance of a rightly ordered constitutional monarchy.

The development of the free market was one of the few true social novelties in history, changing the relation not only of person to person and of people to government, but also of human beings to nature. These profound changes disclosed by remarkable new processes of human interaction were totally unassimilable in classical political thought. Evolution and development—irreversible processes of change—were concepts that lay outside classical theory and the history of the ancient constitution. In these, change was equated with degeneracy. The theories assumed that all possible social arrangements were known. A mixed constitution was the best of these arrangements; any deviation led to decline. The whole vocabulary of corruption and tyranny drew its force from a peculiar attitude toward change, which depended in turn upon a rejection of the idea of novelty, of unknown but possible new developments in human affairs.[16]

16. Pocock, "Civic Humanism," 86–88.

Thus, the case that lay between the men who ran England in the eighteenth century and their critics was not simply one of being for or against the use of patronage, but rather of being for or against a national engagement in the market economy, an engagement that required the support of private enterprise, aggressive national policies, and the elimination of obstacles to increasing the productive power of groups within society. The exigencies of opposition politics forced Walpole's critics to hone a fine ideological weapon out of the intellectual traditions that still commanded allegiance from members of the English upper class. These ideas in turn reinforced an antimodern cast of mind. They gave preeminent place to the achievement of stability, made virtue and knowledge essential to the maintenance of social order, and called for a rigid institutional arrangement to check the tendency of government to increase its power at the expense of the subjects' rights and liberties.

The roots of liberal social thought did not lie in past politics or classical theories of government, but rather can be traced to the first writings on the free-market economy. The subject for investigation disclosed itself in a succession of innovations in trade, manufacturing, the mobilization of labor, and the exchange of coins and bills. It fell to Englishmen in the seventeenth century to integrate random observations of these into a model of the new economy, building from a body of ordinary, everyday commentary an analytical framework for explaining market relations. Max Weber's observation that all sciences emerge in response to problems applies with special relevance to economics.[17] In the 1620s the first of many crises—this time a depression in the clothing industry—prompted Thomas Mun and Edward Misselden to adumbrate an abstract model of the "circle" of trade. Because Mun's conception of international trade became an intellectual crutch for later balance-of-trade thinkers, historians have tended to overlook the radical implications of his and Misselden's analysis of commerce. Their intention was not to discourage foreign imports but to demonstrate the ineffectiveness of the royal exchange in regulating the flow of money. Overshooting this limited goal, Mun asserted in very dramatic terms

17. Walter Eucken, *The Foundations of Economics: History and Theory in the Analysis of Economic Reality* (London, 1950), 303.

that market relations were autonomous: "Let the Statute for employ-
ments by Strangers stand in force or be repealed; Let the meer
Exchanger do his worst; Let Princes oppress, Lawyers extort, Usurers
bite, Prodigals wast," treasure will follow trade, and, to underscore
his point, he added, "And this must come to pass by a Necessity
beyond all resistance." [18] In Mun's pamphlets the shipment of goods
and exchange of payments became parts of an overall commercial
flow whose essential movements were independent of political direction.

In succeeding decades the market in goods and labor slowly
replaced the traditional, direct consumption economy. Commerce
with its free-floating price and profit system spread from the cities
to the countryside. A new network of economic communications
superimposed itself upon the kingdom, breaking down the barriers
of local markets, creating new linkages, spreading incentives, and
exerting pressures directly upon the landowner, the farmer, the
wage-laborer, the trader, and the craftsman. Individual tastes registered anonymously through purchases acquired a new, if hidden,
power. Human volition superseded political direction as the principal determinant of productivity and distribution. As the ultimate
consumer moved further and further from the producer, the process
that joined the two became the object of study, and writers began
to investigate the interconnections of their commercial economy.
By the end of the seventeenth century, key assumptions about
market relations had entered the public discourse in a way that
decisively influenced all subsequent social thought.

Unlike the drawing of an "English face of Machiavelli" or the
elaboration of an insular classical republicanism, the economic literature of the period rarely dealt directly with political questions, but
the model of economic relations that was taking shape had profound
implications for theories of social order, sovereignty, individual
rights, and the relation between natural and positive law. From
Mun through Locke, seventeenth-century economic writers cast
their work in a rationalistic mode, which led eventually to that
most radical of all conceptions: the idea of a natural social order
embedded in human nature and worked out through the voluntary,

18. Thomas Mun, *England's Treasure by Forraign Trade* (London, 1664), 218–219.

but natural, interaction of individuals. As William Letwin observed, "it was difficult enough to make chemistry and physics into sciences . . . it was exceedingly difficult to treat economics in a scientific fashion, since every economic act, being the action of a human being, is necessarily also a moral act."[19] Yet as early as 1675 Roger Coke announced that the legal prohibitions on the export of money were useless because neither man nor nation "ever will attain their ends by forceable means, against the Nature and Order of things."[20] Charles Davenant went further and connected the setting of prices with the law of self-preservation. In the "Naturall course of trade, each commodity will find its price," he said, explaining further that "the supreme power can do many things, but it cannot alter the Laws of Nature of which the most original is, that every man should preserve himself."[21]

Central to the effort to analyze market relations was the conviction that there existed a determinable order behind the multifarious acts of buying and selling. Since every bargain reflected a human decision, it was a consistent human response that provided regularity and made possible the idea of there being economic laws akin to physical laws. From this observation came the conclusion that anarchy was not the inevitable alternative to external control. To be sure, governments could still design laws to achieve specific national goals, but the impression was gaining ground that only those statutes that worked within the economic order could be executed successfully. Without making a frontal attack upon political authority, those who wrote about the economy had created in the realm of fact a check to the capacity of kings to thwart the profit-maximizing activities of the plain members of society. In the tracts and treatises on trade published by the hundreds in the closing years of the seventeenth century, the market was treated as the chief regulator of economic life, providing necessary information, encouraging long-range planning, and rewarding ingenuity and efficiency.

19. William Letwin, *The Origins of Scientific Economics: English Economic Thought 1660–1776* (London, 1963), 148.

20. Roger Coke, *England's Improvements* (London, 1675), 57.

21. Charles Davenant, "A Memorial Concerning the Coyn of England [1693]," in *Two Manuscripts by Charles Davenant*, ed. Abbott Payson Usher (Baltimore, 1942), 21–22.

Utilitarian arguments drew in their train an assortment of assertions about human economic propensities and their effect. Contradictory positions emerged when opposing interest groups found penmen to take their case to the public. The issue that became most salient was how compatible private interests were with the good of the whole. Few disputed that men pursued their private gain in the marketplace, but those groups whose interests required legislative interference evoked the traditional rhetoric for social restraint. One writer insisted that "the making of a great profit on a particular trade may be fit for particular men to consider . . . but was never yet thought a consideration worthy the legislators providing for," because, as he went on to explain, "the great profit which particular men may make, is for the most part directly opposite to the interest of the publick." [22] John Cary reiterated conventional wisdom on this point when he reminded his readers of the importance of managing trade well, because a nation may grow poor, "whilst private Persons encrease their Fortunes." [23]

Those who pressed for a national policy of economic freedom were forced to develop a new rationale to pit against the prudence of the ages. The one that took shape began first with the assertion that wealth could best be achieved by increasing the volume of English trade and outselling foreign competitors in an expanded market. This advocacy of prosperity through growth was then linked to a new theory of human behavior that assumed an innate tendency to work harder and with more ingenuity when tempted by new consuming tastes. Writers attributed this economic rationality to human nature with more and more confidence as the seventeenth century progressed. Thus, John Briscoe claimed that people have a quick sense of "the Profit of their Labour, and will bestow their Cost and Pains in Proportion to the Worth of the Subject Matter and the Benefit they gather from their Industry." [24] Nicholas Barbon echoed the sentiment when he praised England's "Gothick" monarchy, "for men are most industrious, where they are most free, and

22. "A Discourse concerning the East-India Trade . . . a Joint-Stock Company [1697?]," in *A Collection of Scarce and Valuable Tracts . . . of the Late Lord Somers,* ed. Walter Scott, 13 vols. (London, 1813), X, 642.
   23. John Cary, *An Essay on the State of England in Relation to Its Trade* (Bristol, 1695), 1.
   24. [John Briscoe], *A Discourse of Money* (London, 1696), 22.

secure to injoy the Effects of their Labours."[25] England's "great Happiness," according to John Houghton, came not from jealous oversight of the French trade, but from the desire to consume, which puts "all upon an Industry, makes every one strive to excell his Fellow."[26] Arguing for a reduction in the interest rate, Sir Josiah Child extolled the capacity of competition to be a "spur to invention, as well as Industry and Good Husbandry."[27]

Confident of the human propensity to improve society as people improved themselves, economic writers could press for economic freedom. Beneath these arguments was the radical contention that there was a natural social order that rendered useless efforts to direct human endeavors. If England wished to enjoy the same prosperity as the Dutch, one writer insisted, it must not attempt to do by compulsion "which with them is done by nature."[28] There can be no unprofitable trades for the nation, Sir Dudley North maintained, because if they are unprofitable "men leave it off," later adding that "no People ever yet grew rich by Policies; but it is Peace, Industry, and Freedom that brings Trade and Wealth, and nothing else."[29] An anonymous pamphleteer associated the restraint of trade with an earlier, ignorant age "when Navigation was judged a Mystery next to that of the Black Art," but, he continued, "as Trade and Commerce became familiar in the World, the Wisdom of Government made the Privileges of Trade universal to their Subjects."[30]

These writers had caught hold of a dynamic rhythm in economic growth. Pushing hard for the acceleration of commercial activities, they became apostles for change—change in the number and kinds of merchants, changes in the tempo and patterns of marketing, change in the range and quantity of goods produced and sold. The acquisitive instinct, long suffered as a barely repressible vice, now shared in the respectability that naturalness acquired in seventeenth-

---

25. [Nicholas Barbon], *A Discourse of Trade* (London, 1690), 51.

26. John Houghton, *A Collection of Letters for the Improvement of Husbandry & Trade* (London, 1681), 60.

27. [Sir Josiah Child], *A Short Addition to the Observations Concerning Trade and Interest of Money* (London, 1668), 14.

28. *Interest of Money Mistaken* (London, 1668), 21.

29. [Sir Dudley North], *Discourses upon Trade* (London, 1691), viii, v.

30. *The Linnen and Woollen Manufactory Discoursed . . . and may now affect England* (London, 1691), 3–4.

century thought. The acceptance of private profit-seeking as a kind of natural force also tended, like Mun's earlier assertion of autonomous trade flows, to redirect attention from the central authority and its comprehensive purposes to the market behavior of individuals seeking satisfaction of personal goals. English economic commentators were articulating a new social reality in which the self-seeking drive appeared more powerful than institutional efforts to mold people's actions. The exploration of this new theme, moreover, was conducted in the scientific mode appropriate to natural phenomena.

A critical point in the model of the free-market economy developed at that time was the construction to be placed upon self-interest. If, as a growing number of writers began to assert, the market followed laws that were like those of the physical universe, regular and dependable, what provided this regularity? The only possible source given the social nature of the market was human nature—the existence of uniform human tendencies like self-interest and the striving for self-improvement through economic efforts which Adam Smith immortalized. And, although the complete role of self-interest was never clearly worked out, as in *The Wealth of Nations,* the parts were suggested. What was also significant in this description of self-interest was its resoundingly materialistic formulation. Not through the cultivation of virtue or wisdom did one fulfill self-interest, but, rather, through ambition, desire, and a rising standard of living achieved by individual application of industry, ingenuity, and effort.

Without addressing political or social questions, the economic writers of the late seventeenth century created a rationale for individual freedom along lines that subtly undermined the traditional social order. The oversight of one's superior became a less dependable guide toward productive activities than the promptings of personal ambition. General expectations of greater productivity led to the encouragement of all to become more ingenious and industrious. Both opinions carried leveling ideas. Commercial freedom, defended in the early seventeenth century as part of the subjects' rightful liberties, found new support at the close of the century because it promoted the general material welfare. Economic individualism acquired legitimacy as writers suggested that growth lay with releasing the economic energies of ordinary people.

For some writers the compatibility of competition, the motive of gain, material prosperity, and domestic harmony within the kingdom suggested that trade could create peace in the world. John Graunt, for instance, heralded the era of the new, honest, harmless policy of providing for peace and plenty, contrasting it with the former preoccupation of men to study how to supplant and overreach one another.[31] Stressing the mutuality of trade, Henry Robinson counseled moderation to his fellow Englishmen lest they be like Alexander the Great.[32] Critical of the Spanish and Portuguese for restricting entrance to their New World possessions, Rice Vaughan prophesied that "future times will find no part of the Story of this Age so strange, as that all the other States of *Europe* . . . have not combined together to enforce a liberty of Trade in the *West Indies;* the restraint whereof is against all Justice."[33] Trade had the same benign qualities for Coke: "but though all Nations be not of the same Religion, yet all Nations subsist in Society and Commerce; and as every man stands in need of being supplied by another, so does every Country. To restrain therefore the Society and Commerce of Nations to those of the same Religion, is to violate an Institution of God in the conservations of Humane Society, and to deny the benefits which places mutually receive from one another."[34] The most famous expression of this rising sentiment appeared in North's *Discourses Upon Trade,* where the nations of the world were compared to persons within one nation and "the loss of a Trade with one Nation, is not that only . . . but so much of the Trade of the World rescinded and lost, for all is combined together."[35]

Under the pressure of several hotly debated economic issues, these strains of economic analysis coalesced into a liberal consensus in the 1690s. At least a dozen different writers presented a prescription for economic growth which assumed that market relations possessed an order based upon dependable tendencies of human nature and that individual economic freedom promoted sustained commercial

31. John Graunt, *Natural and Political Observations* (London, 1662), 67–68.

32. Henry Robinson, *Englands Safety in Trades Encrease* (London, 1641), 57–58.

33. Rice Vaughan, *A Discourse of Coin and Coinage . . . and the Reasons* (London, 1675), 134.

34. Coke, *England's Improvements.*

35. [North], *Discourses upon Trade,* viii.

development. Left alone, market participants would increase the range of goods available under the stimulus of desire and competition. The consequence would be an expansive program of more goods at lower prices reaching a larger pool of potential buyers. The implications for the moral and social basis of the kingdom were obvious. Prosperity was linked to upward mobility and the ambitions of the common person. Self-interest was given a constructive role as a regulator of individual activity and a goad to industry and ingenuity.

These ideas, however, ran ahead of social developments. There were not enough jobs to bring everyone into the commercial economy. Woolen manufacturers and landlords were still concerned with the problem of wresting labor from a technically free working class, and William III's ascension triggered a fierce rivalry between France and England. In a series of pivotal acts, Parliament between 1696 and 1724 seized the initiative and redirected English economic development.[36] To the political stability that J. H. Plumb has described as coming swiftly to England was added the economic buttress of a national commercial policy, and "Mercantilism" with a capital "M" was created to supply the theoretical underpinnings.[37] The ambit of freedom for the individual entrepreneur grew throughout the eighteenth century, but Parliament directed the flow of investments and trade through protective legislation and statutory augmentation of the navigation system. Visions of a benign world of free trade, such as North projected, were replaced by the muscular prose of balance-of-trade theorists. The forward thrust of liberal economic reasoning was arrested, but an intellectual legacy was left for the champions of a market society to draw upon.[38]

In this reshuffling of economic ideas at the end of the seventeenth century, Locke played a critical role. It is perhaps not too much of

36. For the shifts of economic orientation see P. G. M. Dickinson, *The Financial Revolution in England: A Study in the Development of Public Credit 1688–1756* (London, 1967), 6–14; Ralph Davis, "English Foreign Trade, 1700–1774," *Economic History Review*, 15 (1962), 295–303; "The Rise of Protection in England, 1689–1786," *Economic History Review*, 19 (1966), 306–317.

37. J. H. Plumb, "The Growth of the Electorate in England from 1600 to 1715," *Past and Present* (1969), 90–116; *The Growth of Political Stability in England 1675–1725* (London, 1967).

38. See Chapters 1 and 2.

an exaggeration to say that he sacrificed certain observations about the nature of money in order to assert in the most uncompromising terms that the most basic market relations were beyond the power of King or Parliament to change. As one of his contemporaries observed, Locke claimed that governments "had no more power in Politicks than they have in Naturals."[39] A succession of economic theorists had contributed to the credibility of this claim by redefining the social acts of working, paying, buying, selling, contracting, investing, and lending as parts of a natural order. When Smith gathered the material for his stunning demolition of "the mercantile system," the most controversial part of his case did not need to be made! The propensity of human beings to seek their self-improvement through truck and barter and the inexorable momentum toward efficiency and expansion through natural market behavior— in short, the psychological foundation for his system—had already been laid in the seventeenth century. Working without an intellectual tradition and addressing themselves principally to practical problems, these writers had presented their most subversive propositions as facts arrived at through observation and inference. In the political sphere their most important contribution lay in what they denied: the capacity of government to alter basic economic relations and to control for better or worse the pursuit of profit.

The productive resources that were developed in the seventeenth century had called forth an expansion of the market both internally and externally. Continued prosperity required new levels of consumption, as North, Barbon, Houghton, Humphrey Mackworth, Francis Gardner, and Henry Martyn had so correctly explained at the end of the seventeenth century. These writers were no more flattering in their descriptions of the poor than their contemporaries, but they were sufficiently detached from the social sensibilities of the upper class to recommend envy, ambition, emulation, and the acquisition of new consuming tastes as the most promising means of spreading economic rationalism throughout the society. They treated members of society as market participants, ascribing to all the capacity for rational behavior. Most important, they projected

39. [Henry Layton], *Observations Concerning Money and Coin, and especially those of England* (London, 1697), 15.

into the future a vision of material progress wrought not through virtue and independence but rather through natural self-interest. Contrary to other reformers, the economic liberals claimed that the work habits of the poor were sooner changed through hope of gain than hope of heavenly reward. While their theoretical insights went undeveloped for another eighty years, their social assumptions were picked up and elaborated by those men and women who had hitched their wagons to the star of economic growth.

This upwardly mobile group from the lower ranks of society—craftsmen, mechanics, tradesmen, commercial farmers, and proprietors of small manufacturing firms—prospered during the middle decades of the eighteenth century. D. E. C. Eversley has pinpointed the widening of this stratum as the most significant change in English society. Within a thirty-year period the number of families with an income between £50 and £400 increased enough to make the purchasing power of "this free, mobile, prudent section of the population" a principal force behind the industrial revolution.[40] Similarly, Harold Perkin has called attention to those English men and women in the eighteenth century who moved from the lower classes to an aspiring middle class. Behind their demographic and economic growth Perkin found a psychological force propelling them toward consumption and the acquisition of a conspicuous, respectable status.[41] More recently Neil McKendrick has argued that the social ambitions and cravings of lower-class English men and women pushed wives and children into the labor market where they were able to swell significantly the aggregate family earnings.[42] Behind the dramatic increase in home demand in the eighteenth century there stands a crucial shift of social preferences, as the desire to enhance purchasing power replaced the traditional propensity of the poor to work only long enough to meet subsistence demands.

40. D. E. C. Eversley, "The Home Market and Economic Growth in England, 1750–1780," in *Land, Labour and Population in the Industrial Revolution*, ed. E. L. Jones and G. E. Mingay (New York, 1967), 259.

41. H. J. Perkin, "The Social Causes of the British Industrial Revolution," *Transactions of the Royal Historical Society*, 18 (1968), 135–136.

42. Neil McKendrick, "Home Demand and Economic Growth: A New View of the Role of Women and Children in the Industrial Revolution," in *Historical Perspectives*, ed. Neil McKendrick, 187–202.

These men and women had no reason to identify themselves with the historic ranks of English society. They did not share the distinguished family origins of their social superiors. Nor did they possess the great wealth of financiers and merchants. They were not candidates for that "sponsored mobility" through which elites had recruited the talented from the lower orders throughout the ages.[43] What this group represented was a redrawing of the social structure, a bulge beneath the apex, insistently growing and awkwardly unassimilable into traditional social groupings. Clearly inferior to the educated, independently wealthy members of the upper class, they were equally set apart from the underemployed poor. Through their own exertions they had secured a stake in their country's prosperity. Their loyalties lay with future possibilities. A return to the good old days of prescribed place and uncorrupted virtue held little appeal for them.

In the fifty years before the Revolution, the American colonies underwent a period of striking economic growth.[44] Despite the popularity of the austere truths of classical republicanism, American colonists from all walks of life were infected by new economic ambitions in the middle decades of the eighteenth century. British commercial policies had greatly enhanced the wealth-making prospects of Americans. The much-maligned Navigation Acts protected colonial entry into a number of profitable trades, and the colonists responded to this enlarged scope for economic initiative and throve. During the middle years of the century there was simple expansion: more people—immigrant families, indentured servants, slaves, and a large natural increase   along with more acreage brought under cultivation and a larger volume of exports. In the third quarter of the century there was a rise in the standard of living, made possible in part by developments in the English economy. Long-term credit and cheaper manufactured goods brought both capital and new consuming tastes within the reach of the great body of ordinary colonists. The flow of English investments spilled over its regular channels and reached new commercial debtors among small farmers

43. Lawrence Stone, "Social Mobility in England, 1500–1700," *Past and Present* (1966), 21.

44. Marc Egnal, "The Economic Development of the Thirteen Continental Colonies, 1720 to 1775," *William and Mary Quarterly*, 32 (1975), 191–222.

and tradesmen. The buoyancy of the great Atlantic trade stimulated a continuous exploitation of the natural resources of North America. Recent studies have begun to document the impact of mid-century European food shortages upon American agriculture.[45] New urban networks were laid down in the South. Land reserves disappeared in New England. Commodity exports rose to impressive new levels. Access to markets provided strong inducements to colonists to invest their resources in market ventures, while at the same time creating new partisans of economic growth. The number of farmers, the variety of crops, and the diversity of markets meant, moreover, that no one group of colonists could cut off the economic opportunities of others. Thus there was no check to the inherent tendency of the market influence to permeate the entire society.

The pervasiveness of colonial landholding in the seventeenth century had led to an enlarged electorate; the commercial transformation of the economy in the eighteenth century politicized that electorate. The colonial gentry did not possess the power of Whig magnates to control the legislative process. Rather they were forced to establish conciliatory relations with their constituents.[46] Unwittingly gentlemen contributed to the political education of ordinary voters when they mobilized their support. Economic issues almost always became political ones. As community after community became embroiled in factional disputes, the inner spring of profit and power came under the scrutiny of the plain members of society. Awareness of the self-interested response of elite officeholders sapped the moral base of deference in the colonies, but it also suggested a commonality upon which a new political system might be built.

The capacity of the market to introduce strife in colonial communities has been well documented; less well explored is the way in which participation in a developing economy permitted ordinary men to extend their powers and turn their practical accomplishments

45. Carville Earle and Ronald Hoffman, "Staple Crops and Urban Development in the Eighteenth-Century South," *Perspectives in American History*, 10 (1976), 7–78; James G. Lydon, "Philadelphia's Commercial Expansion, 1720–1739," *Pennsylvania Magazine of History and Biography*, 91 (1967), 401–418.

46. Gary B. Nash, "The Transformation of Urban Politics 1700–1765," *Journal of American History*, 60 (1973), 605–632; John C. Rainbolt, "The Alteration in the Relationship between Leadership and Constituents in Virginia, 1660 to 1720," *William and Mary Quarterly*, 27 (1970), 411–434; Dietmar Rothermund, *The Layman's Progress: Religious and Political Experience in Colonial Pennsylvania, 1740–1770* (Philadelphia, 1961).

into claims for greater esteem. As men persevered in pursuing material gain, some writers began to describe self-interest as a legitimate force. This new social perspective was most frequently expressed when economic policies were debated. Georgia settlers, for instance, argued for an unrestrained access to the market as a basic economic right in their struggles with the philanthropic Trustees.[47] Paper money and land-bank schemes provoked justifications which echoed the liberal affirmations of English economic writings at the end of the seventeenth century. The specific themes that were to prove subversive of traditional notions of social order on both sides of the Atlantic were the endorsements of consumption, the expectation of continued material advance, and the encouragement of individual initiative. Offering "A Word of Comfort to a Melancholy Country," John Wise entered the fray over paper money as a proponent of an expanded currency for "a Wise and Bustling People." Starve the farmer out of his profits, Wise said, and "you will then much disanimate one of the best Servants to the Crown, and the Means of your Plenty, your Safety, and Flourishing Condition."[48] Francis Rawle in Pennsylvania also endorsed the idea of economic animation from the bottom up, and Benjamin Franklin made explicit the importance of paper money to the prosperity of ordinary colonists. Specie shortages, he said, only aided the engrossers of land.[49] In the Massachusetts General Court, Robert Zemsky found that backbenchers tended to turn all issues into economic ones and resisted the leadership of the elite committeemen who ran the Court to gain their ends.[50] The insistent pressure to extend economic opportunity in most colonies led to modifications in debtor legislation as well as land and tax policies.[51] In New York the participation of artisans

47. [Thomas Stephens and Richard Everhard], "A Brief Account of the Causes that Have Retarded the Progress of the Colony of Georgia in America . . . on the Same Subject [1743]," *Collections of the Georgia Historical Society*, II (1892), 87–161.

48. [John Wise], "A Word of Comfort to a Melancholy Country [1721]," in *Colonial Currency Reprints 1682–1751*, ed. Andrew McFarland Davis, 4 vols. (Boston, 1911), II, 186.

49. Richard A. Lester, "Currency Issues to Overcome Depressions in Pennsylvania, 1723 and 1729," *Journal of Political Economy*, 46 (June 1938), 350; [Benjamin Franklin], "A Modest Enquiry into the Nature and Necessity of a Paper-Currency [1729]," in *Colonial Currency Reprints*, ed. Davis, II, 347, 342–343.

50. Robert M. Zemsky, "Power, Influence, and Status: Leadership Patterns in the Massachusetts Assembly, 1740–1755," *William and Mary Quarterly*, 26 (1969), 513–518.

51. Peter J. Coleman, *Debtors and Creditors in America: Insolvency, Imprisonment for Debt, and Bankruptcy, 1607–1900* (Madison, 1974), 6–7.

and small proprietors in public debates registered itself in new references to "a middle class" ranged between the older division of rich and poor.[52] The fights over land, banks, and taxes made people acutely aware of the tension between prosperity and social cohesion, but they also encouraged them to find a new principle of order. Particularly astute observers of the American scene, like Franklin and Robert Livingston, early conceded the dominance of self-interest and stoically accepted the limited moral horizon implied. Conservatives bemoaned the leveling tendencies and decried the unsettling effect of change on property. Champions of commerce also emerged and, like the seventeenth-century English economists, linked material progress to the upward strivings of ordinary men and women.

Policy debates were not the only avenues for expressing the ideas and values of the aspiring members of the middling ranks. Two of the most prolific writers of the period, Daniel Defoe and Richard Steele, purveyed the mores of the upwardly mobile in novels and essays. As Kramnick has shrewdly observed, Defoe and Steele went far beyond the mere recounting of middle-class success stories to claim for their heroes and heroines the rewards that England's chief families were accustomed to monopolizing. Disdained by their literary and social superiors, Defoe and Steele found their readership among the growing bourgeois reading public who shared their optimism, their enthusiasm for economic progress, and their approval of a new distribution of profit and power.[53] Franklin's father had a well-worn copy of Defoe's *Essay upon Projects,* and perhaps to return the compliment for his colonial popularity Defoe had Moll Flanders emigrate![54]

52. Beverly McAnear, "Mr. Robert R. Livingston's Reasons Against a Land Tax," *Journal of Political Economy,* 48 (1940), 73.

53. Kramnick, *Bolingbroke and His Circle,* 188–200, 201–204. Although Isaac Kramnick includes Bernard Mandeville among Robert Walpole's supporters, Mandeville should be distinguished from the proponents of economic liberalism, for his ideas were an endorsement of neither economic rationalism nor economic growth through lower-class mobility. See Nathan Rosenberg, "Mandeville and Laissez-Faire," *Journal of the History of Ideas,* 24 (1963), 186–187.

54. In his autobiography Benjamin Franklin wrote that the *Essays upon Projects* "gave me a Turn of Thinking that had an influence on some of the principal Events of my life," *The Autobiography of Benjamin Franklin,* ed. Leonard W. Labaree, Ralph Ketcham, Helen C. Boatfield, and Helene F. Fineman (New Haven, 1964), 58.

There was little in the self-assertions of economic disputants or the vulgar association of economic competence with social worth to appeal to the arbiters of taste in Augustan England. And here it is important to question the character of the Opposition literature which Neo-Whig historians have found so important to the articulate colonial mind. Pocock has suggested that insufficient attention has been given to the fact that the language and concepts taken from the English Opposition were clearly premodern. His admonition is salutary. However, set against the articulation of a liberal vision of society, both the Dissenters and Bolingbroke's Country party are more understandable as antimodern. Writing in the midst of dramatic economic and social changes, they evoked the classical theory of mixed government to stay the course of modernization and to forestall an accommodation to the economic development that would undercut the values they esteemed and the social order that supported those values. The qualities of the liberal model of society that attracted intelligent but uncultivated men and women on the make were exactly those that made that model distasteful to their betters. Where Bolingbroke and Jonathan Swift decried the vulgarization of taste and the spurning of England's natural leaders, moralists bemoaned the destruction of the bonds of community. Radical Whigs like John Trenchard and Thomas Gordon rejected material progress because it was not based upon the triumph of virtue.[55] In a frequently quoted passage from *Cato's Letters,* Trenchard and Gordon criticized charity schools for giving poor children ambitions above their station and making them unfit for the servant class to which they were destined.[56] Similarly Pocock has found the eighteenth-century Harringtonians to be conservative, anticapitalist proponents of a static economy of masters and servants.[57] Richard Paine, Granville Sharpe, James Burgh, and John Cartwright were concerned with questions of conscience and moral will. Commerce figured in their thinking as the source of vanities, luxury, and irreligion, and the English Dissenters, according to Staughton Lynd, were "particularly receptive to the libertarian asceticism of Rousseau's

55. Kramnick, *Bolingbroke and His Circle,* 243–252.

56. Staughton Lynd, *Intellectual Origins of American Radicalism* (New York, 1968), 35.

57. J. G. A. Pocock, "Machiavelli, Harrington, and English Political Ideologies in the Eighteenth Century," *William and Mary Quarterly,* 22 (1965), 575.

teachings on' education, on luxury, on natural piety, and the Wisdom of the heart."[58] In this their concerns were echoed in the colonies where, as John Crowley has demonstrated, the tensions between virtue and commerce were more often stretched on a religious frame than on the political one of Opposition writers.[59]

The intertwining of evangelical piety and lower-class claims to equal social consideration makes it difficult to differentiate the language of Protestant salvation from that of secular liberalism, but the evidence indicates that revolutionary zeal for regeneration from republicanism passed swiftly into a stronger feeling for the democratization of opportunity that a particular kind of republicanism made possible.[60] It was this pressure coming from the upwardly mobile that divided the American gentry and turned the resistance movement into a revolution. The liberal vision of society as a reflection of a natural economic order challenged two crucial concepts in the reigning colonial ideology: rationalism and self-interest. Among the colonial gentry, it was assumed that only gentlemen were capable of rational behavior; the lower orders were creatures of passion. Rationality stemmed from learning and reflection. The economic theorists, however, had claimed that in their economic dealings all men acted as rationalists, carefully calculating the means to their ends and accepting the order and discipline necessary for success. Similarly, the idea of self-interest underwent a metamorphosis. No one doubted its salience in American life; the question was the construction to be put upon it. For members of the colonial elite the pervasiveness of the motive of gain was cause for cynicism at best, despair at worst.[61] But what struck the colonial gentry as a lamentable human failing was hailed by their inferiors as an extension of individual freedom. As Bernard Friedman and Gary B. Nash

58. Lynd, *Intellectual Origins,* 32.

59. J. E. Crowley, *This Sheba, Self: The Conceptualization of Economic Life in Eighteenth-Century America* (Baltimore, 1974), 76–85.

60. Gordon S. Wood, *The Creation of the American Republic 1776–1787* (Chapel Hill, 1969), 471–483; James Henderson, "The Structure of Politics in the Continental Congress," in *Essays on the American Revolution,* ed. Stephen G. Kurtz and James H. Hutson (Chapel Hill, 1973), 183–184.

61. McAnear, "Mr. Robert R. Livingston's Reasons Against a Land Tax"; Robert M. Weir, "'The Harmony We Were Famous For': An Interpretation of Pre-Revolutionary South Carolina Politics," *William and Mary Quarterly,* 26 (1969), 474–479.

have detailed, the popular agitators in the urban politics in America elevated their goals to a universal law of self-interest.[62] Although the gentry was predisposed to see lower-class striving as a dangerous leveling tendency and the city crowds' exuberant political activity as proof of irrationality, the upwardly mobile themselves were asserting something new about human society. Having improved their lot in an open contest, they endorsed the liberal vision of a society of undifferentiated competitors.

To the tradesmen, mechanics, and newly launched merchants of America, the British measures of the 1760s represented not corruption, but intrusion. The rhetoric they employed in their protests revealed a deep animus toward Great Britain and a much greater detachment from the intellectual traditions of the Mother Country than their superiors showed. A member of the Maryland gentry at the time of the Stamp Act crisis confided to a friend that "the ties of blood, religion, or patriotism will not avail against self-interest."[63] But on the streets the popular leaders put the assertion of self in a much nobler light. As one of the New York Sons of Liberty declared, "*Self Interest* is the grand Principle of all Human Actions; it is unreasonable and vain to expect Service from a Man who must act contrary to his own Interests to perform it." Another spoke of "the principle of self Preservation, self love, [as] tending in the highest degree to the general Benefit of the Whole and every Part."[64] Here again self-interest is seen as a universal and benign regulator of human conduct.

The vision of free trade also reappeared. Christopher Gadsden, leader of the Charleston Sons of Liberty, contrasted in 1766 "a free and open trade" with one limited to "discontented monopolizing selfish Great Britain," and then, stirred by the thought, he exclaimed, "What a boundless & alluring prospect of advantage must even the most distant Idea of an open Trade to all . . . the

62. Bernard Friedman, "The Shaping of Radical Consciousness in Provincial New York," *Journal of American History*, 56 (1970), 781–801; Nash, "Transformation of Urban Politics." On this point see also the essays by Eric Foner, Dirk Hoerder, and Edward Countryman in *The American Revolution: Explorations in the History of American Radicalism*, ed. Alfred F. Young (DeKalb, Ill., 1976).

63. As quoted in Ronald Hoffman, *A Spirit of Dissension: Economics, Politics, and the Revolution in Maryland* (Baltimore, 1973), 91.

64. As quoted in Friedman, "Shaping of Radical Consciousness," 789, 792.

World be to the Americans."[65] Patrick Henry echoed this sentiment in imagery that evoked the shackled slaves of his Virginia. "Why should we fetter commerce?" Henry asked. "If a man is in chains, he droops and bows to the earth, for his spirits are broken . . . but let him twist the fetters from his legs, and he will stand erect . . . Fetter not commerce," Henry went on, "let her be as free as the air."[66] The rhetorical flourishes here convey the almost rhapsodic association some Americans drew between material ambitions and the spirit of freedom. The irenic and egalitarian themes that had appeared socially subversive to upper-class Englishmen struck just the right note with Americans seeking to set their undoubted commercial strength in the proper moral frame. They suggest also why the social theories that grew out of the observation of market behavior offered the means of freeing liberty itself from a long captivity in English history.

There was more than the British connection at risk for the gentry in the resistance movement. Also threatened was a conception of the people as simultaneously too irrational to govern and too removed from ambition to be tempted to power. When radicals defended resistance with the language of liberalism their words spoke to revolution as well as rebellion. The blows that cut the tie with Britain could also pierce the thinly disguised social control that went along with the gentry's romanticizing of the people as a bulwark of virtue.[67] In the mobilization of ideas in the 1760s there were both the origins of a modern ideology for America as well as the roots of the regenerative republicanism that Bailyn and Wood have so carefully retraced.

When the colonists began to protest the statutes which trumpeted Parliament's intention to revamp the empire, they had at their disposal not one social theory, but two: the ornate concept of constitutional balances and civic virtue of classical republicanism, and the simple—simplistic even—affirmations about human nature by the economic observers. The colonial gentry, future Loyalists and

---

65. "Two Letters by Christopher Gadsden, Feb., 1766," ed. Robert M. Weir, *South Carolina Historical Magazine,* 75 (1974), 175.

66. William Wirt Henry, *Patrick Henry: Life, Correspondence and Speeches,* 3 vols. (New York, 1891), II, 192.

67. Buel, "Democracy and the American Revolution," 187–190.

Patriots alike, read the Stamp Act in the light of Opposition truths about tyranny and corruption. But the colonial gentry as a group could contain neither the polemic nor the protests. Like all perceptions of reality, the one which they had adopted constrained as well as liberated. Its anticommercial bias, rooted in the politics of Walpole's England, prevented an appreciation of the progressive social developments of the eighteenth century. Encoded as it was in a gloss on English history, it could provoke only resistance, but the American Revolution developed its revolutionary character not by redeeming the rights of Englishmen, but by denying English sovereignty and the conceptual order which tied liberty to the English constitution. Deliverance from the strictures of classical republicanism came from the ideology of liberalism, from a belief in a natural harmony of benignly striving individuals saved from chaos by the stability worked into nature's own design. First expressed in very local clashes over economic rights in the middle decades of the eighteenth century, this naturalistic recasting of human experience appeared as the universal law of self-interest among radical agitators in the 1760s and acquired final validation as part of the plan of nature and of nature's God in Thomas Jefferson's apotheosis to individual liberty. The association of trade with a natural social order, so forcefully asserted in *Common Sense,* made it possible to democratize liberty by dissociating it from upper-class fears of popular strivings. By substituting a universal law of self-interest for a historical theory about cycles of corruption, American radicals were able to deny the political relevance of the distinctions between the few and the many. Their new social theory not only justified a revolution against an intrusive sovereign, it also offered ordinary people an escape from the self-denying virtue of their superiors.

America was not to see a replay of the English politics of court and country because liberalism found an occasion for winning converts. Alexander Hamilton conveyed very well a sense of dismay at the appearance of this rival paradigm. Writing during the War for Independence, Hamilton reported that "there are some, who maintain, that trade will regulate itself, and is not to be benefitted by the encouragements, or restraints of government." Such persons, Hamilton continued, "will imagine, that there is no need of a common directing power," and he concluded, "This is one of those wild speculative paradoxes, which have grown into credit among us, contrary to the uniform practice and sense of the most enlightened nations."[68] The paradox for Hamilton was the idea of order without an orderer or, as he put it, "a common directing power." Yet this was exactly the appeal of a market society for Americans—its capacity to enlist the voluntary efforts of men and thereby permit the dismantling of the customary institutions of control. This possibility gave to liberalism that utopian quality which infected men of all ranks. John Stevens, scion of a prominent New Jersey family, understood what Hamilton had failed to comprehend. In 1787, Stevens wrote an essay chiding those who thought that the United States would relive the history of other nations. Reversing the flow of truth from past to present, Stevens saluted the future when America would have the honor of teaching mankind what he called "this important, this interesting lesson," that man is actually capable of governing himself.[69] The microcosm and macrocosm condensed in Stevens' statement is instructive, for the Americans' claim to self-government was both personal and political and rested on the faith that there existed a natural order which began inside the individual.

Exploring the themes of virtue and commerce, Pocock has observed that "men cannot do what they have no means of saying they have done; and what they do must in part be what they can say and conceive that it is."[70] Historians, then, must pay due attention to the "languages" available to participants in any given historical moment. Bailyn and Wood discovered the resonating phrases of the English Opposition in the rhetoric of the Revolution. It was a language with roots at least a generation old, according to Bailyn. They had been planted in the colonial gentry through the classical education given the young men and nourished through the persistent

68. Continentalist No. V (April 1782), in *The Papers of Alexander Hamilton,* ed. Harold C. Syrett and Jacob E. Cooke, 15 vols. (New York, 1961–), III, 76.

69. [John Stevens], *Observations on government* (New York, 1787), 53.

70. Pocock, "Virtue and Commerce in the Eighteenth Century," 122; Bailyn, *Ideological Origins of the American Revolution,* 23–26; Jack P. Greene, "Political Mimesis: A Consideration of the Historical and Cultural Roots of Legislative Behavior in the British Colonies in the Eighteenth Century," *American Historical Review,* 75 (1969), 337–360. For the problems that the gentry's ideas pose for explaining the revolution see Pauline Maier, "Why Revolution? Why Democracy?," *Journal of Interdisciplinary History,* 6 (1976), 715.

effort of members of the colonial elite to emulate their English counterparts, to yield to that mimetic urge which Greene has so well detailed.[71] When men outside the close-knit colonial establishments entered the public discourse in the Stamp Act crisis they frequently employed the language which the economic liberals had developed in the late seventeenth century. The straightforward assertions and simplistic psychological truths found confirmation in the education received by mechanics, tradesmen, and farmers. The social origins of this protean theme in American revolutionary ideology, however, should not obscure the intellectual appeal that economic liberalism had to men from all walks of life. The vision of the democratization of material well-being contributed to the idealistic strain that Wood has identified with republicanism, for it was not just a government of laws which Americans celebrated in their newfound enthusiasm for republican forms in 1776, but specifically the use of constitutions to limit government power and thereby release the energies of republican citizens. This view of limited government drew its theoretical support from the seventeenth-century English economic writers who had demonstrated the existence of social relations independent of formal institutions. A new image of human nature—*homo faber,* Edward Hundert has termed it—was joined with a conception of society knit together not by rank or religion but by profitable labor. Liberalism in America became more than an ideological gloss on market economics; it was a description of a modern utopia which could garner the loyalties of a broad range of Americans. In the absence of a visible past and of institutions to enforce deference, the workings of the market—no respecter of persons—had gone a long way toward creating an undifferentiated society of private negotiators. America was rich with new possibilities. The economic theory of England's first liberals offered a language for discussing them, and the American Revolution created the need for an ideology which could lead men with a good conscience from a defense of the rights of the English to an articulation of the rights of man.

71. E. J. Hundert, "The Making of *Homo Faber:* John Locke between Ideology and History," *Journal of the History of Ideas,* 33 (1972), 3–22. See also Alan Ryan, "Locke and the Dictatorship of the Bourgeoisie," *Political Studies,* 13 (1965), 219–230.

7

John Adams and the
New Republican Synthesis

EARLY AMERICAN historians have created a new republican synthesis which attempts to explain how colonial agitators became Founding Fathers.[1] The historians who have produced this synthesis began by exploring the central role which certain key ideas had in shaping the revolutionary events from the 1760s to the close of the eighteenth century. They also have moved toward an understanding of the interaction of thought and action. The resulting synthesis is a blend of idealist and behaviorist concepts in which ideas are seen as having operative force through their control of experience. A particular society affirms certain facts and values because of their capacity to explain realities, but once adopted the ideas impose themselves upon subsequent social perceptions. Random experiences become ideologized, given meaning through the medium of a chosen intellectual formulation. The new republican synthesis, thus, is more than a reconstruction of past thought; it is the description of a socially ordered consciousness which mediated between belief and

1. The principal contributors to this synthesis have been Caroline Robbins, Bernard Bailyn, Gordon Wood, Richard Buel, Edmund Morgan, and Cecelia Kenyon. The most penetrating analysis of the blending of the idealist and behaviorist approaches is Gordon S. Wood's "Rhetoric and Reality in the American Revolution," *William and Mary Quarterly*, 23 (1966), 3–32. For a review of the literature over the past two decades see Robert E. Shalhope, "Toward a Republican Synthesis: The Emergence of an Understanding of Republicanism in American Historiography," *William and Mary Quarterly*, 39 (1972), 49–80.

behavior in the revolutionary era. Specifically, the new synthesis suggests that colonial experiences predisposed Americans to certain truths about republican government which in turn controlled their responses to later events.

As an explanation for the interaction of experience and reflection applied to a specific historical period, the new republican synthesis has much to offer. Its creation demonstrates the influence which the last half-century of scholarship in the social sciences has had upon historians. The mindless determinism of single social forces has been displaced by more supple concepts about the determining power of cultural perspectives, common assumptions and selective world-views. Attention has been directed away from the universal and refocused on the particularizing force of shared experiences. Following the leads of anthropologists and sociologists, historians are trying to locate the roots of society's cohesion in the social organization of experience.[2]

For the historians who have built the new republican synthesis, the seminal ideas which American colonists affirmed came from the English Dissenting tradition. Through the lens of this intellectual formulation, colonists viewed their world, identified the threats to their goals, arranged their social priorities, and screened out behavior incongruent with its basic affirmations. More than anything else the Dissenting tradition offered a critique of power and a rationale for self-government and individual liberty. In this view the American Revolution did not just formalize a break with Great Britain; it precipitated an immediate acceptance of republicanism with an explicit rejection of monarchy and an English-style aristocracy.[3] By assuming that a commitment to republican principles created a common frame of reference within which American political figures operated after Independence, the authors of this synthesis, however, have created a conceptual limbo for the angry political battles of Washington's administration. There is little within the

2. See Peter L. Berger and Thomas Luckmann, *The Social Construction of Reality* (New York, 1966).

3. John R. Howe, Jr., "Republican Thought and Political Violence in the 1790s," *American Quarterly*, 19 (1967), 153; James Morton Smith, "The Transformation of Republican Thought, 1763–1878," in *Indiana Historical Society Lectures, 1967–1970* (Indianapolis, 1970), 42.

explanatory power of the new republican synthesis to show why veterans of two decades of popular politics became absorbed with fears of radical democracy on one side and aristocracy and monarchy on the other. Why, if there was an instantaneous conversion to republicanism, did the leading contenders for power during Washington's presidency break openly and angrily with one another because of their hostility to each other's basic political values?

These questions bear directly on the well-known changes in John Adams' political philosophy. Adams, whose contributions to the Massachusetts constitution of 1780 furnished important evidence about American republicanism, emerged in 1787 as a defender of the old, rejected rationale for England's mixed monarchy. Although Adams published his new position at the end of an eight-year residency in Europe, the current historiographical emphasis upon the particularizing effect of the American colonial experience has encouraged a neglect of his European experiences.[4] Yet the thoughts which Adams poured into his three-volume *Defence of the Constitutions of Government of the United States of America* were not anomalous, as Gordon Wood has recently described them.[5] They possessed the well-defined forms of the debates which engaged European reformers throughout Adams' long stay abroad. Reacting hostilely to the democratic theory put forward by the great French minister Baron Anne Robert Turgot, Adams had reassessed the political affirmations he had formed as a revolutionary leader. Under the pressure of this reassessment, he embraced the conservative reform position staked out by the *anglomanes,* as the French proponents of English institutions were called. In defining anew the essential components of a well-ordered state, Adams was also strongly influenced by Jean Louis De Lolme's *The Constitution of England.*

Reconstructing the European context for the changing political philosophy of John Adams points up a weakness of the new republican synthesis without, I hope, detracting from its great value in recapturing the sensibilities of the Revolutionary period. Treating

4. See especially John R. Howe, Jr., *The Changing Political Thought of John Adams* (Princeton, 1966), 45–60, 147; Gordon S. Wood, *The Creation of the American Republic, 1776–1787* (Chapel Hill, 1969), 568ff.

5. Ibid., 580. Wood entitles section 4 of chapter 14 "The Anomaly of the *Defence of the Constitutions.*"

the gestation period of American republicanism in cultural isolation has denied implicitly the continued interaction of Americans and Europeans. Focusing too exclusively upon the particularities of a specific society, the historians working with this synthesis have overemphasized the degree to which American experience was actually apprehended as being separate and self-contained. Eighteenth-century Americans were still profoundly influenced by their belief in the unity of human experience and the general application of universal truths. These assumptions propelled Americans into an order of reality with roots deeper than their immediate colonial past.

The Americans who struggled to form a new political ethos in the closing decades of the eighteenth century had a far different conception of social behavior than do contemporary scholars. They did not share the view that societies were separated from one another by decisive assumptions which channeled efforts and conditioned responses. Instead they operated within an empiricist scientific tradition in which universal laws operated inexorably. It may be clear to us that their models of social behavior were theoretical and their general principles a priori, but this was not their self-image. They brought to human history the ahistoricity of a natural scientist. Not having a sense that a historical event cannot be understood independent of when it happened, they collected historical instances as a naturalist collects fossils—as empirical data to be worked into general laws. The most that they would concede to human variety was the diversity of the physical world where different conditions prevailed but nevertheless were understandable within a unified structure of knowledge. For them there was no possibility of cultural autonomy where variants in human experience might be cultivated in self-sustained isolation. Every country needed a correct knowledge of the universal natural laws operating in human society because all were affected equally by them. No particular group was immune to the false notions of other people. Discovering universal truths about government was a common undertaking imposed upon all conscientious men.

IT WAS WITH this attitude toward political wisdom that Adams began his long, uninterrupted stay in Europe in November 1779.

The possibility of an American victory over Great Britain had begun to seem probable, and politically aware Europeans recognized the implications of such an event. By all measurable standards Great Britain should have been able to suppress the rebellion. If conventional forces failed, perhaps the power of enlightened principles was real. For the first time the moribund institutions of Europe appeared vulnerable. After independence was won, America became the object of a rigorous scrutiny. An increasing number of European intellectuals moved into circles where discussions centered on constitutional reform. This was the setting for the crystallizing of Adams' mature political convictions. Against the yardstick of European hopes, he took measure of his own conclusions about political possibilities. The problem now was not to challenge the prescriptive ruling right of an imperial government; it was to combat the French arguments for radical social reform based on the destruction of political inequalities. What his long stay in Europe did was to redirect Adams' attention away from the problems of institutionalizing self-government toward the European social theories which acquired credibility with the successful American Revolution.

Of crucial importance to Adams' own reevaluations were his relations with the radical French reformers. Franklin in his pursuit of European friends for the United States had developed a glittering circle of French acquaintances—the two Dukes de La Rochefoucauld, the Duchess d'Enville, Mme. d'Houdetot, Abbés Mably and Morellet, the great Turgot and his young disciples, Pierre Samuel Du Pont and the Marquis de Condorcet. For Turgot and his associates a restructuring of French institutions had appeared a necessity ever since Turgot's reforms as controller-general had been blocked by a combination of the specially privileged groups of France. In the years that followed his dismissal from office, Turgot had developed a political theory which challenged the idea Montesquieu made popular, the idea that the nobility and church (Montesquieu called them "different bodies") were indispensable buffers between ruler and ruled. Turgot's followers became convinced that truly national programs would never be developed as long as there existed centers of power and privilege independent of the central authority. Hence they watched American development carefully to see if the colonists were sufficiently enlightened to establish national governments. Turgot's disappointment with the state constitutions stemmed from his fear that the bicameral legislatures and elected governors were "pale imitations" of England's king and lords. Adams had a full opportunity to listen to the theoretical positions put forward over the dinner tables of these French reformers. Reminiscing on these days, he recalled that "Mr. Turgot, the Duke de La Rochefoucauld and Mr. Condorcet and others admired Mr. Franklin's Constitution and reprobated mine."[6] To the Turgotists, Pennsylvania with its one-house legislature represented the healthy, egalitarian, popular sovereignty they hoped to see institutionalized in America, while the Massachusetts constitution which Adams circulated for reading appeared as a lingering shadow of English conservatism.

Adams was shocked by the Turgotists' shallow grasp of political truths. He could only regard them as closet philosophers, woolly-minded idealists, men totally without any conception of man as a political animal. Feisty, combative, dogmatic John Adams saw clearly the threat which such notions of political equality and unchecked legislative power could do to the world. He deplored their hopes of achieving political purity simply by eliminating the special privileges of the nobility, their belief that human nature would respond freshly to a new political environment, their unwarranted assumption that the future could be radically different from the past. In the European discussions and writings at the time, there was only one alternative to pit against the egalitarian simplicity of radical French formulations: the example of England. Increasingly after 1785, two models of reform possibilities for Europe took shape: the Turgotist vision of national power expressing popular will through a single lawmaking body, and the English constitution with its division of power among the king, the nobility, and the untitled representatives of the nation's dominant interest groups.[7] In the rhetoric of the day, the French radicals represented a hope for genuine change and an enlightened rehabilitation of human nature. The *anglomanes* claimed history, not philosophy, as their teacher and professed to seek the maximum of liberty and civil order

6. *The Works of John Adams*, ed. Charles Francis Adams (Boston, 1850–1856), IX, 623.
7. See Chapter 9.

in a world unavoidably marred by selfish interests, vanity, and power struggles.

Turgotists wanted, above all, to gather the fundamental power of the people into one center. The *anglomanes,* on the contrary, feared such a concentration of power, believing that civil peace rested upon the careful fracturing and balancing of the diverse forces in society. The participants in these discussions did not discover the congruence between English forms, French forms, American forms; this was forced upon them by their assumption that there were common natural laws for all men.

Evidence that Adams formed his mature opinions about political organization in response to the polemical battles among European reformers during his long residency abroad abounds. First of all there is his diary, which sizzles with angry indignation at the Europeans' fuzzy-minded thinking. There are the letters in which Adams confided to friends his fears and his hopes. There is the chronicle of his own reading during the 1780s, left for posterity in a spicy, jabbing commentary scrawled across the margins of his books. There is the *Defence* itself, which proclaims in a lengthy eighteenth-century title that the book will defend the American state constitutions against the criticism of Turgot.[8] The most convincing proof of the influence of the European discussions upon Adams' ideas, however,

---

8. *The Adams Papers,* ed. L. H. Butterfield et al. (Cambridge, Mass., 1961), III, 28, 88–89, 91, 100–101, 110–111, 121; *The Works of John Adams,* ed. Adams, V, 491–496; ibid., X, 522–523, 26–36, 38–46; Zoltan Haraszti, *John Adams and the Prophets of Progress* (New York, 1964), 9, 21, 23, 45, 139–155. For the customary explanation that Shays's Rebellion prompted Adams to write the *Defence,* see *The Works of John Adams,* ed. Adams, I, 423–431; Haraszti, *John Adams and the Prophets of Progress,* 35; and, more recently, Page Smith, *John Adams* (Garden City, N.Y., 1962), II, 688. Both John and Abigail Adams contributed to the Shays's Rebellion theory with statements citing it as the prompting cause of the *Defence,* but Adams' letters written during the composition of the first volume do not support this theory. See Adams to Thomas Jefferson, Nov. 30, 1786, in *The Adams-Jefferson Letters,* ed. Lester J. Cappon (Chapel Hill, 1959), I, 163; Adams to James Warren, Jan. 9, 1787, in *Warren-Adams Letters,* Massachusetts Historical Society *Collections,* 75 (Boston, 1925), II, 280. Reminiscing in a letter to Samuel Perley, June 19, 1809 (*The Works of John Adams,* ed. Adams, IX, 623), Adams wrote of the *Defence:* "I never thought of writing till the Assembly of Notables in France had commenced a revolution, with the Duke de La Rochefoucauld and Mr. Condorcet at their head, who I knew would establish a government in one assembly, and that I knew would involve France and all Europe in all the horrors we have seen."

is the internal evidence of his great debt to De Lolme who became for *anglomanes* all over western Europe the most compelling advocate of England's balanced constitution. Nor did Adams fail to give credit to De Lolme. "Who can think of writing upon this subject after De Lolme, whose book is the best defence of the political balance of three powers that ever was written," he wrote in the *Defence*.[9] What Adams did in his much lengthier three volumes was to use the histories of Italian republics, Swiss cantons, and Germanic tribes to demonstrate the inexorability and universality of De Lolme's assertions.

De Lolme was a disappointed democrat who at the age of twenty-seven had emigrated from his native Geneva after the Geneva revolutionary crisis of 1768.[10] Less than three years from the time of his arrival in London, he had completed his *La Constitution de l'Angleterre,* the book that made his reputation and served for three generations of European readers as a model explanation of the peculiar political felicity of England.[11] De Lolme began his investigation with the assumption that England had what all Europe yearned for: the rule of law, the protection of individual rights, and the enjoyment of public stability without the price of repression. He asked how this happy state of affairs had come about and how it operated in and through English society. His answer was that in England the interaction of history and geography had produced a constitution which accommodated perfectly the nature of man. The differing estates, the lust for power at all levels, the restraint necessary in both the governed and the governing, the adaptability to modern change—all had found their place in the gothic richness of

9. *The Works of John Adams*, ed. Adams, IV, 358.

10. Facts about De Lolme found in standard works such as the *Dictionary of National Biography* have a common origin in Dr. Coote's introduction to the 1807 edition of De Lolme's *The Constitution of England*. See also Robert R. Palmer, *The Age of the Democratic Revolution: The Challenge* (Princeton, 1959), 135–136. Palmer is the first scholar since Correa Walsh (*The Political Science of John Adams* [New York, 1915]) to note the influence of De Lolme on Adams.

11. Published originally in De Lolme's native French in an Amsterdam edition of 1771, the first English edition (London, 1775) was followed by three slightly revised editions, the last (1874) becoming the model for all subsequent English editions. References in this article are to the London edition of 1793. A canvass of European and American libraries has turned up 45 editions in 99 years: 28 in English, 12 in French, 2 in German, and 1 each in Dutch, Spanish, and Russian.

the English constitution. Hardly a novel interpretation, but De Lolme brought it up to date and described its workings in marvelously persuasive prose.

De Lolme's influence upon Adams can best be summarized by considering the nature of the shift in Adams' political position. At the outset of his career in 1775, when he was giving advice to the colonial leaders involved in drafting new republican constitutions, Adams had recommended a type of balanced government in which the executive and the two houses of the legislature were empowered to check one another. In this first model of balanced government, Adams had prescribed a complete popular sovereignty where the people either directly or indirectly chose all of the officeholders. Writing to Richard Henry Lee, he said:

> Let a full and free representation of the people be chosen for a house of commons.
>
> Let the house choose, by ballot, twelve, sixteen, twenty-four, or twenty-eight persons, either members of the house, or from the people at large, as the electors please, for a council.
>
> Let the house and council, by joint ballot, choose a governor, annually, triennially, or septennially, as you will.
>
> Let the governor, council, and house, be each a distinct and independent branch of the legislature, and have a negative on all laws.[12]

In the *Defence,* which appeared eleven years later, Adams had drastically changed his concept of balance in government. Now it was not intragovernmental institutions which checked one another, but different elements in the society at large—the rich and the few—whose power was pitted against one another through a bicameral legislative body. What began as a check against the power ambitions of all men without respect for rank and state had ended up as an acceptance of permanent social inequalities integrated purposefully into the fabric of the political structure itself. So too in this same period had Adams drastically revised his estimate of the efficacy of elections. Writing to a delegate of the Second Continental Congress in January 1776, he declaimed, "there is not in all science a maxim more infallible than this, where annual elections end, there slavery begins." In 1787 he confided to Jefferson, "Elections, my dear sir, Elections to offices which are great objects of Ambition,

12. *The Works of John Adams,* ed. Adams, IV, 186.

I look at with terror." [13] The mechanism which had made popular, representative government possible was now suspect.

Less basic to his philosophy but more illustrative of how far Adams had slipped from his American moorings was his espousal in the *Defence* of the marks of deference, rank, position, and permanent privilege as political instruments to secure and perpetuate the political balance between the few and the many. Adams, who in 1765 had praised his forebears for having "had an utter contempt of all that dark ribaldry of hereditary, indefeasible right," filled his *Defence* with long passages extolling the absolute necessity of permanent elites: distinctions were inherent in human nature, he insisted, "legislation is not yet perfect enough to alter or to remedy, but by making the distinctions themselves legal, and assigning to each its share." "In every state, in Massachusetts, for example, there are inequalities which God and nature have planted there, and which no human legislator ever can eradicate." [14]

The influence of De Lolme's *Constitution of England* can be traced to the year and a half before Adams began writing the *Defence.* Although Adams' own copy of the book has never been found, his papers contain twenty-four closely copied verbatim notes from the 1784 edition of De Lolme's study, thus leaving a twenty-month maximum period between the publication of this edition and September 1786, when Adams began writing the *Defence.* [15] The notes are an accurate mirror of Adams' debt, for in them he gleaned De Lolme's central themes later developed in the *Defence:* the necessity of investing the executive power in one, exalted office; the importance of balancing the constitution through institutions representing the one, the few, and the many; and the paradox of increasing freedom by limiting the range of popular power. It is in this section of *The Constitution of England,* which Adams so carefully copied, that

13. Ibid., IV, 205; *The Adams-Jefferson Letters,* ed. Cappon, I, 213–214.

14. *The Works of John Adams,* ed. Adams, III, 454; ibid., V, 261; ibid., IV, 392.

15. Adams took notes from the 1784 edition because he included material which De Lolme had added to this edition, the last one revised by the author. Adams' notes cover pp. 1–98 of *The Constitution of England* in twelve pages, pp. 151–165 in four, and pp. 195–225 in fourteen. The notes can be found in the center of Reel 188, *Miscellany,* The Microfilms of the Adams Papers, Boston, 1959. The thirty-two pages of notes are in several hands and unfortunately were microfilmed out of order. Editor Marc Friedlaender supplied me with the correct sequence of signatures, which is 1, 7, 6, 8, 2, 3, 4, 5.

De Lolme explained the peculiar virtues of the English constitution in preventing the people from either encroaching on the executive power or engrossing the legislative function, both tendencies described as the most commonly fatal blows to republics. [16] In De Lolme's view it was not enough to have a separation of powers or a check upon the legislative power by means of a bicameral arrangement. The executive and the upper house must be removed from the control of the people. Indeed, they must be exalted not only by the constitution, but by a full measure of pomp and circumstance to impress the unattainability of their position upon the people. [17]

De Lolme did not believe that the legislature should have any share in the executive power, and it is interesting to find Adams criticizing the new federal constitution for giving the Senate a right of consent to executive appointments. [18] It is in this section of *The Constitution of England,* which Adams copied almost word for word, that De Lolme explained why the hereditary aspect of the chief magistrate and upper legislative house was so important. It was De Lolme's contention that the very homage paid a king and aristocracy preserved the civil rights of all, for it put these dignities beyond the reach of ambitious men who might overturn the constitution. De Lolme, extrapolating from the English experience, concluded that all societies sooner or later produced a single strong leader and a few powerful families, who by virtue of their ability would be able to consolidate their wealth and power and render them hereditary. He argued that it was better to admit this inevitability from the start and prepare a constitution which could balance and control all three elements in civil society: the one, the few, and the many. England, he summarized, had shown the world how this could be done, while at the same time giving to each only that degree of political power necessary to the functioning of the whole order. [19] Adams, following De Lolme, predicted the emergence within fifty

16. Although Palmer (*Age of the Democratic Revolution,* 273) says that Adams emphasized more explicitly the importance of a strong executive, I can find nothing in the *Defence* as emphatic as the section in *The Constitution of England* (191–213) copied by Adams.

17. De Lolme, *The Constitution of England,* 199–208.

18. Ibid., 191–192; Adams to Thomas Jefferson, Nov. 10, 1787, in *The Adams-Jefferson Letters,* ed. Cappon, I, 210.

19. De Lolme, *The Constitution of England,* 472–477.

years of family-based political parties for each of the thirteen states, one representing the people, the other the aristocrats.[20] Incessant civil war would ensue, he prophesied, if the states were not wise enough to change their constitutions.

Despite their rejection of radical reform, both Adams and De Lolme were liberal in the sense of cherishing public freedom and venerating the rule of law. The rein on their hopes was tied to their assumptions about man and civil society. It is certainly not irrelevant that they were natives of the two great repositories of Calvinist ethics: Geneva and Massachusetts Bay. Both men represented a kind of secularized Calvinism in which the basic and unchangeable corruption of man's nature determined the possible and the probable in politics. The ever-present foe to order and justice was man himself. The French intended to liberate man, and such a specter prompted Adams to make a critical retreat from his earlier position. Unlike the writers on English government in the radical Whig or Dissenting tradition, De Lolme favored an increase of government power to meet the needs of freedom and order. Nor was he reluctant to extend the prerogatives of the king. When Adams echoed him on this point, he was moving away from the liberal hope that curbing the powers of government would be the best way to protect civil liberty.

What Adams was at pains to insist upon in the *Defence* was that social and political equality is an impossible goal. "God Almighty has decreed in the creation of human nature an eternal aristocracy among men. The world is, always has been, and ever will be governed by it. All that policy and legislation can do is to check its force," he wrote in the margin of one of his books, and the sentiment is echoed in the *Defence*.[21] Quoting in full Machiavelli's assertion that society must recognize existing elites by giving them corresponding ranks in government, Adams elevated it to a "great truth, this eternal principle, without the knowledge of which every speculation upon government must be imperfect."[22] Adams never entertained the idea in the *Defence* that a constitution might safely ignore the ranks and orders in society. "To presume that an unmixed demo-

20. Haraszti, *John Adams and the Prophets of Progress*, 201.
21. *The Works of John Adams*, ed. Adams, V, 183.
22. Ibid., V, 183.

cratic government will preserve the laws," he wrote in the last volume, "is as mad as to presume that a king or senate will do it." [23]

Many may have shared Adams' description of the problem of power in a society. It was his solution that marked him as an aristocrat, for Adams' cure, following De Lolme's, was to create what America had never had: institutions giving permanent political power to an assigned group, "standing bodies," as he called them. Oblique as are many of Adams' comments on the need for "standing powers"—one of them is an index reference to the horrifying history of an Italian republic listed under "America, an excellent warning for"[24]—brought together they indicate that Adams expected America to follow Europe in its social patterns. Adams' sense of history was cyclical. He could predict continuities, but he was at a loss to understand what was becoming. At one point he drew attention to the democratization of landholding in the United States. But for him this was not going to be the basis for new institutions; rather it was evidence of the immaturity of the American states. He did not believe that the distinguishing social features of America in his day would continue. Despite all that was novel in the American experience, Adams anticipated nothing so much as a replay of an Italian tragedy. If he allowed that the America of 1787 did not have clearly defined ranks and orders of men, he predicted their appearance within half a century. [25]

Reasoning from these assumptions, Adams created American parallels for De Lolme's points where none existed. For example, De Lolme had described the House of Lords as acting sometimes as a safety valve for the popular hero, the one man capable of rocking the English boat. Elevated to the peerage, his waxing power would be checked. The success of the people's favorite might be brilliant, even formidable, De Lolme theorized, "but the Constitution, in the very reward it prepares for him, makes him find a kind of ostracism." [26] Adams, in a passage which is frequently quoted from the

23. Ibid., VI, 141.

24. See *Defence* (London, 1788), III, 530. Charles Francis Adams did not republish the original index.

25. *The Works of John Adams,* ed. Adams, V, 238, 255, 261, 426; VI, 10–11, 66–67, 117–118.

26. De Lolme, *The Constitution of England,* 201–205.

Defence, took De Lolme's idea and rewrote it thus: "The rich, the wellborn, and the able acquire an influence among the people that will soon be too much for simple honesty and plain sense, in a house of representatives. The most illustrious of them must, therefore, be separated from the mass, and placed by themselves in a senate; that is, to all honest and useful intents, an ostracism."[27] Nothing in the American political situation indicated that popular leaders would accept an "ostracism" as they perforce had to in England or that, if they did, they would be any less threatening in an American senate than an American house of representatives. When Adams affects this language of European writers and describes the people as simple, honest, and virtuous, one suspects that his mind is on his histories of the Swiss cantons and not the vibrant realities of the Massachusetts General Court.

De Lolme seems also to have impressed Adams with the appreciation of aristocratic trappings which he had earlier disliked. In 1783 when the Society of the Cincinnati was something of a cause célèbre, Adams had been one of its most vigorous critics, calling it "the first step taken to deface the beauty of our temple of liberty . . . against the spirit of our governments and the genius of our people."[28] In 1784 Adams scribbled a note in the margin of a book saying that the Order of the Cincinnati was "a horrid proof and instance" of Turgot's reflection that the secret interests of powerful individuals can frustrate the efforts of good citizens.[29] Yet when he wrote the third volume of the *Defence* three years later, he was happy to cite the Cincinnati as evidence of the universality of the human love for distinctions and a development quite compatible with a well-constructed government.[30]

Similarly in 1785, when writing to Dr. John Jebb, Adams had scorned the idea of exalting leaders: "[People] must be taught to reverence themselves, instead of adoring their servants, their generals,

27. *The Works of John Adams,* ed. Adams, IV, 290. The passage is quoted without reference to De Lolme in Haraszti, *John Adams and the Prophets of Progress,* 35; Palmer, *The Age of the Democratic Revolution,* 58, 273; J. R. Pole, "Historians and the Problem of Early American Democracy," *American Historical Review,* 67 (1962), 644; Howe, *The Changing Political Thought of John Adams,* 169–170.

28. Haraszti, *John Adams and the Prophets of Progress,* 330, n.33.

29. Ibid., 51.

30. *The Works of John Adams,* ed. Adams, V, 488–489.

admirals, bishops and statesmen . . . Instead of adoring a Washington, mankind should applaud the nation which educated him."[31] Yet when preparations were being made for Washington's inauguration four years later, Adams struck a distinctly sour note among his fellow officeholders by suggesting elaborate titles and ceremonies for the same Washington. In these instances De Lolme proved to be a siren song for Adams, pulling him away from his grasp of American sensibilities.

The impact of De Lolme, however, is inseparable from the context for the maturing of Adams' political philosophy. Arriving in Europe as an experienced leader in popular politics, Adams responded with characteristic intensity to the debates on constitutional reform going on among his acquaintances in France, Holland, and England. The question at issue, as we have seen, revolved around competing estimates of the permanence of elite power and the possibilities of making radical social changes through political reconstruction. This question engaged Adams, completely overshadowing all of his other thinking about constitutional arrangements. De Lolme proved to be a compelling influence not because of the uniqueness of his analysis on history and politics, but because he had developed a comprehensive rationale for conservative reformism which gave coherence and precision to Adams' own strongly felt convictions.

Demonstrating Adams' debt to De Lolme is important because it reestablishes the full ideological force of his later writings. Adams was not responding in these years as a solitary political observer, privately reevaluating his political position. The ideas he expressed in the *Defence* are anomalous only to American debates over the federal constitution. Within the context of contemporary European discussions, Adams' ideas vibrate with meaning, and when, during Washington's first administration, the French Revolution broke out, the questions Adams tackled in his *Defence* were pushed to the foreground of political life in the new American nation.[32] Jacobin

31. Ibid., IX, 540.

32. Edward Handler (*America and Europe in the Political Thought of John Adams* [Cambridge, Mass., 1964]) deals with Adams' experiences in Europe, but, not recognizing the critical importance of De Lolme's writings in the French polemics about reform, Handler creates the misleading impression that Adams and the French were locked in political debate. Adams himself claimed that such luminaries as Lally-Tollendal and Condorcet responded to his teachings. Actually Adams figures in these men's writings rarely and only as an echo of De Lolme, who is central to their debates.

and Angloman became the familiar epithets in the partisan battles of the 1790s precisely because the constellation of ideas associated with revolutionary France and conservative England were meaningful to the men arguing over social values in Philadelphia and New York.

At the center of the controversy was the question of elites. Were they vestiges of a benighted age or inexorable outgrowths of human society? Could political constitutions safely ignore them as social phenomena or must they be institutionalized on the most socially advantageous terms to preserve liberty and order? No one doubted their existence. It was their permanence, their origins, and their capacity to protect or destroy the cherished values of freedom, liberation, truth, justice, and brotherhood that were at issue. The common effort to fight for independence—even to create a more perfect union—had not yet found a supplementary coalescence of opinion about what kind of society the new United States should and would become. The consensus upon social values was less complete, and being less complete was less effective as a moderating force. One explanation for the passion of partisan politics in the 1790s lies in the fact that American leaders were deeply divided upon questions which went beyond a choice of political forms and touched more profound convictions about man and civil society. The angry tensions that characterized politics through that decade were generated by the real fears men had about the future. It was in this setting that Adams' Cassandra-like polemics about the doom awaiting unmixed democracies was received. When Adams recommended that "standing bodies" be introduced into the executive and the upper house of the American legislatures, he was endorsing a political form which still commanded attention. It was precisely because Adams could not be dismissed as a renegade American patriot that his opponents in the 1790s worked so hard to paint him as the political aristocrat he was.

The French Revolution was the catalyst in breaking up the consensus among the leaders of the American Revolution because it carried with it an insistent philosophical question that had not yet been resolved. Equality and liberty had been joined in such a way as to challenge all other formulations of natural rights. Adams had recognized this challenge when the Turgotists were developing their ideas, and in his view their basic premise was false. These

French reformers, as we have seen, tied their endorsement of a single central legislative assembly to a concept of nationhood and popular power which was truly radical. They had discovered a new social leveler—man's innate reasoning capacity—and with it they expected to create a nation unmarred by inequalities and private interests. In their view the separate bodies, standing orders, or mediating groups extolled by anglomaniac philosophers were created by chance developments and perpetuated through violence. Once man's reason cut through the veil of mystery and superstition created by others, they believed that man would enter into a new era in which social institutions would reflect the natural order of things. Such a view of human development necessarily posed questions about the American Revolution. Was it to be viewed as the peculiar result of Anglo-American historical events or was it a symbolic earnest money payment toward the new social order which would bind Americans to enlightened souls everywhere?

Placing the American Revolution in the context of a worldwide revolutionary movement suggested that what was truly authentic about the revolution were the social changes it wrought and implied that America's destiny was linked with a worldwide effort to destroy the oppressive institutions of the past. This implication was thrust into political discussions because those Americans in favor of greater social equality quickly espoused the cause of France, just as European reformers had earlier identified with the American Revolution. On hand in Europe when this association was first made, Adams fiercely rejected the connection. When the outbreak of the French Revolution spread the ethos of "liberty, equality, and fraternity" across the Atlantic, other Americans saw the dangers of this association. They disliked the suggestion that what was truly significant about the American Revolution was its importance for the world. The full dimension of the threat was driven home when they saw their fellow Americans enthusiastically embracing the radical notion that genuinely new departures in human society were not only possible, but likely. The French Revolution revealed to Americans in the 1790s the limits of their consensus, and the frenzied distemper which characterized the exchanges between the sympathizers and critics of the French Revolution was a measure of how profound their differences appeared to them.

The area of consensus in American politics in the 1790s could be more accurately described as constitutionalism, or a belief in the constituent power of the people. Few writings in the 1780s and 1790s denied that political institutions should be based on reasoned decision and voluntary adoption. Force, superstition, and blind tradition were recognized on all sides as the bane of man's historic lot. Most writers also shared the stance of the political scientist, agreeing that governmental forms were amenable to investigation and analysis. In the eighteenth century men believed in natural social laws which were both knowable and inexorable. It was this conviction that gave utility to historical knowledge. Past events were so much evidence for confirming general laws. History was not a seamless whole, but a casebook of examples susceptible to ad hoc extrapolation. The *Defence,* with its endless extracts from histories, memoirs, disquisitions, and treatises—all wrenched from their original context—presents impressive testimony to this point of view. And surely there is no more remarkable evidence of the belief in the unity of human experience than Adams' *Discourses on Davila* in which he lectured his countrymen on current politics through the vehicle of an Italian historian's account of the French civil wars of the sixteenth century!

Adams' belief in reasoned political choice had the effect of confusing both his contemporaries and historians, for Adams insisted that he was not a monarchist because he never denied the people's right to choose. "Popular sovereignty," he explained in the *Defence,* permitted "the people to choose the best form of government, not just a democratic one." "The people," Adams claimed, "have as clear a right to erect a simple monarchy, aristocracy, or democracy, or an equal mixture, or any other mixture of all three," adding significantly, "and the wisest nations that ever lived, have preferred such mixtures, and even with such standing powers as ingredients in their composition."[33] In a similar vein, when he changed his opinion on the Order of the Cincinnati Adams criticized its founders for failing to consult the people. "If these gentlemen had been of opinion that titles and ribbons were necessary in society, . . . they should have taken measures for calling conventions of the people, where it should

33. *The Works of John Adams,* ed. Adams, VI, 117ff.

have been determined, first, whether any such distinctions should be introduced; secondly, how many such orders; thirdly, what number of individuals of each; and, lastly, there should have been in convention a general election of noblemen for each of the thirteen states."[34]

Believing as he did in reasoned political choice, Adams relied on the spread of sound information on government to bring into being his cherished mixed government. If the American people would only acquire an understanding of politics, he was certain they would adjust their institutions accordingly. Commenting on the limited value of the new federal constitution, Adams wrote, "A people who could conceive and can adopt it we need not fear will be able to amend it, when by experience, its conveniences and imperfections shall be seen and felt." His faith that this would happen was rooted in a conception of political philosophy which was akin to that of the sciences. Correct ideas would force out misinformation much as major advances in the physical and biological sciences are accepted. "A science," Adams explained, "certainly comprehends all the principles in nature which belong to the subject. The principles in nature which relate to government cannot all be known, without a knowledge of the history of mankind. The English constitution is the only one which has considered and provided for all cases that are known to have generally, indeed to have always, happened in the progress of every nation; it is, therefore, the only scientific government."[35] Here is where De Lolme's presentation of the English constitution was able to influence Adams decisively. Polybius had written all that was theoretically valuable about a mixed government in the second century before Christ. Countless writers had extolled English institutions in the seventeenth and eighteenth centuries, but De Lolme had told the story again from the perspective of a political scientist. Neither Adams nor De Lolme responded to the mystic chords Burke tried to sound when threatened by French radicalism. They were much more analytical in their approach to the threat, applying remedies to known constitutional diseases,

34. Ibid., V, 488–489.
35. Ibid., VI, 118–119.

using the past as a guide to what will work in the future rather than as an unseen hand in the destinies of the present.

In a very real sense Adams' tendentious three volumes of historical extracts is a pamphlet masquerading as a tome. Listening to respected French philosophers discourse on political changes, Adams perceived the true dimension of the problem facing his generation. Perhaps it is fair to say that in the company of European radical reformers he saw that the American Revolution had launched a thousand dangerous hopes. He responded passionately to the debate among French reformers and, like the conservative reformers in France, he found in De Lolme's precise explanation of English institutions the antidote which could save his countrymen from their own folly. He was not unmindful of the storm his book would cause. Sending a presentation copy to Franklin, he wrote, "if it is heresy, I shall, I suppose, be cast out of communion. But it is the only sense in which I am or ever was a Republican, and in such times I hold the concealment of sentiments to be no better than countenancing sedition."[36] Such an inflated view of the situation might be ascribed to Adams' well-known penchant for exaggerating evils, were there not such overwhelming evidence of the apocalyptic attitude that prevailed. Even as late as 1809 Jefferson flailed out angrily when he heard that Adams had pooh-poohed the idea that monarchy had been an issue in the 1790s. The fears of these men seem illusory now, but all evidence suggests that the ghost of permanent, institutionalized elites had not been laid.

When in retirement in 1813 Adams and Jefferson revitalized the friendship ruptured in angry public politics during the 1790s, they turned immediately to the philosophical differences which had divided them twenty years earlier. Tactfully, yet resolutely, the two old friends went over the ground again, gingerly approaching the question of whether elites were of such a permanent character as to require institutionalization and whether the scientific mode of inquiry held out hope of fundamentally affecting the human condition. "One of the questions . . . on which our parties took different sides," Jefferson wrote to Adams,

36. *The Works of Benjamin Franklin,* ed. John Bigelow (New York, 1904), XI, 298–299.

was on the improvability of the human mind, in science, in ethics, in government etc. Those who advocated reformation of institutions, pari passu, with the progress of science, maintained that no definite limits could be assigned to that progress. The enemies of reform, on the other hand, denied improvement, and advocated steady adherence to the principles, practices and institutions of our fathers, which they represented as the consummation of wisdom, and the akmé of excellence, beyond which the human mind could never advance.[37]

In his next letter Jefferson reviewed the party differences which developed between the Second Continental Congress and Washington's administration, beginning with the first stage when he and Adams had stood together on the side of independence, through the second stage when they were both for the new federal constitution to the organization of the new government when, as Jefferson described it: "the line of division was again drawn . . . into two parties, each wishing to give a different direction to the government; the one to strengthen the most popular branch, the other the more permanent branches, and to extend their permanence. Here you and I separated for the first time."[38]

For the next ten years Adams and Jefferson explored these two intertwined questions of social forms and human knowledge. Their common eighteenth-century cast of mind in these letters is striking: classical illusions, universal truths, general principles, and Ciceronian assertions flowed from their pens. Their similarities are more marked in 1813 than their differences, and this fact suggests that the birth of a purely American frame of reference awaited the death of the Enlightenment. Until the eighteenth-century cultural perception of universality gave way to the nineteenth century's appreciation of the particular, the fear of a permanent elite becoming institutionalized appeared justified. Men in the 1790s had believed aristocracy to be a possibility not because the American environment had ever been hospitable to prescriptive social arrangements, but because aristocracy was a part of the historic human order which eighteenth-century Americans accepted as a given. The Dissenting tradition, with its roots in Calvinist theology and natural law philosophy,

37. *The Adams-Jefferson Letters,* ed. Cappon, II, 332.
38. Ibid., 336.

had encouraged the colonists to analyze their experience in terms of a traditional formulation of human possibilities. Arriving at a genuinely American consensus on society and politics involved in large part shaking off the underlying assumptions of constancy and universality of that Dissenting tradition.

8

The American Heritage—
The Heirs and the Disinherited

BEFORE THERE was a constitutional convention in Philadelphia in the summer of 1787, there was a little rebellion in western Massachusetts in the fall of 1786. Two decades of research on the lives of ordinary men and women have made more palpable what was involved in that series of court closings in Hampshire and Worcester counties and how the military response to Daniel Shays's ragged platoons affected the lives of those who marched in opposition to the state's hard-money policies. In the same twenty years we have also entered more sympathetically into the conceptual universe of the men—for the most part, members of the old colonial elite—who suppressed the Shaysites. It is clear in retrospect that it was the shared aspirations of a particular group of American leaders that led to "the more perfect union" created by the Constitution. The essential fragility of that union has been a dominant factor through most of the history of the United States.

The characterization of the 1780s as a period of crisis comes from the writers of the Constitution themselves, most particularly from the authors of the Federalist Papers. The alarm those men experienced was real. James Madison felt it. George Washington expressed it, as did Edmund Randolph and Alexander Hamilton. By no means universal, their sense of crisis represented a particular response of specific leaders in some of the states. Among the gentry of Virginia, it was marked. In fact almost all of the efforts to reform the Articles of Confederation came from Virginia, starting with the casual gathering at Mount Vernon, progressing through the meeting the following year at Annapolis, and culminating in the Philadelphia convention.[1] The leaders of Massachusetts did not share those apprehensions. Their legislature had provided for a speedy retirement of the state's revolutionary debt. Creditors used the courts to distrain tools and to foreclose mortgages. Perhaps because the fighting had shifted southward early in the Revolution, it had not been necessary for Massachusetts' leaders to make concessions to those men who wanted easy money and low taxes. Their drastic measures for repaying the state's revolutionary debt boomeranged in the Berkshires. Shays's Rebellion carried the consciousness of crisis to New England. Indeed it might be considered a fortuitous analogue to the Stamp Act in its consequent uniting of nationalists from Virginia and from Massachusetts. Very quickly the court closings in western Massachusetts were converted into a symbolic event.[2] The name Shays's Rebellion, which came from the writings of the nationalists, has carried a heavy load of ideological meaning ever since, a meaning which we might now begin to unburden ourselves of.

The worries that the events in western Massachusetts provoked had in fact been growing stronger since the end of the war. The state constitutions drafted in the wake of the Declaration of Independence had concentrated governmental power in the legislatures. At the same time, ordinary voters began electing ordinary men to represent them. Because every state was faced with a revolutionary debt to pay off, taxes—their size, incidence, and forms of payment—loomed large in postwar politics. Most voters had their capital tied up in land. Coin was scarce and the level of personal indebtedness high. Faced with popular demands for paper money with legal-tender provisions, for insolvency acts, and for stay laws, legislators in many states adopted policies favorable to their interests and to the interests of their hard-pressed constituents. Many

1. H. James Henderson, "The Structure of Politics in the Continental Congress," in *Essays on the American Revolution,* ed. Stephen G. Kurtz and James H. Hutson (Chapel Hill, 1973), 190–192.

2. Van Beck Hall, *Politics without Parties: Massachusetts, 1780–1791* (Pittsburgh, 1972); David P. Szatmary, *Shays' Rebellion: The Making of an Agrarian Insurrection* (Amherst, Mass., 1980).

of those measures had been passed during the Revolution when gentry leaders had curried popular favor in order to secure support for the war. After the Revolution an increasingly articulate populace garnered enough votes to legislate without help from their social superiors. Controversies over land grants, electoral districts, and tax policies were resolved in favor of popular majorities in well over half the states. Hope that the upper houses of the legislatures would act as a check on the popular will had been swiftly dashed. Deference—the acquiescence to the authority of one's social superiors—was disappearing with remarkable rapidity. Viewed from the perspective of established leaders, those developments were the stuff of crisis. The emphasis that the authors of the Federalist Papers put on the weakness of the Articles of Confederation has obscured the fact that it was the strength and vigor of state governments that had created the sense of crisis among the old revolutionary elite.[3]

The democratization of the state governments was a sudden development—one with plenty of antecedents but nonetheless sudden in its full flowering during the immediate postwar years. There were constitutional implications in that shift of power. As the number of plain farmers and of representatives from the western parts of the states increased, majorities formed around the popular goals of increasing access to land, establishing land banks, and deferring the retirement of the public debt until personal financial security had been achieved. In pursuit of those immediate ends, state legislatures more than once vaulted the limits of their state constitutions. Their laws not only interfered with the value of money and with the certainty of private contracts, they also suggested a legislative indifference to constitutional restraints.[4]

America in the 1780s had constitutions—a baker's dozen of them—but not a culture of constitutionalism. As yet there had

---

3. James Madison, Alexander Hamilton, and John Jay, *The Federalist Papers* (New York, 1937), 88. On state governments during the Confederation period, see Jackson Turner Main, "Government by the People: The American Revolution and the Democratization of the Legislatures," *William and Mary Quarterly*, 23 (1966), 391–407; *Political Parties before the Constitution* (Chapel Hill, 1973); Merrill Jensen, *The New Nation* (New York, 1950).

4. Main, "Government by the People"; *Political Parties before the Constitution;* Jensen, *New Nation.*

developed no special aura around the notion of a constitution, despite the great attention that French and English writers had paid to America's phenomenal outburst of constitution-writing. In several states the constitutions themselves had become the focal point of controversy. Veneration of constitutions did not figure prominently in public discourse, and campaigns to rewrite the state constitutions had begun with their ratification. In Pennsylvania pro- and anticonstitutional parties dominated political life until the constitution was rewritten in 1790. Conflicts over the national domain among the states held up the signing of the Articles of Confederation until all of the fighting for which the Confederation had been formed was over. That negligent attitude toward constitutions is surprising in view of the emphasis that was placed on the British constitution and on its part in guaranteeing liberty. Many people worried about the cavalier attitude adopted by legislative majorities toward the constitutions that empowered them. Even Thomas Jefferson, who supported the democratization of politics, feared the waxing power of the Virginia legislature. "The concentrating of the power of government in the same hands," he wrote in his famous *Notes on the State of Virginia,* was "precisely the definition of despotic government . . . 173 despots would surely be as oppressive as one . . . An elective despotism was not the government we fought for."[5]

It is all too tempting to think that alarmed gentry leaders were reacting as an established interest group resisting pressure from below. And of course in a sense they were, but they were also responding as men thoroughly imbued with eighteenth-century ideas about civil order. It is surely one of the strengths of current ideological interpretations of the past that they promote an appreciation of the complexity of human motivation.[6] Men and women rarely do things out of a single motive. Rather they seem impelled to

5. Thomas Jefferson, *Notes on the State of Virginia,* ed. William Peden (Chapel Hill, 1955), 120; H. James Henderson, "Constitutionalists and Republicans in the Continental Congress, 1778–1786," *Pennsylvania History,* 36 (1969), 119–144; J. R. Pole, *Political Representation in England and the Origins of the American Republic* (New York, 1966); Jack N. Rakove, *The Beginnings of National Politics: An Interpretive History of the Continental Congress* (New York, 1979).

6. For a discussion of the ideological approach, see Gordon S. Wood, "Rhetoric and Reality in the American Revolution," *William and Mary Quarterly,* 23 (1966), 3–32; see also Chapter 11.

act when a range of concerns prompts them. The ideological approach has also called into question the concept of self-interest unmediated by cultural perceptions of wherein one's interests lie.

Recent efforts to understand why the popular state majorities of the revolutionary era created a sense of crisis have led to a remapping of the conceptual world of well-educated Anglo-Americans. Particularly salient in that universe was the metaphor of balance used to describe an order among contending forces. In diplomacy it was the balance of power; in domestic relations it was the balanced constitution. Such a constitution held in check the opposing forces within society, specifically those of the talented few and the ordinary many. That concept rested on the assumption of natural inequality. Drawn from a variety of political treatises stretching forward from Aristotle through Machiavelli, James Harrington, and the century's own Montesquieu, the classical model of a balanced constitution was tied to a rather ornate conception of the politician as the embodiment of male virtue (it should be remembered that virtue came from the Latin word for man, *vir*). Citizens represented a special body of men, distinguished from women, children, and laborers by their social and economic independence.[7] The natural power lusts of human beings made civil society fragile, but the existence of two social groups available for checking each other supplied a solution entirely compatible with the gentlemen's notion of their special place in society. In much the same way as war makes gallantry possible, so the frailty of civil order created a function for civic virtue. And just as those in love with military valor are rarely pacifists, so those filled with admiration for balanced government had little faith in an undifferentiated citizenry.

Those classical republican concepts circulated more easily among gentlemen, for they had read Greek and Roman texts as schoolboys. They also were inclined to accept the theory of natural inequality embedded in the classical gloss on the British constitution. Achieving stability by balancing the superior talents of the few against the numerical strength of the many meant, of course, that the few acted as the statesmen, judges, and generals who ran govern-

7. The meaning of civic virtue for eighteenth-century Anglo-Americans has been detailed in J. G. A. Pocock, *The Machiavellian Moment: Florentine Political Thought and the Atlantic Republican Tradition* (Princeton, 1975).

ment, whereas ordinary people acted solely to check any undue augmentation of elite power. Property played a key, if chameleonic, role in the classical republican recipe for stability. It rooted men in their society and was supposed to liberate them for the practice of politics. Implicit in such a theory was the expectation of deriving a secure living from one's property. If truly independent financially, gentlemen could fulfill their destiny on the public stage, while their ordinary human brethren fulfilled theirs in the less noble, private pursuits of planting and reaping, buying and selling, saving and investing. It is difficult to measure just how real the classical republican categories of thought appeared to the seaboard merchants, tidewater planters, and prosperous farmers who composed the American elite. Nonetheless, their public statements were filled with republican themes: order is fragile; power lusts fill all men; virtue is imperiled by ambition and desire; only those immune from the pressures of everyday want can be trusted with responsibility.[8]

Developments since the emergence of an integrated European trade had made economic life more ebullient than placid and nowhere more so than in the North American colonies.[9] Property rooted men in their society until they decided to move. Deriving an income from that property required constant attention to cues about prices and preferences in distant markets. American participation in the Atlantic trade world undermined the economic stability on which classical republican political ideals rested. The implications of the still new commercial system, however, had not yet been fully elaborated in intellectual formulations. Earlier assumptions remained imbedded in sensibilities, causing the James Madisons and George Washingtons of the day to look with real concern on the legislative manipulation of currency and on the obvious self-interest of debtor-made laws. The state constitutions that had been

8. Istvan Hont and Michael Ignatieff, "Needs and Justice in the *Wealth of Nations:* An Introductory Essay," in *Wealth and Virtue: The Shaping of Political Economy in the Scottish Enlightenment,* ed. Istvan Hont and Michael Ignatieff (Cambridge, 1983), 1–44; Isaac Kramnick, "Republican Revisionism Revisited," *American Historical Review,* 87 (1982), 629–664; Pocock, *Machiavellian Moment,* esp. 333–552.

9. Marc Egnal and Joseph A. Ernst, "An Economic Interpretation of the American Revolution," *William and Mary Quarterly,* 29 (1972), 3–31; John J. McCusker and Russell R. Menard, *The Economy of British America* (Chapel Hill, 1985), esp. 258–276; Thomas M. Doerflinger, *A Vigorous Spirit of Enterprise* (Chapel Hill, 1986).

written immediately following the Declaration of Independence had not elicited reverence, thus rendering uncertain their explicit limitations on the exercise of government power. Viewed through classical republican prisms, the pattern of state politics was not new-modeled democracy but long-feared anarchy. Unbalanced state constitutions were plunging society back into the cyclical turbulence predicted for those benighted people who had not learned from the past. Despite their experience with the dynamic changes of the eighteenth century, many of America's revolutionary elite still thought in terms of decline and degeneration. Comfortable with their own long-established use of power in a status-structured society, they found the similar use of power in the interest of an undifferentiated people unsettling. And when they gave expression to those unsettled feelings, they did so in the language of classical republicanism, pointing to unbalanced constitutions, to the insecurity of property, and to the weakness of authority.

The presuppositions and prejudices of eighteenth-century Americans ordered their reality, but that reality was not orderly. American society at the end of the eighteenth century was undergoing dramatic change without a coherent social theory to explain it. More and more the important arena for social action was the area of free bargaining and voluntary association rather than the polity described in classical texts. Hence, inherited ways of thinking lost their material base. Institutions created to secure old goals of solidarity slowly became irrelevant; others took on new significance. The protection of property in a world predicated on the economic stasis of classical republicanism, for instance, aimed at securing the virtue of the rulers and the rule of the virtuous. The protection of property rights in an economy of enhanced productivity and greater risk taking guaranteed the gains of successful market participants.[10]

Looking at the classical republican worldview as an orientation to reality, it is possible to imagine that the Founding Fathers' reaction to social change involved enthusiasm and fear, selective blindness and anticipatory appreciation. With sensibilities rooted in the past and with information formulated from experience, the

10. That function of the Constitution is explored fruitfully in Donald J. Pisani, "Promotion and Regulation: Constitutionalism and the American Economy," *Journal of American History,* 74 (1987), 740–768.

men and women of the late eighteenth century were forced to live with constant social change and with divided intellectual loyalties. Historians have drawn on the sociology of knowledge and on cultural anthropology to reconstruct how structured consciousness influences social action. Their findings have contributed to a reassessment of the connections between belief and behavior. Seeking usable generalizations, social scientists have written of systems of thought and symbolic meaning. A more accurate metaphor for what historians have found would be a patchwork of thought. The elements in an ideology are joined together like a quilt, their design coming from selection and repetition, not from logic.[11] Thus the elements of classical republicanism found in eighteenth-century writings attest to the persistence of ideas no longer capable of illuminating reality.

The fifty-five delegates who gathered at the Pennsylvania State House may have thought within the cultural matrix of classical republicanism, but they knew well the character of ordinary American voters and how that character limited their choices. Had they been able to assure the preponderating influence of gentlemen in the upper house, they could have used bicameralism as a check on popular power. The decline of deferential social habits had robbed the distinction between the few and the many of its political function. Faced with that intractable reality, the "Demi-Gods" meeting in Philadelphia came up with a liberal solution to their classical republican problem of balance. Unable to call on clearly demarcated social groups to check each others' usurpations of power, the Constitution's drafters took a different tack. They limited the power of government. To be sure they created a national government where none had existed, but they nonetheless departed from British precepts and from classical republican formulas by defining the power granted to both state and federal legislatures. To maintain those novel constitutional limits on power, they innovatively wrote tactics for checking power abuses into the constitutional privileges of the

---

11. See, for example, Wood, "Rhetoric and Reality"; Peter L. Berger and Thomas Luckmann, *The Social Construction of Reality: A Treatise in the Sociology of Knowledge* (New York, 1966); and Robert F. Berkhofer, Jr., "Clio and the Culture Concept: Some Impressions of a Changing Relationship in American Historiography," in *The Idea of Culture in the Social Sciences*, ed. Louis Schneider and Charles M. Bonjean (Cambridge, 1973), 77–100.

departments of government, relying on the self-interest of individual officeholders to preserve the boundaries among the legislature, the executive, and the judiciary. "Ambition must be made to counteract ambition," Madison wrote in Federalist No. 51. "The interests of the man must be connected with the constitutional rights of the place." [12]

Self-interest was accepted as a functional equivalent to civic virtue, but at the same time the scope of government, particularly the power of state government to legislate in economic matters, was severely limited. If the old balance of the few and the many could not be reestablished, a new balance of opposing interests would not be asked to do as much. Article 1, Section 10, of the Constitution indicates just how much was taken away from the states. Listed there are the disallowed powers that had wreaked such havoc in postrevolutionary politics: the power to coin money, to emit bills of credit, to make anything but gold and silver coin legal tender, to pass laws impairing the obligation of contracts, or to lay any import or export duties. The Constitution created a national government to replace a confederation of sovereign states, but it limited the power of that national government through the enumeration of powers. At both levels of the new federalism the Constitution provided for a more limited government, especially in the economic realm. Thomas Paine had popularized a novel distinction between society and government in the opening lines of *Common Sense*. "Society," he wrote, "is produced by our wants, and government by our wickedness; the former promotes our happiness *positively* by uniting our affections, the latter *negatively* by restraining our vices." The Constitution institutionalized that division by restricting the ambit of legislation as it simultaneously enlarged the constitutionally protected domain of free association. Thus the liberalism of the Constitution inheres less in the unleashing of interest group politics than in the enlargement of the sphere of voluntary action, what Jefferson later called "the empire of liberty." [13]

The Constitution closed the door on simple majoritarian government in the United States. Popular majorities animated by what people wanted to do at a particular moment would be forever con-

---

12. Madison, Hamilton, and Jay, *Federalist Papers,* 337.

13. Thomas Paine, *Common Sense,* ed. Isaac Kramnick (New York, 1976); Merrill Peterson, *Thomas Jefferson and the New Nation* (New York, 1970), 771.

strained. The Constitution created a fundamental law, and that law severely restricted the range of government power. The same founding document made it extraordinarily difficult to change the distribution of power. Despite the celebration of popular sovereignty in America, the sovereign people were restrained once the Constitution was ratified. Perhaps nothing in the Constitution has worked more against democracy than the amendment process. One-quarter of the states plus one can always veto the affirmed choice of three-quarters of the states minus one. If the denying states are not very populous, perhaps a tenth of the citizenry can block the will of the remaining nine-tenths. In place of a politics of active involvement, the Constitution provided for the distant administration of national law. And even that centripetal force was minimized when Jefferson dismantled the Federalist program after his election.

What was left for nationalist sentiment to feed on was an abstract union embodied in a written Constitution. The culture of constitutionalism forthwith took the place of a powerful central government as the nation's unifier. Whereas the state constitutions remained political documents to be repeatedly rewritten and amended, the United States Constitution was elevated to a revered status. The still unreconciled and profound differences among the revolutionary elite found an outlet in partisan politics in the 1790s, while expressions of fidelity to the Constitution provided the ideological glue for the loosely bound United States. With that promising material, John Marshall created a judicial tradition that separated law from politics and made of the Constitution an effective arbiter of democratic will. Whereas classical republicanism had promoted a fear of power and a respect for the liberty-securing promise of civil society, American ideology increasingly fostered the disparagement of government and a reverence for the Constitution just because it protected the domain of natural liberty from the now suspect powers of government.[14]

14. Jennifer Nedelsky, "Confining Democratic Politics: Anti-Federalists, Federalists, and the Constitution," *Harvard Law Review*, 96 (1982), esp. 358–360. As R. Kent Newmyer has detailed, even John Marshall's substantial work was insufficient to impose order on the Constitution's many judicial interpreters in the first three decades of the nineteenth century. R. Kent Newmyer, "Harvard Law School, New England Legal Culture, and the Antebellum Origins of American Jurisprudence," *Journal of American History*, 74 (1987), 814–835.

It is hard to believe that there was ever a possibility of a fully participatory democracy in the United States. Or perhaps more accurately, it appears unlikely to most scholars that such a participatory democracy would have decisively changed the course of national development once the crucial connections among capital, technology, and resources had been made in the nineteenth century. Such an attitude draws strength from a historiographical tradition that overdetermines the outcome of industrial capitalism. Whether from a Marxist or from a liberal perspective, the transformative force of industrialization has been treated as an inexorable succession of structural changes sweeping through the purposive realm of politics. Empirically, the similarity today of capitalist economies in western Europe and the United States bolsters the American predisposition to minimize the influence that different political institutions might have exercised. Against that view, I would argue that every difference makes a difference. Unlike eighteenth-century Europe, the United States had the material for democratic politics in 1787. A large proportion of adult white men held land, voted, and engaged in debates on issues elsewhere considered the province of officials. Foreign visitors in the eighteenth century invariably commented on the vitality of public discussions and on the political confidence of ordinary men.[15] Had the states been left with the economic powers they had before the ratification of the Constitution, the momentum of popular politics would not have been checked. Never having lost the normal scope of legislative power, the states could more easily have maintained the traditional connection between the government and the economy, exercising in the economic realm a responsibility that they continued to exercise in matters of morals when they legislated intrusively on drinking habits, on marriage choices, on sexual practices, on race relations, and on a whole range of other personal liberties that have received constitutional protection only in the last few decades. Moreover, without constitutional protection, it seems unlikely that private property rights would ever have achieved their rhetorical status as sacred. That is not to suggest that the majority of Americans disliked the market economy or that

15. For comments of a foreign visitor, see, for example, Davis J. Brandenburg, "A French Aristocrat Looks at American Farming: La Rochefoucauld-Liancourt's *Voyages dans les Etats-Unis*," *Agricultural History*, 32 (1958), 163.

commercial expansion would not have taken place. It is to say that people acting in their capacity as citizens with the power of the state at their collective disposal could have had a larger part in making decisions. The social and the economic would not have been constitutionally divided, and ordinary men in America could have shaped the course of commerce as part of government and not simply as individual buyers and sellers.

Creating a national government was an open-ended goal. We speak of strengthening the government in 1787 as though there was only one way to do it, which is another legacy of the Federalists. There were alternatives to the one issuing from Philadelphia. The dismay of Antifederalists at the specific provisions of the Constitution arose as much as anything from their regret at the roads not taken. Much less coherent than the Federalists, the Antifederalists, nonetheless, articulated a defense of democracy that serves to remind us of a different American political tradition. A more sympathetic reading of Antifederalist polemics restores the sense of possibilities that has been deadened by two centuries of veneration for the Constitution; it also revives for consideration Antifederalist skepticism about a contemporary crisis in the sovereign states. The "crisis" urged on the public by the Federalists, and frequently believed in since, did not alarm the men who opposed the Philadelphia draft constitution. They insisted that Americans lived in peace and tranquility, secure enough to consider reform in a leisurely manner. They did not share the same apprehensions that popular politics would degenerate into majority tyranny, or, more accurately, they considered the tensions between liberty and participatory democracy supportable. No less concerned than the Federalists with the expanding horizons for individual, self-improvement held out by commercial progress, the Antifederalists did not posit a fundamental incompatibility between legislative activism and private-property rights. Hence they did not see the necessity of resolving the tension between the two in favor of the economic freedoms of the individual.[16]

Nothing weakens a position so much as losing. If that is generally

16. Herbert J. Storing, *What the Anti-Federalists Were For: The Political Thought of the Opponents of the Constitution* (Chicago, 1981); Nedelsky, "Confining Democratic Politics."

the case, it is *a fortiori* so when the victorious side prevails in the formation of a new government. The opinions of the Antifederalists have been trapped in the ambergris of one political decision. Their views have not, like those of the Federalists, lived on to be incorporated with the history of a success. Yet now that that success is not at risk, their writings are reminders that other constitutions could have been written. Like the history of science, the history of the United States Constitution has been largely written as the history of its progress.

MARTIN DIAMOND once told his students that the history of the United States could be told as the creation of an American heritage and the fight among the heirs. He thus wittily encapsulated a familiar view in the 1950s: that the two major political parties had divvied up the moral capital of the United States, dividing equality and liberty between them. At a time when the two-party system was hardly less awe-inspiring to Americans than the Constitution, it was comforting to think of each political party drawing on a different trust fund. I am tempted to rewrite Diamond's line and say that the history of American constitutionalism can now be told as the creation of the American heritage and the fight between the heirs and the disinherited.

It is fascinating to think of the recent events that have made possible that reassessment. One can catalogue the predisposing factors: the civil rights campaign, the interest in ethnicity, the women's movement, and the wide-ranging attacks on establishment values. In addition there has been a quiet revolution in the American professoriat. The G.I. Bill introduced working-class men and women—many of them second- and third-generation immigrants—to college education, and the subsequent expansion in higher education opened up university jobs to them. No longer the preserve of upper-middle-class WASP men, history faculties began to reflect the ethnic and racial diversity of the nation at large. The computer facilitated the social historians' reconstruction of the lives of ordinary Americans through the quantitative analysis of vital records. All of those developments have influenced the lines of inquiry pursued by historians who entered the profession in the 1960s. Those historians came from different backgrounds, and they brought fresh questions that, nonetheless, bore a family resemblance to those asked by their patrician predecessors: Where are my forebears in the American past, and what was their place in that past?

The idea of looking at the history of the Constitution as a fight between the heirs and the disinherited opens up some interesting perspectives. First of all because there was an American heritage—a national trust fund of political ideals—there were the roles of heirs and disinherited to be played out. This explains the loyalty of the disinherited to the Constitution and indicates why the same Constitution that has been a bastion for the elite has also been a sanctuary for the oppressed. Reformers have rarely turned against the Constitution—William Lloyd Garrison's burning of the document is an inflammatory exception—because the Constitution has represented a standard of justice to be held up to those with power. They have been able to draw from two ideological fonts: that of inalienable rights articulated in the Declaration of Independence and in the Bill of Rights, and that of fundamental law determining the proper distribution of power embodied in the Constitution. The merging of those two sources of meaning has intensified the constitutionalism of most American reform groups. Had the Constitution been the sole womb of political values in America, its conservative bias would have alienated the disinherited. As it is, equality and liberty, justice and freedom, have lived together for so long in the American imagination that we think of them as legally married, even well-matched. The promiscuous blending of those traditions accounts as well for the discomfort felt when Charles A. Beard disentangled the two and depicted the Constitution as a thermidorean response to the revolutionary ideals of the Declaration of Independence. That Beard's interpretation held sway for but a generation in the two hundred years of writing on the Constitution indicates just how powerful is the appeal of a single American heritage.

The Constitution has also provided a civilized arena for power struggles framed by the concept of civil rights. The Bill of Rights—to return to my metaphoric fight between the heirs and the disinherited—created a codicil to the founders' will, decisively shaping the character of reform in the United States. The existence of a constitutional arena for conflict suggests why a Thurgood Marshall or a Catherine MacKinnon goes to law school; it also helps explain the coolness some radicals feel for the critical legal studies movement. Fundamental law may be a fundamentally flawed concept, but its acceptance by the heirs has created a hostage for the disinherited. And both have shared in the dismissive attitude toward government implicit in Paine's distinction between society and government. The "people's power" evoked by protesters in the 1960s found little resonance in the nation at large, no doubt because Americans are used to thinking of majority will as a threat, against which the Constitution is their sheet anchor.

Despite the reformers' use of the Constitution, the heirs and the disinherited have not had an equal payoff from the inheritance. Probate judges, to continue my metaphor, have usually found for the heirs. The existence of a constitutional standard of justice may have mobilized a succession of reform groups, but it has been even more effective in protecting those who benefit directly from its dispensations. The Constitution has not only structured power in the United States; it has also structured the bad faith of the powerful. The mystification of fundamental law has enabled its beneficiaries to pose as the conservators of tradition. The New England leaders dealt with in R. Kent Newmyer's article had not shed their belief in the superiority of the few. They continued to worry about what would maintain order in a society lacking an established church, an attachment to place, and the uncontested leadership of men of merit. Into that void they poured an avalanche of words, the most powerful of which turned out to be the ones that created a legal science for interpreting the Constitution. Once their jurisprudential nationalism triumphed with the victorious Union Army, judges and lawyers began emphasizing the Constitution's organic connection to the American experience as distinguished from its origins in a contract of states.[17] Thus mystified, the Constitution was ratchetted up another notch above the level of participatory, democratic politics.

The very inequality of the opposing sides—those defending a conservative, sometimes literal, reading of the Constitution and those articulating a more radical, underlying meaning—accounts for the emphasis on strategy found in recent articles on the labor and

17. Newmyer, "Harvard Law School."

the civil rights movements. Had there not been a fundamental law set above majoritarian politics, many of the goals of reform groups could have been achieved through the direct use of legislative power. Instead reform movements in America have often taken on the character of military maneuvers in a fixed terrain. There has been no similar civil rights movement in Great Britain, not because there are no civil rights there, but rather because Parliament has full legislative power. British reformers have availed themselves of that power. In a single vote Parliament abolished slavery in the British Empire. Nowhere in the government of the United States was there ever lodged the power to abolish slavery. As the custodians of rights, the handful of interpreters of the Constitution have exercised far more power than the electorate.

The American heritage and the fight between the heirs and the disinherited tells but part of the story. An equally important reality in the history of America is the fact that the Constitution entered a culture already fully fitted out with symbolic systems and sacred texts. References to the newness of the nation should not obscure the age of the thirteen societies that composed the United States. Classical republicanism did not reign alone. The most important source of meaning for eighteenth-century Americans was the Bible. From centuries of biblical interpretations came Calvinism, Arminianism, Unitarianism, evangelicalism, antinomianism, and millenarianism. All of those Christian traditions were rich with conceptual imagery, potent symbols, and prescriptive models for behavior. The Bible as it was variously interpreted in America's proliferating denominations provided the basis for justifying the inferiority of women, for explaining the differences among the races, and for structuring familial relations, not to mention for conveying the sexual taboos of western Christendom. The culture of constitutionalism that emerged during the first fifty years after ratification had to be reconciled with those already established traditions, a process fraught with ambiguities, if not with outright contradictions. Martha Minow has explored those fascinating ambiguities, showing how implicit assumptions about male domination have encumbered the path to rights for children and women.[18]

18. Martha Minow, "We, the Family: Constitutional Rights and American Families," *Journal of American History,* 74 (1987), 959–983.

It has always been in the interest of the heirs to blend constitutional interpretations with those of the common law and of the Bible, just as it has usually been in the interest of the disinherited to point out the contradiction between the equality of natural rights philosophy and the acceptance of older hierarchies. For many of the heirs, the rights discourse was an irritating intrusion into a settled, biblically ordained order. Hardly less pregnant with meaning than the Bible for eighteenth-century Americans was the common law, whose commanding presence challenged the newly minted political arrangements of the Constitution. Like the Bible, the common law provided little support for natural rights philosophy. For no Americans was that more important than for the industrial workers whose "rights" were subsumed under the common law's rules for masters and servants. Against the prescriptive rights of employers, workers in the emerging industrial economy appealed alternately to their variant of republicanism and to individual rights, as Leon Fink describes. Writing about a contemporary example, Staughton Lynd reveals the enduring fragility of any political community in the face of the atomizing tendencies of American liberalism.[19]

The radical potential offered after 1789 was the opportunity to rethink the judicial imperatives of the Bible and of the common law and to replace them with legislation, a program embraced by the codifiers of the early nineteenth century. The prescriptive hierarchy of men over women, however, worked against the cooperation of black men and disfranchised women, as Ellen DuBois so poignantly details. Having earlier sought the vote as a fundamental right, women, after the ratification of the Thirteenth Amendment, constructed arguments around their peculiar situation. "The shift from arguments based on the common humanity of men and women," she writes, "to arguments based on fundamental differences of the sexes has its parallel in virtually every feminist epoch." Whether "disinherited" men—blacks or workers—have been opportunistic or sexist in dissociating their cause from that of

---

19. Leon Fink, "Labor, Liberty, and the Law: Trade Unionism and the Problem of the American Constitutional Order," ibid., 904–925; Staughton Lynd, "The Genesis of the Idea of a Community Right to Industrial Property in Youngstown and Pittsburgh, 1977–1987," ibid., 926–958. See also Karen Orren, *Belated Feudalism: Labor, the Law, and Liberal Development in the United States* (Cambridge, 1991).

women, the chilling effect has been the same. Similarly the common law protected employers from the efforts of late-nineteenth-century workers to achieve collective goals. "Instead of fleeing from the common law with ringing invocations of the Declaration of Independence or other appeals to natural rights doctrine," Fink asserts, "labor at the turn of the century painstakingly sought to turn inherited legal doctrine to practical advantage." With the rejection after the Civil War of the concept of the Constitution as a compact of states, constitutionalism merged with historicism to form the American variant of immanent values unfolding in space and time. Here again the haze of veneration that obscures the original reception of the Constitution hides as well the conceptual problems involved in integrating the Constitution into the didactic traditions of eighteenth-century America.[20]

Against the philosophical depiction of the Constitution as a disembodied ideal working itself out in history, Beard launched his interpretation of the Constitution. "Man, as a political animal acting upon political, as distinguished from more vital and powerful, motives," he wrote, "is the most unsubstantial of all abstractions."[21] In order to free his generation from its veneration of the Constitution, Beard ironically rejected the validity of political motives. Attempting to recapture the revolutionary potential of 1776 for the working classes of 1913, he demystified the Constitution by reducing the purposes of the constitutional movement to the pecuniary motives of the Founding Fathers. Reading Federalist No. 10 as a gloss on economic liberalism, he implicitly denied that politics could rise above individual self-interest. John P. Diggins has made a case for Beard's concern about the lack of public authority in his America. But Beard, nonetheless, brought the Founding Fathers down from their pedestals by ridiculing the community of interests that had informed their efforts. He thus began a historio-

20. Ellen DuBois, "Outgrowing the Compact of the Fathers: Equal Rights, Woman Suffrage, and the United States Constitution, 1820–1878," *Journal of American History*, 74 (1987), 849. Fink, "Labor, Liberty, and the Law," 915; Kathryn Preyer, "Jurisdiction to Punish: Federal Authority, Federalism and the Common Law of Crimes in the Early Republic," *Law and History Review*, 4 (1986), 223–335.

21. Beard, as quoted in Max Lerner, "The Constitution and Court as Symbols," *Yale Law Journal*, 46 (1937), 32.

graphical tradition that construed human motivation through a radical individualism that did not exist in 1787. The drafters of the Constitution were cultural innovators when they relied on self-interested individualism to provide the checks and balances once supplied by well-defined social classes.[22]

The historians of republicanism who in recent years have revised our understanding of the framing of the Constitution have made it possible to measure just how dramatic a cultural change the liberal elements in the Constitution effected. They have also discovered in the American past a form of community that holds out the promise of revitalizing contemporary politics.[23] Two hundred years later, it is the dysfunctional aspect of relying on self-interest that is most apparent, not the theoretical brilliance of the original intent.

THE CONSTITUTION removed a broad range of legislative powers in the economic domain from the state legislatures where popular majorities most effectively wielded power. The subsequent division between law and politics, elaborated by John Marshall and then by Joseph Story, gave to the Constitution a moral stature denied the political process.[24] Fundamental law became hypostasized as a source of justice removed from the workaday world of partisan elections and legislative bargaining. Majority will in action lost the normative standing accorded the people as the onetime ratifiers of the Constitution. Over time a culture of constitutionalism emerged that blended the Constitution with the higher law tradition of the common law. Both conservatives and reformers—both the heirs and the disinherited—contributed to the veneration of the Constitution. By the end of the nineteenth century, the Constitution had become the symbolic protector of Americans' natural rights. And that tradition had merged with larger themes of Western civilization: belief in a uniform human nature and belief in objective standards of justice.

22. John P. Diggins, "Power and Authority in American History: The Case of Charles A. Beard and His Critics," *American Historical Review,* 86 (1981), 701–730.

23. Gordon S. Wood, *The Creation of the American Republic, 1776–1787* (Chapel Hill, 1969); Pocock, *Machiavellian Moment;* Frank Michelman, "The Supreme Court, 1985 Term: Foreword: Traces of Self-Government," *Harvard Law Review,* 100 (1986), 4–77.

24. Newmyer, "Harvard Law School."

Thomas L. Haskell outlines the perils that those concepts face in the intellectual milieu of the late twentieth century. The question he poses—why the paradoxical persistence of rights talk in an age of interpretation—joins the history of the American Constitution to the contemporary crisis of Western metaphysics. The pivot for Haskell's argument is Friedrich Nietzsche's query: What is the difference between "I want *x*" and "I have a right to *x*"? By asking that, Nietzsche challenged the credibility of the natural law tradition that assigned to human reason the capacity to establish objective truths that could be used to distinguish between power and right. Developments in almost all disciplines since Nietzsche's time have intensified his radical skepticism. Belief in reason operating independently of the historically situated reasoner has been under attack for over a century. Anthropological investigations of the multifarious human cultures on the globe have called into question Western civilization's claim to speak for the entire human race. At the same time, analyses of what is involved in reading and writing, in speaking and hearing, have transformed language into a medium for creating, rather than for discovering, reality. To paraphrase Haskell, the paradoxical coexistence in recent American culture of statements implying objectivity and of a deep skepticism about the theoretical possibility of achieving such objectivity makes contemporary moral discourse incoherent. Even though the new appreciation of culture suggests that conventions, not revelations, rule American concepts of justice, the persistence of rights talk implies an aspiration to base moral arguments on appeals to reason. Despite the sympathetic reading he gives Nietzsche, Haskell does not agree that rights claims sink or swim with the Western flagship of objective knowledge. The recognition that reason does not exist independently of time and place does not deny its existence within time and place. Haskell asserts that rights can be viewed as conventions, as vital components of America's constitutional culture, that are exportable as ideals worthy of persuasive talk. Haskell argues that we can, with John Rawls, accept a conception of justice because of its congruence with a deeper understanding of ourselves.[25]

25. Thomas L. Haskell, "The Paradoxical Persistence of Rights Talk in the 'Age of Interpretation,'" *Journal of American History,* 74 (1987), 984–1012.

A deeper understanding of ourselves can lead to a heightened awareness of the contradictions that rage within and without. We can levitate ourselves intellectually outside our cultural universe long enough to recognize that such contradictions exist. That does not, however, liberate us from their hold. The national commitment to a constitutional order grounded in natural rights was grafted onto a culture that was profoundly racist and sexist. That contradiction has exercised a dynamic power for two centuries. Reformers have repeatedly sought to expose it; conservatives have evoked a concept of nature that restored the hierarchy once maintained by tradition. The crisis of natural rights discourse in the age of interpretation is not confined to the realization that fundamental law has no secure foundation in objective knowledge. It also resides in the refutation of specific assertions of Western philosophy, particularly its creation of human nature in its own image. Westerners have built their science as well as their institutions on specific propositions about human nature that our expanded knowledge of other societies denies. As Jacques Derrida has noted, we are living through "a de-centering of European culture" when Western metaphysics is being "forced to stop considering itself as the culture of reference." [26] Yet the very desire to ground belief in objective knowledge and the accompanying despair that it cannot be done suggest that renunciation of the center comes hard. The more troubling question may well be whether or not we can maintain our cultural center of gravity unweighted by belief in the universality of the characteristics of the autonomous Western man.

Anthropological studies of culture offer a powerful challenge to the belief in the universality of Western norms. But more than intellectual insight is involved. It will require an unprecedented act of humility for defenders of Western civilization to accept the fact that their view of nature is merely a convention. Mere convention cannot prove that constitutions are superior to customs, science to myth, individualism to corporatism, progress to stasis, experimentation to contemplation, or law to politics. Exploring those preferences as conventions leads away from universal propositions toward

26. Jacques Derrida, "Structure, Sign and Play in the Discourse of the Human Science," in *The Languages of Criticism and the Sciences of Man,* ed. Richard Macksey and Eugenia Donato (New York, 1970), 251.

particular mores. To convince others involves leveling appeals to experience and the abandonment of didactic demonstrations of proof. An appreciation for cultural differences offers a powerful solvent to Western hubris, and therein lies hope—a hope especially welcome to those who have felt the sting of universalist assumptions. But the decentering of which Derrida speaks affects the heirs and the disinherited of America's constitutional order quite differently. For the heirs, an elegiac mood prevails; the loss of the possibility of certainty is grave. For the disinherited, there is the possibility of liberation from a language of rights accompanied by a practice of denial. For both, doctrine will have to yield to explanation. A rich opportunity beckons, that of looking at the history of the United States Constitution as the record of a people contending about power, identity, and justice.

9

The American Model for the
French Revolutionaries

THE AMERICAN Revolution created a sentimental bond between the new American nation and French reformers who saw in American events a confirmation of their own ideas. With the philosophy of the Enlightenment they could lift the American Revolution out of its provincial context, and the American Revolution in turn invested their discursive thought with a reality it had not known before. Because the Franco-American alliance protected the publication of American works from the customary ban on foreign political writings, French reformers were able to make the first real breach in government censorship. Several European periodicals catered to the demand for news of America, and translations of the American state constitutions circulated widely.[1] After the Declaration of Independence one French writer after another took up his pen to analyze the significance of the American Revolution, debating small points of American political forms as matters that impinged on his deepest commitments. "Not a book on America was printed between 1775 and 1790 but ended with a sort of homily," Bernard Faÿ observed.[2]

---

1. See Gilbert Chinard, "Notes on the French Translations of the 'Forms of Government or Constitutions of the Several United States,' 1778 and 1783," in American Philosophical Society *Year Book* (Philadelphia, 1943), 88–106, and, for a detailed study of French ideas of America, Durand Echeverria, *Mirage in the West: A History of the French Image of American Society to 1815* (Princeton, 1957). All thirteen state constitutions were translated and published even though Connecticut and Rhode Island retained their colonial charters.

2. Bernard Faÿ, *The Revolutionary Spirit in France and America,* trans. Ramon Guthrie (New York, 1927), 194.

The obvious need for changes in the superannuated Bourbon monarchy had turned many prominent Frenchmen into reformers. Outwardly they were working for specific goals—penal reform, abolition of slavery, religious toleration, freedom of the press—but implicitly their activity suggested the need for the liberalization of French public life. Able men were eager to apply the knowledge of their enlightened age to the problems resulting from France's anachronistic government. However, to apply this knowledge, to think in terms of national problems, or to debate alternative solutions involved of itself a reformation of French society. It was this growing realization that made the American epoch from Revolution to Constitution seem both pertinent and prophetic. In the eyes of many Frenchmen, here was the first modern example of popular self-government and free institutions. Given the universalist assumptions of eighteenth-century thought, there was nothing incongruous about Frenchmen looking for guidance from a cluster of onetime colonies perched on the edge of a wilderness three thousand miles away. Indeed, to many French reformers the *tabula rasa* of American history was an asset, a return to first principles.

Events in France after 1787 had made the American political experience more relevant. The king, bowing to the pressure for a convocation of the Estates-General, issued an *arrêt* asking Frenchmen of all orders to communicate and publish their observations on the future meeting of the Estates. This invitation lifted the gate on a half-century of dammed up political energies, and Frenchmen responded with a flood of publications that did not stop until their revolution had run its course. Lafayette wrote Washington in early 1788 that he hoped France would soon have a constitution and a bill of rights.[3] Arthur Young, the English agronomist, reported that no one whom he met in his travels across France believed that the Estates-General could meet "without a revolution in the government ensuing."[4] Lafayette and his fellow reformers did not of course have the field to themselves. As Robert R. Palmer and others have demonstrated, the revolutionary movement in France began on the right not the left, and the king was first brought to bay by the chal-

---

3. Lafayette to Washington, Jan. 1, 1788, in *The Letters of Lafayette to Washington, 1777–1799,* ed. Louis Gottschalk (New York, 1944), 335.

4. Arthur Young, *Travels in France during the years 1787, 1788, and 1789 . . .* (Dublin, 1793), I, 130.

lenge from the privileged bodies of France, the nobilities of robe and sword.[5] After the failure of this *révolte nobiliare* the initiative passed to reformers bent on a more drastic overhauling of the nation's institutions. This chapter is concerned with one of the forces that swept France into successive revolutionary stages in 1788 and 1789. Specifically, I will try to assess the role that the American example played in the disputes which divided the reform group that emerged in 1789 as the principal political force. Because the American example was cultivated for partisan purposes to combat the influence of English ideas, I shall also examine in some detail the effort to promote England as a model for French reform.

The common assumption that France was at last to receive a modern constitution quickened an interest among reformers in both America and England. More important, the growing awareness that the French body politic was to be renovated forced a precision of terms upon a reform literature which had been hitherto a vehicle for discontent. It quickly became apparent that French reformers were not of one mind. Men who had worked together on common causes discovered fundamental differences in their projections of what France should become. Agreeing that her institutions were archaic, they differed on what in France's past must be jettisoned and what could be safely carried into the new era. These differences, which surfaced in late 1787, affected the reception of American as well as English influences. Where earlier both could have been admired, now they were consciously used to polarize sympathies within French reform sentiment. As they became more pertinent to political developments, they were turned into opposing symbols representing distinct and divergent goals. By early 1789 two models of civil society were competing for acceptance among those dedicated to the reform of French institutions. One was a generous appraisal of the English constitution and the other a radical reading of the American experience. Powerful enough to organize men's thoughts and define party positions, these models epitomized the liberal alternatives open to Frenchmen on the eve of their revolution. When the

5. Robert R. Palmer, *The Age of the Democratic Revolution: A Political History of Europe and America, 1760–1800* (Princeton, 1959), I. See also Ralph W. Greenlaw, "Pamphlet Literature in France During the Period of the Aristocratic Revolt (1787–1788)," *Journal of Modern History,* 29 (1957), 349–354.

French deputies in the National Assembly were called upon to consider that body's first constitutional proposals in the fall of 1789, the English and American models were the reference points for their debates.

The frequent appearance of the American name in these debates suggests that American principles and precepts were powerful determinants of French opinion, but actually the American name was used to convey certain carefully selected ideas. As Adam Ferguson noted, "If nations actually borrow from their neighbours, they probably borrow only what they are nearly in a condition to have invented themselves."[6] America and England were useful to Frenchmen just because France was ready to "invent" her own political forms. The fact of the American Revolution had had an enormous impact; the example of how Americans formed governments furnished key concepts, but America for those French reformers who invoked her name in 1789 was not nearly so much a source of guidance as she was a means of checking the growing admiration for English institutions.

Despite the bitter rivalry between France and England, educated Frenchmen had long honored England as the most free of all European nations.[7] Both Voltaire and Montesquieu, the two giants of the French Enlightenment, had specifically singled out England as the home of liberty. Frenchmen associated England with parliamentary government and public freedom. For traveling Frenchmen, a visit to England was an exhilarating experience. Englishmen seemed to have the best of two worlds: vigorous political institutions capable of accommodating change blended with a popular respect for tradition that invested English forms with an awesome, dignified beauty. The public discussions of France's future in the months before the convening of the Estates-General rekindled an enthusiasm for England among French intellectuals. The young Marquise Henriette Lucie de La Tour du Pin, daughter-in-law of the minister of war,

6. Adam Ferguson, *An Essay on the History of Civil Society* (Basel, 1789; originally published 1767), 257.

7. Gabriel Bonno, *La constitution brittanique devant l'opinion française de Montesquieu à Bonaparte* (Paris, 1931); David Williams, "French Opinion concerning the English Constitution in the Eighteenth Century," *Economica*, 10 (1930), 295–308; and Harold J. Laski, "The English Constitution and French Public Opinion, 1789–1794," *Politica*, 3 (1938), 27–42, offer interesting and conflicting points of view.

recalled in her memoirs being surrounded by reformers who wished to pattern a French constitution after that of England. The craze for everything English made an impression on her in 1788 as it did on Gouverneur Morris a year later when he wrote that "everything is à l'Anglais and a Desire to imitate the English prevails alike in the Cut of a Coat and the Form of a Constitution."[8] Mme. de Staël said that one heard a great deal more about the constitution of England than that of France. Louis Philippe, comte de Ségur, concluded that it was not English fashions that were loved but rather that the taste for English fashion was a way of veiling the real French longing for English liberty. Contemporaries called this passion for things English anglomania, and pro-English reformers like Trophime Gérard de Lally-Tolendal, Stanislas de Clermont-Tonnerre, Armand de Montmorin, Chrétien de Malesherbes, Jean Joseph Mounier, Pierre Victor de Malouet, Jean Baptiste Suard, and Jacques Mallet du Pan were consequently dubbed the *anglomanes,* a term that referred to those Frenchmen who wished to pattern a new France after the old England.[9]

This enthusiasm for England led to the belated discovery in France of Jean Louis De Lolme's study, *La Constitution de l'Angleterre,* a book that played a major role in the *anglomanes'* campaign to win popular support for reform *à l'anglaise.*[10] De Lolme, a Genevan and one of the first political exiles of "the age of the democratic revolution," had produced a learned apotheosis of the English political balance of king, Lords, and Commons. He wrote lucidly, and his arguments were very persuasive to Frenchmen struggling with the

---

8. Henriette Lucie de La Tour du Pin de Gouvernet, *Journal d'une femme de cinquante ans, 1778–1815* (Paris, 1907), I, 141–142; Morris to Washington, Mar. 2, 1789, Gouverneur Morris Papers, I, Library of Congress.

9. Elie Carcassone, *Montesquieu et le problème de la constitution française au XVIIIe siècle* (Paris, 1927), 662; Louis Philippe, comte de Ségur, *Oeuvres complètes de M. le comte de Ségur . . .* (Paris, 1824), I, 150–152. I am using the term *anglomane* to refer to a particular political persuasion and not to indicate an enthusiasm for English thought as used by Peter Gay, *The Enlightenment: An Interpretation* (New York, 1967), 12.

10. Jean Louis De Lolme, *La Constitution de l'Angleterre* (Amsterdam, 1771). The ban on foreign political writings prevented a wide circulation in France of the original edition of Amsterdam (1771), according to Pierre Samuel Du Pont, *Lettre à M. le comte Charles de Scheffer de 20 août 1773* (Paris, 1788), I. Fourteen years elapsed before another French edition was published.

problems of change in an essentially conservative society. He was particularly effective in arguing that the old and the organic in English institutions should be admired not because of some mystic association with the past—as the conservatives of church and state maintained about traditions—but rather because of their demonstrable value in preserving English liberty.

What De Lolme did was supply a rationale for French *anglomanes* who recognized the need for drastic reform but appreciated the permanence of social customs. He did not invent the idea of securing liberty and stability through the balancing of the one, the few, and the many. That was an eighteenth-century gloss on Polybius' mixed republic, but he did move from the general theory of balancing political power among existing social groupings to a minute inspection of how this balance had evolved through England's history and had been preserved through English customs. The similarity between England and France was obvious to contemporaries. They were the advanced nations of Europe. Both were monarchies with privileged noble classes. Both had educated and ambitious middle classes. Frenchmen whose sensibilities were rooted in the old regime could hardly help but feel the force of De Lolme's argument that a king and aristocracy were inevitable components of mature societies which men would do better to accept than fight.

Mounier, one of the *anglomanes'* best thinkers, made De Lolme's explanation of the English government the basis of his *Considérations sur les gouvernements*.[11] Mallet du Pan hailed De Lolme's book with a two-part tribute in his *Mercure de France*.[12] Charles Alexandre de Calonne, the exiled royal minister, commended De Lolme to the king in his *Lettre addressée au roi*.[13] Paul Philippe Gudin de la Brenellerie patterned his discussion of the English Parliament after De Lolme in his *Essai*.[14] Bertrand Barère, the future Jacobin, cited De Lolme's *Constitution de l'Angleterre* as the cause of French anglomania in

11. Jean Joseph Mounier, *Considérations sur les gouvernements et principalement sur celui qui convient à la France* (Paris, 1789), 22.

12. *Mercure de France* (Paris), Jan. 17, 24, 1789.

13. Charles Alexandre de Calonne, *Lettre addressée au roi par M. de Colonne, le 9 février 1789* (London, 1789), 100, 131.

14. Paul Philippe Gudin de la Brenellerie, *Essai sur l'histoire des comices de Rome, des Etats Généraux de la France et du Parlement d'Angleterre* (Philadelphia, 1789), III.

1787,[15] and Dominique Joseph Garat went so far as to claim that De Lolme's popularity equaled that of Rousseau.[16] Armand François, comte d'Allonville, tutor to the dauphin and an unreconstructed defender of the status quo, blamed the revolution on reformers who tried to imitate the English constitution because of the writings of the "romancier L'Olme."[17] From right and left De Lolme's book was recognized as an influence in shaping opinion. For the *anglomanes* it was a godsend—a reasoned defense of the English constitution, a triumph of scholarly persuasion, and a runaway best-seller.

De Lolme, the *anglomanes,* and their evident success in promoting the English constitution posed a serious threat to those Frenchmen who had long ago weighed the institutions of England and found them wanting. Good as she was in comparison to other European monarchies, she was not good enough in their enlightened day, and the need to prove her false appeared urgent if France was to be saved from a serious blunder. These critics of England were the ones who introduced a model of America as an alternative to England, but their disenchantment with the workings of the English constitution was older than the American Revolution. The *américanistes* coalesced as a group around the figure of Anne Robert Turgot, the famous reforming intendant whom Louis XVI had chosen for the office of controller-general in 1774. Turgot's efforts to liberate the French economy from the dead hand of the past had provoked the wrath of the privileged orders—the church, the nobilities of robe and sword, and the owners of myriad economic boons which hopelessly bogged down the production and distribution of French commodities. They persuaded the king to dismiss Turgot, and his fall signaled the end of hope for reform within the existing royal structure. Turgot and his followers, especially Antoine Caritat, Marquis de Condorcet, and Pierre Samuel Du Pont, then turned to questions of political reform, developing a theory of civil society which owed

15. Bertrand Barère de Vieuzac, *Mémoires de B. Barère, membre de la Constituante, de la Convention, du Comité de salut public, et de la Chambre des représentants,* ed. Lazare Hippolyte and Pierre Jean David d'Angers (Paris, 1842), 366.

16. Dominique Joseph Garat, *Mémoires historiques sur la vie de M. Suard, sur ses écrits et sur le XVIIIe siècle* (Paris, 1820), I, 196–197.

17. Armand François, comte d'Allonville, *Mémoires secrets de 1770 à 1830* (Paris, 1838), II, 2–3.

much to their economic ideas.[18] The natural harmony that they found in the physical world they projected into the social world. Like the physical world, society, they believed, was ruled by natural laws which if freed from human interference would operate to the benefit of all.

Implicit in such theories is the idea of the oneness of man, the similarity of his aspirations, the mutuality of his political and economic needs. Thus in the abstract, these men around Turgot rejected the idea that there were significant differences among men demanding special usages. As a practical matter, the privileged classes of France had proved over and over again to be the effective obstacle to all reform, so in theory and in practice, they must be circumvented. In place of the privileged orders of France, Turgot's group named the people as the proper legislators of France. Uncontaminated by the "special bodies" of privilege, the people, they believed, would be incapable of having interests distinct from those of the nation as a whole. From this it followed that France needed a political structure with one, unitary legislative body. Unicameralism became a major political goal. Although the third estate of commoners was France's political equivalent of the people, the ideal which the Turgot group developed appealed to many in the church and nobility as well. Drawn together by the idea of reconstructing the archaic French monarchy into a modern, humane, and unified nation, these men wrote voluminously on the subject. The vitality of these ideals as ideals should not be overlooked, even though they may have served some individuals as vehicles of social mobility or personal profit.

Such thinkers could not help but be critical of England, since there was no place in their reasoning for a sympathetic assessment of the virtues of the English constitution. The cherished procedures of the English parliamentary system were designed for a legislative process that accommodated different, often conflicting, interests within the country. Because the English had managed to preserve some degree of liberty and flexibility seemed no reasonable justifica-

18. Both Condorcet and Du Pont published biographies of Turgot in 1787 as well as posthumous publications of his works which can be found in Anne Robert Jacques Turgot, *Oeuvres de Turgot . . .*, ed. Gustave Schelle (Paris, 1913–1923; originally published 1808–1811).

tion for reproducing the excrescences along with the excellences of the English constitution. Moreover, any call for imitating England conjured up to them a government which conferred special political power on the very groups that had blocked all change in France for half a century. How much better to make a clean sweep of ancient forms and begin anew with enlightened principles. Why speak of the best that exists, Du Pont wrote in 1788, why not seek the best that is possible? [19] America nourished just this kind of hope for a new departure, and the group around Turgot—Du Pont, Condorcet, Mirabeau, the ducs de La Rochefoucauld—were among the first Frenchmen to take an interest in the American cause. They were friends of Franklin, and when Jefferson arrived to succeed Franklin, they became his friends. After Turgot's death in 1781, they continued as a group of kindred spirits. When the general French reform movement divided into distinct partisan groupings, these early admirers of America were joined by Pierre Louis, comte de Roederer, Lafayette, Adrien Duport, Abbé Sieyès, Guy Jean Target, and Talleyrand to form the nucleus of the *américaniste* group of 1789.

The differences that divided France's most articulate reformers on the eve of the revolution were fundamental—irreconcilable in theory as they proved to be in fact. The *anglomanes,* although they wished to reform the existing French society, considered a politically privileged group a necessary component of a well-constructed constitution. The *américanistes* were committed to political equality and popular sovereignty. They rejected tradition and the "lessons of the past" and were confident that France could be newly fashioned on the principles of natural law. The *anglomanes* believed that special interests were rooted in the nature of man and the complexity of society. Their opponents believed that force and chance had made some men masters and others servants. To the *anglomanes* history was a teacher; to the *américanistes,* a prison. The crux of their differences was the question of aristocratic power, but the debate swirled around the choice of forms for the legislature in a new constitution. A bicameral legislature was a symbol of balanced power with a house

19. *Analyse des papiers anglois,* ed. Honoré-Gabriel de Riquetti, comte de Mirabeau (Paris, 1787–1788), II, 267. For a thorough discussion of the anglophobic aspects of the *américanistes'* ideas, see Frances Acomb, *Anglophobia in France, 1763–1789* (Durham, N.C., 1950).

for the privileged few and a house for the unprivileged many, each with a veto in the lawmaking process. Unicameralism, on the other hand, was the institution for the brave, new world of the *américanistes* where the people would look after the interests of the nation. True to their physiocratic origins, they defined the people as the *propriétaires*, or landowners, a classification which included the many poor French peasants as well as the wealthy noblemen.

An important element in America's usefulness to the *américanistes* was the rejection of England implicit in her very existence. Her successful revolution gave the lie to the jaded pessimism of European conservatives. America, however, was valuable to the former *Turgotists* and *Economistes* who temporarily marched under the banner of *l'Amérique* only insofar as her practices and principles supported their program to free France from the moribund grasp of the French privileged classes. The strategy was not without its snares, the most serious being the lack of a clear-cut American endorsement of unicameral legislatures. Turgot himself had first criticized Americans for this in a letter to Richard Price. He charged the American states with perpetuating "useless imitations of English usages," referring to the office of governor and the two houses of the state legislatures as "separate bodies" in the traditional sense of French estates. "They undertake to balance these different authorities," Turgot wrote in 1778, "as if the same equilibrium of powers which has been thought necessary to balance the enormous preponderance of royalty could be of any use in republics, formed upon the equality of all the citizens." [20] No amount of American influence ever dislodged Turgot's followers from this position. John Adams, who shared Franklin's French acquaintances, grumbled when he recalled some years later that "Mr. Turgot, the Duke de la Rochefoucauld, and Mr. Condorcet and others, admired Mr. Franklin's Constitution and reprobated mine." [21] Pennsylvania had a unicameral legislature at the time.

20. Richard Price, *Observations on the Importance of the American Revolution* . . . (Boston, 1784), 75–77. It was as an appendix to this essay that Price made public Turgot's letter of March 1778 in the London edition of the same year. It was published in French in Honoré-Gabriel de Requitti, comte de Mirabeau, *Considérations sur l'ordre Cincinnatus* (London, 1784), and, according to Barère de Vieuzac, *Mémoires*, ed. Carnot and d'Angers, 366–392, was circulating in manuscript form as late as 1787.

21. John Adams to Samuel Perley, June 19, 1809, in *The Works of John Adams*, ed. Charles Francis Adams (Boston, 1850–1856), IX, 623.

The embarrassment of American bicameralism was aggravated by the new federal constitution for the United States, copies of which reached France in November 1787. This time, however, the *américanistes* confided their criticisms to private correspondents, particularly Franklin. Condorcet bemoaned the introduction of "the aristocratic spirit" in America and stoically concluded that if the constitution was the best that could be obtained then it must be regarded "as among the necessary evils." Du Pont and Louis Alexandre de La Rochefoucauld d'Enville also expressed their disappointment to Franklin, who agreed that two houses were not necessary, but reminded his French friends that the writers of the constitution were so different and "their prejudices so strong and so various, and their particular interests, independent of the general, seeming so opposite, that not a move" was not contested.[22] This was wasted commentary, for the *américanistes* held firmly to the conviction that the people could have no permanent interest contrary to the good of the nation as a whole.

The serviceability of the American name became even more doubtful with the seriatim publications in London of John Adams' *Defence of the Constitutions of Government of the United States of America.*[23] At the very time that the *américanistes* were trying to scotch the idea that aristocratic privileges should be perpetuated, an American hero and diplomat publicly endorsed the rationale for politically privileged elites. Pretty much an echo of De Lolme, Adams hailed the concept of balancing the power of the few against the power of the many as "this great truth, this eternal principle, without the knowledge of which every speculation upon government must be imperfect." Adams cited De Lolme's study as the best defense of the political balance of three powers ever written, and England, he maintained, had the only scientific government because it alone encompassed all things known to civil society and provided for all cases likely to appear in the progress of every nation, the "progress"

22. Franklin to Du Pont, June 9, 1788; Condorcet to Franklin, July 8, 1788; La Rochefoucauld to Franklin, July 12, 1788, in *The Works of Benjamin Franklin,* ed. John Bigelow (New York, 1904), XI, 433, 434–435, 436–437. See also Franklin to Le Veillard, Apr. 22, 1788, in *The Writings of Benjamin Franklin,* ed. Albert Henry Smyth (New York, 1906), IX, 645.

23. John Adams, *A Defence of the Constitutions of Government of the United States of America* (London, 1787–1788), I–III.

of every nation having already been disclosed to Adams by the records of the past. "To presume that an unmixed democratical government will preserve the laws," Adams intoned with characteristic dogmatism, "is as mad as to presume that a king or senate will do it."[24]

Perhaps the *américanistes* would have ditched the American model altogether had there not come to their hands an American pamphlet that could be turned to account against both De Lolme and Adams. In the winter of 1787, James Madison sent Philip Mazzei a copy of John Stevens' *Observations on Government, including some Animadversions on Mr. Adams's Defence . . . and on Mr. De Lolme's Constitution of England.*[25] Mazzei, a kind of Italian Tom Paine who was close to Jefferson's Paris establishment and the favorite salons of the *américanistes,* immediately sensed the utility of Stevens' pamphlet for his French friends and carried it to Du Pont and Condorcet. They decided to prepare a translation, and the presses that were slated to have turned out a translation of Adams' *Defence* were used instead for the *américanistes'* most ambitious publishing venture: a book-length annotated French translation of Stevens' pamphlet entitled *Examen du gouvernement d'Angleterre, comparé aux Constitutions des Etats-Unis . . .*[26] Madison apparently had written Mazzei that the pamphlet's pseudonym, "A Farmer of New-Jersey," belonged to New Jersey's most eminent writer and current governor, William Livingston. The French editors published this attribution in their introduction, so the name they put on hundreds of Gallic tongues was Livingston not Stevens.[27]

24. *The Works of John Adams,* ed. Adams, V, 183; IV, 358; VI, 117–118, 141.

25. See Philip Mazzei to James Madison, Feb. 4, 1788, in Richard C. Garlick, Jr., *Philip Mazzei, Friend of Jefferson: His Life and Letters* (Baltimore, 1933), 117; Philip Mazzei, *Memoirs of the Life and Peregrinations of the Florentine Philip Mazzei, 1730–1816,* trans. Howard R. Marraro (New York, 1942), 278–279. The book (with notations in Mazzei's hand) is a part of the Jefferson collection in the Library of Congress.

26. John Stevens, *Examen du gouvernement d'Angleterre, comparé aux Constitutions des Etats-Unis . . .* (London, 1789). See Joyce Appleby, "The Jefferson-Adams Rupture and the First French Translation of John Adams' *Defence," American Historical Review,* 73 (1967–1968), 1084–1091.

27. Stevens, *Examen,* v–vi. The best recapitulation of Stevens' claim to authorship is in Richard P. McCormick, *Experiment in Independence: New Jersey in the Critical Period, 1781–1789* (New Brunswick, N.J., 1950), 278–279. Jefferson corrected the attribution in his copy. There is strong evidence that American bibliographers of the nineteenth century picked it up from *Examen.*

Stevens' pamphlet was useful to the *américanistes* because Stevens attacked Adams for his imitation of De Lolme's faulty notions, saying that Adams sounded more like a European than a native of Massachusetts, for true Americans had faith that self-government could be achieved without leaning upon a king or aristocracy for stability. There was no proof that elites—standing powers, Adams called them—were inevitable, Stevens argued, and certainly there was no logic in making them more powerful than they already were. "By introducing 'independent and self-existing powers' in the government," Stevens wrote, "an interest is erected in the state distinct and separate from that of the community at large." "This martialing of power against power, in battle array," he concluded, "does not accord with my idea of perfection in government."[28] There was an element in Stevens' thinking that was very much akin to that of his French translators and altogether missing in Adams: a vivid sense of the possibilities of the future, an apperception of vital, substantial change in the society that was in the process of becoming. Adams exhorted his countrymen to read history for its lessons, while Stevens pointed to the hopefulness in America's unprecedented experiments in popular participation in government, near perfect political equality, guaranteed civil rights, and written constitutions. America, Stevens rhapsodized, should have "the honor of teaching mankind this important, this interesting lesson, THAT MAN IS ACTUALLY CAPABLE OF GOVERNING HIMSELF."[29] Unlike the French *américanistes*, however, Stevens did not disavow American bicameralism. What he did oppose was the use of the two houses of the legislature as the political preserve of social groups, the few and the many, the elite and the mass.

The American pamphlet accounted for only 66 pages of the French *Examen*. The additional 225 pages were devoted to notes and appendices clearly designed to link Stevens' arguments with the particular issues agitating French reformers in 1789. Much more explicitly than Stevens had done, the French editors drew attention to Adams' debt to De Lolme. Undoubtedly they wished to burden De Lolme with the responsibility for Adams' defection from the true American

28. John Stevens, *Observations on Government* . . . (New York, 1787), 28–29.
29. Ibid., 53.

political faith. However, the majority of the notes ignored Adams altogether and concentrated on the ideas of De Lolme and the nature of the true English government. Already Du Pont and Condorcet had published three items attacking De Lolme's *Constitution de l'Angleterre*,[30] and *Examen* is but a continuation of that attack, making more explicit the difference between the *anglomanes* and the *américanistes* on the question of the legislature. Ignoring Stevens' comments on bicameralism, the French editors drove home their point that to imitate England's Parliament was to divide the law-making power between two social groupings, while to create a unicameral legislature was to give reality to the concept of a nation uncontaminated by privileged power.

So effective were the *américanistes* in fitting Stevens' pamphlet to their own polemical needs that commentators ever since have cited the New-Jersey Farmer's preference for a unicameral legislature, despite the fact that Stevens specifically endorsed a bicameral system. It was for his alleged preference for unicameralism that Sieyès referred to *Examen* in the third edition of his famous *Qu'est-ce que c'est le tiers état?*[31] A hundred years later Bernard Faÿ characterized *Examen* (which he erroneously attributed to Robert Livingston) as a "brief and violent pamphlet which, in the name of pure democracy, took up the defense of Turgot's thesis and condemned the system of two legislative bodies as being a useless impediment to the machinery of government."[32] The French editors' silence about Stevens' true views was golden in this case, for they translated his lines on bicameralism without comment, while they jabbed away with rewarding results at De Lolme and the deplorable aristocratic bias of the English constitution.

When *Examen* made its appearance, anglomania was reaching its zenith. The fiery republican journalist Mademoiselle de Kerialo declared that the English constitution appeared to Frenchmen as the

---

30. Du Pont first criticized De Lolme's book in a commissioned letter that was published as *Lettre à M. le comte de Scheffer,* and in *Analyse des papiers anglois,* ed. Riquetti, Mar. 22, Apr. 1, 1788. Marie Jean Antoine Nicolas Caritat, marquis de Condorcet, attacked De Lolme's thesis in his *Lettres d'un Bourgeois de New-Haven à un Citoyen de Virginie, sur l'inutilité de partager le pouvoir législatif entre plusiers corps* (Paris, 1788), also published in Philip Mazzei, *Recherches historiques et politiques sur les états-unis de l'Amérique Septentrionale* (Paris, 1788).

31. Joseph Emmanuel, *Abbé Sieyès* (Paris, 1789), 97.

32. Faÿ, *Revolutionary Spirit,* trans. Guthrie, 279.

"chef d'oeuvre" of the human race in the early months of 1789.[33] The *américaniste* Roederer wrote that the English constitution appeared "to serve as the right model to France, and English liberty was regarded as the optimal political liberty."[34] The comtesse de Beaumont recalled the enthusiasm for the English constitution among the guests of her father, the foreign minister, Montmorin. She even remembered with relish how the Abbé André Morellet, an *anglomane*, had spiritedly attacked "some superficial publicists" for their criticism of England.[35] The importance of *Examen* as a volley against the *anglomanes* was recognized immediately. First reviewed in France's only daily newspaper, the *Journal de Paris*, *Examen* was greeted as a corrective to the seductive prose of De Lolme which might cure the French public of its dangerous adulation of the English constitution.[36] With Stevens' pamphlet, the *américanistes* had successfully constructed a model of America which could evoke her inspirational appeal without wedding their program to aspects of American government of which they disapproved.

The *anglomanes* struck back. Morellet prepared a twenty-three page critique for the *Mercure de France* which asserted that the French editors were far harder on De Lolme than the "Farmer of New-Jersey" had been. Lally-Tolendal claimed that *Examen* had aided those who already despised England. Mounier attacked *Examen* for its contradictions and charged the French nation with being fickle, one day adoring the English constitution, the next day affecting hatred for it.[37] By the time the National Assembly turned its attention to the reform of France in the summer of 1789, the months of pamphlet warfare had provided the terms, the authorities, and the arguments for the debates that followed.

Through the summer, while the Bastille was stormed, the feudal

33. Bonno, *La constitution brittanique*, 193.

34. Pierre Louis, comte de Roederer, *L'Esprit de la révolution de 1789* (Paris, 1831), 57.

35. Agénor Bardoux, *Etudes sur la fin du XVIIIe siècle. La Comtesse de Beaumont* (Paris, 1889; originally published 1884), 94, 126.

36. Feb. 13, 1789, later reprinted in the May 23, 1789 issue of *Mercure de France* (Paris), under the initials M.G., probably Dominique Joseph Garat's.

37. André Morellet's *Mercure de France* review was reprinted as *Lettre écrite à l'occasion de l'ouvrage intitulé: "Examen du gouvernement d'Angleterre"* (Paris, 1789); Trophime Gérard, marquis de Lally-Tolendal, *Mémoire de M. le comte de Lally-Tolendal, ou Seconde lettre à ses Comméttans* (Paris, 1790), 8; Mounier, *Considérations sur gouvernements*, 37.

privileges abolished, and the *Declaration of the Rights of Man and the Citizen* adopted, a committee dominated by *anglomanes* prepared a constitution which was largely an imitation of England's, with an upper house of lifetime, royally appointed members, and an absolute royal veto. When Mounier had finished reading the committee's constitutional proposals to the delegates, the *américaniste* Louis de Noailles suggested that the two major issues—the composition of the legislature and the nature of the king's veto—be debated first, after which, he claimed, all else would go smoothly.[38] With this proposal accepted, the showdown for which the *américanistes* and the *anglomanes* had long been preparing began.

America and England were referred to often in the ensuing weeks of debate: the American model as a support for a unicameral legislature and a suspensive veto, and the English model in support of a privileged upper house in a bicameral legislature and an absolute royal veto. Summarizing the differences in *Le Point du Jour,* Barère said that the English model vaunted the equilibrium of opposing and independent powers while the American model sought only liberty in a single legislative body uniting all interests in the nation.[39] The effectiveness of the gallicized *Observations on Government* was made obvious by the frequent references to Livingston, the supposed "Farmer of New-Jersey." Moreover, the *américanistes* had succeeded in pushing the burden of defending the corruption and oligarchic nature of the English system onto the *anglomanes.* Delegates from all over France repeated the charges that the *américanistes* had popularized in the months before. M. Sales said that the English did not enjoy political freedom. Pétion de Villeneuve challenged Montesquieu and the whole batch of English admirers. M. l'Epau disclaimed any similarity between England and France. Barnave insisted that it was no longer necessary to negotiate among independent powers within the state as the English had done.[40] M. Castellane rose to say that England was not admired for its double veto and hereditary magistracy, but rather because of its public spirit and the fact that Englishmen loved liberty and had the habit of living under the empire of laws. "Those who wish to have two

38. Louis de Noailles, *Le Point du Jour* (Paris), lxvi, II, 239.
39. Ibid., lxviii, II, 255–256.
40. Ibid., lxix, lxxi, II, 261–307.

houses are led astray by the very authors whom they appeal to for admiration," another delegate asserted, ending grandly, "Begone sentiment of the inconsequential De Lolme, of Montesquieu who could not escape from the prejudices of the robe. Begone vote of the Anglo-American M. Adams . . . they impress us no longer."[41] M. Laudine raised the question that the English might well correct their constitution were they given a chance to repudiate their House of Lords which is so useful to the king and so useless to the people. More explicitly, M. Lanjuinais announced: "If America has perfected the English government, then we ought to be able to perfect hers."[42] M. Thouret characterized Adams as a "blind partisan of the inequality of rights" as he castigated the English constitution.[43]

In vain did the *anglomanes* argue that France might copy good English principles without adopting bad English practices. Mounier urged the delegates who praised America to be consistent and recognize the extent of the American copying of English forms, a point echoed by other *anglomanes*.[44] Lally-Tolendal told the delegates that a comparison between France and the United States was too ridiculous to attempt to establish and urged them to attend to the fact that Adams and even Livingston, the New-Jersey Farmer, had associated stable government with the balance of three powers.[45] Nicolas Bergasse insisted that the Americans were approaching more closely the constitution of England.[46] Throughout the debates the *anglomanes* referred to the American example far more than their *américaniste* opponents, who preferred to dwell upon the failings of English government and the fallacies of the theory of balanced government. The *anglomane* argument that the Americans had adopted the very bicameral legislative system that the *américanistes* opposed became something of a debater's point, bypassing the con-

41. *Réimpression de l'Ancien Moniteur*, ed. Henri Plon (Paris, 1858), I, 540.

42. *Mercure de France* (Paris), Sept. 12, 1789; Assemblée Nationale, *Journal des débats et des décrets, 29 août 1789–29 août 1790* (Paris, 1789), I, 13–15.

43. *Point du Jour* (Paris), lxxi, II, 292.

44. *Mercure de France* (Paris), Sept. 12, 1789. See also Nicolas Bergasse, *Discours de M. Bergasse, sur la manière dont il convient de limiter le pouvoir législatif & le pouvoir exécutif dans une monarchie . . .* (Paris, 1789), 45.

45. Trophime Gérard, marquis de Lally-Tolendal, *Pièces justificatives contenant différentes motions de M. le comte de Lally-Tolendal* (Paris, 1789), 117–118.

46. Bergasse, *Discours*, 45.

trolling fact that the *américanistes* had learned from French, not American, experience.

As the time for voting on the first constitutional plan neared, the debates narrowed to the balanced government theory itself and the marshaling of authorities for and against it. The Abbé Jean Siffrein Maury, whom Barère cited as a great orator, pleaded with his fellow delegates to follow the masterpiece of political construction, the English constitution.[47] Lally-Tolendal declared in a rhetorical flourish that he would speak with "Lycurgus and Polybius, with Cicero and Tacitus, with Montesquieu, Gibbon, De Lolme, Blackstone, Adams, and Livingston himself," so sure was he that the "liberty and tranquillity of the people rests in the balancing of the three powers of the one, the few, and the many."[48] In response to this parading of authorities, La Rochefoucauld concluded that if one wished to pit writer against writer, there were enough celebrated men for each position. "Montesquieu could be refuted by Rousseau, Adams by Livingston."[49] Thus the names of the two Americans were mingled with those of the giants of political philosophy on the floor of the National Assembly. When all the possibilities had been debated and the vote finally called for, the delegates were overwhelmingly in favor of a unicameral legislature: 849 to 89. "One God, One King, One National Assembly" was the slogan of the hour. The *anglomane* members of the constitutional committee resigned their positions.

In reality the fight over two houses was determined when the first and second estates joined the third estate to form France's first modern legislative body. To set up a two-house legislature with all the implications of recreating a politically powerful nobility smacked too much of a step backward whatever the logic of the theorists or the utility of the English example. Barère recalled in his *Mémoires* that he had cautioned an *anglomane* committee member during the summer not to "think for a moment to obtain the power to create two chambers, which, by their likeness to those of England,

47. *Point du Jour* (Paris), lxx, II, 292.

48. Lally-Tolendal, *Seconde lettre*, 136. See also Assemblée Nationale, *Rapports du comité de Constitution, présentés à l'Assemblée Nationale, le 31 août 1789* (Versailles, [1789]), 23–24.

49. Louis Alexandre, duc de La Rochefoucauld d'Enville, *Opinion de m. le duc de La Rochefoucauld . . .* [7 septembre 1789] (Versailles, 1789), 7, 12.

would re-establish the clergy and nobility and make them stronger, more influential, more reactionary and more aristocratical than ever." He added significantly, "public opinion would forbid such a thing."[50] The assessment by the reporter for the *Moniteur* reveals even more sharply the polemics of the preceding months: "Former nobles did not want a new nobility created; democrats did not want one at all, and others believing that no state could exist without the mysterious equilibrium of three powers voted for one house to destroy the constitution."[51] The *Journal de Paris* characterized the idea of an upper house as "the asylum of the old aristocracy or the cradle of a new one."[52] These opinions, responsive of course to deeply felt fears among the National Assembly delegates, had nonetheless been carefully cultivated. A well-conceived polemical attack upon English political institutions had clarified and sharpened the issues involved in drafting a constitution and advertised an alternative to political privilege. Two German witnesses of the French Revolution, Ernst Brandes, who wrote for the *Berliner Monatsscrift,* and August Rehberg, a Hanoverian, credited the *américaniste* campaign with dissuading Frenchmen from following the English example. De Lolme and the English constitution were the vogue in France, Brandes maintained, until the party, "nourished by the combined maxims of J. J. Rousseau, the North American legislators, and the *économistes,"* gained a decisive preponderance with the help of Stevens' pamphlet.[53] Writing three years later in 1793, Rehberg, who shared Brandes' admiration of De Lolme, gave pretty much the same interpretation for the change of public opinion, citing *Examen* as a factor in the decline of De Lolme's and Adams' influence.[54] The English model was never seriously considered again. For the *américanistes,* who had deftly played off a deliberately vague image of a fresh, new democratic nation against the explicit flaws of old, oligarchical England, the victory was decisive.

50. Barère, *Mémoires,* ed. Carnot and d'Angers, 232.

51. *L'Ancien Moniteur,* ed. Plon, I, 441.

52. *Select documents illustrative of the history of the French revolution,* ed. L. H. Wickham Legg (Oxford, 1905), I, 143.

53. Ernst Brandes, *Considérations politiques sur la Révolution de France* (Paris, 1791), 80–88.

54. August Wilhelm Rehberg, *Untersuchungen über die Französische Revolution* (Hanover, 1793), II, 56–65.

Events after 1789 have largely obscured these early controversies—as though historians cannot quite accept as real the
polemics over constitutional questions when they know that beneath
the reasoned discourses were forces capable of destroying a whole
succession of constitutions. But men lead their lives forward, not
knowing what is to come, and the Frenchmen who debated the
future of France in these months were grappling with fundamental
problems of political reconstruction with a sense of urgency that
came from their conviction that their decisions would be critical.
The *américanistes* fought their *anglomane* opponents as a threat
equally as grave as the reactionary blindness of the court party. In
so doing they moved the revolution a little farther to the left. When
the American Revolution broke out, Turgot and his associates
already had the conceptual forms into which to pour the raw data
of American experience. Moreover, they had already rejected the
balanced government theory exemplified by England's constitution
and extolled by Montesquieu. So fixed were their political principles that when American statesmen failed to purify their governments of vestigial institutions, the French *américanistes* confidently
shaped their American model to conform to reason rather than
reality.

The *anglomane-américaniste* dispute makes explicit the disagreements within French reforming groups. These disagreements hinged
on different estimates of man and of civil society and on the possibility of genuinely new departures in the future. In this, these
French controversies of 1787, 1788, and 1789 are a preview of the
Angloman-Galloman quarrels in America in the 1790s. The debates
over the form of the legislature should also remind us that the issue
of bicameralism had nothing to do with the tepid practicality of
one house checking the other in the internal workings of the law-
making process. What was at stake was the legitimatizing of different social groups within society, the giving to the privileged few
that "more than equal" power of vetoing the decisions of the many.
Stevens took issue with Adams not for espousing a two-house legislature, but rather for using this legislative form to perpetuate and
strengthen social cleavages. French *anglomanes* lectured their readers
that the elite would not mingle in a new government on the same
basis as all other subjects; the *américanistes* could not accept this

prediction and rejected bicameralism just because it would give to the few the means of checking the will of the whole.

With strange, almost unnerving, empathy, John Stevens sat down in his farm in Hoboken and wrote a pamphlet which was immediately useful to a group of French reformers who were fighting the same political propositions that worried Stevens. This fact tells us of a cultural unity in the eighteenth century that colored very strongly the way men on both sides of the Atlantic viewed their world. Universalist assumptions about man and society cemented this unity—"truths the same for all good souls," Du Pont called them in the introduction to *Examen*. Both France and America aspired, as Stevens put it, "to teach this interesting lesson . . . that man might actually govern himself." Their classrooms proved to be quite different, however, and their revolutions so similarly conceived did more than anything to destroy the cultural unity and make way for an appreciation of the particular. Madame d'Houdetot, in a letter to Jefferson, showed just how quickly a perceptive observer could grasp the implications of different national experiences. "The characteristic difference between your revolution and ours, is that having nothing to destroy, you had nothing to injure, and labouring for a people, few in number, incorrupted, and extended over a large tract of country, you have avoided all the inconveniences of a situation, contrary in every respect. Every step in your revolution," she emphasized in anticipation of Louis Hartz's thesis, "was perhaps the effect of virtue, while ours are often faults, and sometimes crimes." [55] In the field of action there was a limit to what nations could borrow from one another, a fact which had not been apparent in the realm of ideas.

55. Mme. d'Houdetot to Jefferson, Sept. 3, 1790, in *Les Amitiés Américaines de Madame d'Houdetot, d'après sa correspondance inédite avec Benjamin Franklin et Thomas Jefferson*, ed. Gilbert Chinard (Paris, 1924), 56.

10

The "Agrarian Myth" in the Early Republic

THE YEAR 1943 marked the two-hundredth anniversary of the birth of Thomas Jefferson and the occasion for bestowing yet another honor on the Sage of Monticello. Amid salutes to Jefferson's politics and philosophy, historians and agronomists seized the opportunity to herald his contributions to scientific agriculture. Quoting from Vice-President Henry A. Wallace, M. L. Wilson claimed that farmers identified Jefferson with "the application of science to agriculture," and he then admiringly listed Jefferson's scientific achievements: the invention of a threshing machine, the improvement of the plow, the introduction of Merino sheep, and the advocacy of soil conservation.[1] August C. Miller, Jr., called Jefferson the father of American democracy and "a scientific farmer and agriculturist in the most comprehensive sense" of the term.[2] On this bicentennial anniversary, according to A. Whitney Griswold, people paid tribute to Jefferson as "preeminently and above all a farmer." Noting that Jefferson's enthusiasm for farming had always included commerce, Griswold agreed with William D. Grampp that Jefferson's concern about marketing farm commodities had

1. M. L. Wilson, "Thomas Jefferson—Farmer," *Proceedings of the American Philosophical Society,* 87 (1944), 217–219.

2. August C. Miller, Jr., "Jefferson as an Agriculturist," *Agricultural History,* 16 (1942), 65.

made him an ardent proponent of international free trade.[3] Thus, like the Department of Agriculture experts who gathered in the auditorium that bore his name, Jefferson in 1943 was depicted as an early-day New Dealer, a modernizer dedicated to helping ordinary farmers become efficient producers.

In 1955—just twelve years later—Richard Hofstadter published *The Age of Reform,* and Jefferson was captured for an altogether different historiographical tradition. Looking for the roots of the nostalgia that flowered with the Populists, Hofstadter described how Jefferson and other eighteenth-century writers had been drawn irresistibly to the "noncommercial, nonpecuniary, self-sufficient aspects of American farm life." The Jeffersonians, Hofstadter said, had created an "agrarian myth" and fashioned for the new nation a folk hero, the yeoman farmer, who was admired "not for his capacity to exploit opportunities and make money," but rather for his ability to produce a simple abundance. Underlining the mythic aspect of this literary creation, Hofstadter noted the actual profit orientation of the farmers who, he said, accepted the views of their social superiors as harmless flattery.[4]

The instantaneous popularity of Hofstadter's "agrarian myth" owes a good deal more to trends in the writing of history than to the evidentiary base upon which it rested. That in fact was very shaky. Hofstadter directed his readers to two writers, neither of whom drew the distinction he had made between the romantic myth of rural self-sufficiency created by writers and the reality of farming for profit acted upon by ordinary men. Griswold, whom Hofstadter claimed had produced "a full statement of the agrarian myth as it was formulated by Jefferson," in fact explored Jefferson's views on agricultural improvements and commercial expansion in order to point out that what had made sense in Jefferson's day no longer held true in the twentieth century.[5] The second writer to whom Hofstadter referred, Chester E. Eisinger, addressed Hofstadter's

3. A. Whitney Griswold, *Farming and Democracy* (New York, 1948), 18–19, 26–32; William D. Grampp, "A Re-examination of Jeffersonian Economics," *Southern Economic Journal,* 12 (1946), 263–282.

4. Richard Hofstadter, *The Age of Reform from Bryan to F.D.R.* (New York, 1955), 23–24, 30.

5. Ibid., 25; Griswold, *Farming and Democracy,* 12–15.

theme of national symbols, but his freehold concept can be readily differentiated from Hofstadter's agrarian myth. Tracing the appearance of independent freehold farmers to the destruction of feudal tenures, Eisinger explained how in England the same commercial forces that destroyed the manorial system had also worked to eliminate the small, freeholding producer. In America the reality of vacant land gave substance to a vision of a society of independent farmers; so the freehold concept, like so many other ideas, got a new lease on life by crossing the Atlantic. Where Hofstadter stressed the appeal of yeoman self-sufficiency, however, Eisinger linked the freehold concept to the emerging capitalistic economy. In the era of commercial agriculture, he wrote, "not only could a man possess his own farm, but he was his own master, rising and falling by his own efforts, bargaining in a free market."[6] Thus where Hofstadter's introductory chapter juxtaposed the agrarian myth and commercial realities, Eisinger distinguished between the poetic yearning for a bygone age of peasants and the modern reality of market-oriented farmers. All of Hofstadter's sources had traced the eighteenth-century literary preoccupation with farming to the rising population and the consequent importance of food production, but Hofstadter snapped this connection between material reality and intellectual response by stressing the purely mythic power of what two of his students have since characterized as the ideal of "'the self-sufficient' yeoman dwelling in a rural arcadia of unspoiled virtue, honest toil and rude plenty."[7]

Without looking firsthand at the literature of the 1790s, Hofstadter wrote his thesis about the nostalgic politics of the Populist era back into the earlier period. His indifference to a time that provided only a backdrop to the central drama in the age of reform is understandable. Indeed, what sustained the attractiveness of the yeoman ideal was not Hofstadter's book but a much stronger

6. Chester E. Eisinger, "The Freehold Concept in Eighteenth-Century American Letters," *William and Mary Quarterly*, 4 (1947). See also Chester E. Eisinger, "Land and Loyalty: Literary Expressions of Agrarian Nationalism in the Seventeenth and Eighteenth Centuries," *American Literature*, 21 (1949), 160–178; "The Farmer in the Eighteenth-Century Almanac," *Agricultural History*, 28 (1954), 107–112.

7. Stanley Elkins and Eric McKitrick, "Richard Hofstadter: A Progress," in *The Hofstadter Aegis: A Memorial*, ed. Stanley Elkins and Eric McKitrick (New York, 1975), 316.

tide coursing through scholarship on eighteenth-century America. As a quick survey of titles and expository prose produced in the last thirty years will reveal, *yeoman* has become a favorite designation for the ordinary farmer of postrevolutionary America. Losing its definition as a rank in a hierarchical society of tenants, yeomen, gentlemen, and lords, it has become instead a code word for a man of simple tastes, sturdy independence, and admirable disdain for all things newfangled. In this form the yeoman archetype has become particularly congruent with the recent work of those social historians who have sought to reconstruct the basic character and structure of colonial society.

Using continuous records on family formation and landholding patterns, such scholars have given special attention to the collective experience of whole communities. The models of the social scientists that they have employed, moreover, have encouraged them to look for the similarities between early American society and its counterpart in Europe. Where earlier historians had emphasized the idea of an America born free and modern, the new practitioners of social history have been more open to the possibility that America too had once been a traditional society. Indeed, they have found that, like traditional men and women of sociological theory, colonial Americans created the community solidarity and familial networks that encouraged resistance to change.[8] Instead of the contrast between old-fashioned and up-to-date that had been employed to describe the essentially external transformation from rural to industrial America, writings of the past few decades have concentrated on the connection between visible social action and invisible cultural influences. Traditional society as an abstract concept has been invested with the normative values of stability, cohesion, and neighborly concern, while the changes that came with economic development have been characterized as intrusive, exploitive, and class-biased. Where Hofstadter played off myth against reality, the new interpreters of early America are more likely to insist that a genuine conflict existed between farm communities and the modern world of money, markets, and merchants.

8. For a review of this literature, see John J. Waters, "From Democracy to Demography: Recent Historiography of the New England Town," in *Perspectives on Early American History: Essays in Honor of Richard B. Morris,* ed. Alden T. Vaughan and George Athan Billias (New York, 1973), 222–249.

It is this more refined and subtle model of rural life that has turned the Jeffersonians into nostalgic men fighting a rearguard action against the forces of modernity. Thus J. G. A. Pocock has named Jefferson as the conduit through which a civic concept of virtue entered "the whole tradition of American agrarian and populist messianism."[9] Less concerned with political issues, James A. Henretta has stressed the farmers' concern with protecting the lineal family from the centrifugal forces of individual enterprise and economic competition.[10] According to Lance Banning, the Republican party appealed to "the hesitations of agrarian conservatives as they experienced the stirrings of a more commercial age," while John M. Murrin has concluded that the Jeffersonians were like the English Country opposition on political and economic questions because "they idealized the past more than the future and feared significant change, especially major economic change, as corruption and degeneration."[11] For Drew R. McCoy the tension between tradition and innovation is more explicit. The Jeffersonians, he said, were forced to reconcile classical ideals with social realities; their ambiguities and contradictions reflected "an attempt to cling to the traditional republican spirit of classical antiquity without disregarding the new imperatives of a more modern commercial society."[12] In *The Elusive Republic,* McCoy has recovered the centrality of commercial policy in the Jeffersonians' program, but he has assumed that the values of civic humanism gave shape and direction to their recommendations.

In contrast to these characterizations of early national attitudes, I believe that the new European demand for American grains—the crops produced by most farm families from Virginia through Maryland, Pennsylvania, Delaware, New Jersey, New York, and up the Connecticut River Valley—created an unusually favorable oppor-

9. J. G. A. Pocock, "Virtue and Commerce in the Eighteenth Century," *Journal of Interdisciplinary History,* 3 (1972), 134. See also Pocock, *The Machiavellian Moment: Florentine Political Thought and the Atlantic Republican Tradition* (Princeton, 1975), 529–533.

10. James A. Henretta, "Families and Farms: *Mentalité* in Pre-Industrial America," *William and Mary Quarterly,* 35 (1978), 3–32.

11. Lance Banning, *The Jeffersonian Persuasion: Evolution of a Party Ideology* (Ithaca, 1978), 269; John M. Murrin, "The Great Inversion, or Court versus Country: A Comparison of the Revolution Settlements in England (1688–1721) and America (1776–1815)," in *Three British Revolutions: 1641, 1688, 1776,* ed. J. G. A. Pocock (Princeton, 1980), 406.

12. Drew R. McCoy, *The Elusive Republic: Political Economy in Jeffersonian America* (Chapel Hill, 1980), 10.

tunity for ordinary men to produce for the Atlantic trade world. Far from being viewed apprehensively, this prospect during the thirty years following the adoption of the Constitution undergirded Jefferson's optimism about America's future as a progressive, prosperous, democratic nation. Indeed, this anticipated participation in an expanding international commerce in foodstuffs created the material base for a new social vision owing little conceptually or practically to antiquity, the Renaissance, or the mercantilists of eighteenth-century England. From this perspective, the battle between the Jeffersonians and Federalists appears not as a conflict between the patrons of agrarian self-sufficiency and the proponents of modern commerce, but rather as a struggle between two different elaborations of capitalistic development in America. Jefferson becomes, not the heroic loser in a battle against modernity, but the conspicuous winner in a contest over how the government should serve its citizens in the first generation of the nation's territorial expansion.

Anyone searching for the word *yeoman* in the writings of the 1790s will be disappointed. A canvass of titles in Charles Evans' *American Bibliography* failed to turn up the designation *yeoman* in the more than thirty thousand works published in the United States between 1760 and 1800. The word *yeomanry* appeared only three times, all in works by a single author, George Logan.[13] Noah Webster, America's first lexicographer, defined *yeoman* as "a common man, or one of the plebeians, of the first or most respectable class; a freeholder, a man free born," but went on to explain that "the word is little used in the United States, unless as a title in law proceedings . . . and this only in particular states." *Yeomanry,* on the other hand, was much used, according to Webster, and referred to the collective body of freeholders. "Thus the common people in America are called the yeomanry."[14] For Webster, an ardent Fed-

13. Charles Evans, C. K. Shipton, and R. P. Bristol, comps., *American Bibliography,* 14 vols. (New York, 1959); George Logan, *Letters Addressed to the Yeomanry of the United States* (Philadelphia, 1791); *Five Letters, Addressed to the Yeomanry of the United States Containing Some Observations on the Dangerous Scheme of Governor Duer and Mr. Secretary Hamilton* (Philadelphia, 1792); *Letters Addressed to the Yeomanry of the United States Containing Some Observations on Funding and Bank Systems* (Philadelphia, 1793).

14. Noah Webster, *An American Dictionary of the English Language,* 2 vols. (New York,

eralist, the word retained the social distinction of its British provenance but conveyed nothing as such about farming. I have never found the word *yeoman* in Jefferson's writings; it certainly does not appear in his one book, *Notes on the State of Virginia,* where undifferentiated people in political contexts are called "citizens," "taxpayers," or "electors"; in economic references, "husbandmen," "farmers," or "laborers"; and in social commentary, "the poor," "the most discreet and honest inhabitants," or "respectable merchants and farmers." When Jefferson spoke in theoretical terms, ordinary persons were often discussed as "individuals," as in a passage where he says the dissolution of power would leave people "as individuals to shift for themselves." [15] Like Jefferson, the writers who filled Evans' bibliography with titles chose such socially neutral nouns as *farmers, planters, husbandmen, growers, inhabitants, landowners,* or more frequently, simply *countrymen,* a term whose double meaning reflected accurately the rural location of the preponderance of American citizens.

The absence of the word *yeoman* is negative evidence only, although its occasional use by contemporary Englishmen and New Englanders suggests a lingering reference to a status designation. [16] The error in current scholarly usage, however, is not lexical, but conceptual; it points Jefferson and his party in the wrong direction. Despite Jefferson's repeated assertions that his party was animated by bold new expectations for the human condition, the agrarian myth makes him a traditional, republican visionary, socially radical perhaps, but economically conservative. The assumed contradiction between democratic aspirations and economic romanticism explains why his plans were doomed to failure in competition with the hard-headed realism of an Alexander Hamilton. To this form of the argument, interpretive schemes much older than Hofstadter's have contributed a great deal. Viewed retrospectively by historians living

---

1828), s.v. "Yeoman" and "Yeomanry." See also Noah Webster, *A Compendious Dictionary of the English Language* (Hartford, 1806), where *yeoman* is defined as "a gentleman-farmer, freeholder, officer."

15. Thomas Jefferson, *Notes on the State of Virginia,* ed. William Peden (Chapel Hill, 1955), 125, 127, 130, 164–165, 213.

16. For the use of *yeoman* in this period, see *Boston Gazette,* Apr. 15, 1790, Mar. 3, 1794, May 25, 1796; *Independent Chronicle* (Boston), Dec. 15, 1786, Apr. 9, 1789.

in an industrial age, Jefferson's enthusiasm for agriculture has long been misinterpreted as an attachment to the past. So dazzling were the technological triumphs of railroad building and steam power that the age of the marvelous machines came to appear as the great divide in human history. Henry Adams offers a splendid example of this distorting perspective. Describing the United States in 1800, Adams said that "down to the close of the eighteenth century no change had occurred in the world which warranted practical men in assuming that great changes were to come." The connection between industrial technology and a modern mentality for him was complete, for he then went on to say, "as time passed, and as science developed man's capacity to control Nature's forces, old-fashioned conservatism vanished from society." [17] In fact, an American who was forty years old in 1800 would have seen every fixed point in his or her world dramatically transformed through violent political agitation, protracted warfare, galloping inflation, and republican revolutions. Yet for Adams the speed of travel held the human imagination in a thrall that the toppling of kings could not affect.

Two interpretative tendencies have followed from this point of view. One has been to treat proponents of agricultural development as conservative and to construe as progressive those who favored manufacturing and banking. The contrast between Jefferson cast as an agrarian romantic and Hamilton as the far-seeing capitalist comes readily to mind. The other retrospective bias has been the characterization of industrialization as an end toward which prior economic changes were inexorably moving. Both classical economic and Marxist theory have contributed to this determinism, which recasts historical events as parts of a process, as stages in a sequential morphology. Under this influence the actual human encounter with time is reversed; instead of interpreting social change as the result of particular responses to a knowable past, the decisions men and women made are examined in relation to future developments

---

17. Henry Adams, *The United States in 1800* (Ithaca, 1955), 42. Contrast this with Duc François de La Rochefoucauld-Liancourt's firsthand observation that America was "a country in flux; that which is true today as regards its population, its establishments, its prices, its commerce will not be true six months from now." David J. Brandenburg, "A French Aristocrat Looks at American Farming: La Rochefoucauld-Liancourt's *Voyages dans les Etats-Unis*," *Agricultural History*, 32 (1958), 163.

unknown to them.[18] The situation in America at the end of the eighteenth century is exemplary.

Ignorant of the industrial future, Americans were nonetheless aware that their economy was being reshaped by the most important material change of the era: the rise of European population and the consequent inability of European agriculture to meet the new demand for foodstuffs. After 1755 the terms of trade between grain and all other commodities turned decisively in favor of the grains and stayed that way until the third decade of the nineteenth century.[19] In *Common Sense,* Thomas Paine dismissed colonial fears about leaving the security of the English navigation system by saying that American commerce would flourish so long as "eating is the custom of Europe."[20] Eating of course had long been the custom of Europeans. What made their eating habits newly relevant to Americans was their declining capacity to feed themselves. More fortunate than most of her neighbors, England benefited from a century and a half of previous agricultural improvements, so that pressure from her growing population meant that harvest surpluses, which had once been exported, after mid-century were consumed at home. The withdrawal of English grains, however, created major food deficits on the Iberian Peninsula. No longer able to rely upon Britain's bounteous harvests, the Spanish and Portuguese began looking anxiously across the Atlantic to North America. The impact of food shortages had a differential impact upon European nations, but for Americans the consequences, particularly after 1788, were salubrious. The long upward climb of prices enhanced the value of those crops that ordinary farmers could easily grow.[21] Combined with the

18. For a critique of this tendency in economic history, see Robert E. Mutch, "Yeoman and Merchant in Pre-Industrial America: Eighteenth-Century Massachusetts as a Case Study," *Societas,* 7 (1977), 279–302.

19. B. H. Slicher Van Bath, "Eighteenth-Century Agriculture on the Continent of Europe: Evolution or Revolution?," *Agricultural History,* 63 (1969), 173–175.

20. [Thomas Paine], *Common Sense, Addressed to the Inhabitants of America,* in *The Writings of Thomas Paine,* ed. Moncure Daniel Conway, 4 vols. (New York, 1894–1896), I, 86.

21. For some important interpretative points in regard to agricultural productivity and to exports as its measure, see Claudia D. Goldin and Frank D. Lewis, "The Role of Exports in American Economic Growth during the Napoleonic Wars, 1793 to 1807," *Explorations in Economic History,* 17 (1980), 6–25; William N. Parker, "Sources of Agricultural Productivity in the Nineteenth Century," *Journal of Farm Economics,* 49 (1967), 1455–1468; and

strong markets in the West Indies for corn and meat products, the growth of European markets for American foodstuffs had the greatest impact on the ordinary farmer who pursued a mixed husbandry.

The first and most conspicuous response to these economic changes came in the prerevolutionary South where large planters and small farmers alike began planting wheat instead of tobacco. While soil exhaustion offered an incentive to make the switch, rising prices for grains financed the conversion. In the frontier areas of the Piedmont and Shenandoah Valley, selling grain and livestock surpluses offered a speedy avenue of integration into the Atlantic trade world.[22] As historians have recently made clear, this change-over to grains in the Upper South involved more than agricultural techniques, for the marketing of wheat and corn had a decisive influence upon the area's urban growth. The switch to grains and livestock along the Eastern Shore, the lower James, the upper Potomac, and in the Piedmont promoted in two decades the cities, towns, and hamlets that had eluded the Chesapeake region during the previous century of tobacco production. Equally important to the character of these new urban networks was capturing what Jacob M. Price has termed "the entrepreneurial headquarters" of the grain trade. Unlike tobacco, the capital and marketing profits for the commerce in food remained in American hands.[23] For planters and farmers the switch to wheat could mean liberation from British factors and merchants who controlled both the sales and purchases of Tidewater tobacco planters. Such a possibility can be read in more personal terms in the writings of the young planter George Washington, who pledged himself to economic freedom by raising wheat.[24] Fanning out from Baltimore, Norfolk, and later Richmond,

Andrew Hill Clark, "Suggestions for the Geographical Study of Agricultural Change in the United States, 1790–1840," in *Farming the New Nation: Interpreting American Agriculture, 1790–1840,* ed. Darwin P. Kelsey (Washington, 1972), 155–172.

22. Robert D. Mitchell, *Commercialism and Frontier: Perspectives on the Early Shenandoah Valley* (Charlottesville, 1977), 40, 173–178; Malcolm J. Rohrbough, *The Trans-Appalachian Frontier: People, Societies, and Institutions, 1775–1850* (New York, 1978), 99–106.

23. Carville Earle and Ronald Hoffman, "Staple Crops and Urban Development in the Eighteenth-Century South," *Perspectives in American History,* 10 (1976), 5–78; Jacob M. Price, "Economic Function and the Growth of American Port Towns in the Eighteenth Century," *Perspectives in American History,* 8 (1974), 121–186.

24. James Thomas Flexner, *George Washington: The Forge of Experience, 1732–1775* (Boston, 1965), 279–284.

an array of market towns sprang up to handle the inspection, storage, processing, and shipping of the grains and livestock being pulled into the Atlantic trade from the rural areas of North Carolina, Virginia, Maryland, and Pennsylvania. During these same years Philadelphia and New York, both drawing on a grain-raising hinterland, surpassed Boston in population, wealth, and shipping.[25]

The dislocations of the American Revolution were followed by a five-year depression, but in 1788 a new upward surge in grain and livestock prices ushered in a thirty-year period of prosperity. Even in England the shortfall between grain production and domestic demand led to net grain imports for twenty-seven out of these thirty years. Southern European demand remained strong. A printed solicitation for American business sent from a Barcelona firm in 1796 described American wheat and flour as much esteemed and constantly in demand "in this Place & Province, which," as the handbill explained, "in years of abundance never produces more than for four Months provisions."[26] In the longer run, sustained profits in grain-raising encouraged investments in agricultural improvements and prompted heroic efforts to increase output. By 1820, especially in England, Belgium, and the Netherlands, food production again had caught up with population growth, and prices returned to the levels of the mid-1790s.[27] Higher yields abroad, not the end of the Napoleonic Wars, curbed demand for American farm products.

Coinciding as it did with the adoption of the United States Constitution, the new climb of food prices meant not only that the market could penetrate further into the countryside but also that the national government could extend its reach with improvements in communication and transportation systems. In the single decade of the 1790s, America's 75 post offices increased to 903, while the mileage of post routes went from 1,875 to 20,817. The number of

25. Price, "Economic Function and the Growth of American Port Towns," 151–160.

26. Arabet, Gautier, and Manning handbill, Barcelona, May 18, 1796, File 1215, Miscellaneous Material Regarding Philadelphia Business Concerns, 1784–1824 (Eleutherian Mills Historical Library, Wilmington, Del.). British imports of American grain can be followed in Great Britain, Parliamentary Papers (Commons), "An Account of the Grain of All Sorts, Meal, and Flour, Stated in Quarters, Imported into Great Britain in Each Year from January 5, 1800 to January 5, 1825" (no. 227), 1825, xx, 233–267. For the earlier period, see Great Britain, Parliamentary Papers (Commons), "Accounts Relating to Corn, Etc." (no. 50), 1826–1827, xvi, 487–501.

27. Slicher Van Bath, "Eighteenth-Century Agriculture," 175.

newspapers more than doubled; circulation itself increased threefold. In the middle of the decade turnpike construction began.[28] With each decadal increase in grain prices, the distance wheat and flour could be carted profitably to market increased dramatically. At 1772 price levels, farmers and grain merchants could afford to ship flour 121 miles and wheat 64 to reach the grain-exporting seaports of Norfolk, Baltimore, Richmond, Philadelphia, and New York. Between 1800 and 1819 the range had extended to 201 miles for flour and 143 for wheat. For the farmer who wished to earn his own teamster's wage, the distance could be extended further.[29] The population doubled during the first twenty-three years of the new national government, but even more important to the burgeoning trade in American foodstuffs, the preponderance of American farmers lived within marketing range of the inland waterways that flowed into the sea-lanes of the great Atlantic commerce. As the volume of grain exports grew, country stores replaced rural fairs, and millers, bakers, butchers, brewers, and tanners turned from the custom trade of their neighbors to the commercial processing of the farmer's surpluses.

For the gentlemen planters of the Upper South, the switch to wheat represented a calculated response to new market opportunities, but for the mass of ordinary farmers the growing demand for foodstuffs abroad offered an inducement to increase surpluses without giving up the basic structure of the family farm. The man with seventy-five to one hundred acres who relied principally upon his own and his family's labor to grow Indian corn and wheat and to tend his livestock and draft animals could participate in the market with increasing profits without taking the risks associated with cash crops.[30] European population growth had enhanced the

28. Allan R. Pred, *Urban Growth and the Circulation of Information: The United States System of Cities, 1790–1840* (Cambridge, Mass., 1973), 58–59, 80, 153.

29. Ibid., 114. Max G. Schumacher has calculated the "approximate maximum commercial range from Baltimore and Philadelphia of wheat and flour dependent on land-carriage" for price levels in 1755 and 1772. I extended Schumacher's ratios to the price range from 1800 to 1819. Max G. Schumacher, *The Northern Farmer and His Markets during the Late Colonial Period* (New York, 1975), 63.

30. As this relates to Maryland, see Paul G. E. Clemens, *The Atlantic Economy and Colonial Maryland's Eastern Shore: From Tobacco to Grain* (Ithaca, 1980). See also Mitchell, *Commercialism and Frontier*, 234; David Maldwyn Ellis, *Landlords and Farmers in the Hudson-Mohawk Region, 1790–1850* (New York, 1967), 76–82; Sarah Shaver Hughes, "Elizabeth

value of the little man's harvests, not that of the rich man's staples. It also blurred the old textbook distinction between the commercial agriculture of the South and the subsistence farming of the North. The wheat farmer's replication of European crops was no longer a commercial liability, for it was exactly the foods and fibers indigenous to Europe that were in demand. Published prices current of American produce in Liverpool, Amsterdam, Le Havre, Bordeaux, Barcelona, Saint-Domingue, and Havana convey the situation: wheat, flour, Indian corn, clover seed, flaxseed, hemp, deerskins, beeswax, staves, and timber all commanded good prices, while West Indian markets took beef, pork, fish, cider, apples, potatoes, peas, bread, lard, onions, cheese, and butter as well. The mixed husbandry through which the farmer supplied his family also fed into the stream of commerce that linked rural stores and backcountry millers to the Atlantic commerce. To be sure, as Diane Lindstrom has pointed out, the farmer's family remained his best customer, but this held true well into the nineteenth century.[31]

The diversity of demand for American farm commodities in the generation after 1788 encouraged the adoption of the up-and-down husbandry that had revolutionized English and Dutch agriculture a century earlier. Here diversification, not specialization, held the key to raising crop yields and maintaining soil fertility in an age without chemical fertilizers.[32] Livestock and wheat raising required dividing land among meadows, pastures, and fields. When these were rotated, yields could be increased and fertility maintained. Livestock

---

City County, Virginia, 1782–1810: The Economic and Social Structure of a Tidewater County in the Early National Years" (Ph.D. diss., College of William and Mary, 1975), 406–407; David C. Klingaman, *Colonial Virginia's Coastwise and Grain Trade* (New York, 1975). For some of the theoretical implications of the market involvement of self-sufficient family farms, see Mutch, "Yeoman and Merchant," 279–302.

31. Diane Lindstrom, "Southern Dependence upon Western Grain Supplies" (M.A. thesis, University of Delaware, 1969), 10. Printed prices current and merchant handbills can be sampled in manuscript files 1303, 667, 1097, 1144, 1215, and 1457 (Eleutherian Mills Historical Library). Comparisons were made between advertised export items and farm account books in the collections at the Delaware State Archives (Dover); the University of Delaware Library Special Collections (Newark); and the Historical Society of Delaware (Wilmington).

32. Eric Kerridge, *The Agricultural Revolution* (London, 1967), 39–40, 107, 214–215, 299, 347–348.

fed with soil-enriching grasses could also produce manure for fields of wheat and corn. While foreign visitors judged American farmers improvident and wasteful, American writers insisted that European practices had been adapted to American needs. Fertility in the grain- and livestock-producing areas evidently held up.[33]

Economies of scale had practically no bearing on the enhancement of the harvests that produced the food surpluses of the eighteenth and early nineteenth centuries. Attention to detail was the key. As the agricultural writer John Dabney explained, the farmer who does not "cart out his summer dung, nor plough those lands in the fall, which he means to feed in the following spring" could not grow rich.[34] In no other husbandry was it more true that the best manure was the tread of the master's foot. Moreover, the capital investments that could improve output—folding animals, bringing uncultivated land under the plow, laying down new pastures—could be made by the ordinary farmer willing to exchange leisure for off-season

33. For a foreign view of American agriculture based on a tour in 1794–1795, see William Strickland, *Observations on the Agriculture of the United States of America* (London, 1801). A rebuttal is provided by William Tatham, *Communications Concerning the Agriculture and Commerce of America* (London, 1800). The controversy over William Strickland's report to the English Board of Agriculture is covered by G. Melvin Herndon, "Agriculture in America in the 1790s: An Englishman's View," *Agricultural History,* 49 (1975), 505–516. Other contemporary writers who stressed both the differences and the profitability of American agriculture were Timothy Matlack, *An Oration Delivered March 16, 1780* (Philadelphia, 1780), 14–16; François Alexandre Frederick, duc de La Rochefoucauld-Liancourt, *Voyages dans les États Unis d'Amérique Fait en 1795, 1796, et 1797,* 8 vols. (Paris, [1799]), I, 101–117; II, 325; III, 50; John Spurrier, *The Practical Farmer* (Wilmington, Del., 1793); John A. Binns, *A Treatise on Practical Farming* (Frederick-town, Md., 1803); George Logan, *Fourteen Experiments on Agriculture* (Philadelphia, 1797); and J. B. Bordley, *Essays and Notes on Husbandry and Rural Affairs* (Philadelphia, 1801). Estimates on yields vary widely. William Guthrie estimated that yields in Delaware after fifty years of planting continued at levels of 15 to 25 bushels per acre for wheat and barley and 200 for Indian corn. William Guthrie, *A New System of Modern Geography,* 2 vols. (Philadephia, 1795), II, 458. Sarah Shaver Hughes confirmed Gurthrie's conclusion that fertility held up; Hughes, "Elizabeth City County, Virginia," 90–91. An elaborate tabular computation of wages, prices, and yields done by La Rochefoucauld-Liancourt indicates yields ranging from 8 to 25 bushels per acre for various areas in the Delaware, Maryland, and Pennsylvania wheat-raising belt. "Tabulation of Commerce in the United States, 1795–1797," file 501, P. S. Du Pont Office Collection (Eleutherian Mills Historical Library).

34. [John Dabney], *An Address to Farmers* (Newburyport, Mass., 1796), 5. John Dabney continued: "A complete Farmer is also a man of great carefulness and solicitude; without care, the severest labor on the best of Farms, will never produce riches or plenty."

labors.[35] Increasing surpluses required, above all, a better management of time and a close watch on the market. Here too the range of farm commodities in demand redounded to the benefit of the small farmer, for each nook and cranny had a potential use. Hemp, according to John Alexander Binns, could be raised on every conceivable hollow just as beehives, whose wax commanded good prices in England, could be lodged near the ubiquitous stands of white clover.[36] The relative success of the farmers who harvested wheat in the Middle Atlantic states can be gauged by Stanley L. Engerman's findings that the wealth of the North surpassed that of the South for the first time in the period from 1774 to 1798.[37] Without any of the qualities that characterized commercial agriculture in the colonial period—slave labor, specialization, large holdings—northern farmers had been brought into the thriving trade in foodstuffs.

Although high food prices greatly increased the ambit of the market, soil and climate more rigidly delimited the domain of up-and-down husbandry. The optimal mix of livestock and grain raising depended on crops of timothy, alfalfa, and clover, which were not easily grown in the Lower South where heavy rains leached the land, leaving severe lime deficiencies. Hot, humid summers exposed cattle to ticks and mosquitos which kept herds small. Agricultural improvements in these areas had to await later developments in fertilizers and soil amendments.[38] In New England the thin soils and rocky terrain also barred farmers from effectively competing with the rich farmlands of the South and West. Even before the Revolution, Massachusetts had become an importer of

35. For theoretical discussion of this point, see Stephen Hymer and Stephen Resnick, "A Model of an Agrarian Economy with Nonagricultural Activities," *American Economic Review*, 59 (1969), 493–506.

36. John A. Binns, *A Treatise of Practical Farming* (Richmond, 1804), 63. Dabney maintained that a farmer could clear £6 profit from an acre of flax. Dabney, *Address to Farmers*, 51. Substantial British imports of American beeswax are reported in Edmund C. Burnett, "Observations of London Merchants on American Trade, 1783," *American Historical Review*, 18 (1913), 776.

37. Stanley L. Engerman, "A Reconsideration of Southern Economic Growth, 1770–1860," *Agricultural History*, 49 (1975), 348–349.

38. Julius Rubin, "The Limits of Agricultural Progress in the Nineteenth-Century South," *Agricultural History*, 49 (1975), 362–373.

wheat.[39] The New England situation did not encourage the embrace of an expansive, market-oriented, food-raising economy. In time the reexport trade breathed new life into the mercantile sector, but manufacturing, with its very different cultural imperatives, held out the long-range prospect for development.[40] Thus, despite the easy entry into the mixed husbandry of grain and livestock raising, climate and topography drew the borders around the wheat belt that passed through Virginia, Maryland, Delaware, Pennsylvania, New Jersey, and New York. As long as food prices remained high, the conventional divisions of North and South, subsistence and commercial, yielded to a core of common interests among American farmers, food processors, and merchants in this favored region.[41]

The acknowledged novelty of the new American nation's political experiments has too often obscured the equally strong sense contemporaries had that they were entering a new economic era as well. Gouverneur Morris, for instance, called his fellow countrymen of 1782 "the first born children of extended Commerce in modern Times."[42] Americans were repeatedly characterized as eager market participants—certainly when it came to spending and borrowing—and commerce itself was associated with a remarkable augmentation of wealth-producing possibilities. "The spirit for Trade which pervades these States is not to be restrained," George Washington wrote to James Warren in 1784. Jefferson, eager to build canals linking the Chesapeake to the interior valleys of Virginia, wrote Washington that since all the world was becoming commercial, America too must get as much as possible of this modern source of wealth and power.[43] Timothy Matlack predicted for an audience in

39. Klingaman, *Colonial Virginia's Coastwise and Grain Trade,* 38.

40. Charles L. Sanford, "The Intellectual Origins and New-Worldlinesss of American Industry," *Journal of Economic History,* 18 (1958), 1–16.

41. For a discussion of the problem of discriminating between a subsistence and a commercial agriculture, see Clark, "Suggestions," 166.

42. Gouverneur Morris to Matthew Ridley, Aug. 6, 1782, quoted in Clarence Ver Steeg, *Robert Morris: Revolutionary Financier* (Philadelphia, 1954), 166–167.

43. George Washington to James Warren, Oct. 7, 1785, *The Writings of George Washington, from the Original Manuscript Sources, 1745–1799,* ed. John C. Fitzpatrick, 39 vols. (Washington, 1931–1944), XXVIII, 290–291; Thomas Jefferson to Washington, Mar. 15, 1784, *The Papers of Thomas Jefferson,* ed. Julian P. Boyd et al., 19 vols. (Princeton, 1950–1974), VII, 26.

Philadelphia the rise of America to a "Height of Riches, Strength and Glory, which the fondest Imagination cannot readily conceive," going on to specify that "the Star-bespangled Genius of America . . . points to Agriculture as the stable Foundation of this rising mighty Empire."[44] Without any major technological breakthrough, the late-eighteenth-century economy nonetheless suggested to men that they stood on the threshold of major advances.

By isolating in time and space the golden era of grain growing in the early national period, one can see more clearly the material base upon which Jefferson built his vision of America, a vision that was both democratic and capitalistic, agrarian and commercial. It is especially the commercial component of Jefferson's program that sinks periodically from scholarly view, a submersion that can be traced to the failure to connect Jefferson's interpretation of economic developments to his political goals. Agriculture did not figure in his plans as a venerable form of production giving shelter to a traditional way of life; rather, he was responsive to every possible change in cultivation, processing, and marketing that would enhance its profitability. It was exactly the promise of progressive agricultural development that fueled his hopes that ordinary men might escape the tyranny of their social superiors both as employers and magistrates. More than most democratic reformers, he recognized that hierarchy rested on economic relations and a deference to the past as well as formal privilege and social custom.

The Upper South's conversion from tobacco to wheat provided the central focus for Jefferson's discussion of commerce and manufacturing in his *Notes on the State of Virginia*. Throughout the Tidewater, planters were shifting from the old staple, tobacco, to the production of cereals. Made profitable by the sharp price increases occasioned by European and American population growth, foodstuffs were much less labor-intensive than tobacco and were therefore suitable for family farms. Large and small Virginia planters became integrated into the new grain-marketing network that connected American producers from the James to the Hudson with buyers throughout the Atlantic world. As Jefferson wrote, wheat raising "diffuses plenty and happiness among the whole," and it did so, he

44. Matlack, *Oration*, 25.

noted, with only moderate toil, an observation that evokes the unstated, invidious comparison with slave labor.[45] Whether talking about consumption or production, he took for granted the importance of the market in influencing developments. For instance, he predicted that wheat would continue to replace tobacco because growers in Georgia and the Mississippi Territory would be able to undersell their Chesapeake competitors. Similarly the weevil might threaten the profits of the Virginia wheat grower, for the expense of combating the infestation would "enable other countries to undersell him." Looking to the future, Jefferson hailed the "immensity of land courting the industry of the husbandman," but he assumed that the husbandman would participate in international trade. Popular taste, that final arbiter for Jefferson, guaranteed that Americans would "return as soon as they can, to the raising [of] raw materials, and exchanging them for finer manufactures than they are able to execute themselves." The country's interest, therefore, would be to "throw open the doors of commerce, and to knock off all its shackles." At the same time it was entirely natural to Jefferson to mix shrewd assessment of market realities with homiletic commentary. Thus, he said, relying on European manufacturing would forestall the corruption of "the mass of cultivators," and he condemned tobacco raising as "a culture productive of infinite wretchedness."[46]

Working with a completely commercial mode of agriculture, Jefferson projected for America a dynamic food-producing and food-selling economy which promised the best of two worlds: economic independence for the bulk of the population and a rising standard of living. Even the word *farmer* captured some of the novelty of the new prospect. As William Tatham explained to his English readers, the cultivator "who follows the ancient track of his ancestors, is called a *planter*" while he "who sows wheat, and waters meadows, is a *farmer*."[47] The concrete policy measures that emanated from this prescription for American growth were both political and economic:

45. Jefferson, *Notes on the State of Virginia,* 168.

46. Ibid., 164–168, 174. For a description of the Founding Fathers as having "commerce-phobia," citing Jefferson's expressions of enthusiasm for free trade as the result of his years in France, see James H. Hutson, "Intellectual Foundations of Early American Diplomacy," *Diplomatic History,* 1 (1977), 6, 8.

47. Tatham, *Communications Concerning the Agriculture and Commerce of the United States,* 46.

making new land in the national domain accessible to the individual farmer-owner, using diplomatic initiatives to open markets around the world, committing public funds to internal improvements, and, negatively, opposing fiscal measures that bore heavily upon the ordinary, rural taxpayers.[48] William N. Parker has described just what these policies meant to mid-nineteenth-century agriculture: "an ambitious farmer might buy more farms, but he gained no economies by consolidating them" because "enterprise was too vigorous and too widely diffused, competition for finance, land, and labor too intense to permit large concentrations of wealth in land." The larger farmer, moreover, "suffered the disadvantages of the liberal land policy and the prevailing sentiment in favor of the settler."[49]

Jefferson was not alone in joining political democracy to economic freedom; these themes coalesced in a number of local movements that in time found a national base in the opposition to Hamilton's program. Typical of this new view was Logan's declaration that the sacred rights of mankind included farmers deriving "all the advantages they can from every part of the produce of their farms," a goal that required "a perfectly free commerce" and "a free unrestricted sale for the produce of their own industry."[50] In a similar spirit John Spurrier dedicated *The Practical Farmer* to Jefferson because of his interest in agricultural science and his efforts "to promote the real strength and wealth of this commonwealth" on rational principles.[51] Writing at the same time, Tench Coxe described the overwhelming importance of farming to America. Capital and labor investments in agriculture were eight times those in any other pursuit, he estimated. More pertinently, he gave almost exclusive attention to the range of foodstuffs produced by family labor from Virginia to Connecticut.[52]

48. For excellent discussions of Thomas Jefferson's commercial policies, see Merrill Peterson, "Thomas Jefferson and Commercial Policy, 1783–1793," *William and Mary Quarterly,* 22 (1965); Richard E. Ellis, "The Political Economy of Thomas Jefferson," in *Thomas Jefferson: The Man, His World, His Influence,* ed. Lally Waymouth (New York, 1973), 81–95.

49. William N. Parker, "Productivity Growth in American Grain Farming: An Analysis of Its 19th Century Sources," in *Reinterpretation of American Economic History,* ed. Robert Fogel and Stanley L. Engerman (New York, 1971), 178.

50. Logan, *Five Letters,* 25, 28.

51. Spurrier, *Practical Farmer,* iii.

52. Tench Coxe, *A View of the United States of America* (Philadelphia, 1794), 8–9, 87–99.

The nationalism implicit in these descriptions of America's economic future helps explain the breadth of the Republican movement, and the emphasis upon the commercial value of the grains, livestock, and beverages produced on family farms indicates how market changes affected early national politics. Jefferson's own nationalism was closely tied to the issues of international free trade and the disposition of the national domain. In this he was representative of the Virginia nationalists who dominated American politics after 1783 and led the campaign to establish "a more perfect union" four years later. With peace and the failure of William Morris' impost scheme, attention in the Continental Congress passed to matters of vital concern to Virginians—the taking-up of western land and the marketing of America's bounteous harvests. Both goals encouraged a national perspective. To expel the British from the Northwest, to ease the Indians out of the Ohio Territory, to negotiate new commercial treaties abroad—these things required more than confederal cooperation. Just how long-range their view was can be gauged by the passions aroused by the idea of closing the port of New Orleans at a time when settlers had reached Kentucky. The implicit social values of this southern program, as H. James Henderson has pointed out, were secular rather than religious, anticipatory rather than regressive, individualistic rather than corporate. The leaders of the Old Dominion "looked forward to continental grandeur rather than back to ancestral virtue." [53] East of the Hudson there was little support for an expansive American republic. The stagnating Massachusetts economy made the past a more reliable guide to the future than dreams of a new age of prosperity and progress. In the middle and southern states, however, the depressed 1780s reflected less the limits of growth than the failure to unlock America's rich resources.

From Georgia to New York a hinterland ran westward that gave the new American nation what no other people had ever possessed: the material base for a citizenry of independent, industrious propertyholders. And Virginia, the largest and wealthiest state, produced the leaders who turned this prospect into a political program. Most

53. H. James Henderson, "The Structure of Politics in the Continental Congress," in *Essays on the American Revolution,* ed. Stephen G. Kurtz and James H. Hutson (Chapel Hill, 1973), 88.

national leaders recognized the economic potential in America; the question that emerged was how and in deference to which values would this potential be realized. The issues that clustered around the opening of the national domain reveal very well how choices would affect the character of American society. Manufacturing, proponents argued, would provide jobs for sons and daughters at home; uncontrolled movement into the west would scatter families.[54] Recognizing the class difference in migration rates, an article addressed to the working people of Maryland urged support for the Constitution on the grounds that the common people were more properly citizens of the United States than of any particular state, for many of them died far away from where they were born.[55] The congressional debates on the Land Act of 1796 swirled around the question whether these sons and daughters who moved west would become independent farmers or the tenants of land speculators. The geographic base of the Jeffersonian Republicans can be traced in the votes for 160-acre sales.[56] Because grains were raised throughout the United States and required ancillary industries for their processing and sale, the Republican program was neither regional nor, strictly speaking, agrarian. It should be emphasized that it involved neither American isolation nor a slowed pace of growth. It was in fact a form of capitalism that Jefferson seized as the ax to fell Old World institutions because free trade offered the integrative network that social authority supplied elsewhere. Hamilton's response to the Louisiana Purchase makes this point negatively: the extension of America's agricultural frontier, he maintained, threatened to remove citizens from the coercive power of the state.[57]

The Revolution had made possible Jefferson's vision of a great, progressive republic, but developments during the first years of independence brought to light two different threats to its fulfillment.

54. "On American Manufactures," *American Museum or Repository of Ancient and Modern Pieces, Prose and Poetical*, I (1787), 18.

55. *Pennsylvania Gazette*, Apr. 2, 1788, 3.

56. Rudolph M. Bell, *Party and Faction in American Politics: The House of Representatives, 1789–1801* (Westport, Conn., 1973), 85–89; Murray R. Benedict, *Farm Policies of the United States, 1790–1950: A Study of Their Origins and Development* (New York, 1953), 12–15.

57. Gerald Stourzh, *Alexander Hamilton and the Idea of Republican Government* (Stanford, 1970), 192–193.

The one was old and predictable: the tendency of the rich and mighty to control the avenues to profit and preferment. The other came from the very strength of common voters in revolutionary America. The war effort itself had democratized politics, and without royal government, the broad prerevolutionary suffrage was translated into comprehensive popular power.[58] Emboldened by the natural rights rhetoric of the resistance movement, political newcomers began to challenge the old merchant oligarchies in the cities, while their counterparts in state legislatures pushed through radical measures affecting taxation, inheritance, insolvency, debt retirement, and land sales.[59] The ensuing conflicts, which Progressive historians made familiar as part of the struggle between rich and poor, aroused fears that cannot be categorized so easily. The new aggregate power of the people channeled through popularly elected legislatures alarmed men as philosophically different as Jefferson and Hamilton, as unlike temperamentally as Benjamin Rush and Robert Livingston. When ordinary Americans used their new voting power to push for legislation favorable to themselves, they made committed democrats as well as conservatives apprehensive. The anxieties expressed during the late 1780s cannot be ascribed solely to an elitist distrust of the poor, the ill-born, and the untalented many. Men destined to become the champions of political equality found the augmentation of power in the first state governments a genuine threat. A historiographical tradition that reads all fears of popular, unrestricted governmental power as evidence of upper-class sympathies is in danger of missing the most compelling political goal to emerge in late eighteenth-century America: the limitation of formal authority in deference to individual freedom. Disaggregating society, the Jeffersonians redirected the sovereign people away from exercising power as a body and toward enjoying free

58. Jackson Turner Main, "Government by the People: The American Revolution and the Democratization of the Legislatures," *William and Mary Quarterly,* 23 (1966), 391–407; John Shy, "The American Revolution: The Military Conflict Considered as a Revolutionary War," in *Essays on the American Revolution,* ed. Kurtz and Hutson, 21–56; Edward Countryman, "Consolidating Power in Revolutionary America: The Case of New York, 1775–1883," *Journal of Interdisciplinary History,* 6 (1976), 645–677.

59. Jon C. Teaford, *The Municipal Revolution in America: Origins of Modern Urban Government, 1650–1825* (Chicago, 1975); Jackson Turner Main, *Political Parties before the Constitution* (Chapel Hill, 1973).

choice as private persons. Leaders of both the Federalist and Republican parties had cooperated in 1787 because a national political framework and a unified economy were essential to their differing conceptions of America's future. The new government created by the Constitution, however, proved to be a double-edged sword for the democratic nationalists. Strong enough to provide the conditions for freedom and growth, it could also be used to concentrate power and thereby raise a new national elite.

In resisting Hamilton's policies the Republicans eschewed the very divisions that historians have dwelt upon in explaining party formation. Far from pitting merchants against farmers, rich against poor, or the commercially inclined against the self-sufficient, the Jeffersonians assumed that a freely developing economy would benefit all. The eradication of privilege and the limitation of formal power would stimulate the natural harmony of interests. Thomas Paine with his usual directness gave expression to this liberal view in the fight over Robert Morris' bank. In a republican form of government, he wrote, "public good is not a term opposed to the good of individuals; on the contrary, it is the good of every individual collected . . . the farmer understands farming, and the merchant understands commerce; and as riches are equally the object of both, there is no occasion that either should fear that the other will seek to be poor."[60] Making a slightly different point, the Jeffersonian congressional leader, Albert Gallatin, opposed the Federalists' 1800 bankruptcy bill because its provisions could not be restricted to merchants. In America, he argued, "the different professions and trades are blended together in the same persons; the same man being frequently a farmer and a merchant, and perhaps a manufacturer."[61] What was distinctive about the Jeffersonian economic policy was not an anticommercial bias, but a commitment to growth through the unimpeded exertions of individuals whose access to economic opportunity was both protected and facilitated by government. Treated for so long as a set of self-evident truths, the flowering of liberal thought in America owed much to specific

---

60. [Thomas Paine], *Dissertations on Government: The Affairs of the Bank; and Paper Money,* in *The Complete Writings of Thomas Paine,* ed. Philip S. Foner, 2 vols. (New York, 1945), II, 372, 399–400.

61. *Annals of the Congress,* 5 Cong., 3 sess., Jan. 14, 1799, 2650–2651.

developments. The advantageous terms of trade for American farm commodities, the expulsion of Europeans and Native Americans from the trans-Appalachian west, the people's commercial tendencies that Jefferson described—all these made men and women receptive to a new conception of human nature that affirmed the reciprocal influences of freedom and prosperity. What had given a sacred underpinning to Locke's contract theory was his assumption that men living under God's law were enjoined to protect the life, liberty, and property of others as well as their own. Jefferson perceived that Locke's identity of interests among the propertied could be universalized in America and thereby acquire a moral base in natural design. It was indeed a *novus ordo seclorum*.

11

Republicanism
and Ideology

REPUBLICANISM slipped into the scholarly lexicon in the late 1960s and has since become the most protean concept for those working on the culture of antebellum America. In its initial appearance republicanism referred to a body of ideas said to have animated the men of the revolutionary generation. Drawn from the vivid polemics of the English opposition, republican ideology filled Americans with a horror of arbitrary power and a fear of the incipient corruption of the British constitution. Since the men who led the colonial resistance movement presided over the affairs of the new nation for the next fifty years, it could reasonably be inferred that they would carry their republican worldview with them into the nineteenth century, letting it set the agenda for political discourse for years to come. And so it has been. The recent discovery of republicanism as the reigning social theory of eighteenth-century America has produced a reaction among historians akin to the response of chemists to a new element. Once having been identified, it can be found everywhere. Thus for more than two decades scholars have used republicanism to revise conventional wisdom on the debates over the Constitution, the opposition politics of the 1790s and the partisan divisions of the Jacksonian era.[1] Similarly old nuclei

1. James H. Hutson, "Country, Court, and Constitution: Antifederalism and the Historians," *William and Mary Quarterly,* 38 (1981), 337–368; Lance Banning, *The Jeffersonian Persuasion* (Ithaca, 1978); Rowland Berthoff, "Independence and Attachment, Virtue and

of American historiography, like the significance of the frontier, the role of women, the politics of New England clergy—even the actions of Washington's officer corps—have been formed into new compounds with the addition of republicanism.[2]

I would like to discuss what republicanism has meant to American historians. Packed into the concept are hypotheses about the nature of social experience which would have been unthinkable to an earlier group of scholars. For this reason republicanism can be used fruitfully as a trace element for following the very ambitious contemporary effort to integrate our knowledge of the past with new and highly sophisticated models of human behavior. As an attentive, and by no means impartial, observer of the dramatic revisions wrought under its influence I have noted that republicanism has actually had two careers, the first as a reference to certain ideas said to have reverberated through the eighteenth and early nineteenth centuries, and the second issuing from its close connection with another resonating concept, ideology. This has meant that two revisions have been progressing simultaneously: the one dealing with a new description of what men believed in the early modern Anglo-American world, and another involving a new explanation of how ideas enter into the making of events. The concept of republicanism which points to the ornate rhetoric of classical political theory is thus bound up—extricably, I think—with a complex of theories about language and consciousness. In its first career republicanism has swept the colonial house of intellect clean of those wonderfully accessible slogans about no taxation without representation and retrofitted it with a sterner, chaster set of truths about the fragility of civil order and the ferocity of uncivil passions. In its second career it has surreptitiously inserted into our history the conviction that reality is socially constructed.

Interest: From Republican Citizen to Free Enterpriser, 1787–1837," in *Uprooted Americans,* ed. Richard L. Bushman et al. (Cambridge, Mass., 1979), 97–124. For two excellent evaluative essays on republicanism, see Robert E. Shalhope, "Toward a Republican Synthesis: The Emergence of an Understanding of Republicanism in American Historiography," *William and Mary Quarterly,* 29 (1972), 49–80; "Republicanism and Early American Historiography," *William and Mary Quarterly,* 39 (1982), 334–356.

2. Drew R. McCoy, *The Elusive Republic* (Chapel Hill, 1980); Linda Kerber, *Women of the Republic* (Chapel Hill, 1980); Nathan O. Hatch, *The Sacred Cause of Liberty* (New Haven, 1977); Charles Royster, *A Revolutionary People at War* (Chapel Hill, 1979).

The wildfire popularity of republicanism indicates how keenly historians feel the need to talk about the ineffable aspects of past politics. This helps explain why we hear more and more about political ceremonies and less and less about political campaigns, why we now evoke sympathies and symbols to discuss party divisions where evidence about voters' occupations would once have been more pertinent. Because scholarly statements about the sentiments of Jefferson, Adams, Hamilton, and a host of lesser figures have congealed with assertions about the dynamic interplay of belief and behavior, republicanism has come to represent a declaration of independence from older scholarship in American political history. Indeed, our approach has now been revolutionized by two linked assumptions. The first deals with how interests enter the political arena. Men and women respond to their interests according to how they interpret those interests, it is now said. Therefore ideas intervene and mediate between circumstances and responses to those circumstances. The second assumption deals with the character of interpretive schemes and points to the fact that interpretive frameworks are constructed from general convictions about the nature of human experience, moving out from this base to political affirmations. Where the decisionmaking individual once stood at the center of our analysis of politics, ideology has pushed to the fore the social forces that presumably have shaped the consciousness of the individuals we study. With this change of perspectives, American historians have burned their bridges not to the past—but rather to past ways of looking at our past.

Because republicanism contains a theory of social psychology embedded in a description of the worldview in the revolutionary era, it has provided us with a foil against which to examine our previous accounts of this period. We can see more clearly now the liberal bias in our historiography. From the original histories of the American Revolution written by contemporaries through the Consensus writings of the 1950s, the eighteenth-century acts of nationbuilding have been construed as the doings of forward-looking, self-improving men.[3] First, American patriots as individual lovers of

3. David Ramsay, *History of the United States from their First Settlement as English Colonies, in 1607, to the Year 1808,* 3 vols. (Philadelphia, 1818); Carl L. Becker, *History of Political Parties in the Province of New York, 1760–1776* (Madison, 1909); Robert E. Brown, *Middle-Class Democracy and the Revolution in Massachusetts* (Ithaca, 1955).

liberty banded together as a whole people to repel English tyrants. The Beardian revision disaggregated the whole American people into interest groups, but the individuals remained self-consciously self-improving. The patriot leaders in progressive historiography became American capitalists, asserting themselves against their British counterparts while inadvertently drawing into the conflict ordinary colonists who, like the children in Locke's "Second Treatise," came into their political manhood and began agitating for rights on their own behalf. With a later emphasis upon consensus rather than conflict, our histories merged the contentious leaders and democrats into members of a prosperous middle class long used to possessing themselves, their property, and the vote.

In all of these accounts, ideas figured as unproblematic elements in the minds of the participants. First they were true principles, then—in the muckraking era of the early twentieth century—they became window-dressing rationalizations, and finally, in the self-congratulatory national mood after World War II, obvious propositions about human behavior. Men—sometimes even women— were depicted as choosing ideas much as they bought and sold in the free market, according to the value received. The only time that ideas presented difficulties for scholars was when people clung to those beliefs that egregiously contradicted liberal affirmations about independence, autonomy, progress, and natural rights. In such instances, custom, ignorance, superstition, dogma, or upper-class intimidation could be invoked to explain the deviations from the self-evident. Thus the differences between historians using the concept of republicanism and their predecessors is not over the importance of ideas, but rather the character of ideas in social experience. For this reason the work of the past two decades tells us as much about the mind of the late twentieth century as of that of the late eighteenth.

With the publication of Bernard Bailyn's *The Ideological Origins of The American Revolution,* the study of the American Revolution was itself revolutionized, although curiously the word *republicanism* does not figure prominently in his text. What Bailyn did was to effect that fusion of substantive and theoretical meaning that republicanism has come to represent. In a single study he turned around the entire field working on eighteenth-century America. By joining earlier work on the English Commonwealthmen to a powerful explanation of how ideas enter into the realm of history-making events, he made ideology the central concept in our current accounts of the break with Great Britain. In his analysis of revolutionary rhetoric Bailyn dropped themes into our history which like dye in a vat have permeated and colored our writings on the whole era stretching from the Stamp Act crisis through the Jeffersonian presidencies. More significantly he replaced the tired old notion of intellectual influence with the exciting concept of ideology. Ideas, Bailyn maintained, only influence political action when they are part of a socially created structure. The Cassandras of the British Opposition shaped events in America because their opinions organized attitudes otherwise too vague to be acted upon, because, as he said, they crystallized otherwise inchoate discontent. Ideas, to use Bailyn's metaphor, compose themselves into intellectual switchboards wired so that certain events almost surely will provoke particular reactions. The colonial elite, confronting the Parliamentary reforms of the 1760s, for example, was compelled to interpret the new measures as signs of a tyrannical impulse in England because this unexpected exercise of power tripped existing fears about the unbalancing of the constitutional order which preserved Englishmen in their liberties and estates.[4]

It remained for Bailyn's student Gordon Wood to connect explicitly the conceptual order of the American patriots to the classical republican tradition in England. This, he did, in *The Creation of the American Republic* which carried the story of Americans' engagement with republicanism through the drafting of the Constitution. Concentrating as they did upon the founding acts of independence and constitution-making, Bailyn and Wood left unexamined the genesis of the English ideology they found flourishing in the colonies. Content to explore how classical republicanism organized the consciousness of the most influential generation in American history, they presented the source of the founders' ideology as a kind of grab bag of radical Whig notions about power, rights, and virtue. It was left to J. G. A. Pocock to provide a central nervous system for the

4. Bernard Bailyn, *The Ideological Origins of the American Revolution* (Cambridge, Mass., 1967); "The Central Themes of the American Revolution: An Interpretation," in *Essays on the American Revolution*, ed. Stephen G. Kurtz and James H. Hutson (Chapel Hill, 1973).

new skeleton of American political culture which they had fashioned. And this he did in *The Machiavellian Moment*. A keystone in Pocock's scholarship, *The Machiavellian Moment* completed the arches raised in his *Ancient Constitution* and *Politics, Language and Time.*[5] Like Bailyn, Pocock had simultaneously thought about what eighteenth-century men actually believed as well as how beliefs figure in the historical drama of situation, action, and reaction. Unlike Bailyn, Pocock has pursued these questions as part of a larger enterprise—an investigation of the spiritual crisis that accompanied the birth of the modern world.

In his *Ancient Constitution* Pocock explored the emergence of civic consciousness among those Englishmen centrally involved in their country's century of revolution. Following the twin histories of the common law and Parliament, he showed how the idea of citizenship emerged when the king could no longer count on the unthinking obedience of his subjects. According to Pocock, after the execution of Charles I and the subsequent failure of the Puritans' Elect Nation, Englishmen came face to face with the temporality of their polity. Then they turned to that great theorist of fortune and design, Machiavelli. Although Pocock did not draw from the anthropological work of Clifford Geertz, his findings accord with Geertz's contention that ideologies emerge and take hold at precisely the time when a society begins "to free itself from the immediate governance of the received tradition."[6] Only Pocock's English did not so much free themselves as find themselves unhappily free. They are emphatically not like the Parliamentarians who move through Whig history confidently championing a new era of government by the consent of the governed. In Pocock's account, England's leaders reached backward for classical models to teach them how to stay the march of time. At once enamored of their unchanging constitution and deeply aware of the demonic force of rebellion, they looked to the residual wisdom of the past for a theory of how to remain in place. And they found it in the classical writings of Aristotle and Polybius and their Renaissance interpreters.

5. J. G. A. Pocock, *The Machiavellian Moment: Florentine Political Thought and the Atlantic Republican Tradition* (Princeton, 1975); *The Ancient Constitution and the Feudal Law* (Cambridge, 1957); *Politics, Language and Time* (New York, 1960).

6. Clifford Geertz, "Ideology as a Cultural System," in *The Interpretation of Cultures* (New York, 1973), 219.

From Machiavelli's analysis of ancient politics the English gentry, according to Pocock, took the idea of civic virtue. The exercise of civic virtue enabled men to realize their human potential at the same time it imposed form on the flotsam and jetsam of human events. Only men secure in their property could be virtuous, and only through the exertions of such virtuous men could property be made secure.[7] Thus the classical republican outlook of England's ruling class denied a place in the polity for the capitalist carriers of change and made every advance in economic development appear as evidence of fortune's zone of irrationality.[8] Shrewdly aware that both Marxists and liberals drew their intellectual hubris from a common assumption that they understood progress, Pocock removed the place for progress from the Anglo-American worldview. Taken as a whole, his work can be seen as a formidable indictment of the reductionism in liberal and Marxist historiography.

Both Pocock's theoretical assumptions and his findings about English political discourse are essential to his stunning interpretation of how material advance was received in the homelands of capitalism. Theoretically, Pocock says that the conceptual language of a society structures both personality and the world. People do not choose their beliefs so much as they feel an affinity for an explanation of experience which thereafter entails them in its multiple meanings. "Men cannot do what they have no means of saying they have done," he has said, "and what they do must in part be what they can say and conceive that it is."[9] Social languages thus confine more than they liberate. The precedent-shattering economic innovations did not seem like precedent-shattering economic innovations because there was no conceptual language for understanding them as such. Instead they appeared as threats to that balance of the one, the few, and the many which alone secured order and liberty for Englishmen. Innovation involved change and change evoked fears of the disruption of the constitutional balance. This was especially the case, Pocock says, because the new wealth-generating activities of the late seventeenth century became entangled actually and in men's minds with fiscal schemes which

---

7. Pocock, *Machiavellian Moment*, 184.

8. Ibid., 461.

9. J. G. A. Pocock, "Virtue and Commerce in the Eighteenth Century," *Journal of Interdisciplinary History*, 3 (1972), 122.

extended the range and size of the king's patronage.[10] The purely economic features of the commercial revolution were subsumed under the political rubric of corruption, since it was a maxim of classical republicanism that only those capable of subordinating their own interests to the well-being of the whole could perform the crucial job of protecting the constitution. English classical republicans could not say that it was otherwise.

Thomas Hobbes and John Locke had provided an alternative way of talking about private men and public policy, but Pocock maintains that Locke's notorious indifference to history rendered him a nugatory influence in his day. Dispensing with Locke in this manner has cut the taproots of the liberal tradition in both England and America, forestalling until a later day the triumph of the natural rights philosophy in America and a bourgeois revolution in England. No Locke, no Marx, it seems, and the shot heard around the world went backward. As Pocock wrote with characteristic audacity, "an effect of the recent research has been to display the American Revolution less as the first political act of revolutionary enlightenment than as the last great act of the Renaissance."[11]

The sweep of Pocock's revision is breathtaking. Against the pull of two centuries of unexamined assumptions about the reception of economic progress, he has succeeded in giving us eighteenth-century men firmly planted in their own time, facing an uncertain future with the sensibilities of their predecessors in the foreground and the values of their descendents properly out of sight. As he wrote about his *Machiavellian Moment,* it was concerned with "ways in which men perceived change in their times, rather than with our endorsement of their perceptions."[12] Pocock's formidable erudition has contributed to his achievement, but so have his brilliant insights on the functioning of political languages. Here Thomas Kuhn's analysis of how scientists order their research around models of nature offered him an appropriate template for understanding the structuring of political thought.[13] Indeed what Geertz was to Bailyn, Kuhn was

10. Pocock, *Machiavellian Moment,* 122–126, 426.

11. Pocock, "Virtue and Commerce," 124.

12. J. G. A. Pocock, *"The Machiavellian Moment* Revisited: A Study in History and Ideology," *Journal of Modern History,* 53 (1981), 61.

13. Pocock, *Politics, Language and Time,* 14–15; Thomas S. Kuhn, *The Structure of Scientific Revolutions* (Chicago, 1962).

to Pocock. Rejecting the liberal treatment of ideas as discrete units which people picked up and dropped according to need and preference, all four scholars maintained that ideas exerted influence as parts of wholes, paradigms in Kuhn's lexicon, and then only because the whole illuminated reality. Those who share a paradigm form a community. Kuhn's scientific practitioners became analogues for Pocock's English gentry. For each group a common language made coherent social action possible. As Pocock explained, social thought involved both linguistic and political processes because any socially organized way of thinking became a means for distributing authority, as well as communicating ideas. Political languages distribute authority as and because they communicate the wisdom of the society. With those who lived by the strictures of classical republicanism only men secure in landed property were free to practice civic virtue. Power thus flowed to those men and away from entrepreneurs and financiers, and everyone understood why. Pocock recognizes that the symbolic and evasionary aspects of rhetoric distinguish the language of politics from the language of a disciplined inquiry. However, their similarities lie in the control implicit in both. As he wrote, "the individual's thinking may now be viewed as a social event." [14] Kuhn showed Pocock the way to discomfit both liberal and Marxist historians. The reigning paradigm of classical republicanism denied liberals their forward-moving, freedom-loving makers of history—the innovator as hero—while it confronted Marxists with a ruling class speaking a language which wrote rising capitalists out of the political script.

The republican revisionists have self-consciously reached out for social scientific models to free intellectual history from its distortingly rationalistic assumptions about the life of the mind. In the sympathetic analysis of belief systems done by anthropologists they found the means for studying thought as a social phenomenon. What anthropologists also offered was a concept of ideology which concentrated upon the means rather than the causes or consequences of specific beliefs. Approached as "systems of interacting symbols, as patterns of interworking meanings," ideology was fashioned into a concept which could integrate social psychology with linguistic analysis, or in the language of historians, motivation with docu-

14. Ibid.

mentation.[15] The anthropologists' concept of ideology was particularly helpful to those studying early America because in presenting what eighteenth-century people actually thought, historians had all too often collapsed the colonial past into the historian's present. The ideological approach encouraged a dispassionate sympathy for those beyond one's ken; it invited scholars to look for structured meaning; and it moved American historiography beyond the filiopietistic evaluation of nation-building acts. As Bailyn commented, it was now possible to understand both the English and the colonial positions in the Revolution.

Like all fruitful borrowings the concept of ideology lighted up whole new areas which could not be seen before. While earlier scholars may have sensed that thinking was a social activity, or that assertions about reality were interconnected, or that individuals interpreted their experience through preconceived notions, these propositions had never before been systematically explored and applied to concrete historical texts. With the concept of ideology, intellectual historians were able to break away from an arid debate over causality in which pecuniary interests were arrayed against political convictions as mutually exclusive causes of action. Ideology invited an examination of the processes of thinking which necessarily linked belief and behavior. But the concept of ideology which has fused with the recent recovery of republican thought remains a borrowing. Its limitations are inherent in that fact. Anthropologists observing small, cohesive, and frequently nonliterate societies emphasized the uniformity of a people's worldview and linked that uniformity to the maintenance of stable cultures. Comprehensiveness and statis have been inseparable from their theoretical interpretation of ideology. Yet neither seventeenth-century England nor eighteenth-century America were tightly knit or cohesive societies. The high level of literacy in both countries encouraged the free circulation of printed material. Neither censorship nor limited access to printing presses existed to inhibit the publication of divergent, even inflammatory, points of view. The English gentry, who considered themselves the kingdom's natural leaders, could no more control the reading public's taste for Daniel Defoe than their American counterparts could curb the popularity of an incendiary pro-

15. Geertz, "Ideology as a Cultural System," 207.

paradigms do not permit pluralism

pagandist like Thomas Paine. Both countries were intellectually as well as culturally pluralistic. The conceptual world of the elite permeated all classes, but it could not and did not exclude competing views—views which in time exercised greater interpretive powers for those differently positioned in society. By insisting upon the hegemony of a particular political tradition on theoretical grounds, the republican revisionists have resisted seeing that in pluralistic, uncensored, literate societies, the ideological predispositions of human beings have an opposite effect. Instead of insuring social solidarity, competing ideologies thwart it and embarrass the efforts of government to secure order. The eighteenth century, as Bailyn has pointed out, was an ideological age. In no small part this was because the changing nature of work and wealth in western Europe was forcing into the open different conceptions of society and politics.

Reviewing the reception of his *Machiavellian Moment* ten years after its publication, Pocock reiterated his principal contentions. The financial revolution outweighs the Glorious Revolution in the history of ideology; neo-Harringtonian concepts guided how the English and their colonial brethren perceived change; and the potential for reading Locke as the interpreter of a new order was missed because contemporaries viewed commercial growth through the conceptual lenses of classical republicanism.[16] All three of these propositions depend upon the theoretical assumption that one language of social analysis precludes the coexistence of others. Yet there were other languages available and used. As important as the financial and glorious revolutions were in the history of ideology the commercial revolution was even more important. Here a paradigm like Kuhn's scientific ones had to be invented. The worries about the Bank of England and the national debt in no way precluded men from responding to the abounding evidence of economic change in politically explosive ways. Indeed, many writers managed to think in both languages, pointing out the dangers of political corruptions from extended patronage while analyzing the new market economy with a totally different vocabulary.[17]

16. Pocock, "*Machiavellian Moment* Revisited," 65.

17. Joyce Appleby, *Economic Thought and Ideology in Seventeenth-Century England* (Princeton, 1978). See especially references to Robert Filmer, Francis Gardiner, John Briscoe, and Roger Coke.

Dozens of publications on economic topics appeared each year in the closing decades of the seventeenth century. Out of a half-century of writing about the novelties of farming techniques, in internal marketing, and in foreign trade came the means for talking about society as a natural and spontaneously ordered system. To these observers of commercial change what was most remarkable was not the new scope of political corruption but rather the propensity for men and women to discipline themselves in their economic dealings. To some these apparently universal traits suggested that human beings carried within them the natural antidote to the ancient disease of anarchy. In these pamphlets natural law was transmogrified from an ethical into a scientific category, one which elevated previously vulgar material pursuits into dependable regulators of human behavior. Work—uncoerced, productive, rewarding in the new language of economics—became the integrator of society.

Even as sophisticated a man as John Locke did not escape infection from the visionary aspects of this new paradigm. Among his papers is a scribbled note in which he observed that if everyone in the world worked, the world's work could be done routinely in half a day.[18] It is difficult to imagine a more vivid indicator of the inherent leveling tendencies of the market economy. Since these new observations were cohering during a period of remarkable economic expansion, the possibility of unchecked economic advance occurred to some, strengthening the enthusiasm of the advocates of economic change while laying the foundation for the idea of progress. Totally new too was the frank delight in the artifacts issuing from the presses, potteries, and looms of England. No account of the reception of economic development can ignore the sheer aesthetic pleasure—the incitement to the imagination—created by the printed calicoes, decorated plates, colored maps, and mechanical gimmicks that circulated in great abundance.[19] To claim that these writings are not political is to miss what was truly revolutionary in the liberal worldview: the replacement of the economy for the polity as the fundamental social system. Pocock has maintained that the classical republican paradigm provided no role for the capitalist as citizen; it is equally true that liberalism returned the favor by diminishing

18. Locke Manuscripts, Cambridge University Library, Cambridge, England.
19. This subject is explored in Chandra Mukerji, *Graven Images* (Chicago, 1983).

the importance of citizenship itself. Thomas Paine's differentiation of society and government in the opening paragraph of *Common Sense* makes this reevaluation of the public and private realms explicit: "society is produced by our wants and government by our wickedness; the former promotes our happiness positively by uniting our affections, the latter negatively by restraining our vices."[20] With characteristic audacity Paine reduced the virtues of classical republicanism to simple policing, while elevating free association to a new moral plane. But without the reconceptualization of the nature of society worked out during the preceding century, his stunning deflation of classical republicanism would not have been persuasive.

To reassert the significance of a liberal mode of society grounded in observations of economic advance and articulated through the language of science is not to return to the *status quo ante revisionism.* The recovery of classical republican modes of thinking in the colonies has changed forever our understanding of early America. Further, because republicanism has been propelled into our consciousness by the engine of ideology we can leave behind that place where, as Louis Hartz put it, the American historian functioned as "an erudite reflection of the limited social perspectives of the average American."[21] Not the least of the merits of the ideological approach is the possibility it affords of dealing with liberalism as a cultural artifact. When scholars recognize in self-interest as conceptual a notion as classical republicanism's civic virtue, we can be certain that the new insights about the social construction of reality have been absorbed. Like fish unaware of water, we American writers have moved about in a world of invisible liberal assumptions. The clarity with which republicanism has been delineated enables us to detect the elements of liberalism in our own thinking and hence to identify them as they entered into public discourse during the eighteenth century.

Republicanism has become an integrative theme for a vast amount of recent research in social history. In part this is because those historians who have studied the lives of ordinary men and women have found in classical political truths a cluster of values congruent with the lives of early Americans. Although classical republicanism

20. *Selections from the Works of Thomas Paine*, ed. Arthur Wallace Peach (New York, 1928), 4.
21. Louis Hartz, *The Liberal Tradition in America* (New York, 1955).

has been traced to the most politically powerful and sophisticated men in the eighteenth century, its emphasis upon virtuous leaders and the subordination of self-interest reflected the popular mentality as well, we are told. The new recognition in intellectual history that human thinking is structured also accords with the social historians' own discovery of social patterning. Since it is largely through charts, graphs, and tables that the historically inaudible have been described, the texts of classical republicanism have been welcomed for their audibility. In the reigning assumptions of classical republicanism, moreover, social historians have found the antidote to the instrumental logic and demystifying rationality of that Lockean liberalism which has dominated historical writing for so long. The presence of republicanism in the American past has provided roots at last for a genuine alternative to the worldview generated by liberal capitalism, a need all the more pressing for those scholars working on periods before industrialization.

While most scholars would agree that the possibility of institutionalizing the civic values extolled in classical republicanism ended with the ratification of the Constitution, the vitality of republican ideals not only persisted but continued to embarrass the progress of liberal values in America. What remains to be sorted out are the circumstances and influences which account for the appeal of different constructions of reality. Yet to be resolved is whether ideology functions to crystallize inchoate feelings, as Bailyn describes it, or whether we are dealing with ideologies which reflect choices made by diverse groups in an intellectually pluralistic society. Is it true that men and women must wait for a language to give voice to their understanding of experience? Or are purposes and—less constructively—tensions in the multiple systems within which we must live the driving force behind the articulation of new truths? Marx said that social categories cannot be transcended in thought until they have been questioned in practice while Pocock stresses that men cannot do what they have no means of saying they have done. The one does not exclude the other, but recognition of the twin possibilities is no substitute for hard thinking about the relationship of structured consciousness and personal intentions. Only when these questions have been addressed will we be able to account for the changes in the way men and women think as well as how they acted upon those changes.

12

What Is Still American in Jefferson's Political Philosophy?

SHORTLY after leaving the presidency, Thomas Jefferson undertook the translation of a manuscript by the French philosopher Antoine Louis Claude Destutt de Tracy. At the same time he prevailed on his friend William Duane to publish it anonymously, and in due course Tracy's *Commentary and Review of Montesquieu's Spirit of Laws* appeared in Philadelphia.[1] For Tracy this American imprint offered his ideas safe conduct into the hostile territory of Napoleonic France. For Jefferson the *Review of Montesquieu* became a new weapon in his old war against pernicious ideas. He sent copies to friends and got the book adopted as a text at the College of William and Mary while venturing the hope that it might be placed in the hands of every American student as "the elementary and fundamental" work on the science of government. Such an outcome, Jefferson confided to Lafayette, would more than repay the five hours daily he had expended on Tracy's manuscript over the course of three months. To Pierre Samuel Du Pont de Nemours he revealed more clearly his motives: "The paradoxes of Montesquieu have been too

1. Jefferson originally asked Robert Walch, journalist and publisher, to do the translation; see Silvia Bedini, *Thomas Jefferson and His Copying Machine* (Charlottesville, 1984), 17. Merrill D. Peterson, *Thomas Jefferson and the New Nation: A Biography* (New York, 1970), 947–948; Jefferson to Duane, Aug. 12, 1810, in *The Writings of Thomas Jefferson*, ed. Andrew A. Lipscomb and Albert Ellery Bergh (Washington, D.C., 1903–1905), XII, 407–408.

long uncorrected."[2] Probably not many young men in America still read Montesquieu, but Jefferson's unabated desire to combat his influence offers us an Ariadne's thread through the ideological labyrinth of the early national period. In addition, Jefferson's endorsement of Tracy's economic theory gives us an idea of his mature thinking on commercial development and its moral implications. These well-documented reactions to the work of Montesquieu and Tracy raise serious doubts about the wisdom of the recent scholarly effort to assimilate Jefferson into the Country party tradition of eighteenth-century England.[3]

During the years of constitution-writing in America, Montesquieu's name acted as a code reference to the small-republic theory and the principle of the separation of powers. European readers, on the other hand, associated Montesquieu with an elaborate rationale for aristocratic power. All of these positions emerged from his schematic analysis of governmental types in *The Spirit of the Laws*. The maintenance of liberty and order in a society of any size, Montesquieu had said, required a "standing body" to mediate between the king and the people. Taking England as his model, he showed how the English constitution not only disentangled the executive, legislative, and judicial functions of government but also balanced the power of the people and the nobility. Here Montesquieu pro-

2. Jefferson to Duane, Jan. 22, 1813, ibid., XIII, 213–214; Jefferson to Joseph Milligan, Oct. 25, 1818, ibid., XIX, 263; Jefferson to Thomas Cooper, Jan. 16, 1814, ibid., XIV, 54–63; Jefferson to Lafayette, May 17, 1816, ibid., XIX, 237–238; Jefferson to Du Pont de Nemours, Nov. 29, 1813, in *Correspondence between Thomas Jefferson and Pierre Samuel du Pont de Nemours, 1798–1817,* ed. Dumas Malone (Boston, 1930), 145. On Tracy's motives, see Emmet Kennedy, *A Philosophe in the Age of Revolution: Destutt de Tracy and the Origins of "Ideology"* (Philadelphia, 1978), 210.

3. J. G. A. Pocock, "Virtue and Commerce in the Eighteenth Century," *Journal of Interdisciplinary History,* 3 (1972), 133–134; *The Machiavellian Moment: Florentine Political Thought and the Atlantic Republican Tradition* (Princeton, 1975), ix, 529–533; Lance Banning, *The Jeffersonian Persuasion: Evolution of a Party Ideology* (Ithaca, 1978); Forrest McDonald, *The Presidency of Thomas Jefferson* (Lawrence, Kan., 1976); John M. Murrin, "The Great Inversion, or Court versus Country: A Comparison of the Revolution Settlements in England (1688–1721) and America (1776–1816)," in *Three British Revolutions: 1641, 1688, 1776,* ed. J. G. A. Pocock (Princeton, 1980); Rowland Berthoff, "Independence and Attachment, Virtue and Interest: From Republican Citizen to Free Enterpriser, 1787–1837," in *Uprooted Americans: Essays to Honor Oscar Handlin,* ed. Richard L. Bushman et al. (Boston, 1979).

duced an eighteenth-century gloss on the ancient theory of politics
that had been revived by Machiavelli and anglicized by James Harrington. The sovereign authority of the English king-in-parliament
thus became the modern version of the constitutional balance of the
one, the few, and the many recommended by Aristotle and
Polybius.[4] Fractured and checked in this way, the august power of
government could be moderated, which for Montesquieu was the
great goal of politics. Republics, however, by their very nature had
no such tripartite division, and the moderating influence had to
come from another source. A virtuous citizenry could sustain a
republic through the disorders endemic in human society, but this
essential civic virtue could survive only among a people of frugal
habits who lived in a limited area where a rough equality of property
prevailed. From this chain of reasoning came Montesquieu's celebrated small-republic theory.[5]

Our knowledge of the significance of the Renaissance revival of
classical political thought has been enormously enriched by J. G. A.
Pocock, who has traced the tangled threads of civic humanism from
sixteenth-century Florence through the political clash between the
Court and Country parties in eighteenth-century England to what
he considers the replay of that conflict in America in the 1790s.
Sensitive to the way ideas suggest and legitimate lines of action,
Pocock connects the emergence of civic-humanist values to the political disorders of seventeenth-century England. Because the traditional monarchy left English subjects with no duties save obedience,
the Civil War necessitated a search for ideas to inform a new consciousness.[6] After the failure of the Puritan commonwealth,
Englishmen turned to classical political theory for explanations that
could accommodate their reverence for the ancient constitution to
the imperatives of a modern ruling class. There they found a chaste
model of civil society where men exercised their virtue by putting
the common good before their own and thus realized their fulfillment as Aristotle's political animal. Civic humanism offered a concept of public life that served the moral as well as the intellectual

4. Pocock, *Machiavellian Moment*, 478–485.
5. Charles Secondat, Baron de Montesquieu, *The Spirit of the Laws*, trans. Thomas
Nugent (New York, 1962; originally published Paris, 1748), 20–22, 40–48.
6. Pocock, *Machiavellian Moment*, 333–347.

needs of the English gentry. However, the ancients did not give of their wisdom without a price. Their precepts were inseparable from the dreary record of tyrannies, rebellions, and usurpations from which they were gleaned. Human nature is flawed; civil order is always at risk; cycles of degeneration await all societies. History furnishes the important lesson that the rule of law alone preserves liberty and the balancing of the few and the many alone preserves the law. From this classical paradigm, Pocock believes, most Englishmen took their political soundings, discovering therein reasons for alarm as well as prescriptions for stability. This paradigm also generated the suspicion of novelty and the fear of self-interest. Politics had to be reduced to ethics if it were not itself to be reduced to corruption. This "sociology of civic ethics," according to Pocock, "had to be restated with paradigmatic force and comprehensiveness for the eighteenth-century West at large," and it fell to Montesquieu's *Spirit of the Laws* to do the job.[7]

Despite its character as a learned treatise, Montesquieu's book was immediately drawn into polemical warfare, in large part because his depiction of England's mixed monarchy was more ideological than empirical. His source of information had been the leader of the English Country opposition, Henry St. John, Viscount Bolingbroke, who had fashioned the theory of balanced government into an attack on the ruling Whig oligarchy. With the wisdom of the ancients at his back, Bolingbroke contended that his enemies at court were not merely wrong, but highly dangerous, that indeed their consolidation of executive power placed the entire British constitution in jeopardy.[8] Montesquieu's Bolingbrokean bias made the *Spirit of the Laws* highly useful to the Country party in England, while in France it offered new weapons for the fight against the absolutism of Louis XV. His theoretical justification for the autonomy and authority of political elites lent support to the campaign to strengthen the power of the French *parlements,* the provincial courts staffed by a hereditary magistracy.[9] These partisan responses, however, had little effect on Montesquieu's reception in

7. Ibid., 484, 527.

8. Isaac Kramnick, *Bolingbroke and His Circle: The Politics of Nostalgia in the Age of Walpole* (Cambridge, Mass., 1968), 142–152.

9. Ibid., 150–152.

America, where he exercised the influence of a mighty savant of the age of enlightenment and was, as Pocock puts it, "the greatest practitioner" of the "science of virtue." [10]

Jefferson began reading Montesquieu in 1774, when he was thirty-one and a member of the First Continental Congress. He devoted more space in his commonplace book to the *Spirit of the Laws* than to any other work. [11] Sixteen years later he began to write about its "falsehoods" and "heresies." To Tracy he admitted that his initial admiration was shaken only when he recognized so much of "false principle and misapplied fact" as to render equivocal the whole. Thereafter he took increasing note of the "inconsistencies," "apocryphal facts," and "false inferences" that, in his judgment, marred Montesquieu's great book. [12] In view of Jefferson's reputation as a guardian of virtue, an admirer of simplicity, and a patron, if not a person, of frugality, this mounting criticism of Montesquieu may seem puzzling. In fact, the two men began with diametrically opposed assumptions about human nature, which in turn impinged on their conception of the problem of order, and, more important to Jefferson, the prospect for political equality.

Jefferson became aware of the elitist implications of Montesquieu's civic humanism during his years in Paris. [13] When he took up his duties as American minister in 1785, most educated Frenchmen believed that reform of their antiquated institutions was imminent. Debates in the famous Paris salons frequented by Jefferson swirled around the questions raised by this expectation. Must a newly constituted French monarchy include a role for the nobility, as Montesquieu had insisted? Did political realities dictate that the French legislature contain both a house for the people and a house for the privileged few, as in England? In the two years preceding the convocation of the Estates General, reform-minded Frenchmen

10. Pocock, *Machiavellian Moment*, 484.

11. *The Commonplace Book of Thomas Jefferson: A Repertory of His Ideas on Government*, ed. Gilbert Chinard (Baltimore, 1926), 9, 31–37.

12. Jefferson to Thomas Mann Randolph, May 30, 1790, in *The Writings of Jefferson*, ed. Lipscomb and Bergh, VIII, 31; Jefferson to Duane, Aug. 12, 1810, ibid., XII, 408; Jefferson to Nathaniel Niles, Mar. 22, 1801, ibid., X, 232; Jefferson to Cooper, July 10, 1812, ibid., XIII, 177–178; Jefferson to Tracy, Jan. 26, 1811, ibid., 13. See also Peterson, *Thomas Jefferson and the New Nation*, 948.

13. *Commonplace Book*, ed. Chinard, 31–37.

divided into hostile camps. One comprised the *anglomanes,* who said yes to Montesquieu and his balanced-government theory; the other, the *américanistes,* said no, and rallied to the slogan "one king, one nation, one house." They also spurned the lessons encoded in the English example and maintained that Montesquieu's "standing bodies" had been the principal obstacles to improvements in France.[14] Jefferson's sympathies lay wholly with the latter group, among whom he made warm friends. Though the question at hand concerned bicameralism, it unavoidably touched the entire classical paradigm: the esteem for ancient wisdom, the hostility to change, and the acceptance of ranks and orders as permanent features of human society. The civic-humanist tradition also fostered suspicions about commercial development and economic innovations, which both Jefferson and his *américaniste* friends strongly favored.

The *américanistes* were drawn from the ranks of the *économistes,* who had long agitated for agricultural improvements and a free trade in grain. They disliked England's mercantilistic policies as much as its aristocratic constitution. America's unique economic situation, in their view, helped explain the bold political experiments of the new nation; both made the United States a powerful symbol of reform.[15] Shortly before he died, Anne Robert Jacques Turgot, the famous leader of the *économistes,* had expressed to Richard Price his dismay at the slavish imitation of English forms to be found in the American state constitutions. Published after Turgot's death, this letter provoked John Adams, then minister at the Court of St. James, to write a three-volume rebuttal. Appearing in the midst of the French debates on political reform, Adams' *Defence of the Constitutions of Government of the United States of America* clearly ranged him on the side of the *anglomanes.*[16] Fearing that the *Defence* would tarnish the fresh image of America, Jefferson's French friends, possibly with his connivance, rushed into print with an anonymous American pamphlet that explicitly dissociated Adams' veneration

14. See Chapter 9.

15. See Pierre Samuel Du Pont de Nemours' article in *Ephémèrides du citoyen,* VI (1770), 210–211; Durand Echeverria, *Mirage in the West: A History of the French Image of American Society to 1815* (Princeton, 1957), 24–26, 56.

16. Joyce Appleby, "The Jefferson-Adams Rupture and the First French Translation of John Adams' *Defence,*" *American Historical Review,* 63 (1968), 1084–1091.

of Old World political theory from mainstream American thought. "Had Mr. Adams been a native of the old, instead of the new world," the author, John Stevens, wrote, "we should not have been so surprised at his system." [17] Having shed their provincial status by revolution, Americans like Stevens were ready to give ideological import to what were once considered egregious departures from European norms. Novelty no longer frightened them.

The political perceptions of Adams, like those of Jefferson, had been sharpened during his long sojourn in Europe. Writing the *Defence* on the eve of his return home, Adams was acutely aware that his ideas might not be well received in the United States. In a letter accompanying a presentation copy sent to Benjamin Franklin, he declared somewhat defensively, "if it is heresy, I shall, I suppose, be cast out of communion. But it is the only sense in which I am or ever was a Republican." [18] Fortunately for Adams, his fellow New Englanders shared his preoccupation with the civic-humanist values of the classical republican tradition. In the years immediately following the end of the war, they had dwelt obsessively on the necessity of civic virtue and the threats posed by the riotous appetites of a liberated people. As Nathan O. Hatch detailed, clergymen of both evangelical and rationalist strains had revitalized John Winthrop's sense of mission by fusing the themes of an embattled Calvinism with the secular ideals of classical republicanism. Originally directed against the French Canadian menace, this civil millenarianism offered a rationale for opposing the British and for turning the resistance movement in Massachusetts into "the sacred cause of liberty." American independence presented these Puritan descendants with yet another occasion for putting their countrymen to the question, "Are we a virtuous people?" Without endorsing formal political privilege, upper-class New Englanders insisted on the traditional deference of the many to the few. Both classical political theory and conventional Christian dogma heightened fears about individual self-interest. Like members of the English Country party, many New Englanders espied in the quickening pace of commercial life the triumph of license and luxury.

17. [John Stevens], *Observations on Government, Including Some Animadversions on Mr. Adams's Defence of the Constitutions of Government* . . . (New York, 1787), 25–26.

18. *The Works of Benjamin Franklin*, ed. John Bigelow, XI (New York, 1904), 298–299.

Such concerns lay ready to trigger powerful emotions when the many actually spoke. Thus the court closings by western farmers led by Daniel Shays evoked the old refrains of "savage independence," "unthinking multitude," and "the sad corruption of republican virtue." The civil millenarianism that put Massachusetts in the Revolutionary vanguard, however, laid the groundwork for that unbending Federalism that would later set New England at odds with the rest of the nation. [19]

As Jefferson's and Adams' references to heresy suggest, contemporaries continued to think in terms of orthodoxy, while republicanism itself became a protean concept. With the first stirrings of American intellectual independence, republicanism flooded its classical channels, especially outside New England. In response to these new currents James Madison worked out an answer to Montesquieu's small-republic theory in his Federalist No. 10. Drawing on the experience of a socially diverse and economically expansive people, he argued that the mortal effects of majority faction could best be controlled in a large pluralistic society through the competition of interests. In Madison's eyes, Adams' endorsement of the ancient doctrine of balanced government represented a betrayal of American political forms. Four years after the publication of the *Defence* he charged that Adams, "under a mock defence of the Republican Constitutions of his Country," had attacked them with all his force. [20] Such hyperbole can be ascribed to partisan rhetoric, but the assertion of theoretical differences in the meaning of republicanism deserves investigation, especially because some historians of the early national period have claimed that the classical model that Adams endorsed dominated American politics well into the nineteenth century.

Jefferson's metaphorical response to Shays's Rebellion—"the tree of liberty must be refreshed from time to time with the blood of patriots and tyrants"—alerts us to a set of values easily distinguished from those flourishing in Adams' New England. In his conception of human nature, his expectation of progress, his enthusiasm for economic growth, and his irreverence toward the past, Jefferson

19. Nathan O. Hatch, *The Sacred Cause of Liberty: Republican Thought and the Millenium in Revolutionary New England* (New Haven, 1977), 13–18, 36–55, 121.

20. Madison to Jefferson, May 12, 1791, in *The Writings of James Madison*, ed. Gaillard Hunt (New York, 1904), VI, 50.

explicitly distanced himself from the civic humanism that Adams had espoused. Far from fearing a decline of virtue in his fellow Americans, he laid it down as an axiom that they would remain healthy in spirit and body so long as they pursued farming. "Corruption of morals in the mass of cultivators," he wrote in a much-quoted passage in the *Notes on the State of Virginia,* "is a phenomenon of which no age nor nation has furnished an example." As Hatch has observed, most New Englanders would have gaped in disbelief at such faith in the beneficent influence of a social occupation.[21] Jefferson had freed himself from worries about the moral fiber of his countrymen by embracing a different construction of reality. Abandoning the eternal Adam of Christianity as well as the creature of passions portrayed in ancient texts, he had embraced a conception of human nature that emphasized its benign potential.

Where traditional thinkers traced the source of social evils back to wayward human propensities, Jefferson reversed the influence and ascribed the lowly state of man to repressive institutions. Nowhere better described than in Daniel Boorstin's *The Lost World of Thomas Jefferson,* this naturalistic view was at once mechanistic and moral.[22] The environment could create vice and virtue—typically, Jefferson described tobacco-raising as "a culture productive of infinite wretchedness"—but the innate qualities of man held out great promise.[23] The purpose of government was therefore not to raise power to check power but rather to ensure the conditions for liberating man's self-actualizing capacities. If the authoritarian institutions of the past could be reformed, then a different and happier future could be imagined. Again he reversed the priorities implicit in the classical tradition. The private came first. Instead of regarding the public arena as the locus of human fulfillment where men rose above their self-interest to serve the common good, Jefferson wanted government to offer protection to the personal realm where men might freely exercise their faculties. It is to this complex set of values that

21. Jefferson to William Stephens Smith, Nov. 13, 1787, in *The Papers of Thomas Jefferson,* ed. Julian P. Boyd et al. (Princeton, 1950–   ), XII, 356; Jefferson, *Notes on the State of Virginia,* ed. William Peden (Chapel Hill, 1955), 164–165; Hatch, *Sacred Cause of Liberty,* 108.

22. Boorstin, *The Lost World of Thomas Jefferson* (New York, 1948).

23. Jefferson, *Notes,* ed. Peden, 166.

one must look for the reasons behind Jefferson's prolonged campaign against the heresies of Montesquieu.

Montesquieu's veneration of ancient wisdom ran athwart Jefferson's oft-expressed optimism that the future would outshine the past; the American celebration of the balanced government theory in the *Spirit of the Laws* led Jefferson to fear that his countrymen would accept as inevitable the dominance of a new elite of wealth and privilege. Coining the term "Americanism," he put it to polemical use as an alternative to an Anglo-inspired "aristocracy."[24] As a Virginia politician during the Revolution, Jefferson had given highest priority to laws that would prevent concentrations of landed wealth. "Legislators cannot invent too many devices for subdividing property," he wrote to Madison from Paris, going on to suggest progressive taxes for large holders, with total exemptions for small ones. Looking back in his autobiography on his own legislative record, he claimed to have created a system "by which every fibre would be eradicated of antient or future aristocracy." Tradition held no charms for him, nor did precedent. He was not at all surprised that "time and trial have discovered very capital defects" in the Virginia constitution when it had reached the ripe old age of eight years. Even more indicative of the iconoclastic cast of his mind was his idea of submitting the country's laws to a plebiscite every generation. By lifting the dead hand of the past Jefferson expected to give life to the latent human capacity for personal fulfillment. Science and education pulled his carriage of hopes, as he revealed when he ordered a composite portrait of the life-sized busts of Bacon, Locke, and Newton. They had, he told John Trumbull, laid the foundation for the physical and moral sciences and should not be confounded "with the herd of other great men," because they were "the three greatest men that have ever lived, without any exception."[25]

More than any other figure in his generation Jefferson integrated a program of economic development and a policy for nation-building

24. In a letter to C. F. C. de Volney, Feb. 8, 1805, Jefferson predicted that Delaware would be split until "Anglomany with her yields to Americanism" (*Writings of Jefferson,* ed. Lipscomb and Bergh, XI, 68). The *Oxford English Dictionary* credits Jefferson with coining the word "Americanism" but cites an 1808 passage as the first one.

25. Jefferson to Madison, Oct. 28, 1785, in *Papers of Thomas Jefferson,* ed. Boyd et al., XV, 384–398; Jefferson to Trumbull, Feb. 15, 1789, ibid., XIV, 561.

into a radical moral theory. What emerges from his own writings is a fairly coherent description of the kind of economic base that would support a democratic republic. Believing that industrious, self-reliant farmers made superior citizens, Jefferson advocated measures to increase the number of freeholders. He ingeniously suggested a fifty-acre qualification for voting in Virginia, coupled with a proposal to give fifty acres to every landless white adult male. His efforts to abolish primogeniture represented yet another way to diffuse property-holding.[26] He successfully opposed the speculative land companies in working out the details of Virginia's cession of western claims, and he guided the first land ordinance through the Continental Congress. There he wrote into American policy the goals of easy access to the national domain and speedy statehood for the territories. Where classical economic theory stressed that the poor could not act as citizens because they were dependent on the will of others, Jefferson unmasked the self-fulfilling prophecy in that formulation. Assessing the party divisions in the Constitutional Convention, he charged that many then had believed the experience of Europe "to be a safer guide than mere theory." Many too had come to accept the political domination of the poor by the rich and had further aimed at constraining "the brute force of the people" by hard labor, poverty, and ignorance.[27] As early as 1784, Jefferson had charted a different course: use constitutional and statutory measures to make the poor independent. Here his environmentalism merged imperceptibly into his convictions about the basic human endowment. What today would appear as social engineering presented itself to Jefferson as a liberation of those natural forces long held in check by the Old World artifices of monarchy, nobility, and established religion.

More basic to the issues here, Jefferson was an early advocate of the commercial exploitation of American agriculture. His vision of a nation of farmers involved him in long-range programs for expanding international free trade in basic farm commodities. The marketing of American surpluses engaged his attention from his days as Virginia's representative in the Continental Congress, through his years in Paris, as secretary of state, as president, and

26. *Papers of Thomas Jefferson,* ed. Boyd et al., I, 362; ibid., II, 308.
27. Jefferson to William Johnson, June 12, 1823, in *The Writings of Thomas Jefferson,* ed. Paul Leicester Ford (New York, 1892–1899), X, 226n–227n.

as adviser to his successors. In the *Notes* Jefferson adumbrated a prescription for American growth which he followed with some consistency through a long political career. Here he extolled the production of wheat because it "feeds the labourers plentifully, requires from them only a moderate toil . . . and diffuses plenty and happiness among the whole." Farmers, he assumed, would participate in the world market, not seek self-sufficiency. Their rising standard of living would lift them from the miserable life of their European counterparts. His countrymen, Jefferson predicted, would go back to buying European manufactured goods after the Revolution, while moving rapidly westward to exploit the natural resources that could pay for them.[28] No partisan of Spartan endurance, he exonerated Americans from the charge of lukewarm patriotism by pointing to "the pennyless condition of a people, totally shut out from all commerce . . . and therefore without any means for converting their labor into money."[29] It was not the slave-worked staple crops that fueled Jefferson's hopes but the prospects opened to ordinary farmers. The burgeoning Atlantic trade in grains gave him the material base for a program that was both national and democratic.

The steady increase of world population that had raised the price of wheat prompted the pessimism of Thomas R. Malthus, but Jefferson stuck by his guns of optimism. Indeed, what is fascinating in both Jefferson's and Madison's responses to Malthus is their complete transformation of the problem. Expecting a diminishing return from agriculture, Malthus asserted that population would outstrip food; assuming an enhanced capacity to feed people, Madison and Jefferson instead feared that there would be more people than jobs.[30]

28. Jefferson, *Notes on the State of Virginia*, ed. Peden, 164, 168.

29. Jefferson to Johnson, Oct. 27, 1822, in *Writings of Jefferson*, ed. Ford, X, 222–223.

30. Madison to Jefferson, June 19, 1786, in *The Papers of Thomas Jefferson*, ed. Boyd et al., IX, 659–660. See also Drew R. McCoy, "Jefferson and Madison on Malthus: Population Growth in Jeffersonian Political Economy," *Virginia Magazine of History and Biography*, 88 (1980), 259–276. Although McCoy argues that there was a "significant interest in population growth in late eighteenth- and early nineteenth-century America" (261), his review of Jefferson's four references to Malthus indicates that Jefferson held to his "basic vision of a predominantly agricultural America that would continue to export its bountiful surpluses of food abroad" (268). See also Peterson, *Thomas Jefferson and the New Nation*, 771–773. No American publication on the subject of Malthus appeared until twenty years after the 1798 appearance of *An Essay on the Principle of Population*.

Writing to Jean Baptiste Say in 1804, Jefferson explained why Americans would be exempted from Malthus' gloomy prophecies. The uncultivated expanses of the national domain promised harvests increasing "geometrically with our laborers." Americans would then be able to produce surpluses "to nourish the now perishing births of Europe, who in return would manufacture and send us in exchange our clothes and other comforts."[31] It was the same formula he had proposed a score of years earlier in the *Notes*. Meanwhile he had wrested much of the land in the northwest from speculators, ensured the political parity of new states, and presided over the dismantling of the national financial establishment that had threatened to narrow the ambit of economic freedom for ordinary Americans.

In an article on Virginia's Revolutionary leadership Marc Egnal describes the coalescence of a party of expansionists among the Virginia gentry. Quick to identify themselves with "America's cornucopian future," burgesses from the Northern Neck and the piedmont took the lead in claiming the Ohio Valley. After the British made good that claim in the French and Indian War, these same expansionists fought the efforts of Parliament to control their hunger for land. Committed to expansion, they pursued what Egnal characterizes as "forthright measures against any power that hindered the colonies from becoming prosperous, self-assertive states."[32] In tracing the bold plans of the Lees and Washingtons who led the expansionist party, Egnal provides roots for Jefferson's enthusiasm for economic progress. In a letter to George Washington, Jefferson dismissed doubts about America's commercial future on the ground that the people had had too full a taste for manufactured comforts to be closed off from them. "We must," he wrote in 1784, "endeavor to share as large a portion as we can of this modern source of wealth and power."[33] Where Jefferson went beyond the expansionists was in imagining how the agricultural prospects of America could

31. Jefferson to Say, Feb. 1, 1804, in *Writings of Jefferson*, ed. Lipscomb and Bergh, XI, 2–3.

32. Marc Egnal, "The Origins of the Revolution in Virginia: A Reinterpretation," *William and Mary Quarterly*, 37 (1980), 404, 416, 424–428. See also H. James Henderson, "The Structure of Politics in the Continental Congress," in *Essays on the American Revolution*, ed. Stephen G. Kurtz and James H. Hutson (Chapel Hill, 1973), 187–191.

33. Jefferson to Washington, Mar. 15, 1784, in *Papers of Thomas Jefferson*, ed. Boyd et al., VII, 26.

nurture the unfolding of a human potential long blocked by poverty and ignorance. Virginia's size, its population, its suitability for raising food, and its access to the West help explain why Virginians spearheaded the drive for a constitutional convention and won eight of the first nine presidential elections under the new federal government. The nationalism of Virginians drew sustenance from a favorable material situation, but it was the genius of Jefferson to give that vision of expansion a powerful moral character.

Jefferson's optimism and the hopes it promoted came out most clearly when he pushed against the limits of reform advocated by his radical French friends. As Gilbert Chinard long ago pointed out, Jefferson rejected Du Pont's premise that it was the *propriétaires* who formed the political nation. "You," he chided Du Pont, "set down as zeros all individuals not having lands," adding significantly that the landless "are the greater number in every society of long standing." Governments, Jefferson insisted, did not exist to protect property but rather to promote access to property or, more broadly speaking, opportunity. It was in deference to this distinction that he changed Locke's "life, liberty and property" to make the Declaration of Independence affirm the natural rights to "life, liberty, and the pursuit of happiness." A decade later, when Lafayette submitted to him a draft declaration of rights for France, he again excised the offending word, property. Investing faith in the profoundly revolutionary ideal of a natural capacity for personal autonomy, Jefferson resolutely put his influence to work to minimize social distinctions, eschewing as well the didacticism that came too readily to upper-class reformers. Writing to Du Pont at age seventy-three, he acknowledged that they shared a paternal love for their people, "but you love them as infants whom you are afraid to trust without nurses; and I as adults whom I freely leave to self-government."[34]

The linkage between Jefferson's basic assumptions about human nature and his ideas about commerce can be traced through the *Review of Montesquieu* upon which Jefferson lavished so much attention after he left the presidency. Describing Tracy's book as the "most profound and logical work" addressed to the present genera-

---

34. *The Correspondence of Jefferson and Du Pont de Nemours,* ed. Gilbert Chinard (Baltimore, 1931), lxiii; Jefferson to Du Pont, Apr. 24, 1816, in *Correspondence between Thomas Jefferson and Pierre Samuel du Pont de Nemours,* ed. Malone, 184.

tion, he predicted that it would finally reduce Montesquieu to his true value.[35] Tracy's own intellectual debts were owed to Thomas Hobbes, John Locke, and Adam Smith, whose cold analyses of social relations he warmed with infusions of a moralism reminiscent of Jean-Jacques Rousseau. From Hobbes he took his fundamental stance on human nature: men are creatures of will. Their liberty consists in the power of executing that will and accomplishing their desires, and their happiness in the gratification of the will. Hence happiness and liberty are the same. The pursuit of self-interest is both natural and irresistible, but Tracy escaped from the Hobbesian war of all against all by asserting that in a free government men would pursue possessions by exercising their own faculties rather than by invading the rights of others. This resolution reflected Jefferson's own environmentalism and his expectation that the reform of social institutions would activate hitherto suppressed human capacities. Like Frenchmen of an earlier generation, Tracy considered America's political forms as revolutionary breakthroughs: representative democracy was "a new invention, unknown in Montesquieu's time." With this new type of government came written constitutions, which Tracy described in Lockean rather than classical terms. They did not exist to establish a balance of power, as in the ancient constitution of England, but rather to define the power given to the people's representatives and to fix the limits beyond which they must not trespass. "This," he explained in Madisonian terms, "is democracy rendered practicable for a long time and over a great extent of territory."[36]

Tracy devoted a great deal of attention in both works to economics. Montesquieu, he said, had worked with too narrow an idea of trade. What he should have seen was that because all exchanges are acts of commerce, commerce is "not only the foundation and basis of society but . . . the fabric itself." Tracy declared that to understand economic relations was the principal end of the social sciences. He gave Smith and Say high marks but lamented that they

35. Jefferson to Du Pont, Nov. 29, 1813, in *Writings of Jefferson*, ed. Lipscomb and Bergh, XIX, 195; Jefferson to Cooper, July 10, 1812, ibid., XIII, 177–178; Jefferson to Tracy, Jan. 26, 1811, ibid., 13.

36. [Antoine Louis Claude Destutt de Tracy], *A Commentary and Review of Montesquieu's Spirit of Laws . . .* (Philadelphia, 1811), 97–98, 232, 19–20.

had failed to see that only human beings create the utility that determines market value. Had they grasped this, a hundred thousand superfluous distinctions might have been avoided, including especially the physiocratic notion that agriculture possessed a special value. Emphasizing utility, Tracy gave to the capitalist an importance altogether lacking in Smith's mere accumulator. Whether an entrepreneur used his own labor or commanded the labor of others, he invested natural goods with utility when he organized productive resources and by doing so became a force for good. Tracy elaborated many of these points in his *Treatise of Political Economy,* which Jefferson also translated.[37]

Tracy's eudaemonism explains his rejection of the civic-humanist tradition. Montesquieu, he charged, made virtue consist in voluntary privations, a fundamental error because "no human being is so constituted by nature." We cannot say too often, he wrote, that liberty is happiness and that happiness flows from a civic order that enables men to multiply and perfect their enjoyments. When Montesquieu based republican government on self-denial, he made it depend on "a false and fluctuating virtue . . . which, by exciting men to hardihood and devotedness, renders them at the same time malignant, austere, ferocious, sanguinary, and above all unhappy."[38]

Unlike Smith, whose invisible hand of the market required the competition of self-interested bargainers, Tracy generously gave human beings their own harmonizing qualities of good sense and moderation. He thus avoided both the problem of power and the problem of order. Montesquieu, he conceded, had recognized that taxes were generally bad but had failed to explain how they threatened human happiness: "We desire society to be well organized in order that our enjoyments may be more multiplied, more perfect, and more tranquil; and so long as this end is not well understood, we are liable to a number of errors, from which our celebrated author is not always exempt."[39] The emphasis in Tracy's strictures on taxation fell not on the transfer from private to public funds but rather on the diminution of the means of personal gratification, which he

37. Ibid., 204–211, 183–192; Tracy, *A Treatise on Political Economy* . . . (Georgetown, D.C., 1817).

38. Tracy, *Review of Montesquieu,* 20–24, 184, 35.

39. Ibid., 159–164, 184–185.

considered to be the source of happiness in human society. Reflecting more conventional ways of thinking, he also noted that public expenditures, unless for bridges and roads, were economically sterile and that swollen revenues encouraged corruption and oppression. Far from enhancing productivity, public indebtedness raised the price of money and thereby discouraged investment in agriculture, manufacturing, and commerce. Even more pernicious, paper money required the intrusion of government into the private economic system of voluntary bargains. Montesquieu was also faulted for his preoccupation with international trade and his error in thinking that profits could only be made off strangers. By contrast, Tracy asserted that internal commerce was in all cases much more important, especially for large countries. Moreover, commercial development in a representative democracy would level the rich and raise the poor, causing both "to approach that middle point, at which the love of order, of industry, of justice and reason, naturally establish themselves." [40] Men are thus not naturally corrupt, lazy, or avaricious; they become so only when special privilege exalts the few and depresses the many. If given scope for their innate inclinations, ordinary men would realize their true vocation as sober and industrious producers. This was a gratuitous endowment, as John Adams pointed out, but for believers it offered an escape from the predicament posed by the classical dichotomy between virtue and commerce. [41]

Jefferson had an exalted opinion of Tracy and his work. He thought his ideas should supplant those of Adam Smith and claimed that Tracy had produced "the best elementary book on the principles of government." It marked "an epoch in the science of government" and should be recognized as "the most precious gift the present age had received." [42] By joining this praise with criticism of Montesquieu's shortcomings, Jefferson made clear just what in the

40. Ibid., 240–244, 214–218, 33.

41. Adams to Jefferson, Feb. 2, 1817, in *The Adams-Jefferson Letters: The Complete Correspondence between Thomas Jefferson and Abigail and John Adams,* ed. Lester J. Cappon (Chapel Hill, 1959), II, 506.

42. Jefferson to Duane, Apr. 4, 1813, in *Writings of Jefferson,* ed. Lipscomb and Bergh, XIII, 231; Jefferson to Joseph C. Cabell, Feb. 2, 1816, ibid., XIV, 419; Jefferson to Cooper, Jan. 16, 1814, ibid., 62–63; Jefferson to Tracy, Jan. 26, 1811, ibid., XIII, 13.

Review and *Treatise* prompted these accolades.[43] Considering the extended scholarly treatment of Jefferson's thought, this unbounded enthusiasm for Tracy expressed at the end of his life has special value as an indication of the ideas that he found enduringly attractive.[44] Tracy had dissolved society into its individual human components and given to them a fundamentally economic character. He believed that the individual's experience of will gave birth to the knowledge that one is endowed "with an inevitable and inalienable property, that of its individuality." All notions of riches and deprivations, of justice and injustice, he wrote, should, therefore, be seen as dependent on the idea of personality and the anterior awareness of self.[45] Drained from this analysis were the distinctions of class and rank whose balancing played so central a role in classical republicanism. Instead, Tracy started with natural rights and concluded that because all contracts by definition yielded gain to the contracting parties, society itself rested on voluntary commitments. Rejecting out of hand Montesquieu's elaboration of cultural traits, he insisted to the contrary that "men everywhere hold to their interests, and are occupied with them." Far from being bad, this created an essential identity of interests among men that was founded on their dual and private capacities as producers and consumers.[46]

43. In a different assessment of Tracy's influence on Jefferson, Drew R. McCoy describes Tracy as passing on to Jefferson his fears about European overpopulation (*The Elusive Republic: Political Economy in Jeffersonian America* [Chapel Hill, 1980], 253). Actually this analysis plays a very small part in Tracy's overall social theory and, unlike the long passages on Montesquieu, this section from the *Treatise* is never mentioned by Jefferson.

44. See Morton White, *The Philosophy of the American Revolution* (New York, 1978); Garry Wills, *Inventing America: Jefferson's Declaration of Independence* (Garden City, N.Y., 1978); Ronald Hamowy, "Jefferson and the Scottish Enlightenment: A Critique of Garry Wills's *Inventing America: Jefferson's Declaration of Independence*," *William and Mary Quarterly,* 36 (1979), 502–523. Hamowy's critique of Wills and the issue of the relative influence of Locke and the philosophers of the Scottish Enlightenment raises many points not resolvable here, but it is relevant that Tracy was unequivocal in his natural rights philosophy and on the priority of property rights to government.

45. Tracy, *A Treatise on Political Economy* . . . , 35–36, 46–47. Madison anticipated Tracy on this point when he wrote that "as a man is said to have a right to his property, he may be equally said to have a property in his rights" (*Writings of Madison,* ed. Hunt, VI, 101–103; this line appeared originally in the *National Gazette* [Philadelphia], Mar. 29, 1792).

46. Tracy, *Review of Montesquieu,* 192–205; *A Treatise on Political Economy,* 162, 117.

Clearly something had gone awry with society as it actually was, and Tracy explained this as the consequence of tendencies toward inequality and injustice that could be corrected by eliminating formal privilege and protecting the equality of rights established in nature. More specifically, he detailed how government could free economic life and liberate the active, desiring nature of man by discountenancing paper money, bank companies, and public credit. But unlike the Country party critics of England's funded debt, Tracy fired at his target with guns newly cast in the foundry of modern utilitarianism. The interests of society lay with the interests of the poor, and the interests of the poor lay with greater productivity. Government could contribute to progressive economic development by freeing trade and protecting property rights—those of the worker who owns himself and those of the capitalists who set others to work. In this, as in much else, Tracy exulted in having cleared up the confusions of Montesquieu. "Great talents," he declared, "belong only to our time." An appreciative Jefferson placed the phrase in capitals.[47]

It is against this background that scholarly efforts to construe the Jeffersonians as an American version of the English Country party must be judged. This interpretation rests on the foundation laid in Bernard Bailyn's *The Ideological Origins of the American Revolution*. Bailyn traced the resistance movement of the 1760s to the colonists' peculiar conception of reality. Having absorbed a view of politics from the resonating rhetoric of the English opposition, the Americans considered the new British measures evidence of a conspiracy to destroy their rights. For Bailyn, however, the Revolution was a transforming event that triggered a "critical probing of traditional concepts." In *The Creation of the American Republic* Gordon S. Wood pushed forward the emergence of a native political idiom to 1787, when Americans abandoned their earlier "devotion to the transcendent public good" and accepted Madison's brilliant solution to the problem of majority faction.[48] In the scholarship of the last twenty years, the date for the Americanization of politics has been delayed

47. Tracy, *A Treatise on Political Economy*, 185.

48. Bailyn, *The Ideological Origins of the American Revolution* (Cambridge, Mass., 1967), 56–58, 101–109, 161; Wood, *The Creation of the American Republic, 1776–1787* (Chapel Hill, 1969), 93–97, 179, 418–425, 471–475.

yet another score of years, and the celebrated clashes between Alexander Hamilton and Jefferson have been reinterpreted as a transatlantic mirroring of the battle between the great Court politician, Robert Walpole, and his Country opponent, Bolingbroke.

Pointing out the course others were to follow, Pocock noted in 1972 that if the Federalist-Republican debates are viewed as a replay of English Court and Country struggles, this would necessitate postponing the demise of the Country style in America until the end of the first party system. Turning this reflection into an affirmation, Pocock went on to name Jefferson as the conduit through which a civic concept of virtue entered "the whole tradition of American agrarian and populist messianism."[49] Writing four years later, John M. Murrin made the adoption of the Court-and-Country model an imperative: "The continuing unity and viability of the United States depended, ironically, upon its ability to replicate both sides of the central tensions that had afflicted Augustan England."[50] In a study of the "Jeffersonian persuasion," Lance Banning has discovered a persistent polarity between Court and Country throughout the entire early national period. He attributes the Country cast of Jeffersonian thought to the fact that Americans still lived in "a universe of classical political perceptions."[51] Focusing more tightly on the fiscal alternatives endorsed by Jeffersonians and Federalists, E. James Ferguson has argued that the reaction to Hamilton's policies followed the lines it did because of the pervasiveness of Country-mindedness in America.[52] To Forrest McDonald, the affinities between the Jeffersonians and the English Country party are even closer: they borrowed "*in toto* from such Oppositionists as Charles Davenant, John Trenchard, Thomas Gordon, James Burgh, and most especially Henry St. John, First Viscount Bolingbroke." Warming to his subject, McDonald concludes that "just about everything in Jeffersonian Republicanism was to be found in Boling-

49. J. G. A. Pocock, "Virtue and Commerce in the Eighteenth Century," *Journal of Interdisciplinary History*, 3 (1972), 133–134; *The Machiavellian Moment: Florentine Political Thought and the Atlantic Republican Tradition* (Princeton, 1975), IX, 529–533.

50. Murrin, "Great Inversion," in *Three British Revolutions,* ed. Pocock, 406.

51. Banning, *Jeffersonian Persuasion,* 17–18, 92–93, 273–274.

52. Ferguson, "Political Economy, Public Liberty, and the Formation of the Constitution" (unpubl. paper, Organization of American Historians, New Orleans, 1979), 4.

broke."[53] Thus these historians have depicted the thought of Americans in the 1790s as encapsulated in the conceptual world of Montesquieu's civic humanism.

Banning has made the greatest effort to demonstrate the influence of classical republicanism on the polemics of the 1790s, and his study illustrates the problems involved in the enterprise. The power of English opposition thought is frequently asserted but nowhere traced through the body of any particular man's thought. The prior existence of Country-mindedness, detailed by Bailyn and Wood, forms the principal proof for the continuation of classical politics down to 1815.[54] So pervasive was this inherited mode of thought, Banning says, that newspaper writers could communicate with loose analogies or a suggestive word. "The most telling and ideologically most fundamental criticism of Federalist government was carried by a cryptic code." Corruption, for instance, "conveyed to friends and enemies alike an entire language about social and governmental degeneration." Hamilton's program inevitably provoked concerns in men "shaped by British opposition thought" because certain worries "were never very far beneath the surface of revolutionary minds." Writers in 1792 hammered home the opposition themes in a "few phrases loaded with the apocalyptic connotations" already familiar to Americans. "Without a fully systematic explication, they were comprehended and assented to in every corner of the land."[55] The subliminal aspects of Country ideology thus rendered unnecessary a search for confirming evidence. Banning's assertions, however, are plausible only if one accepts his basic assumption that eighteenth-century British opposition ideas acted as the "structured medium

---

53. McDonald, *Presidency of Jefferson,* 19–20, 161–163, ix. See also James H. Hutson, "Country, Court, and Constitution: Antifederalism and the Historians," *William and Mary Quarterly,* 38 (1981), 337–368; Robert E. Shalhope, "Republicanism and Early American Historiography," *William and Mary Quarterly,* 29 (1982), 334–356.

54. Banning, *Jeffersonian Persuasion,* 93. The only scholarship on the substance of English Country thought is Pocock's *Machiavellian Moment,* to which the historians of the Country interpretation refer. See, for example, Murrin, "Great Inversion," in *Three British Revolutions,* ed. Pocock, 382, 417, 448–449, n.109; McCoy, *Elusive Republic,* 42, 60–61; and Berthoff, "Independence and Attachment," in *Uprooted Americans,* ed. Bushman et al., 124, n.96. Pocock himself appeals to Banning's work to refute Wood's contention that classical politics came to an end in 1787 (*Machiavellian Moment,* 527–531).

55. Banning, *Jeffersonian Persuasion,* 185, 128, 177.

through which Americans continued to perceive the world and give expression to their hopes and discontents."[56] It is precisely this contention that must be proved.

Nothing in Jefferson's statements or policies suggests that he adhered to the agrarian conservatism implicit in classical republican thought. Rather, early in his political career, Jefferson saw in rising food prices the promise of flourishing American trade in grains. Unlike slave-produced staples, foodstuffs could be raised through the mixed husbandry of the family farm. The prosperity of ordinary farmers, Jefferson believed, would form the economic base for a democratic, progressive America. Also unlike the previously dominant staples, wheat could be grown in a wide arc that extended northward from the Upper South through the Middle Atlantic states to the Connecticut Valley. On the issue of exploiting the commercial opportunities in this vast area, Jefferson showed little hesitation. Indeed, in a rather callous appraisal of attitudes toward the War of 1812, he informed Madison that all he need do to shore up popular support was to seize Canada and secure markets for American flour. "The great profits of the wheat crop have allured every one to it; and ever was such a crop on the ground . . . It would be mortifying to the farmer to see such an one rot in his barn. It would soon sicken him to war."[57] The statement measures Jefferson's distance from the Harringtonian view of property as the means to stability and leisure, a possession, according to Pocock, that "anchored the individual in the structure of power and virtue, and liberated him to practice these as activities."[58]

Although Banning recognizes that it would be "an error to conceive of the Republicans as foes of either capital or wealth," he leaves unexplored the way in which their commercial attitudes either exemplified or modified the classical paradigm he finds reigning supreme in late-eighteenth-century America.[59] A more empirical

56. Ibid., 92, 273–274.

57. Jefferson to Madison, June 29, 1812, in *Writings of Jefferson,* ed. Ford, IX, 364. Jefferson's enthusiasm for international free trade can be traced back to his *Notes on the State of Virginia* (174), and cannot be attributed to his French sojourn, as asserted in James H. Hutson, "Intellectual Foundations of Early American Diplomacy," *Diplomatic History,* I (1977), 6.

58. Pocock, *Machiavellian Moment,* 389–391.

59. Banning, *Jeffersonian Persuasion,* 204–205.

and hence more satisfying account of the Jeffersonian stance on economic issues is Drew R. McCoy's *The Elusive Republic.* McCoy finds the Republicans working consistently and aggressively to secure outlets for American produce. He also concludes that their economic program was tied to "an intense concern with the autonomy . . . of the individual." But he starts with the premise that Jeffersonianism reflected "an attempt to cling to the traditional republican spirit of classical antiquity" and turns Jefferson's well-known enthusiasm for westward expansion into a way of reconciling "classical republicanism with more modern . . . realities." Thus what was once seen as the basis for Jefferson's optimism now becomes a reflection of pessimism and anxiety about the future, a device for postponing the day of corruption and degeneration by throwing space in the way of time. Similarly, McCoy imputes to Jefferson a "continuing concern with the natural threat presented by the biological pressure of population growth," a view wholly at odds with Jefferson's repudiation of Malthus' dire projections.[60] Not until the Missouri Crisis and his own bankruptcy did Jefferson, at age seventy-six, express apprehension about the fate of the nation that he had so willingly nurtured.

Jefferson was as absorbed with the details of his free-trade policies as with the grand plans for continental expansion. Free land and free trade spelled progress and prosperity. He was fascinated with scientific advances in farming. The scope of his activities as diplomat, secretary of state, and president pointed to the future, and as Thomas M. Cragan has written, "far exceeded the commercial developments needed to carry away normal American agricultural surpluses."[61] While Jefferson associated luxury with unjust concentrations of wealth, he expected and approved of a rising standard of living, not the frugality so esteemed in the classical tradition. This distinction is nicely captured in a letter to Adams written when

60. McCoy, *Elusive Republic,* 131, 10, 253, 189–195; Jefferson to Say, Feb. 1, 1804, in *Writings of Jefferson,* ed. Lipscomb and Bergh, XI, 2–3; Jefferson to David Williams, Nov. 14, 1803, ibid., 430–431.

61. Cragan, "Thomas Jefferson's Early Attitudes Towards Manufacturing, Agriculture and Commerce" (Ph.D. diss., University of Tennessee, 1965), 310. See also Richard Ellis, "The Political Economy of Thomas Jefferson," in *Thomas Jefferson: The Man, His World, His Influence,* ed. Lally Weymouth (London, 1973), 81–95; Merrill D. Peterson's review of *The Papers of Thomas Jefferson,* XVIII, XIX, in *William and Mary Quarterly,* 32 (1975), 656–658.

they were both in Europe. Reviewing Adams' draft of a commercial treaty with Spain, Jefferson urged that the word "necessaries" be replaced by "comforts." [62] If the Republicans' promotion of international commerce and westward expansion did in fact reflect a Country-minded concern about escaping the terrors of history, we would see them monitor the pace of economic development. Instead, at critical junctures Jefferson and Madison rushed the pace of growth by facilitating access to land, by protecting the reexport trade, and by hastening the market penetration of frontier areas. McCoy's fine research provides a wealth of information about the economic policies and practices of the Jeffersonians, most of it difficult to reconcile with an ideological resistance to social change. The central historical question has been begged: Rather than inquire if the Jeffersonians were Country thinkers, Banning and McCoy begin by asking how the Republicans' Country-mindedness helps explain their political decisions.

Starting with the latter question, Murrin has also examined the modifications in Country ideology between the Revolution and the end of the War of 1812. The Revolution opened American politics to a broader range of questions, he says, but disputes after 1780 "fit neatly within the old Court-Country paradigm." Although the broadening of suffrage threatened to disrupt the classical republican balance between the few and the many, Murrin maintains that this innovation was accommodated intellectually by shifting the constitutional balance from actual groups in society to branches of government. [63] The Jeffersonians, however, did not want to balance government; they wanted to limit it. Their liberal sympathies in this regard were well underscored by Jefferson's remark that "Locke's little book on Government, is perfect as far as it goes." [64] In the eyes of the Country interpreters, however, neither the doctrine of popular sovereignty nor the novelty of limited government brought an end to the dominance of a classical mode in America. The specific formulations may have changed, but the emotional timbre endured because the Country-minded Republicans sought to preserve ancient

62. Jefferson to Adams, Nov. 27, 1785, in *Adams-Jefferson Letters,* ed. Cappon, I, 103.

63. Murrin, "Great Inversion," in *Three British Revolutions,* ed. Pocock, 401, 404–407.

64. Jefferson to Randolph, May 30, 1790, in *Writings of Jefferson,* ed. Lipscomb and Bergh, VIII, 31.

values in a modern world. The American opposition, like its English model, Murrin concludes, "idealized the past more than the future and feared significant change, especially major economic change, as corruption and degeneration." This demonstrates for him that the rest of the world has little to learn from eighteenth-century republicanism, which, "even in its own day, remained more nostalgic than modernizing." McDonald reaches a similar conclusion: Jefferson, like Bolingbroke, sought a return to "some Edenic Past: when all men revered God, respected their fellows, deferred to their betters, and knew their place."[65]

The incompatibility of Country ideology and the positions that Jefferson affirmed throughout his life should be abundantly clear. Much as he equivocated on the questions of slavery and national power, his dislike of social distinctions and political privilege never wavered. Far from idealizing traditional society, he boldly imagined a world without formal hierarchy. The issue cannot be confined to a discussion of the suffrage, for Jefferson's egalitarianism grew out of radical assumptions about human nature. He was temperamentally at odds with the reverence for the past nurtured by civic humanism. He neither venerated old institutional arrangements nor feared experimentation with new ones, and he repeatedly insisted that his was the party of change. Writing to Abigail Adams during his first term as president, he characterized the Republicans as men who feared the ignorance of the people less than the selfishness of their rulers. He rephrased the distinction for John Adams in a letter of the following decade. Looking back on the partisan battles of the 1790s, he differentiated the advocates of reform, who placed no definite limits on social improvements, from the enemies of reform who considered their inherited institutions "the akme of excellence."[66]

The writings of Tracy that Jefferson so ardently promoted also undercut the interpretation of the Jeffersonians as a Country party, for Tracy explicitly attacked the civic-humanist tradition. When he

65. Murrin, "Great Inversion," in *Three British Revolutions,* ed. Pocock, 400–401; McDonald, *Presidency of Jefferson,* 19.

66. Jefferson to Abigail Adams, Sept. 11, 1804, in *Adams-Jefferson Letters,* ed. Cappon, I, 280; Jefferson to John Adams, June 15, 1813, ibid., II, 332. See also Jefferson to Johnson, June 12, 1823, in *Writings of Jefferson,* ed. Ford, X, 226n–227n.

ridiculed Montesquieu's concept of virtue, he rejected its civic character. "Simplicity, habits of industry, a contempt for frivolity, the love of independence," he said, were the endowments of all rational human beings. Against Montesquieu's elaborate formulas for "voluntary privations and self-denials" Tracy pitted the simplicity of innate virtue. His extended commentary on *Spirit of the Laws* points up the error of making virtue a code word in Country ideology. The American critics of classical republicanism did not abandon virtue as a cherished goal but rather redefined it. Their redefinition, however, permitted them to ignore traditional political solutions because they no longer accepted the conventional formulation of the problem. By giving society a natural economic character they were able to believe in virtue with commerce. Decoding old conceptual languages helps us to reconstruct a past reality, but meanings can change while terms remain the same. Virtue is one example; liberty is another. In the eighteenth-century English lexicon liberty referred to constitutional rights, but the liberty that Republicans hurled at Federalists was that of individual self-assertion, tamed by a new conception of human progress. Nor were contemporaries unaware of these differences. "Your Taste is judicious," Adams commented wryly to Jefferson, "in likeing better the dreams of the Future, than the History of the Past."[67]

The first assertion that the Jeffersonians were acting like the English Country party came not from historians in the 1970s but from Federalists in the 1790s.[68] Therein lies a clue to the locus of classical politics in America. Both the Country-minded and the Court-tempered moved into the ranks of respectable Federalism because they shared a traditional political vocabulary. The archetypal

67. Tracy, *Review of Montesquieu*, 20. Adams to Jefferson, Aug. 9, 1816, in *Adams-Jefferson Letters,* ed. Cappon, II, 487. With uncharacteristic optimism Adams predicted that Jefferson and he would find a meeting of minds. See also Jeffrey Barnouw, "American Independence: Revolution of the Republican Ideal. A Critique of the 'Paradigm' of Republican Virtue," in *The American Revolution and Eighteenth-Century Culture,* ed. Paul Korchin (New York, 1982).

68. Banning, *Jeffersonian Persuasion,* 91; Ferguson, "Political Economy," 1. For evidence of Warren's adherence to Montesquieu's position, see Lester H. Cohen, "Explaining the Revolution: Ideology and Ethics in Mercy Otis Warren's Historical Theory," *William and Mary Quarterly,* 37 (1980), 218. Less convincing is Cohen's claim (217) that Madison was an exponent of mixed government and that Jefferson was concerned with civic virtue.

Country leader, Adams, found his prefigured enemy in the classical Court politician, Hamilton. Neither understood the expectations for social change entertained by their Republican opponents. Adams' addiction to moribund theories is notorious; less well advertised are the limits of Hamilton's conceptual world. Two quotations help mark the boundaries of his imagination. In 1784 Hamilton wrote in disbelief that some people maintained that commerce might regulate itself. Such persons, he went on to say, "will imagine, that there is no need of a common directing power" and then labeled the idea "one of those wild speculative paradoxes, which have grown into credit among us, contrary to the uniform practice and sense of the most enlightened nations." Elsewhere he distinguished freedom from slavery by saying that free men consented to the laws by which they were governed.[69] Totally missing from his thinking was the idea that the powers consigned to government might be reduced. Like Hamilton, most Federalists presumed that the world would go on as their histories taught them it always had. When confronted with a passionate assault on these assumptions, they could understand it only by assigning their attackers the historic role of the English opposition.

The composition of the Republican party also indicates that the choice was not between a Jeffersonian *gemeinschaft* and a Hamiltonian *gesellschaft,* as the Court and Country interpretation of early national politics would have it. Commercial farmers, small planters, urban tradesmen, and aspiring professional men poured into Jefferson's party as soon as he sounded the alarm about Hamilton's program.[70] To be fearful, as the Jeffersonians were, of the corruption they saw in public stock speculation was not the same as making corruption

---

69. Hamilton, *Continentalist No. V.,* Apr. 18, 1782, in *The Papers of Alexander Hamilton,* ed. Harold C. Syrett et al. (New York, 1962–1979), III, 76; Hamilton, "A Full Vindication," Dec. 15, 1774, ibid., I, 51–52.

70. Alfred E. Young, *The Democratic Republicans of New York: The Origins, 1763–1797* (Chapel Hill, 1976); John A. Munroe, *Federalist Delaware, 1775–1815* (New Brunswick, 1954); Paul Goodman, "Social Status of Party Leadership: The House of Representatives, 1797–1804," *William and Mary Quarterly,* 25 (1968), 465–474; Norman K. Risjord and Gordon DenBoer, "The Evolution of Political Parties in Virginia, 1782–1800," *Journal of American History,* 60 (1974), 961–984; Frank A. Cassell, "The Structure of Baltimore's Politics in the Age of Jefferson, 1795–1812," in *Law, Society and Politics in Early Maryland,* ed. Aubrey C. Land et al. (Baltimore, 1977), 278–295.

part of the eternal human drama. Because they believed that special privilege had poisoned the natural social harmony, they could look optimistically to a future rid of monarchs and aristocrats. At issue in the nation's first partisan battles were two mutually exclusive but entirely plausible blueprints for national development. The nationalists of both Republican and Federalist persuasions could agree on the establishment of an effective, unified government— even on the major planks of Hamilton's fiscal program—because they both favored growth with commerce. Indeed, the liberal economic order that Jefferson espoused was sustained in part by the success of the Constitution in providing the essential framework for capitalist development: a national market, a uniform currency, and the protection of contracts. Where the nationalists parted company was on the question of whether American growth should be controlled at the center through the manipulation of public credit or should move in response to the private bargaining of ordinary men.

This examination of Jefferson's social thought has been prompted by the accomplishments of the Court and Country interpreters. If they err—as I believe they do—in describing the Jeffersonians as classical republicans, they are surely correct to insist that civic humanism shaped the terms of political debate in the early national period, uniting one group of men and provoking an alternative ideology in another. The close attention they have paid to the conceptual world of Anglo-America has left an indelible mark on historical scholarship. No longer can a mindless liberalism be ascribed to human beings, nor the liberal theory about what is natural be confounded with nature itself. The values and beliefs that informed Jefferson's "Americanism" must be located and made precise. Readily assented to by many, these views could not be taken for granted if only because they conflicted with a venerable political tradition.

In defiance of that tradition, Jefferson rallied his countrymen with a vision of the future that joined their materialism to a new morality. An unstable combination in the classical model, this fusion proved particularly strong in American thought. And Jefferson affirmed it repeatedly. Writing in 1817 to the Frenchman for whom he had so long ago composed his *Notes,* he pointed to American progress as proof of his social theories: "When you witnessed our first struggles in the War of Independence, you little calculated more than we did, on the rapid growth and prosperity of this country; on the practical demonstration it was about to exhibit, of the happy truth that man is capable of self-government." Then, taking aim at his old target, he declared his confidence that "we shall proceed successfully for ages to come, and that, contrary to the principle of Montesquieu, it will be seen that the larger the extent of country, the more firm its republican structure, if founded, not on conquest, but in principles of compact and equality." America's economic base and the concept of a benign human potential sustained Jefferson's optimism, for, as he explained, his hope of an enduring republic was "built much on the enlargement of the resources of life, going hand in hand with the enlargement of territory, and the belief that men are disposed to live honestly, if the means of doing so are open to them." [71]

71. Jefferson to Barré de Marbois, June 14, 1817, in *Writings of Jefferson,* ed. Lipscomb and Bergh, XV, 130–131. The confidence that Jefferson expressed here contrasts sharply with the depiction of his mood after 1814 in Robert E. Shalhope, "Thomas Jefferson's Republicanism and Antebellum Southern Thought," *Journal of Southern History,* 42 (1976), 537–545.

13

Republicanism in Old and New Contexts

WHAT DID Americans in the late eighteenth century mean when they spoke about republicanism? For many men—and this was primarily a male discourse—republicanism represented something new. Thus, Thomas Paine in *Common Sense* referred to the "new republican materials" of the House of Commons on whose virtue depended the freedom of England. Eight years later, Paine defined a republic as a sovereignty of justice, in contrast to a sovereignty of will.[1] Writing at about the same time, an angry critic denounced the Philadelphia stage for insidiously fostering aristocratic values and alluded sarcastically to "our present state of imaginary republican equality."[2] In this man's mind, republicanism entailed the reformation of social mores along democratic lines. Addressing the American Philosophical Society on the subject of innovative farming techniques, Timothy Matlack spoke of "the great Republican Virtues of Industry and Economy."[3] Here Matlack associated republicanism with private virtues and linked them to productivity.

1. Thomas Paine, *Common Sense*, ed. Isaac Kramnick (New York, 1976), and "Dissertations on Government; The Affairs of the Bank; and Paper Money," in *The Life and Works of Thomas Paine*, ed. William M. Van der Weyde (New Rochelle, N.Y., 1925), IV, 234.

2. *Freeman's Journal; or, the North-American Intelligencer* (Philadelphia), Feb. 11, 1784.

3. Timothy Matlack, *An Oration, Delivered March 16, 1780, before the . . . American Philosophical Society . . .* (Philadelphia, 1780), 27.

For John Adams, republicanism retained its historical connection with classical and Renaissance texts. Abigail Adams described her husband's immersion in those texts as his "travelling through the Itallian Republicks."[4] The results of Adams' scholarly perambulations—his *Defence of the Constitutions of Government of the United States of America*—did not, however, restore the pristine meaning of republicanism. We can read James Madison, an equally learned man, lamenting the presence in Adams' *Defence* of so many remarks "unfriendly to republicanism." Four years after its publication, Madison observed to Jefferson that Adams had actually written a "mock defence" of the "Republican Constitutions of his Country," while attacking them with all the force he possessed.[5] Adams no doubt provoked this harsh judgment by insisting on the accuracy of Machiavelli's statement that all republics needed three orders of men. This, he claimed was an "eternal principle, without the knowledge of which every speculation upon government must be imperfect."[6] But clearly Adams expected controversy. He described the *Defence* to Benjamin Franklin as a confession of political faith containing "the only sense in which I am or ever was a Republican."[7]

The passage of time did not clarify the conceptual confusion about republicanism in the early national period. Reading the political pamphlets and private correspondence of the 1790s, one gets the impression that "republican" was a label to be fought over, a prized appellation to claim for one's own views. This is particularly apparent during the political ferment over Adams' reelection that began almost the moment he entered office. In Massachusetts, for instance, a Federalist newspaper exulted that "the inflexible republican virtues of the majority of the people" had foiled the machinations of the Jeffersonians in the Senate,[8] while simultaneously a

4. Adams to Mercy Warren, May 14, 1787, in *The Warren-Adams Letters* . . . (Massachusetts Historical Society, *Collections*, LXXII–LXXIII [Boston, 1917–1925]), II, 290.

5. Madison to Jefferson, June 6, 1787, in *The Papers of Thomas Jefferson*, ed. Julian P. Boyd et al. (Princeton, 1950–), XI, 402; Madison to Jefferson, May 12, 1791, in *The Writings of James Madison* . . . , ed. Gaillard Hunt (New York, 1906), VI, 50–51.

6. *The Works of John Adams* . . . , [ed.] Charles Francis Adams (Boston, 1851), V, 183.

7. Adams to Franklin, Jan. 27, 1787, in *The Works of Benjamin Franklin* . . . , ed. John Bigelow (New York, 1904), XI, 298–299.

8. *Boston Gazette, Commercial and Political*, Nov. 24, 1800.

Jeffersonian editor in Maryland described how the genius of universal liberty had finally combined with the new doctrine of universal rights to draw almost all the people into America's "*modern* republic."[9]

Such quotations leave little doubt that *republican* and *republic* figured prominently, if ambiguously, in the public discourse of the eighteenth century. *Republic* in fact appears as the conceptual equivalent of *union* in the nineteenth century and *nation* in the twentieth. Yet it was only in 1967, with the publication of Bernard Bailyn's *Ideological Origins of the American Revolution,* that historians began to investigate what this protean concept meant to men of the Revolutionary era. It would be surprising if scholars were able to agree upon the meaning of a word that contemporaries themselves used in such disparate contexts. And of course they don't. In part this is because the republican terrain Bailyn discovered turned out to be virtually unknown territory. The pamphlets he examined did not lead him to the familiar lawyerly absorption with constituent powers and prescriptive rights—the accessible principles that could be captured in the slogan "no taxation without representation." Rather, he found himself in the midst of a thicket of references to degeneration and corruption attached to a rhetoric of passionate outrage and unbounded fears. This excursion into the colonial mind convinced Bailyn that Americans had formed their worldview—more particularly, their grasp of political reality—from the republicanism of the English Commonwealthmen. From these Opposition writers of Augustan England, he explained, colonial pamphleteers had put together a social theory that stressed the eternal opposition of liberty and authority, the aggressive nature of power, and the dependence of the common good upon a delicate constitutional balance of the one, the few, and the many.[10] This worldview, which Bailyn evocatively portrayed, was wholly traditional in its emphasis upon the essential fragility of civil order.

Since 1967, the thesis of the centrality of this classical republican model in American thinking has been extended through the consti-

9. "The American: A Country Gazette," Baltimore, 1800, broadside, Historical Society of Pennsylvania, Philadelphia.

10. Bernard Bailyn, *The Ideological Origins of the American Revolution* (Cambridge, Mass., 1967), 34–93.

tutional period, the 1790s, and beyond.[11] Lance Banning best described the revisionist position in 1974: "Most of the inherited structure of eighteenth-century political thought persisted in America for years after 1789. And this persistence was not a matter of a shadowy half-life of fragmentary ideas. A structured universe of classical thought continued to serve as the intellectual medium through which Americans perceived the political world, and an inherited political language was the primary vehicle for the expression of their hopes and discontents."[12] J. G. A. Pocock spelled out the larger implications for the history of the United States: the new research displayed the American Revolution less as the first political act of revolutionary enlightenment than as "the last great act of the Renaissance."[13]

With admirable clarity Banning has epitomized the essential points of the revision that has restored republicanism to the conceptual world of our Founding Fathers. With the same lucidity he has recapitulated my criticisms of the "republican hypothesis" as it pertains to the opposition between the Jeffersonians and Federalists. What remains to be resolved in the scholarly dispute about republicanism in America is whose republicanism are we talking about— that of the Founding Fathers or our own? And if theirs is ours, which one of ours: the chaste and venerable classical republicanism distilled by Harrington for English needs and updated by Montesquieu for eighteenth-century readers, or the liberal republicanism that contemporaries traced to the inquiries of Bacon, Newton, Locke, and Smith. My answer is that both were present and that they represent the contending republican paradigms of Federalists and Jeffersonians. Banning, after generously conceding the presence of some liberal tendencies in those who opposed the Federalists, insists that the Jeffersonians retained their intellectual moorings

11. Gordon S. Wood, *The Creation of the American Republic, 1776–1787* (Chapel Hill, 1969); Lance Banning, *The Jeffersonian Persuasion: Evolution of a Party Ideology* (Ithaca, 1978). See also the special issue on republicanism edited by Joyce Appleby of *American Quarterly*, 37 (1985).

12. Banning, "Republican Ideology and the Triumph of the Constitution, 1789 to 1793," *William and Mary Quarterly*, 31 (1974), 173.

13. J. G. A. Pocock, "Virtue and Commerce in the Eighteenth Century," *Journal of Interdisciplinary History*, 3 (1972), 120.

in English Opposition thought. Only confusion will result, he writes, if we suppose that the analytical distinctions we detect were evident to the thinkers we study. Further, he maintains that it was the striking similarity between Alexander Hamilton's program and the policies of the English "court" party that called forth a "country opposition" in the United States.[14] Here he is following Pocock, who described the polemics over Hamilton's policies as a "replay of Court-Country debates" held in England seventy years earlier.[15]

Our interpretations on this point are mutually exclusive, for in my view it was precisely the recrudescence of both Court and Country thinking in the Washington administration that crystallized the liberal political vision of Jefferson and propelled him into action once he became convinced that in style, purpose, and personnel the new federal government belonged to men like Hamilton and Adams and not to those like Madison and himself. Here I would summon Jefferson's own words. From the year of his presidential election until his death Jefferson wrote about the issues that had been at stake in that famous contest. During this twenty-six-year period his account never varied. The Jeffersonians had liberated themselves from the bondage of old systems. They recognized that theirs was a new era. The advances in science and learning were so striking that the past need no longer haunt men's minds. Hopes for humanity once deemed chimerical could be embraced as practical for those who could free themselves of encumbering prejudices. Writing to Joseph Priestley in 1801, Jefferson criticized his opponents for believing in an education that looked backward, not forward, and hence failed to see what was new in America. "We can no longer say there is nothing new under the sun," he wrote. "For this whole chapter in the history of man is new. The great extent of our Republic is new. Its sparse habitation is new. The mighty wave of public opinion which has rolled over it is new." Exercising more tact with Abigail Adams, he left it to time and experience to determine whether the public good had more to fear from the people or its rulers, pointing out that those who feared the people

14. Banning, "Jeffersonian Ideology Revisited: Liberal and Classical Ideas in the New American Republic" and "Republican Ideology," *William and Mary Quarterly*, 31 (1974), 180–185, esp. 183.

15. Pocock, "Virtue and Commerce," 131.

had long controlled government, while those who feared governments independent of the people represented a new idea. When he
resumed correspondence with Adams himself, Jefferson characterized their parties as composed of reformers and the enemies of
reform who divided on the question of "the improvability of the
human mind, in science, in ethics, in government." [16] Whatever
the truth of these assertions, the language suggests that Jefferson
made sharp analytical distinctions in assessing how lines were drawn
in 1800.

Jefferson was also clear about the import of the new learning, the
innovations, and the novelties that preoccupied him. They marked
a great divide in human history. No longer need eighteenth-century
men be in the thrall of the great philosophers of antiquity, he wrote.
The loss of the political writings of Aristotle or any other ancient
philosopher need not cause regret, he maintained, because the "new
principle of representative democracy has rendered useless almost
everything written before on the structure of government." Similarly
he believed that the new science of economics had brought to light
the essential truths that were transforming the material world. He
insisted upon emphasizing the break in old continuities. Power and
force in international relations, for instance, "were legitimate principles in the dark ages which intervened between ancient and modern
civilisation." Disturbed by contemporaries who failed to appreciate
the significance of the dramatic changes they had witnessed, Jefferson ridiculed those who "look at constitutions with sanctimonious
reverence, and deem them like the arc of the covenant, too sacred
to be touched." Purists about language were equally antediluvian
in his eyes. Dictionaries were mere depositories, while society, he
said, was the great workshop for the smithing of new words. [17] These

16. Jefferson to Priestley, Mar. 21, 1801, in *The Writings of Thomas Jefferson*, ed. Paul
Leicester Ford (New York, 1892–1899), VIII, 54–56; Jefferson to Abigail Adams, Sept.
11, 1804, in *The Adams-Jefferson Letters: The Complete Correspondence Between Thomas Jefferson
and Abigail and John Adams*, ed. Lester J. Cappon (Chapel Hill, 1959), I, 278–280;
Jefferson to John Adams, ibid., II, 332.

17. Jefferson to Isaac H. Tiffany, Aug. 26, 1816, in *The Writings of Thomas Jefferson*, ed.
Andrew A. Lipscomb and Albert Ellery Bergh (Washington, D.C., 1903–1904), XV, 65–
66; Jefferson to James Madison, Aug. 28, 1789, in *The Papers of Thomas Jefferson*, ed. Boyd
et al., XV, 367; Jefferson to Samuel Kercheval, July 12, 1816, in *Writings of Jefferson*, ed.
Ford, X, 42; *The Living Thoughts of Thomas Jefferson*, [ed.] John Dewey (New York, 1940), 9.

are the statements of a man intent on making hard-edged divisions between himself and his opponents. However exaggerated Jefferson's insistence upon the newness of the intellectual terrain may appear to us, it clearly reflected a proposition of central importance to his worldview. There is little evidence here of a mingling of liberal and classical traditions or of a concern for those staple fears of country thought—standing armies, public debts, executive influence, and government by money.

Although Hamilton sounded like a latter-day Robert Walpole, the attacks he provoked owed little to the influence of English Opposition thought because Hamilton's opponents—Jefferson and the largely unknown group that formed around him—had far different goals. They did not look to the past for wisdom; they did not yearn for a government of balanced estates in a society of stable relationships; they did not celebrate participation in the polis. The conceptual language of classical republicanism had little relevance to their social realities and positively impeded their political purposes. It was just because of their disassociation from the cherished convictions of English political thought that Jefferson and his allies had to create an image of the society they hoped to bring into existence. In their depiction of America's future, freedom was expanded by drastically limiting the scope of government so that individual citizens could be empowered to act on their own behalf. Democratic values were invoked not to enlarge the people's power in government but rather to justify the abandonment of the authority traditionally exercised over them. In espousing limited government the Jeffersonians endorsed a redrawing of the lines between the public and private spheres, and this meant reordering their significance for the whole human enterprise. Old and well-documented abuses rendered government suspect because it relied on coercion. The new realm of voluntary associations—for worship, for study, for enterprise—held out the wonderful promise of shedding past oppression. The virtue whose fragility required a carefully balanced constitution grew robust when freed from old systems. Adams certainly knew his man when he brought to Jefferson's attention his good fortune in preferring "the dreams of the Future" to the histories of the past.[18]

18. Adams to Jefferson, Aug. 9, 1816, in *Adams-Jefferson Letters,* ed. Cappon, II, 487.

Jefferson believed devoutly in progress, and like all such devotees he had to explain why the future would be different from the past. His answer lay with the prospect of making fundamental changes in human institutions. The new understanding of nature and society, as well as the evidence that ordinary men could order their lives properly, argued for the possibility of establishing a new direction for social development. This was Jefferson's goal and the reason why his iconoclasm was basic to its attainment. Freedom for him meant liberation. Civilization's spiritual and material advances depended upon free initiatives and creative intelligence. Progress had been impeded just because the public realm had been dominated by the few who used their power to keep the many ignorant. Unlike Country party rhetoric with its lamentations about corruption and decay, Jeffersonian campaign literature ran to hyperbolic descriptions of America's future greatness once universal freedom, equal representation, and natural rights were firmly established.

Because these themes have pervaded American politics ever since, it has been difficult for historians to appreciate their novelty in the 1790s. And so the liberal tradition in America has been treated as a mindless reaction to a supposed New World or—worse yet—construed as what all human beings believe when not constrained by the elaborate intellectual constructions of Old World societies. For both Banning and me, the significance of the recent republican revision has been the discovery that many eighteenth-century Americans thought within a classical republican frame of reference. For me, the importance of this fact is that it enables us to see that liberalism did not sprawl unimpeded across the flat intellectual landscape of American abundance, as Louis Hartz maintained.[19] Hence we can begin to study it as a complex construction of reality put together, as all worldviews are, through a selective interpretation of experience, to serve profound human values.

While on the face of it Banning and I are arguing about facts—which conceptual order animated the Jeffersonian opposition—our differences are encumbered by theoretical issues as well. Since the evidence and arguments around which we have constructed our contrasting accounts of the 1790s are readily available in print,

---

19. Hartz, *The Liberal Tradition in America: An Interpretation of American Political Thought since the Revolution* (New York, 1955).

I think it will be more productive to address these issues.[20] Banning's presentation of the Jeffersonian permeates his entire interpretation. When Bailyn extended the range of Caroline Robbins' original work on the impact of the English Commonwealthmen in colonial America, he integrated this research with the compelling concept of ideology. In his study, the Cassandras of the British Opposition did not just furnish the articulate colonial mind with notions about power, corruption, and liberty. Their literature could be counted as a cause of the American Revolution because it fused "into effective formulations" opinions and attitudes "otherwise too scattered and vague to be acted upon." In this famous passage describing the heady potency of ideology, Bailyn distinguished between mere ideas and those capable of crystallizing inchoate social discontent, turning unrealized private emotions into a public possession and elevating to structured consciousness the mingled urges that stir within us all.[21] This association of ideology with the deep structuring of social consciousness has necessarily affected the reading of texts. When Banning writes that the opponents of Hamilton seized the only political language available to them or that evocative words and phrases were assented to without further explanation because of shared understandings of classical republicanism, he is working within the scholarly conventions established a decade earlier by Bailyn and anatomized before that by Pocock and Quentin Skinner.[22] Disentangling the theory from the evidence in the "republican hypothesis" is basic to understanding Banning's and my differing approaches to the disputes between the Jeffersonians and Federalists.

A myriad of assumptions about how ideas become social facts is packed into Bailyn's statement about ideology, and these assumptions have unavoidably affected how he and his followers have interpreted their evidence. Bailyn's understanding of the role of ideas in history rests heavily upon the work of Clifford Geertz, and Geertz's

20. Centrally in Banning, *Jeffersonian Persuasion,* and Appleby, *Capitalism and a New Social Order: The Republican Vision of the 1790s* (New York, 1984).

21. Bailyn, "The Central Themes of the American Revolution: An Interpretation," in *Essays on the American Revolution,* ed. Stephen G. Kurtz and James H. Hutson (Chapel Hill, 1973), 11.

22. Banning, *Jeffersonian Persuasion,* 185, 41, 177, 127, 148, 164.

thinking on ideology flows from anthropological studies of small face-to-face communities.[23] In these, the sharp differentiation between the social practices under observation and those familiar to the scholarly observers has encouraged scholars to search for the cues behind the patterned actions they were analyzing. In time they found these cues in the consciousness of the people under observation—those unspoken assumptions, visceral reactions, and value-laden convictions that reside within individuals but, from the outside, appear as patterned reactions. The exploration of this link between belief and behavior has produced a theory that emphasizes both the systematic and the social in our thought processes. Our construction of reality is not random but ordered, and it is not ours, even though we experience our knowledge as a personal possession. Just as significantly, society's messages are constantly being conveyed to us through gestures, intonations, symbols, and rituals, as well as by more articulate aspects of human communication. Society, as Geertz has said, supplies the media for expression, and the media mold the expresser.[24] Of central importance to this theory is that language is encoded through social practices. The words used in any particular sentence acquire their meaning through previous discourse; behind their utterance lies a richly textured interpretation of reality. Human reason, in this view, operates within acquired consciousness; it does not stand outside socially conditioned thought as a tool in the service of objective criticism.

Merging with this theory of ideology derived from anthropology have been equally important reflections on the way human knowledge is organized through interpretive schemes. These have been introduced into the scholarship on republicanism through Pocock, who has approached ideology by way of Thomas Kuhn and the sociology of knowledge. What Kuhn offered historians, Pocock explains, was a way of treating social thought as a process both

23. Clifford Geertz, "The Impact of the Concept of Culture on the Concept of Man" and "Ideology as a Cultural System," in his *The Interpretation of Cultures* (New York, 1973). See also Ronald G. Walters, "Signs of the Times: Clifford Geertz and Historians," *Social Research*, 47 (1980), 537–556.

24. Geertz, "Ideology as a Cultural System," in his *Interpretation of Cultures*, 212. "The sociology of knowledge ought to be called the sociology of meaning, for what is socially determined is not the nature of conception but the vehicles of conception."

linguistic and political because thinking could be viewed as a means of distributing authority as well as a system of communication.[25] The complementary insights of Geertz and Kuhn entered scholarly works at the same time that hermeneutics and structuralism were transforming the way all texts were being examined. The net result has been to diminish drastically the independence of the word and the autonomy of the author. Nothing speaks to us directly; every text must be comprehended within the linguistic, conceptual, and social systems that controlled its creation and reception. What becomes paramount for historians is ferreting out the connections that relate the part to the whole. This means that the texts that are the most valuable typify an age while those that deviate from a reigning paradigm may be interesting but less relevant to the enterprise of decoding public discourse. Thus Pocock dismisses Locke's *Second Treatise of Civil Government* on the grounds that his thought was notoriously not organized around historical concepts at a time when his contemporaries were placing their politics in a context of historical change.[26]

Bringing these theoretical insights to bear on Revolutionary America, Pocock has made explicit their impact on the revision under way. The classical view of politics, he writes, was a closed ideology, introducing into eighteenth-century America a Renaissance pessimism concerning the direction and reversibility of historical developments. Any change was likely to evoke fears of corruption and, through corruption, degeneration with its accompanying loss of liberty. The static ideal of the Americans, according to Pocock, was embodied in the word *virtue,* a heroic concept metaphorically braced for attack from the corrupting disruptions embodied in the word *commerce.* So firm was the grip of the notion of the incompatibility of virtue and commerce on the colonial mind that Americans were compelled to interpret change as a threat to their liberties.[27] This was true apparently whether the change issued

25. Thomas S. Kuhn, *The Structure of Scientific Revolutions* (Chicago, 1962); J. G. A. Pocock, "Languages and Their Implications: The Transformation of the Study of Political Thought," in his *Politics, Language and Time: Essays on Politicial Thought and History* (New York, 1971), 14–15.

26. Pocock, "Virtue and Commerce," 129.

27. Ibid., 120–123.

from the English imperial authorities before Independence, the popular involvement with tax and debt policies after the Revolution, or the fiscal program of Hamilton during Washington's administration.

This emphasis upon the social component in thought has had the salutary effect of disengaging intellectual historians from their great texts and plunging them into the systems of communication in which those texts, and lesser ones, acquired meaning. The accomplishments of the ideological school in this regard are major and permanent. However, this achievement should be separated from theoretical assumptions about the constraining effect of those ideas said to have paradigmatic stature. Among scientists sharing a discipline or in small custom-oriented communities a single conceptual order may in fact suppress imaginative deviation. This is far less likely to happen in complex, literate societies. Such societies with their plurality of religions and occupations naturally generate distinct groups with diverging interests. Power relations within them are frequently troubled, and men and women enjoy an access to information that can supply materials for alternative interpretations of reality. Ideologies in such societies rarely enjoy an uncontested supremacy—which is why we so often refer to them as persuasions.

By accepting the idea of a presiding paradigm, ideological historians have created the notion of a collective mind that furnishes the promptings that structure action. Ideologically the society is undifferentiated. Some may benefit more than others from the distribution of authority built into the society's conceptual language, but the distribution nonetheless presents itself as a given embedded in the minds of all. There is no room in this conception of social thought for the kind of ideological warfare that Jefferson injected into national politics. Conflicts instead are psychologized. As Gordon S. Wood explained about Bailyn's findings, the ideas of the Revolutionaries took on an "elusive and unmanageable quality, a dynamic self-intensifying character that transcended the intentions and desires of any of the historical participants."[28] With this theoretical approach, novelties and altered circumstances become intellec-

28. Wood, "Rhetoric and Reality in the American Revolution," *William and Mary Quarterly*, 23 (1966), 22.

tual problems for the whole society. A collective case of cognitive dissonance produces a collective effort to accommodate the nonconfirming evidence. Within each person rage the battles generated by the ideological contradictions of the whole. An ideology once in place, so it seems, imposes itself upon the range of human interests that generated interpretive schemes in the first place.

The ideological historians' emphasis upon the social structuring of communication has greatly enhanced our ability to understand the process of expression, but it has led to a neglect of the motives behind expression, not the least of which is testing the validity of one's assumptions. Human beings think for a purpose, for many purposes. It is possible to explore with an anthropologist's sensitivity the riches of symbolic systems without subscribing to the view that these systems possess a power to inhibit the creation of new symbols. One of the most insistent intellectual demands for men and women in the early modern period was the need to understand the dramatic changes transforming their world. Since these changes carried opportunities as well as threats, interpreting them had unavoidable implications for existing institutional arrangements. But it is just this play of intellectual power and imaginative virtuosity that the ideological approach obscures. Wishing to move beyond the aridly rationalistic search for causes in explanations of great historical events, the republican revisers have come dangerously close to cutting the taproots of human thought. While it is undeniable that human beings begin their thinking with an established worldview, it does not follow that the reality testing that constitutes mature thought will necessarily stay confined within that view. This is *a fortiori* the case if the different groups in an open and pluralistic society are confronting changes powerful enough to reshape the social landscape.

These criticisms of the ideological approach are particularly relevant to the treatment of economic change in the "republican hypothesis." Again Pocock has elaborated the controlling interpretation. In his *Machiavellian Moment* he explains how commerce became arrayed against virtue. Late-seventeenth-century Englishmen confronted a series of fiscal innovations that left the king with a bank, an expandable debt, and the means of buying both an army and a complaisant Parliament. The political nation split along the lines marked out by the classical republican model. Those who embraced the ideal of an uncorrupted domain for political participation reserved to the propertied and independent members of the polity endorsed the alarmist Country position; those receptive to the new engines for national wealth and power accepted the outlook of the Court. Henceforth the reigning republican paradigm controlled the reaction to the accelerating advances in trade. Those who identified with the state welcomed the new wealth-producing systems without removing the onus of corruption from them; those who identified with the independent gentry viewed commerce as the foe of virtue. Since civic virtue was counted upon to maintain the constitutional balance that guaranteed liberty and the survival of the polity, the commercial penetration of England's agricultural economy represented an unalloyed threat.[29]

Revisiting his Machiavellian moment in 1981, Pocock reasserted the primacy of the financial revolution in the history of ideology. It—not the Glorious Revolution, certainly not the commercial revolution—produced the nodes of significance that would dominate political discourse in the Anglo-American world throughout the eighteenth century.[30] Not the least of the astounding historiographical consequences of his revision, he said then, had been the displacement of Locke. Here Locke represents for Pocock a code name for those earlier historical accounts—both whig and Marxist—that interpreted the past from the front to the back and assumed that the great Mr. Locke came into being to prepare the way for modern industrial democracies. This Locke of course can be easily dispensed with, but coming to terms with the Locke who was notoriously ahistorical will require a less heroic view of how ideologies organize consciousness.

It has been a major goal of the ideological historians to move beyond the bootless efforts of materialists and idealists to establish either social facts or conceptions of them as fundamental. By making conceptual languages part of the structure of personality and the world, they have tried to envelop rather than transcend the

29. Pocock, *The Machiavellian Moment: Florentine Political Thought and the Atlantic Republican Tradition* (Princeton, 1975).

30. Pocock, *"The Machiavellian Moment* Revisited: A Study in History and Ideology," *Journal of Modern History,* 53 (1981), 64–66.

epiphenomenal-phenomenal split. "Men cannot do what they have no means of saying they have done," Pocock has written, "and what they do must in part be what they can say and conceive that it is."[31] We sense that that must be true. Indeed, it is not uncommon now to read in scholarly works that a group—usually a subordinate one—did not embark on a particular program because its members did not have a language for discussing new goals. This equating of conceptual languages with the actual structuring of our consciousness is what gives plausibility to the idea of a single, shared worldview operating within a given society. This claim, which has not always been made explicit, undergirds Pocock's and Banning's insistence that the classical republican paradigm controlled how eighteenth-century men reacted to change. With their reconstruction of the conceptual world of classical republicanism we can appreciate just how discordant progressive economic development could be. Men living with sensibilities formed in an agrarian society and struggling to interpret change with an ideology pivoting on the preeminent importance of stasis could only be disconcerted by the intrusive vigor of the market. This much has been established, and the fatuities of whig history can be quietly forgotten. However, by insisting that the only significant intellectual accommodation to change took place within a presiding paradigm, the revisionists have made it difficult to recognize that alongside the Machiavellian conception of citizenship, order, and liberty there grew up another paradigm.[32]

Men did find the means of talking about commerce that over time produced a language totally unassimilable to the social grammar of civic humanism. Indeed, they were forced to do so in part because their political language had no means for discussing the early modern economy as it in fact operated.[33] Classical theory asserted the predominance of politics over all other aspects of social life. This predominance reflected and perpetuated the subordinate position of all other social institutions. Economic life served purely

31. Pocock, "Virtue and Commerce," 122.

32. Ibid. Pocock here suggests that it was unlikely that there would be only one language in use within a given society but goes on to accept that this was so.

33. On this subject see Nicholas Xenos, "Classical Political Economy: The Apolitical Discourse of Civil Society," *Humanities in Society,* 3 (1980).

private, household needs. The political whole was not only greater than the sum of the parts; it alone possessed sufficient unity for a history. Time existed within the polity; outside churned a meaningless sequence of events ruled by fortune. To catalog in this manner the central propositions of classical republicanism is to state the problem. No concepts existed for analyzing a trading system that had not only moved beyond the confines of political boundaries but had created wealth essential to the conduct of politics. There was no classical language for understanding a commercial system that was public, progressive, and orderly. However appealing civic humanism was to English gentlemen involved in public issues, it did not help persons who sought to understand the private transactions that were determining the shape and direction of the Anglo-American economy.

Publications on agriculture, trade, and manufacturing grew in volume and range during the seventeenth and eighteenth centuries, and these writings indicate that the imagination of men who studied commerce was not imprisoned within the classical republican worldview. Many observers were able to see that their economic system represented a wholly new phenomenon. They interpreted the evidence of material advance as part of a complicated transformation requiring new modes of analysis. Men were able to talk about trade, in time to fashion a bold new conceptual language capable of transforming traditional assumptions about the human personality. They created an abstract model of the market. They constructed powerful hypotheses to explain to one another how regularities emerged from the apparently random behavior of market bargainers. They recognized too the implications for their political order in the existence of an international organization for the production and distribution of wealth. They saw that trade engaged men as individuals rather than as members of a polity. And they extrapolated new truths from their observations and attached them to new models of human association. Necessity was the mother of this intellectual invention in part because classical republicanism offered only a language for lamenting, as opposed to understanding, commerce. From the 1620s, when Gerald de Malynes and Thomas Mun exchanged views on the English coin shortage, to the 1776 publication of Adam Smith's masterly synthesis, men thought about the market economy in ways that incessantly impinged upon politics. In exactly the way that Pocock has described the creation of all matrices of language, writers decomposed old meanings about civil order and recomposed the elements of time, citizenship, and the distribution of authority. Outside the polity, they constructed a model of economic life that borrowed its order from nature—the newly conceptualized nature of predictable regularity.[34] As this economy absorbed more and more of the attention of men and women it supplied a new identity for them. By the end of the eighteenth century the individual with wide-ranging needs and abstract rights appeared to challenge the citizen with concrete obligations and prescribed privileges.

In the 1790s, when the Jeffersonian Republicans and Federalists confronted each other, the battle lines had been drawn around opposing conceptions of civil society. The passions mobilized by this contest over national leadership reflected this fact. However diffuse the ideas of ordinary participants, the parties' champions were disciplined and rigorous thinkers, filled with a sense of the portentousness of the events they sought to control. For the Jeffersonians the economy offered an escape from the predicaments implicit in traditional ways of looking at social order. Here was a system operating independently of politics and, like the physical universe, taking its cues from nature. Where politics achieved stability by imposing its structure of power, the economy appeared to elicit voluntary participation as it wove ever more extensive networks of free exchange. It also discovered a rationality in the humblest person whose capacity to take care of himself could be used as an argument for freedom. Like so many other staple concepts in traditional political discourse, freedom underwent a transformation in this newly imagined society of the future. Freedom now could be construed as a universal liberation wherein men—and of course it was a white male vision—were free to define and pursue their own goals.

Only in the United States, with its undeveloped resources and

34. I have discussed this development in *Economic Thought and Ideology in Seventeenth-Century England* (Princeton, 1978).

flexible social norms, could reality lend support to this proleptic vision of a free society. The persuasiveness of the liberal paradigm, however, depended less upon palpable evidence than upon powerful, new, analytical models explaining human psychology, physical causation, and the workings of the market. It would be hard to exaggerate the subversive role abstract reasoning played in this retreat from politics. Science became the lodestar for those who thought they were at the dawn of a new age; modern scientists, not ancient philosophers, guided them into the future; the inquiring mind presented itself as the inexhaustible resource for endless improvement. The importance of the free market to this development cannot be reduced to economics. Nor can Jeffersonians be distinguished from Federalists on the basis of their enthusiasm for economic development. It was the economy's ordering of society with minimal compulsion that stirred the Jeffersonian imagination, not its capacity to produce wealth. Even after the incessant tendency of the unregulated market to make the rich richer and the poor more vulnerable had fully revealed itself, belief in spontaneous harmony died hard, for with it went the expectation that progress inhered in the natural order.

Liberalism and capitalism have undeniable historical links, but the concept of capitalism that we use today only obscures their connection in the eighteenth century. Our postulates about capitalism crystallized in the nineteenth century, when the relentless dynamic of unimpeded economic development became apparent. For us the end of capitalism is the accumulation of capital, the means to that end the capitalist's organization of hired labor, and the social consequence a permanent division between dependent laborers and independent employers. Attached to the notion of a bourgeois ethic, the culture produced by this capitalism appears in an altogether different light from the Jeffersonian vision. Constricting rather than generous, manipulative rather than emancipating, its values never rise above the interests of its beneficiaries. This capitalism shimmers beneath Banning's statements that the Jeffersonians had many reservations about the "eager, unrestrained pursuit of economic opportunity" or the "unrestrained pursuit of purely private interests." Similarly, when he writes that liberalism "is comfortable with economic man, with the individual who is intent on maximizing private satisfactions," it is William Graham Sumner's liberalism, not Jefferson's, that provides the model.[35]

The recovery of classical republican thought has, as Banning writes, enabled us to understand that the Revolutionary generation left "a lasting commitment to ideas that were not part of a liberal consensus."[36] However, by presenting this mode of political discourse as encapsulating Americans within a closed ideology, the republican revisionists have gone beyond their evidence. It is of course possible that Jefferson and his followers were simultaneously liberal and classical, as Banning has argued. However, when we find a man as methodically reflective as Jefferson repeatedly stating that his party distinguished itself by its commitment to scientific advances in the knowledge of government, by its faith in the self-governing capacities of ordinary men, and by its liberation from reverence for the past, it makes good sense to believe him. Not to do so is to interpret his triumph as a defeat and to construe the emergence of liberalism as a disappointing capitulation to the overpowering force of economic development.

Republicanism in the 1780s, according to Gordon Wood, was essentially anticapitalistic, representing "a final attempt to come to terms with the emergent individualistic society that threatened to destroy once and for all the communion and benevolence that civilized men had always considered to be the ideal of human behavior."[37] It is this meaning that scholars have in mind when they speak of the new republican hypothesis that has transformed our understanding of political discourse in eighteenth-century America. Undeniably, *republicanism* continued to convey this complicated message to some, but the men who claimed *republican* for a party title in 1800 had elaborated a new meaning—equally complex—that embraced and celebrated the free individual. No longer seen as a threat, the emerging individualist had become the instrument of progress. What was exhilarating in their world was not the experience of organizing society around new principles—for that they had not had—but rather the hopes such a prospect inspired.

35. Banning, "Jeffersonian Ideology Revisited," 12, 14.
36. Ibid., 13.
37. Wood, *Creation of the American Republic,* 418–419.

When Jefferson hailed his age as a whole new chapter in the history of man, we sense that his opponents' reverence for the past was uppermost in his mind. Indeed, the excitement generated by the election of Jefferson tells us something about the connection between American optimism and the promise of a different future. Jefferson's victory stirred deeply his champions just because his republicanism represented a carefully constructed alternative to the human predicament so forcefully depicted in classical republican texts.

Sources

Earlier versions of the chapters, edited for this book, appeared elsewhere as noted.

1. "Ideology and Theory: The Tension between Political and Economic Liberalism in Seventeenth-Century England," *The American Historical Review*, June (1976), 499–515.

2. "Locke, Liberalism and the Natural Law of Money," *Past and Present: A Journal of Historical Studies*, 71 (1976), 43–69.

3. "Modernization Theory and the Formation of Modern Social Theories in England and America," *Comparative Studies in Society and History*, 20 (1978), 259–285.

4. "Ideology and the History of Political Thought," *Intellectual History Newsletter* (1980), 10–18; J. G. A. Pocock, "An Appeal from the New to the Old Whigs? A Note on Joyce Appleby's 'Ideology and the History of Political Thought,'" ibid. (1981), 47–51; Joyce Appleby, "Response to J. G. A. Pocock," ibid. (1982), 20–23.

5. "Liberalism and the American Revolution," *The New England Quarterly*, 49 (1976), 3–26.

6. "The Social Origins of American Revolutionary Ideology," *The Journal of American History*, 64 (1978), 935–958.

7. "The New Republican Synthesis and the Changing Political Ideas of John Adams," *American Quarterly*, 25 (1973), 578–595.

8. "The American Heritage: The Heirs and the Disinherited," *The Journal of American History*, 74 (1987), 798–813.

9. "America as a Model for the Radical French Reformers of 1789," *The William and Mary Quarterly*, 28 (1971), 267–286.

10. "Commercial Farming and the 'Agrarian Myth' in the Early Republic," *The Journal of American History*, 68 (1982), 833–849.

11. "Republicanism and Ideology," *American Quarterly*, 37 (1985), 461–473.

12. "What Is Still American in the Political Philosophy of Thomas Jefferson?," *The William and Mary Quarterly*, 39 (1982), 287–309.

13. "Republicanism in Old and New Contexts," *The William and Mary Quarterly*, 43 (1986), 20–34.

Index